Time Out

Turin

timeout.com/turin

TIME OUT GUIDES LTD

Published by Time Out Guides Ltd
251 Tottenham Court Road
London W1T 7AB
United Kingdom

First edition 2004

10 9 8 7 6 5 4 3 2 1

Colour reprographics by Icon, Crowne House, 56-58 Southwark Street, London SE1 1UN
Printed and bound by Cayfosa-Quebecor, Ctra. de Caldes, Km 3 08 130 Sta, Perpètua de Mogoda, Barcelona, Spain

Edited and designed by
Time Out Guides Limited
Universal House
251 Tottenham Court Road
London W1T 7AB
Tel + 44 (0)20 7813 3000
Fax + 44 (0)20 7813 6001
Email guides@timeout.com
www.timeout.com

Editorial

Editor Anne Hanley
Deputy Editor Jenny Piening
Listings Editor Roberta Balma Mion
Proofreader Tamsin Shelton
Indexer Jackie Brind

Editorial/Managing Director Peter Fiennes
Series Editor Ruth Jarvis
Deputy Series Editor Lesley McCave
Guides Co-ordinator Anna Norman
Accountant Sarah Bostock

Design

Art Director Mandy Martin
Acting Art Director Scott Moore
Acting Art Editor Tracey Ridgewell
Acting Senior Designer Astrid Kogler
Designer Sam Lands
Junior Designer Oliver Knight
Digital Imaging Dan Conway
Ad Make-up Charlotte Blythe

Picture Desk

Picture Editor Jael Marschner
Deputy Picture Editor Kit Burnet
Picture Researcher Ivy Lahon
Picture Desk Assistant/Librarian Laura Lord

Advertising

Sales Director Mark Phillips
International Sales Manager Ross Canadé
International Sales Executive James Tuson
Advertising Sales (Turin) Conversa
Advertising Assistant Lucy Butler

Marketing

Marketing Manager Mandy Martinez
US Publicity & Marketing Associate Rosella Albanese

Production

Guides Production Director Mark Lamond
Production Controller Samantha Furniss

Time Out Group

Chairman Tony Elliott
Managing Director Mike Hardwick
Group Financial Director Richard Waterlow
Group Commercial Director Lesley Gill
Group Marketing Director Christine Cort
Group General Manager Nichola Coulthard
Group Art Director John Oakey
Online Managing Director David Pepper
Group Production Director Steve Proctor
Group IT Director Simon Chappell

Contributors

History Anne Hanley (*Literary Turin* Gregory Dowling). **Turin Today** Elisabetta Povoledo (*Body builders* Carol Bazzani, Romina Pastorelli). **Art & Architecture** Lucy Maulsby. **Piedmont & Food** Pamela Cuthbert (*Regional wines* Paul French; *Cioccolata* Elisabetta Povoleda). **Where to Stay** Nicky Swallow. **Sightseeing** Carol Bazzani, Romina Pastorelli, Anne Hanley (*In the footsteps of Cavour* Elisabetta Povoledo). **Restaurants** Fiona MacWilliam; *additional reviews* Nicky Swallow. **Cafés & Bars** Anastasia Clafferty, Marino Marolini. **Shops & Services** Natasha Miller. **Festivals & Events** Harriet Graham. **Children** Andrew Turner. **Film** Juliet Richetto (*Trail blazing, On location* Juliet Richetto, Lee Marshall). **Galleries** Helen Weaver (*Art on track, Light show* Carol Bazzani, Romina Pastorelli). **Gay & Lesbian** Juliet Richetto. **Nightlife & Music** Juliet Richetto. **Performing Arts** Harriet Graham. **Sport & Fitness** Andrew Turner. **Trips Out of Town: Introduction** Anne Hanley. **Piedmont by Season** Andrew Turner. **Ivrea & Biella** Anastasia Clafferty, Marino Marolini (*Cult status* Jenny Piening). **Vercelli** Anastasia Clafferty, Marino Marolini (*Piedmont paddies* Paul French; *Pope Felix* Anne Hanley). **Asti & Il Monferrato** Aaron Maines. **Alba & Le Langhe** Lara Statham (*The pure ones* Jenny Piening; *Middle-aged spread* Paul French; *Truffle snufflers* Nicky Swallow). **The Po Valley** Kirsty Ramsbottom. **Val di Susa** Anastasia Clafferty, Marino Marolini. **The Mountains** Lisa Ariemma. **Directory** Roberta Balma Mion; *Glossary* Anne Hanley; *Further reference* Jenny Piening, Anne Hanley.

Maps LS International Cartography, via Sanremo 17, 20133 Milan, Italy.

Photography by Gianluca Moggi, New Press Photo, except: pages 14, 16, 170 Corbis; page 21 PA Photos; pages 23, 27 Turin Tourist Office; page 83 AKG London; page 139 Kobal Collection; page 169 Alamy.

The Editor would like to thank: Daniela Vitta and Elena Cottini at Studio Mailander, and the Turin city council for help and support. Special thanks to Lee and Clara Marshall.

Contents

Introduction

When the dukes of Savoy moved their dynasty's capital from Chambéry to Turin in the mid 16th century, they gave themselves the kind of clean slate that no other European rulers had ever enjoyed. From what was then a small village on the Po plain at the foot of the Alps, this family could create a city to fit their pretensions, a purpose-built capital for the kings – of Sardinia-Piedmont, then of Italy – that they would later become.

Turin, therefore, is unique. Abandon your preconceptions about quaint Italian towns: if you're looking for the charm of twisting medieval streets then this is not the city for you. Turin is about pomp and circumstance, extraordinary architectonic unity and monumental magnificence.

Strangely however, for much of the 20th century this side of the city was largely overlooked. Instead, Turin was simply Fiat Town, a rather grimy northern Italian conglomeration, a sprawling mass of jerry-built suburbs and factories at the centre of the country's economic miracle. Even the locals were blind to its merits: this, the story goes, was the only Italian town blasé enough about its own monuments to allow a Michael Caine-led team of payroll robbers drive Mini Coopers over them in *The Italian Job*.

It has taken the decline of Turin as industrial locomotive to bring its forgotten facets to the fore.

Post-industrial Turin is a busy place, a city industriously dedicated to finding a new role for itself. It has polished up its historic glories, given its *centro storico* a face-lift. Buoyed by its selection as host of the 2006 Winter Olympics, the city is forging ahead with new transport systems and improved infrastructure. And having set its cultural heritage to rights, it's seeking to create something new, with an unparalleled dedication to encouraging contemporary art, to reclaiming its industrial wasteland and to endowing itself with a slew of exciting, cutting-edge new buildings. Quaint it ain't: but 21st-century Turin is unquestionably a part of Italy worth exploring.

ABOUT THE TIME OUT CITY GUIDES

Time Out Turin is one of the expanding series of Time Out City Guides, produced by the people behind London and New York's successful listings magazines. Our guides are all written and updated by resident experts who have striven to provide you with all the most up-to-date information you'll need to explore the city or read up on its background, whether you're a local or a first-time visitor.

THE LOWDOWN ON THE LISTINGS

Above all, we've tried to make this book as useful as possible. Addresses, telephone numbers, websites, transport information, opening times, admission prices and credit card details have all been included in the listings. And, as far as possible, we've given details of facilities, services and events, all checked and correct as we went to press. However, owners and managers can change their arrangements at any time, and they often do. Before you go out of your way, we'd advise you to telephone and check opening times, ticket prices and other particulars.

While every effort has been made to ensure the accuracy of the information contained in this guide, the publishers cannot accept responsibility for any errors it may contain.

PRICES AND PAYMENT

We have noted where venues such as shops, hotels, restaurants, museums, attractions and the like accept the following credit cards: American Express (AmEx), Diners Club (DC), MasterCard (MC) and Visa (V). Many will also accept travellers' cheques, along with other credit cards.

The prices we've supplied should be treated as guidelines, not gospel. If you find that prices vary wildly from those we've quoted, please write and let us know. We aim to give the best and most up-to-date advice, so we always want to know if you've been badly treated or overcharged.

THE LIE OF THE LAND

Central Turin is a highly compact area, arranged on a grid system that makes finding your way around comparatively easy. The names given by locals to the various areas of the city are derived mostly from the nearest large square, street, landmark

There is an online version of this guide, and guides to over 45 international cities, at **www.timeout.com**.

or church and are, on the whole, without definite borders. For the purposes of this guide, we have adopted our own divisions.

Though Turin's small *centro storico* is best visited on foot, the city does have an extensive public transport system. For information on public transport, see page 217. For a map of bus and tram lines, see page 248. However, as this guide went to press, the transport system was being upgraded and an underground built, throwing the whole network into some disarray. Don't be surprised if your bus is diverted to a very different route or if your tram grinds to a halt long before you reach your destination.

When listing an address for a venue, we have given not only the street address, but also – to make finding your way around easier – the appropriate area into which we have divided the city.

Turin's heavy traffic, restricted areas, one-way systems and parking problems mean that there is little point in having a car in the city. Most larger towns in the Piedmont region can be reached by train. For visiting country areas around Turin, however, a car is definitely an advantage. Where there *is* public transport to outlying districts, we have given full details. But don't count on its being frequent or covering the territory exhaustively.

Our Trips Out of Town section starts on page 165. For information on driving, see page 219; for car rental, see page 220.

TELEPHONE NUMBERS

The phone code for Turin is 011. This must be dialed whether you are calling from outside or inside the city. Do *not* drop the zero if you are calling from abroad. Numbers beginning 800 are toll-free numbers; most can only be called from inside Italy, and some can only be called from within the city or region. For more on telephones and codes, see page 229.

ESSENTIAL INFORMATION

For all the practical information you might need for visiting Turin, including advice on facilities and access for the disabled, emergency telephone numbers and local transport, turn to the Directory chapter at the back of the guide. It starts on page 215.

MAPS

Wherever possible, a map reference is provided for venues listed in the guide, indicating the page and grid reference on which it can be found in our detailed street maps of Turin. There is also an overview map of the city showing our areas and the suburbs around, and a transport map showing the bus and tram system in downtown Turin. The maps section starts on page 239.

LET US KNOW WHAT YOU THINK

We hope you enjoy *Time Out Turin*, and we'd like to know what you think of it. We welcome tips for places that you consider we should include in future editions and take note of your criticism of our choices. There's a reader's reply card at the back of this book for your feedback, or you can email us at guides@timeout.com.

ARMANDO TESTA

SAN TOMMASO 10. ORIGINAL LAVAZZA COFFEE HOUSE
Drinking espresso coffee is often just an enjoyable habit
At San Tommaso 10 it is an experience. Only here can you
order your favourite blend of espresso, drink coffee
Neapolitan style or prepared in a 'moka' and choose from 2
delicious specialities, all coffee flavoured of course. And
only here, where the first Lavazza coffee was born, can you
taste 'èspesso', the first espresso that you can eat

VIA SAN TOMMASO, 10 - TORINO - TEL. 011.53.42.01
OPEN MONDAY TO SATURDAY FROM 0800 TO 2400
TO FIND OUT MORE VISIT WWW.SANTOMMASO10.COM

LAVAZZA
ITALY'S FAVOURITE COFFEE

In Context

Roman foundations:
Porta Palatina. *See p58.*

History

From dynastic capital to industrial boom-town.

Paleolithic and, in particular, neolithic settlements abounded in the region where, according to Roman chronicles, Ligurian tribes tended sheep for milk and wool, husbanded woods, mined and panned for gold. Trade routes had long criss-crossed this expanse of plain, hill country and mountain so that the Romans – when they had secured their hold over the area during the reign of Augustus in the 20s BC – were able to superimpose their military roads over already well-worn tracks. The Roman highways brought new importance, and new Roman names, to those pre-existing settlements that were to become today's Piedmontese cities. The newly conquered territory was arranged around settlements at Augusta Bagiennorum, Augusta Praetoria (Aosta, capital of the Val d'Aosta region north of Piedmont) and Augusta Taurinorum (Turin, *see p50* **Sightseeing**).

When a settlement on the site of today's Turin originally saw the light of day is unclear, thanks to millennia of thorough going make-over work. In the mid 16th century, round about the time when the ruling Savoy family was to transfer its capital from Chambéry to Turin, a mythical origin for the city seemed desirable; a stone carving dedicated to the Egyptian goddess Isis was fortuitously unearthed during construction work. Savoy savants argued that followers of Isis were clearly responsible for introducing the cult of the bull (*toro*) god Apis to the area where Turin now stands. Locals snorted in derision.

On less shaky ground, chronicles relate that the great Carthaginian general Hannibal, having crossed the Alps with his pachyderms, swooped on the little settlement, laid siege to it for three days, then razed it in 218 BC. After which nothing is heard of the place until

Julius Caesar found it convenient as a stepping stone on his way to conquer Gaul – and, later, Britain – in 58 BC.

Augustus' colony of Augustus Taurinorum was laid out according to the usual Roman grid plan, with decumani running east–west and cardines north–south dividing the rectangular settlement into 72 insulae (blocks). The decumanus maximus corresponded more or less with the stretch of via Garibaldi between Palazzo Madama (see p54) and via della Consolata. The main cardine ran south from the Porta Palatina (see p58).

But Augustus Taurinorum remained a minor outpost, a furthest-flung bulwark between the Italian peninsula and Gallic territory. It was subject to all the vicissitudes of the declining and falling empire and the advent of Christianity: a cathedral was built where the Duomo (see p58) now stands in the third to fourth centuries. When Barbarian hordes began getting itchy feet in the fifth century, Turin was easy meat. The Burgundians hacked their way through in 492, only to be dislodged some decades later by the longobardi (Lombards). This well-primed Germanic war-machine made its raping and pillaging way down the Italian boot, and having conquered, made Turin and its surrounding area into a duchy with a Lombard stooge in the ducal seat. The area was then left in relative peace for two centuries until the Frankish king Charlemagne overthrew the status quo in 773. With his usual passion for reorganising feudal bureaucracy, Charlemagne replaced Turin's duke with a count who was subject to the marquis of Ivrea (see pp171-9).

THE RISE OF THE SAVOYS

The end of the Carolingian line (ie Charlemagne's descendants) in the late ninth century brought fragmentation through what had been Charlemagne's empire, and north-west Italy was no exception. The Val d'Aosta was taken in hand by its bishops and nobles, whose loyalty lay with the king of Burgundy. Divided into four sub-zones by northern Italy's Frankish strongman King Berengario II, Piedmont became a jigsaw puzzle of leaders and political systems: Asti (see pp184-91), Tortona, Novara, Vercelli (see pp180-83) and Alessandria established strong independent communes; in Monferrato (see p187) and Saluzzo (see p201), powerful marquisates emerged; around Turin, the counts of Savoy (Savoia) took the upper hand.

Turin and its surrounding region owed its growing importance in the 11th century to a remarkable woman named Adelaide Manfredi. Adelaide collected and outlived husbands from some of northern Italy's most powerful families.

With her third marriage, to Oddone di Savoia, son of Umberto Biancamano (see p8 **The unstoppable Savoys**), she brought together strategically vital lands on both sides of the Alps. This fact did not go unnoticed by the Holy Roman Emperor Henry V; he acted swiftly to stymie this position of power by making Turin an independent commune in the early 12th century, allowing it to finance itself by exacting tolls from anyone using its roads through the Alps; and to boost the local tourist trade, all travellers were obliged to spend at least one night in Turin. By 1280, however, the Savoy family was fully in control of the region, though wisely allowed the communal authorities in Turin to continue to exercise their toll prerogatives. Indeed, the only real threat to Savoy hegemony now came from the Acaias, a minor branch of the Savoy family. But with the

Pietro Micca

Hero of Turin's military struggles he may be, but Pietro Micca was a miner from the hill town of Sagliano, north of Biella (see p174), and not even an army soldier. In fact, he was drafted, along with 20,000 other young piemontesi, after Turin's French foes had effectively dismantled the Savoy forces in 1703. Miners were needed, in particular, to maintain and man the labyrinth of countermine tunnels that ran beneath Turin's Cittadella (see p66), the principal France-facing fortress along the city's defensive walls. And it was here that the brave – or unlucky, depending on which version of events you believe – Pietro found himself on the night of 29 August 1706 when a band of grenadiers from the French forces that had been besieging the city for the previous four months found their way into the tunnels.

Micca lit a fuse to bring down a stretch of tunnel; the French intruders were blocked and the city saved from certain defeat, but the 29-year-old was killed too.

At the time, the only significance attributed to his action was military. But in later years, Pietro became a propaganda tool: a kamikaze of noble ideals, he had sacrificed his own life for his country, the story went. More recently, however, this local hero has been downgraded, becoming a brave soldier, doing his duty (with a fuse that was too short) and unable to run fast enough to escape death.

death in 1418 of the last Acaia heir, all power passed into the hands of Amedeo VIII di Savoia. In 1416 the Savoys' *contea* had been upgraded to a *ducato* (duchy), making the family chief a duke rather than a count. For the next six centuries the Savoys would remain more or less stably in the driving seat.

THE SAVOY CAPITAL

Documents attribute no particular name to the area surrounding Turin until as late as the end of the 12th century when a swathe of hill and plain territory at the western end of the Po valley was described as *Pedemontum* (foot of the mountains). By 1424, when Amedeo VIII di Savoia made his son duke of Piemonte, the name had been Italianised and the area made even larger: the duke's territory stretched from Nice to the Sesia river, which today marks the divide between the Piedmont and Lombardy regions, encompassing the Val d'Aosta too.

As the 15th century dawned, Turin was a key economic and administrative centre with a population of over 10,000. In 1404 it was endowed with a university. Yet it bristled under the anomaly and indignity of not being the

The unstoppable Savoys

Umberto I Biancamano (Humbert the White-handed), who founded the House of Savoy (Savoie in French; Savoia in Italian, adj. *sabaudo*) in the early 11th century, may have been of Burgundian origin. Through the Middle Ages, the counts of Savoy concentrated on amassing territory in the western Alps, east of the Rhône and south of Lake Geneva. **Amedeo V** (1285-1323) had the foresight to forbid the division of Savoy property among offspring, guaranteeing succession of the eldest son. The counts moved east and south, picking up Nice (late 14th century); Piedmont (early 15th century, after a branch of the Savoy family, the Acaia, had ruled it for almost 200 years); and the title of duke in 1416. The Treaty of Utrecht (1713) gave them Sicily (later swapped for Sardinia) and the title of king. In 1814 Genoa became part of the family's dominions.

No longer the men they used to be by the 19th century, wavering Savoys allowed themselves, nevertheless, to be swept along by the liberal fervour gripping Europe, and **Vittorio Emanuele II** fell under the spell of Camillo Benso, count of Cavour (*see p10* **The four horsemen of the Risorgimento**) – wisely for the Savoy House, as it turned out. For this little-regarded, much trampled-over dynasty from the Alps found itself ruling over the whole of the Italian peninsula in 1861 (though the king from Turin never bothered to change his title, becoming Vittorio Emanuele II, first king of Italy). The Savoy glory was short-lived, however. **Vittorio Emanuele III** stood limply by as Mussolini put his Fascist regime, with its oppressive law-and-order methods and odious race laws, in place. When the king finally realised that Mussolini was not a good thing in 1943, he made such a botched job of ousting *Il Duce* and switching to the Allied side that Italy was devastated by the war's worst crossfire. Abdicating in favour of his son **Umberto II** was too little, too late. In 1946 Italians voted to send their ruling family into exile and become a republic.

DUKES (FROM 1416)

1391-1440 Amedeo VIII
1440-65 Lodovico
1465-72 Amedeo IX
1472-82 Filiberto I
1482-90 Carlo I
1490-96 Carlo II Giovanni Amedeo
1496-97 Filippo II
1497-1504 Filiberto II
1504-53 Carlo III
1553-80 Emanuele Filiberto
1580-1630 Carlo Emanuele I
1630-37 Vittorio Amedeo I
1637-38 Francesco Giacinto
1638-75 Carlo Emanuele II (NB Christine of France, widow of Vittorio Amedeo and sister of Luigi XIII, regent from 1638-1663)

KINGS (FROM 1713)

1675-1730 Vittorio Amedeo II (NB Marie Jeanne Battiste de Nemours, widow of Carlo Emanuele, regent from 1675-1684)
1730-73 Carlo Emanuele III
1773-96 Vittorio Amedeo III
1796-(1802) Carlo Emanuele IV
1798-99 French rule
1799 Occupation by Austria/Russia
1800-14 French rule (1808 Camillo Borghese viceroy)
(1802)-1821 Vittorio Emanuele I
1821-31 Carlo Felice
1831-49 Carlo Alberto
1849-78 Vittorio Emanuele II of Italy
1878-1900 Umberto I
1900-46 Vittorio Emanuele III
1946 Umberto II

dynasty's capital: that honour went to Chambéry, in the Savoys' French dominions. Gradually, however, the family transferred its affections – then its seat – to its Italian stronghold. During a 65-year struggle between France and Spain for control over the Italian peninsula (Spain won), the French occupied much of Piedmont and Savoy. But in 1559 the Treaty of Cateau-Cambresis restored the Savoys' territories to their rightful owner and Spanish ally Emanuele Filiberto di Savoia – known as *Testa 'd fer* (Iron-head), for his genius in military strategy – officially made Turin the capital of the family dominions.

At the time, Turin was a largely medieval city of somewhat fewer than 20,000 inhabitants. Emanuele Filiberto and his son Carlo Emanuele I set to work rearranging and fortifying Turin and its region, turning the city into a capital *a tutti gli effetti*, building the Mastio della Cittadella (1564-6; *see p66*), and taking steps against the French presumption that they could march through Piedmont and on down the peninsula as and when they pleased.

To provide trappings of grandeur for their new capital, the Savoy rulers summoned some of the age's greatest artists and architects – not always a blessing at a time when mannerist tastes were eking out the last vestiges of the Renaissance in works that were not always of true genius. Federico Zuccari, a native of Urbino who made his name at the magnificent Palazzo Farnese at Caprarola north of Rome, arrived in Turin in 1605. In 1584 Ascanio Vitozzi was given the job of opening up a whole new suburb along the axis of what is now via Roma. But the greatest architectural triumphs came somewhat later, with the arrival in Turin of Guarino Guarini (1666-81) and of Filippo Juvarra in the early years of the 18th century (*see also p25* **Masters of the Baroque**).

Despite more or less constant low-grade war between 1588 and 1602, a devastating outbreak of plague in 1629-30 and a tendency towards famine on the outer, mountainous reaches of the region, the fertile plains under the Savoys' control were in general well managed, with religious houses overseeing massive *bonifiche* (draining) of marshy plains and the ruling family encouraging industries such as silk, ceramics, carriage-making, linen and glass.

With France and Spain still itching to achieve European hegemony, a strategically vital crossroads such as Savoy might have been expected, at the very least, to perfect the art of hedging its diplomatic bets. Instead, the duchy dithered and double-crossed, sending out signals that were far from clear to the belligerents. After Vittorio Amedeo I died at a young age in 1637, his widow Marie Christine,

The Savoys ruled supreme.

the sister of King Louis XIII of France, became regent (*Madama reale*), and was, naturally, fiercely pro-France. Not so her in-laws who, behind her back, courted the Spanish camp until the French invaded Savoy in 1640 and devastated Turin after a siege. Things calmed down somewhat during the reign of Carlo Emanuele II (who technically ruled from 1638 to 1675, though had no real power until the death of his regent-mother in 1663), who focused his energies on extending the city down to the banks of the Po and on commissioning important works such as Guarino Guarini's Cappella della Sindone (*see p58*), which symbolically and physically linked the seats of temporal and ecclesiastical power in the city.

Turin strayed firmly back into the French fold on Carlo Emanuele's death in 1675 when his widow, Marie Jeanne Battiste de Nemours, became Turin's second *Madama reale*. By 1684, however, her son Vittorio Amedeo II had had enough of this policy and ousted his *madame mère*. His marriage to the French king's niece, Anne d'Orléans, was a piece of diplomatic skullduggery that fooled no one. Ostensibly allied with France, Vittorio Amedeo did a not-so-secret deal with the Spanish-Germanic-English alliance, thus

The four horsemen of the Risorgimento

In the mid 19th century Italy was a patchwork: Bourbons ruled the Kingdom of the Two Sicilies in the South, the Savoy family the Kingdom of Sardinia-Piedmont in the North. Sandwiched between were the backwards, feudal papal states, plus smaller duchies in Tuscany, Modena, Parma and Romagna. Lombardy and the Veneto were under Austrian control. As the winds of liberalism shook Europe's absolute monarchies around 1848, a slew of Italian nationalists emerged, the most able of them in Piedmont – perhaps because they were closest to the revolutionary gale blowing from France, or because they had an easier time of persuading the fading Savoy dynasty to back them. The Risorgimento that led to Italian unification was no movement of the masses: the middle-to-upper class intelligentsia remained firmly in control.

Massimo Taparelli, marchese d'Azeglio (1798-1866), dabbled in painting and literature before falling back on politics where his talents were undoubtedly greater. **Massimo d'Azeglio** was no man of the people: the two mainstays of his very conservative policy were expelling foreign rulers – namely, the Austrians – from Italian soil and uniting the various states of the peninsula under a Savoy monarch. For his role in the battle against the Austrians in 1848, King Vittorio Emanuele II made D'Azeglio prime minister in 1849. He remained in that office for three years, until he met his nemesis in an up-and-coming political spark called Camillo Cavour. Resigning in disagreement with this steamroller of a reformer, D'Azeglio led a quiet life thereafter writing pamphlets on national identity.

If the Risorgimento had a popular front, it centred on **Giuseppe Mazzini** (1805-72), a doctor's son from Genoa and an out-and-out republican. As a young lawyer he defended the poor. When he was unmasked as a member of the secret republican Carbonari society, he was condemned to exile and moved to Marseilles where in 1832 he founded *Giovine Italia* (Young Italy), a patriotic movement inspired by Mazzini's catchphrase 'neither pope nor king'. By 1833 *Giovine Italia* boasted 60,000 members around Italy. But liberal fervour never translated into revolutionary success: a planned uprising in Piedmont in 1833 was crushed before it got off the ground. By 1837 *Giovine Italia* had

fizzled out and Mazzini moved to London, where he set up a school for Italian boys. When in 1844 he claimed that British authorities were reading his mail, Mazzini's intellectual friends took up his case: shamefacedly, the British government admitted to spying on him and passing information to authorities in Piedmont. Mazzini returned home in 1848, when Milan and Piedmont launched a campaign to oust the Austrians from northern Italy; Milanese leaders soon made it clear that his republican stance was out of line. After a brief stretch fighting with the irregular army of Giuseppe Garibaldi, he made his way to Rome, where a republican uprising had driven out the pope; there he was invited to become part of a ruling triumvirate and showed exceptional administrative skills. But the Catholic states of Europe soon moved in to crush the Roman republic, forcing Mazzini back to London where he edited revolutionary papers and hatched unfeasible plots, much to the annoyance of Cavour who, unfairly, called him 'chief of the assassins'. Mazzini made a last-ditch attempt to swim against the monarchist tide in 1870 when he led a republican uprising in Sicily. He was arrested, then released, and made his embittered way to Switzerland.

Giuseppe Garibaldi (1807-82) was the armed wing of the Risorgimento, a loose cannon whose enthusiastic, idealistic contribution to national unity failed to endear him to Risorgimento politicians. Garibaldi hailed from Nice, traditionally a Savoy dominion. A sea captain, he served in the Piedmontese navy until he came under the influence of Mazzini and joined a failed republican uprising. Fleeing a death sentence, he made his way to South America where he threw in his swashbuckling lot with revolutionary forces in Brazil and Uruguay. His fame spread to Europe, where he was lionised as a wild, poncho-clad Romantic. In 1848 Garibaldi returned to Italy and offered the services of his Italian 'Red Shirt' legion to the pope and to Piedmont's king. When both rejected him, he made his way to Milan and Mazzini, and continued his own private guerrilla war against the Austrians well after Piedmont had called a truce. When word reached him that Pope Pius IX had fled Rome, he led his soldiers south. He was elected to the Roman assembly and placed himself in charge of Roman defence. His fight against the French on the Gianicolo hill is the stuff of legend, no less so because his tiny force was routed by vastly superior French numbers, and hacked a valiant retreat through central Italy. Garibaldi was forced into exile, crossing the Atlantic and waiting for a chance to return. By 1854 Piedmont's prime minister Camillo Cavour had realised that the rebel was safer as an ally than an enemy, and that enticing him away from Mazzini's republican influence could only be to the monarchists' advantage. Now a general in the Piedmontese army, Garibaldi helped drive the Austrians out of Lombardy. But the relationship between Garibaldi and the king remained tense: the soldier was struggling for a united Italy, Vittorio Emanuele for an expanded Piedmont.

The king promised, then withdrew, support for a planned attack on the papal states; he infuriated Garibaldi by handing Nice over to France; and he made no move to back him when the 'Hero of Two Worlds' headed for Sicily with 1,000 men – the famous '*mille*' – to begin a conquest of the Bourbon kingdom in southern Italy. In September 1860 the South voted to join Vittorio Emanuele's united Italy. Garibaldi's request to be viceroy of Naples was rejected; the hero – considered a dangerous radical by conservative politicians and a rival to his own popularity by the king – slunk into self-imposed exile on the island of Caprera, from where he launched barbed criticisms. From time to time he emerged to lead another campaign, including the one in 1866 that rid Venice of the Austrians and brought it into the Italian fold. But on all occasions, any support given to him by the state was hushed up unless he won, and his ever-longer island sojourns brought nothing but relief to the king and his ministers.

At the age of 14, **Camillo Benso, conte di Cavour** (1810-61), refused the coveted post of page-boy to Prince Carlo Alberto (the uniform, he said, was ridiculous), thus confirming the fears of his illustrious parents and the suspicions of his tutors at the military academy: that this bright spark of a youth had liberal leanings that needed to be weeded out. His first postings in the Savoy army's engineers were, therefore, in far-flung places. Later, when he was stationed in Genoa, he came under the influence of the liberal intelligentsia, and followed closely events in

neighbouring France where the Bourbon king Charles X had been ousted in favour of liberal Louis-Philippe. Cavour was placed under police surveillance until his father persuaded the powers-that-be to send him back to the sticks; predictably, his son was so frustrated that he left the army in 1831. His family set him to managing country estates where Cavour's long-standing fixations against absolutism, the clergy and the aristocracy were joined by a fervour for improving the lot of the poor. During visits to London and Paris Cavour decided that liberalism and progress were Good, revolution and bloody uprisings Bad, a belief that underpinned his prolific political writings thereafter. As the revolutionary year of 1848 approached, Cavour's newspaper *Il Risorgimento* spoke out in favour of drastic economic and political reform, not to mention war to drive Austria out of Lombardy and the Veneto. Elected to parliament, however, Cavour turned less belligerent; when he championed a peace treaty with Austria, he was taken under the wing of Massimo d'Azeglio's reactionary right-wing coalition and given a cabinet post. But Cavour's heart was firmly moderate: he formed a broad-based centre-left/centre-right alliance, and D'Azeglio resigned.

From 1852 until his death, Cavour became the effective political leader of the realm. It was Cavour's great talent for diplomacy that put the 'Italian question' on the agenda at the Congress of Paris (1856) after the Crimean War. With French help, the Piedmontese evicted Austria from Lombardy; the war sparked revolutionary uprisings across the central Italian duchies and in areas of the papal states, but it was only by ceding Nice and Savoy that Piedmont persuaded the European powers to let it take control of greater swathes of Italy. In 1860 the Bourbon Kingdom of the Two Sicilies came under Savoy control, thanks to a brilliant military campaign by Giuseppe Garibaldi. Garibaldi's popularity made it all the more difficult for Cavour to engineer a peaceful handover of Rome to the newly united state while Garibaldi sought to overthrow the papal regime. Cavour died before a solution was reached; it was not until 1870 that the French dismantled their pope-protecting garrison in Rome, allowing Italian troops to march into what would become the nation's capital.

opening up his territory to vituperative reprisals by the French, from which he was relieved only by the hefty intervention of Imperial (German) troops in 1691.

Vittorio Amedeo failed utterly to learn by the experience. When the War of Spanish Succession erupted in 1700, he allied himself with the French, only to switch sides, bringing a besieging army of 40,000, complete with the latest in heavy artillery, to the walls of Turin. After four months of hardship it was the troops of the Holy Roman Emperor who once again delivered Turin from the furious French. They arrived none too soon: the night before, local hero Pietro Micca (see p7 **Pietro Micca**) had sacrificed his own life as he staved off the final French onslaught by using explosives to bring down the access tunnels beneath the Cittadella (see p66).

FRENCH OCCUPATION

The Peace of Utrecht (1713) was good to the Savoys, granting them the title of king, and adding Sicily to their possessions. In 1720 Sicily was swapped for Sardinia (Sicily went to Austria), but not before the king had visited his southern Italian dominion and made the acquaintance of architect Filippo Juvarra who was to make a huge impact on Turin's urban planning and skyline. The Sicilian designed the Quartieri Militari (see p63), the basilica di Superga (see p91) and the spectacular Palazzina di Stupinigi (see p94).

Early in the 18th century, Vittorio Amedeo's policy of extreme centralisation had a trickle-down effect on the art and architecture of the region. Turin's stately if somewhat cold baroque became the local benchmark: new edifices adhered rigidly to its specifications and existing churches were rebuilt or altered accordingly. With political stability well established and a flourishing industry-driven economy, Turin's population soared, and city authorities responded by extending the city still further, along via Dora Grossa.

By the late 18th century, the House of Savoy was looking frayed, unravelling as the Revolution in neighbouring France went into high gear, and going to pieces as Napoleon descended on the Italian peninsula in 1796. Piedmont's liberals were pleased to see the Corsican general smiting their absolute monarchy; they were less pleased when the French occupiers left Vittorio Amedeo III quietly on his throne – removing his power, granted, but leaving the appearance of it at least. Vittorio Amedeo's successor Carlo Emanuele IV was less happy about playing the French puppet and withdrew to his kingdom in Sardinia, the shouts of joy of his former subjects, ecstatic at his departure, echoing in his ears.

The French failed royally to live up to Piedmontese expectations, sacking the vanquished kingdom so vindictively that in 1799 an Austro-Russian force felt justified in moving back in. But though Austria was rarely averse to reinstating absolute monarchs, in this case it preferred to leave Carlo Emanuele on his Mediterranean island (Sardinia was the only realm in western Europe not overrun by Napoleon), putting Turin under military command. But this situation didn't last long. By 1802 the French were back and Turin had been declared one of the key cities of Napoleon's Italian state. The French emperor even made his brother-in-law, Prince Camillo Borghese, his viceroy there in 1808. Though the fall of Napoleon brought this state of affairs to a close in 1814, the French had used their decade-plus rule to ensure that Turin was transformed from impregnable fortress to amenable town, ripping down the city walls.

The Savoy who was returned to the throne in Turin by the Congress of Vienna was Vittorio Emanuele I. Because he was a novelty he was initially greeted enthusiastically by his subjects. They soon realised, however, that their monarch had been undisturbed by the revolutionary winds of change blowing across Europe. Liberal uprisings in 1821 persuaded Vittorio Emanuele to abdicate in favour of his brother Carlo Felice, who focused his energies on giving his capital impressive landmarks – piazze Carlo Felice, Emanuele Filiberto (now della Repubblica) and Vittorio Emanuele (now Vittorio Veneto) – rather than on a liberal constitution.

IL RISORGIMENTO

The main Savoy line died with Carlo Felice. Carlo Alberto I hailed from the cadet Savoia-Carignano branch, and was rumoured to be liberally inclined – until, that is, he ascended the throne. Certainly, in the arts and sciences Carlo Alberto was a breath of fresh air for the city, giving it its Accademia delle Scienze and Accademia di Belle Arti and opening the Galleria Sabauda (see p71) and the Accademia Albertina (see p78) to the public. But politically speaking he was a ditherer, preferring non-decision to change – this, in a city seething with reformers of the calibre of Massimo d'Azeglio and, in particular, Camillo Benso, Conte di Cavour (see p10 **The four horsemen of the Risorgimento**). The wavering monarch was forced to approve the liberal Statuto Albertino in 1848, and to declare a disastrous war against absolutist Austria the following year, after which he abdicated in favour of his son

Palazzo Carignano, birthplace of kings. *See p72.*

Vittorio Emanuele II, who was to oversee the Risorgimento movement that would lead to the unification of Italy.

As more and more of the Italian peninsula came under Piedmontese control from 1859, a region that had long been 'on the edge' – of Italy, of France, a place of passage – found itself faced with the prospect, then the reality, of being the capital of a united nation stretching, with one or two interruptions, from the Alps to Sicily. The exultation manifested itself in more expansion, more grandiose (or pompous) architecture fit for a European capital, and scenes of joy the like of which had never been witnessed before when the Italian parliament first met in February 1861 in Palazzo Carignano (*see p72*). The joy was matched only by fury when, in 1864, Florence was suddenly declared Italy's capital. The blow to morale apart, banks, arms manufacturers and other suppliers of the Turin national government stared economic disaster in the face. As adminstrative taggerson followed parliament to Florence (and then to Rome in 1870), Turin's population fell, many of its now-bankrupt small businessmen returning to the poor country villages from which they thought they had escaped forever.

THE AGE OF INDUSTRY

But all was not bleak on the economic front. Piedmont's industry had traditionally been mostly of the small-scale variety, meeting the needs of the kingdom. In the 1850s economic reforms introduced by Cavour (*see p10* **The four horsemen of the Risorgimento**) favoured foreign trade – with exports through the port of Genoa in the neighbouring region of Liguria, which had come under Savoy control in 1814 – and boosted larger-scale industry, particularly after the transfer of Italy's capital. The Cavour canal (1860-3) was dug to improve irrigation in the rice paddies (*see p182* **Piedmont paddies**); the Fréjus tunnel (1857-71) provided speedier links with French markets. The 1880s were hard years for Turin, with banks failing, savers losing their nest eggs and a crisis in the agricultural sector. But with extraordinary foresight, Piedmont's political leaders had also focused on providing power for burgeoning large industry: without the electricity supply provided by local companies, it is doubtful whether Piedmont's major textile, metalworking, chemical and agro industries would have been so successful; nor whether the world of business machinery would have taken the turn it did with the foundation in 1908 in Ivrea of Olivetti; nor whether the Fabbrica Italiana Automobili Torino (Fiat), founded in 1899, would have gone on to become one of the world's leading car makers.

Turin also led the cinema world from 1904 (*see also pp139-40*) when Arturo Ambrosio built Italy's first cinema studio, and Giovanni Pastrone founded Itala Film (1908). The Turin-produced *Cabiria* (1914), directed by Pastrone with the help of poet and megalomaniac

Literary Turin

It was not until the 20th century that Turin became a major literary centre. In the 18th and 19th centuries, perhaps owing to the city's crucial role in the complicated power-politics of the day, the writers associated with Turin tended to have as much interest in political affairs as in literature.

The first major writer connected with Turin was the tragedian and poet **Vittorio Alfieri** (1749-1803), who was born in Asti (*see* p185) but educated in Turin until the age of 17, when he began a series of journeys that were to take him all over Europe throughout the course of his life. His desire to be free of the Kingdom of Sardinia-Piedmont was such that he gave up his estates to his sister in exchange for an allowance. A passionate lover of libertarian causes, who advocated the violent overthrow of all tyrants, Alfieri was a Romantic figure born before the Romantic age. His admiration for the free institutions of Britain was paralleled by ardent affairs of the heart with British or British-connected ladies; in 1771 he fought a duel in London with the husband of his lover Penelope Pitt; he later became devotedly attached to the separated wife of Charles Edward Stuart, the Young Pretender.

Although he spent relatively little time in Turin, his influence was felt by subsequent generations, including such political figures as **Cesare Balbo** (1789-1853) and **Massimo D'Azeglio** (1798-1866; *see also* p10 **The four horsemen of the Risorgimento**). The former, who served in the Napoleonic administration of Piedmont, founded a literary academy in the city; Massimo D'Azeglio, who became famous with historical novels on patriotic themes, was a moderate liberal, who desired an Italy free of foreign influence, but was unconvinced by Count Camillo Cavour's (*see* p10 **The four horsemen of the Risorgimento**) programmes for unity. The work that has survived best is his book of memoirs, *I miei ricordi* (published 1867), which is still read for the affectionate descriptions of the Turin of his youth.

The most famous Turin writer of the 19th century is undoubtedly **Edmondo De Amicis** (1846-1908), whose sentimental, patriotic school story *Cuore* (translated both as *Cuore: the Heart of a Boy* and *Heart: a School Boy's Journal*) has been jerking tears ever since it was first published in 1886. De Amicis, who

Turin's greatest, Primo Levi.

was involved in the struggle for Italian unification, includes in this Turin-based novel the figures of immigrants from southern Italy, making an early plea for national solidarity that is still a long way from being achieved.

Guido Gozzano (1883-1916) was the first to discover the poetical side of this city of bourgeois respectability; in his exquisite, gently decadent verse he pays homage to Turin's air of gentle melancholy, while indulging in nostalgia for a mythical Piedmont of the 19th century.

As Turin grew in political and economic importance it began to attract writers from other parts of Italy. One of the first to move to Turin for a mixture of literary and economic reasons was the Veronese writer **Emilio Salgari** (1863-1911), Italy's Jules Verne. Never having travelled outside Italy, apart from an Adriatic cruise, Salgari wrote 85 novels and over 100 short stories of adventure set in far-flung exotic locations. There was thus very little that was specifically *torinese* about his writings; he did, however, initiate what was to become a sad trend among Turin writers, committing suicide after a series of family and financial troubles.

Turin's centre-stage role in 20th-century Italian literature can be ascribed mainly to the presence of one important publishing house: **Einaudi**. It was founded in 1933 by Giulio Einaudi, son of a famous economist and bibliophile, Luigi Einaudi, who was to become, in 1948, the first president of the Italian Republic. Giulio Einaudi (1912-99) had shown an interest in publishing while still at school; with family backing and the support of like-minded friends he launched the firm in the same building that had held the offices of *Ordine Nuovo*, the journal of Antonio Gramsci, founder of Italy's Communist Party. From the very start the publishing firm ran into trouble with the Fascist authorities and in 1935 Giulio Einaudi was arrested, together with an impressive list of colleagues that included all the major names of literary Turin (Leone Ginzburg, Vittorio Foa, Norberto Bobbio, Cesare Pavese and Carlo Levi) and sent to temporary internal exile. However, in 1936 the firm was given permission to start up again, continuing its policy of publishing both new Italian works and a number of major foreign authors, from Charles Dickens and Herman Melville (Pavese had translated *Moby-Dick* in 1932) to Edgar Lee Masters and Gertrude Stein.

With the German invasion of Italy, most of the members of the firm joined the partisan movement. Leone Ginzburg was taken prisoner in Rome, where he died in prison, leaving his wife with three small children. With her family memoir, *Lessico famigliare*, **Natalia Ginzburg** was to become one of the best-known authors on the Einaudi list.

After the war, the publishing house was one of the few that could boast a consistent record of anti-Fascism. Other writers came from outside Turin to join. One was the Sicilian-born poet **Elio Vittorini** (1908-66), who had taught himself to read English and who did more than any other writer at the time to promote American literature, translating (with great literary flair but not always comparable accuracy) such authors as Ernest Hemingway and William Faulkner. **Cesare Pavese** (1908-50) now did less translation work, devoting himself to his own short stories and novels, usually based on his own experience of attempting to adjust to city life after a childhood in the country. He committed suicide in a Turin hotel in 1950, shortly after the publication of his masterpiece, *La luna e i falò* (*The Moon and the Bonfires*).

Italo Calvino (1923-85) was undoubtedly the firm's most valuable acquisition. After his wartime experience as a partisan, he moved to Turin to study at the university, becoming involved with Vittorini's short-lived literary journal, *Il Politecnico*. At Einaudi he became

a key figure, directing its editorial choices; he continued to work for the firm even after moving to Paris in 1964. Calvino's own works struck a new note in post-war Italian fiction; just when grim realism seemed obligatory, Calvino published a trilogy of fantastic, allegorical novels, *I nostri antenati* (*Our Ancestors*), that owed more to the Italian tradition of epic romance than to any contemporary trends in the Italian novel.

The city's greatest native-born writer was **Primo Levi** (1919-87). He lived almost all his life in the same house on corso Re Umberto where he was born. However, the few years he spent away from Turin – in Auschwitz – inevitably became the central subject of his major works, beginning with the harrowing classic *Se questo è un uomo* (1947, *If This Is a Man*). After a life devoted to the task of persistent, courageous testimony, Primo Levi committed suicide in the house on corso Re Umberto on 11 April 1987.

Almost certainly the most enjoyable portrayal of the city of Turin is to be found in two detective stories by the novel-writing duo of **Carlo Fruttero** (from Turin) and **Franco Lucentini** (from Rome), *La donna della domenica* (1972, *The Sunday Woman*) and *A che punto è la notte?* (1979). These two writers, born respectively in 1926 and 1920, began collaborating in the 1960s and were among the first to give literary dignity to the crime-fiction genre in Italy, taking it out of the cheap yellow-back paperbacks to which it had always been relegated. They also collaborated on a number of science-fiction anthologies, helping to promulgate this genre as well. Franco Lucentini brought the partnership to an end in August 2002, committing suicide in his house in piazza Vittorio Veneto in the same way as Primo Levi, throwing himself down the stairwell.

The most important new name in Turin literary circles is that of **Alessandro Baricco** (born 1958), author of *Novecento* (1994), which was turned into a film by Giuseppe Tornatore (*La leggenda del pianista sull'oceano*), and *Seta* (1996, *Silk*). Baricco has brought his musical skills (he started his career as a music critic) to the art of fiction, experimenting playfully in a variety of genres. He has also founded one of Italy's few creative-writing schools, named 'Holden' after the protagonist of *The Catcher in the Rye*.

Gabriele d'Annunzio, remains a celluloid classic. Growing industrialisation brought growing industrial strife in its wake, and Turin was in the vanguard during the *Biennio rosso* (two red years) from 1920 when striking workers occupied factories. When Benito Mussolini came to power in 1923, even industrialists with hitherto impeccable liberal credentials saw him as their saviour, and gave his henchmen carte blanche to put down the protests in any way deemed necessary. Il Duce's drive for a self-sufficient state helped enlarge industries still further, bringing immigrants en masse to Piedmont, especially from the backward, agricultural and poverty-stricken Veneto, and sending jerry-built housing rambling over the once-agricultural lands towards Rivoli (*see p94*) and Venaria (*see p89*).

The crash of 1929 took its toll in this industrialised corner of the world, with Fiat among the few companies riding the storm. Not even the outbreak of war could stop the inexorable rise of this colossus, which turned its hand to producing military equipment.

Occupied by German troops in October 1943 and heavily bombed by both sides before Liberation in April 1945, Turin emerged from the war with 40 per cent of its buildings in rubble and some 1,000 factories destroyed or damaged. Its Resistance movement had been courageous and vital, its blue collar population had had to struggle hard to survive the rigours of the conflict and accompanying food shortages. The city that went to vote in the 1946 referendum on a Savoy ruling house – now fatally compromised by its collaboration with the Fascist regime – was no comfortable burgh of profoundly monarchist leanings; the monarchy was rejected here, and left-wingers did resoundingly well in elections.

Piedmont's economic resurgence in the aftermath of war was nothing short of miraculous and was due, once again, to its electrical power supply, which fuelled the region through its darkest days and into a post-war boom. The lure of jobs in industry was strong in the still-starving agricultural South. Between 1951 and 1961 the city's population soared from 300,000 to one million, sparking what proved to be an urban planning catastrophe for Turin's hinterland. The industrial unrest of the 1970s turned Turin's factories – and Fiat's main Mirafiori plant in particular – into a hotbed of support for the furthest fringes of extra-parliamentary action: in his book *A viso aperto*, Renato Curcio, founder of the extreme-left Red Brigades (BR) terrorists, recalls that the disgusted reaction of blue collar Fiat employees to a controversial metalworkers' contract signed in 1973 was a key factor in pushing the BR into armed insurrection: 'That defeat made us realise that workers' power could no longer be confined within factories… We had to attack the snake at its head, raising the level of our struggle and challenging political power head on.'

Fiat spearheaded Turin's industrial boom.

Turin Today

In the run-up to the 2006 Winter Olympics Turin is trying to shed its singular association with Fiat once and for all.

In the last three decades of the 20th century a radical restructuring of Turin's industrial fabric, an inversion in demographic trends and a prolonged economic downturn sparked profound changes in the city's makeup.

For nearly a century, Fiat had been to Turin what the Catholic Church is to the Vatican City. So the long-drawn-out crisis at the company's auto unit (*see p21* **Whither Fiat?**) had inevitable repercussions on the local economy; little by little, the car maker lost its primacy as the city's main employer. In a radical turnaround for what ha long been Italy's industrial powerhouse, Turin's municipal administration is now the city's biggest revenue generator, and service industries have flourished, accounting for 68 per cent of the city's gross domestic product.

For decades, discussios concerning Turin's future have inevitably tagged on the catchphrase '*dopo Fiat*' (post-Fiat). That '*dopo*' is still at an embryonic phase. Certainly, the city's business community and its local

administrators saw winning the bid for the 2006 Winter Olympics as manna from heaven. 'Remember Barcelona' has become the civic mantra, an acknowledgement of the Spanish city's intelligent and successful handling of the 1992 Olympics, which continued to boost tourism and investment in Barcelona long after the Games were over. The Olympics have also helped to set some definite goals in Turin's scramble to transform Italy's Detroit into a diversified economy. But such a profound metamorphosis is inevitably a slow process.

In the meantime, contemporary Turin remains a work in progess. This is true in a literal sense – construction sites abound, physical manifestations of Turin's socio-economic transformation. Millions of euros have been invested in Olympic facilities, in urban regeneration projects, in transportation infrastructure and in the conversion of more than two million square metres (21.5 million square feet) of divested industrial areas to new use. In ten years, local administrators say,

Body builders

In 1912 **Giovanni Bertone** (www.bertone.it) opened a *carradore* (coach maker's shop) in Turin but soon – and particularly after his son Nuccio joined the family workshop in 1914 – placed his skills at the disposal of the city's new auto manufacturers (*see p21* **Whither Fiat?**). With its extraordinary range of details, Bertone's Fiat 527 Ardita 2500 (1934-6) was a turning point in car design. The company consolidated its reputation producing popular cars such as the Alfa Romeo Giulietta Sprint (1954), the Alfa Romeo 2600 Sprint (1960), the Fiat 850 Spider (1965) and the Lancia Stratos line in the 1970s. Nuccio ran the company until his death in 1997, since when Bertone engineers have continued to produce instantly recognisable models. Latest Bertone designs include the Opel Astra Cabrio (2000) and BMW's C1 motorbike (1999).

Pininfarina (www.pininfarina.it) is named after Battista Farina, known as *Pinin* (Tiny), who in the 1930s transformed his father's body shop into a producer of custom-built cars. But his dream of turning 'luxury' designs into mass-produced vehicles came in 1947 with the Cisitalia Coupé; this sporty number was the first car ever to be put on display in New York's MOMA. Since 1952, thanks to the founder's son Sergio, Pininfarina's name has been synonymous with Ferrari, but the group also designed less exclusive models, including the Fiat 6C 1500 cabriolet (1947), the Austin A40 (1956), the Alfa Romeo 1600 Spider Duetto (1966) and the Jaguar XJ-S (1978). Pininfarina's 2002 models included the Daiwoo Nubira saloon, the StreetKa and the Ferrari Enzo.

Giorgetto Giugiaro (www.italdesign.it) was one of Nuccio Bertone's many protégés. It was while still at Bertone that he created such classics as the Maserati 5000 (1961) and the Chevrolet Corvair Testudo (1963). In 1969 Giugiaro went out on his own with Italdesign, creating over 200 car models – including the Lotus Esprit (1972), Fiat's Panda and Puntos and a range of Volkswagen Golfs – not to mention architectural and design projects including Atrium (*see p228* **Atrium**). Latest car designs include the Toyota Alessandro Volta and the Alfa Romeo Visconti.

Turin will look very different. But grand projects inevitably attract controversy and despite the vision of the high-profile architects – including Mario Botta and Massimiliano Fuksas – called in to assist in the transformation, some critics have suggested that the city's urban redevelopments lack the architectural innovation to make a lasting impact on its contemporary topography.

Physical transformation has gone hand in hand with economic and social revolution. In 1974 Turin counted 1,203,000 residents. It now has around 905,000, after losing almost a quarter of its population in 25 years. Only the steady influx of immigrants from non-European Union countries – in 2003 the city was home to 61,200 legal immigrants; that's 6.7 per cent of the population – buffeted the steady demographic decline. Statistics show that 79 per cent of the resident foreigners are under 40, which could help counter future prognostics that see Turin's population shrinking still further in the next three decades.

The presence of immigrant populations – nearly a third of which hail from North Africa, primarily Morocco – has been most felt in certain neighbourhoods such as San Salvario and Porta Palazzo (*see p60*), and integration has not always been easy, a phenomenon enhanced by the *torinesi*'s legendary tendency to be standoffish. The late 1990s in particular were marked by a series of incidents and since then some social tension has prevailed, especially towards the growing Muslim population.

Social tension also accompanied the progressive decline in Fiat's fortunes throughout the 1970s, '80s and well into the '90s. However, if a point of no return in Turin's history as a one-company-town can be identified it would have to be when the Lingotto plant (*see p86*) – once the pulsing heart of Fiat manufacturing – closed down in 1982. Architect Renzo Piano later transformed the Lingotto into a multi-functional complex that includes a shopping centre, a university faculty, a conference centre and a trade fair facility. For the 2006 shenanigans, the Lingotto is to be connected by means of a foot-bridge to the Olympic Village.

The closing of the Lingotto set off alarm bells that were difficult to ignore. Even as Turin has maintained its position as the Italian capital of the automotive sector, boosted by the presence of world-renowned car designers such as Bertone, Italdesign-Giugiaro and Pininfarina (*see left* **Body builders**), economic diversification has taken several paths.

The city drew upon a long-standing tradition in the telecommunications sector – initially established by companies like Sip, Stet (which went on to become Telecom Italia) and Olivetti in nearby Ivrea (*see p175* **Adriano's legacy**) – to become one of Italy's first hi-tech clusters, or technology districts. Motorola opened a specialised laboratory for cellular phones here in 1999 and there are now nearly 7,000 ICT companies in the area employing more than 50,000 people. Research in the sector – which is also fostered by local universities – is mainly focusing on wireless technologies.

Turin is also putting money where mouths are, promoting oeno-gastronomic trade fairs and taste-seeking tourists. Here again, tradition plays a logical antecedent, because Turin is home to chocolate makers Caffarel, Ferrero (*see p194* **Middle-aged spread**) and Peyrano, to name but three; not to mention Carpano and Campari (*see p122* **No Carpano, no party**), without which aperitivo hour would be a very sad moment of the day indeed.

Trade fairs such as the **Salone del Gusto** (*see p134*), which is sponsored by the Slow Food association (*see p31* **Slow and steady**), which is based in the nearby town of Bra, have made Turin synonymous with food and wine

appreciation. The 2002 Salone del Gusto, held at the Lingotto, attracted more than 138,000 visitors, helping to make oeno-gastronomic tourism one of the cornerstones of the region's economic rebirth.

The gradual weaning of Turin from its Fiat-dependent status has certainly worked in its favour from an image point of view. Turin may have been the backbone of Italian industry but it was hard to push cultural tourism in a city that was seen as industrious but notoriously grey. The new and improved Turin is still grey – you can't fool Mother Nature – but it's bursting with cultural initiatives and is going all out to set off its many artistic gems, from former Savoy residences to the **Museo Egizio** (*see p71*), which boasts one of the most important collections of ancient artefacts in the world.

Support for the new civic cultural zeitgeist has also come from a key alignment of public art museums, private foundations and private art galleries as well as municipal initiatives supporting the arts and a respected trade fair **Artissima** (*see p134*), all of which have contributed to making Turin the contemporary art capital of Italy. With the support of City Hall, Turin is well on its way to being a major player on the international art scene.

Tourism and business also rub shoulders in the symbiotic relationship that exists between the city and celluloid, a liaison that dates back to the late 1890s. From 1906 to 1916 Turin was the world film production capital. Italy's first motion picture studios were built here and production companies like FERT, Ambrosio and Gloria made early cinema history, salient moments of which can be relived first hand at the excellent **Museo nazionale del cinema** (*see p78*) in the Mole Antonelliana. Turin's limelight was later snuffed out by Hollywood-on-the-Tiber, as Rome's Cinecittà studios were known, but a new boom in filmmaking followed the birth of the Torino Film Commission in 2000 as well as the development of the Virtual Reality and Multimedia Park (*see p138*) and LUMIQ studios. Since then dozens of films and television productions have been shot here.

At the beginning of the third millennium, Turin is poised to present its new guise as a modern industrial city. The construction – stalled at the time of writing – of a high-speed train connection with Lyon is touted as the next step towards greater European integration and is seen as fundamental to the city's future development. But even before then, local administrators hope that the 2006 Winter Olympic Games will have given Turin a new outlook in a Fiat-free world.

Whither Fiat?

An oft-repeated slogan attributed to Fiat workers is: 'Agnelli is Fiat, Fiat is Turin and Turin is Italy', a corollary of sorts of the late Gianni Agnelli's own famous quip 'What's good for Fiat is good for Italy'. Rarely have private and public fortunes been so incestuously intertwined (barring, perhaps, those of Italy's current prime minister Silvio Berlusconi). Bereft of its royal family, shamed into exile, Italy's post-war republic anointed Fiat chairman Gianni Agnelli as its capitalist prince, and dedicated substantial resources to helping his company prosper. In return, Agnelli built Fiat into the symbol of the post-war 'economic miracle'. Turin – where Fiat was founded in 1899 – became the capital of this new Italian order, and in so doing inextricably bound its own prosperity to the company's alternating vicissitudes.

In good times, Fiat/Turin thrived. In 1902, the first year of production, 35 employees produced 24 automobiles. By 1916 Fiat had grown so quickly that Europe's largest factory, the Lingotto (see p86), was built to keep up with the increase in demand for passenger and racing cars, along with marine engines, trucks, trams, taxis and ball-bearings. The Mirafiori plant (see p85), inaugurated in 1939, was the first example of a mass production plant in Italy. By the outbreak of World War II, Fiat employed 50,000 workers in Turin.

Post-war Italy saw a renewed boom in business and an increase in workforce. As Fiat continued to pump out small, cheap cars, both in Turin and increasingly in developing

countries and then southern Italy, it broke ground in research. Fiat produced Italy's first jet aircraft, the first turbine-powered car and, more recently, the first common-rail engine.

But growth – and increasing dependency on mechanised assembly lines – brought with it social upheaval. During 1969 alone, industrial action accounted for 15 million hours of lost labour.

The 1970s saw Fiat begin its long process of divestment from Turin. In the following decades the Italian government did what it could to help Fiat, from introducing a form of unemployment benefit specially tailored to the auto giant's needs, to issuing cash incentives for the purchase of new cars. And Italians continued to be loyal Fiat buyers... mostly because an astute pricing policy left them without much of a choice. However, as Italy opened to greater competition in the 1990s Fiat began to flail. Competition in western markets, prompted by the flood of products manufactured in South-east Asia, forced Fiat to diversify.

When Gianni Agnelli (*pictured*) died in January 2003, many believed that his family would sell the heavily indebted auto unit. Instead, the Agnellis – now led by Gianni's brother Umberto – dug into their own pockets and injected new life into Fiat Auto. But, nostalgia aside, the success or otherwise of Fiat no longer determines the survival of the city as it previously did. Where once 130,000 employees worked for the auto giant in Turin, today fewer than 16,000 jobs hang on the company's fortunes.

Fiat. The pleasure of travelling in Italy.

New Panda. Don't call me baby.

Art & Architecture

Baroque grandeur, *stile Liberty* and Fascist monumentality –
Turin's history is echoed in its architecture.

The 20th-century painter Giorgio De Chirico once commented, 'Turin is the most profound, most enigmatic and most disquieting city not only of Italy but of the world.' In the raking shadows of the arcades that line the straight streets of Turin, De Chirico found a strange beauty that he captured in countless paintings. Turin is a city of architecture and urban design, and though important works of art grace the halls of the city's museums, Turin's history is best understood through the built forms that are a testament to the great families and minds that have contributed to the rich history of the city.

More so than any other it was the Savoy (Savoia) family that gave Turin its modern form. At the height of the Savoys' power in the 17th century, Turin's medieval and Renaissance streets and monuments were transformed to meet their taste and standards. While Italian models were a point of reference, Turin has always had a close relationship, politically and culturally, with France, and echoes of French

taste from 17th-century royal residences to 19th-century boulevards betray this rapport. The scale and grandeur of Turin's streets and *piazze* defy visitors' expectations of an Italian city, but bear eloquent witness to the city's history as the capital of the Savoy dynasty (*see p8* **The unstoppable Savoys**), brief status as the capital of Italy, and modern role as a centre of Italian industry.

ROMAN ORIGINS

The chequerboard street pattern of the city centre provides a clear link to Turin's origin as a Roman military outpost. What is today via Garibaldi was once the principle east–west axis (decumanus) of the ancient Augusta Taurinorum and it is likely that the Palazzo di Città (*see p62*) marks the site of the forum. But despite its rigid layout, little of the ancient city remains: there are scant ruins of a theatre (*see p58*) dating from the first century AD near the Palazzo Reale and, nearby, the remains of the Porta Palatina (*see p58*), one of the four original gates of the walled city.

Liberty details on **Casa Fenoglio**. *See p27.*

MEDIEVAL AND RENAISSANCE TURIN

Scant, too, are the traces of medieval Turin. The vaulted nave of the church of San Domenico (*see p62*) only hints at the heights the pointed arch was capable of reaching. Inside the church, the Cappella della Madonna delle Grazie holds the city's only remaining 14th-century frescoes.

It is outside the city that the technical skill and creative energies of medieval artists and architects working in the area can best be appreciated. At the Sacra di San Michele (*see p204*), a dense cluster of buildings dramatically perched on a rocky summit offers a powerful and evocative testament to the isolation of monastic life and the authority of the Church. Details such as the zodiac sculptures that frame the entrance to the lower church and the flying buttresses of the upper church are representative of artistic currents in Romanesque and Gothic sculpture and architecture respectively. The naturalism of the vegetable motifs found here is evidence of the strong artistic connection between France and Turin in this period, and it is likely that some of the sculptors who worked on the great cathedrals of France also found employment here.

During the Renaissance, the extraordinary climate in central Italy exerted a strong gravitational pull on artists and architects, leaving few to practise in this northern city. The cathedral of San Giovanni Battista (1491-8; *see p58* **Duomo**) is Turin's prime Renaissance monument, though the pointed arches inside betray a lingering hint of Gothic. Designed by the Florentine architect Meo del Caprino, the ordered stone façade indicates the presence of a new Renaissance sensibility.

The stars of Renaissance art rarely ventured as far as Turin, though works by Italian Renaissance masters **Antonello da Messina** and **Leonardo da Vinci** are found in Turin collections. It was little-known locals such as **Giovanni Martino Spanzotti** who introduced the Renaissance preference for greater naturalism to Turin and Piedmont. One of the more notable examples of his work is in the church of San Bernardino in Ivrea (*see p171*), where Spanzotti executed a fresco cycle that depicts the life of Christ in 21 scenes. Spanzotti's influence is evident in two works by the notable painter **Defendente Ferrari** also housed within Turin's cathedral: the polyptych of the *SS Crispin and Crispinian* (1505-7) and the *Baptism of Christ* (1510-13). Atmospheric perspective and the physical presence of the figures are all evidence of Renaissance principles of representation. Due to the itinerant nature of the Savoy court, works by these Renaissance artists can be found throughout the region.

THE BAROQUE CAPITAL

Turin is one of the great baroque cities of Europe and owes much of this to the absolute rule of the Savoy family. In keeping with standards of representation established by monarchs such as Louis XIV of France, the Savoys made every effort to translate their political ambition into powerful architectural and urban forms. In the process, most of pre-17th-century Turin was razed and piazza Castello (*see p52*) and the Duomo (*see p58*) became the centre of a new rigidly hierarchical urban system.

Emanuele Filiberto began this trend when he named Turin as the capital of his duchy in 1563, and Carlo Emanuele I, his son and successor, intensified his efforts. Both dukes looked throughout Italy and Europe for architects and artists to celebrate their patronage and rule. It is in this period that the foundations for the royal collection, housed today in the Accademia delle scienze (*see p71*), were laid. Carlo Emanuele I built significantly on his father's collection with new acquisitions from Venice and Flanders and was responsible for bringing

Masters of the baroque

Guarino Guarini

Architect, mathematician, theorist, astronomer and Theatine priest from Modena, Guarino Guarini (1624-83) remains one of the more enigmatic figures of the Italian baroque. Few of his buildings have survived and the history of his travels and studies prior to his arrival in Turin in 1666 remains obscure. Guarini's first project in Turin was the completion of the Theatine order's church of San Lorenzo (*see p53*) where he transformed the existing Latin cross plan into a centrally organised space. The contrasts of red, black and white marble add to the visual complexity and richness of the architectural perform-ance. As is often the case with Guarini's churches, the most breathtaking element is the soaring dome, which, some scholars argue, is inspired by the mosque in Cordoba, Spain. A similar technique was used in the Cappella della Santa Sindone (*see p58*) begun a year later for Carlo Emanuele II. The chapel housed the relic of the Holy Shroud and clearly articulates Guarini's ability to handle a complex symbolic and spatial programme. The chapel suffered considerable damage in a fire in 1997. Though primarily an architect of churches, Guarini was commissioned to design Palazzo Carignano (*see p72*) for Emanuele Filiberto, son of Carlo Emanuele, and the resulting curved brick façade was an inventive response to the sombre Italian palazzo style.

Filippo Juvarra

Of a later generation than Guarini and less indebted to the lessons of baroque Rome, the Sicilian Filippo Juvarra (1678-1736) was influenced by classical currents in French taste. Juvarra's spectacular west façade for the Palazzo Madama (1718-21; *see p54*) with its tall windows and classical references

shows the influence of French architecture and, in particular, seems to echo the formal order of Versailles. The grand staircase, a typical feature of baroque palaces, is a masterful display of spatial organisation. Crowning a hill east of Turin stands Juvarra's royal burial church at Superga (1717-31; *see p91*). The church was commissioned by Vittorio Amedeo II as a votive offering following victory in the Battle of Turin in 1706.

A ring of royal residences outside Turin – Venaria Reale (*see p89*), Stupinigi (*see p93*), Racconigi (*see p92* **Crown of delights**) and Rivoli (*see p94*) – remains as testimony to the wealth and power of the Savoys. Royal architects such as Amedeo di Castellamonte, Guarini and Juvarra all worked on these projects, and the French landscape designer **André Le Nôtre** planned the gardens for the Palazzo Reale and Racconigi. Among the most sumptuous is the hunting lodge designed by Juvarra. The central oval is the fulcrum for diagonally arranged wings that frame the principal entrance. The interior is richly decorated with frescoes and stucco work by artists such as **Charles André Van Loo** and **Giovan Battista Crosato**.

Bernardo Vittone

Bernardo Vittone (1702-70) studied painting in Rome, and after returning to Turin in 1733 was influenced by the work of Guarini and Juvarra. His greatest achievements can be found in a series of small, centrally planned churches in and around Turin: the Chapel of the Visitation in Vallinotto, Santa Chiara in Bra and Santa Maria dl Piazza (*see p65*). Vittone's light-filled domes are complemented by pastel shades that betray the influence of the playful taste of rococo design and the end of the baroque age in Turin.

Early Rationalism at **Palazzo Gualino**.
See p27.

sought-after artists such as **Federico Zuccari** and **Orazio Gentileschi** to Turin.

Under Carlo Emanuele I, following the direction of ducal architect and military engineer **Ascanio Vitozzi**, what was till then a tiny city clinging around the edges of piazza Castello was given its first significant extension to the south and east. In addition, piazza Castello was enlarged and given a regular arcaded perimeter. Vitozzi laid out a system of new streets that connected the centre of power at piazza Castello to the medieval and Renaissance city and to new districts. Laid out shortly before his death, the Contrada Nuova (today via Roma) continued the arcaded perimeter of piazza Castello and established the portico as an identifying characteristic of Turin. Additional streets, including what is now via di Palazzo di Città, connecting piazza Castello to the market-place in front of the Palazzo di Città (*see p62*), gave a new regular order to the hierarchy of the city, and visually and spatially affirmed the Savoy dynasty's absolute grip on power.

Carlo di Castellamonte carried on the work of Vitozzi as the Savoy rulers continued to manipulate the urban fabric to strengthen and legitimate their authority. Marie Christine of France, the widow of Vittorio Amedeo, was a particularly avid builder (it is worth noting that her hold on the throne was also particularly tenuous) and it was during her reign that the major work on the royal residence, the Palazzo Reale (*see p54*), was undertaken. She also authorised the extension of the Contrada Nuova (via Roma) and the creation of the elegant residential piazza San Carlo (1640s) – formerly piazza Reale – with the twin churches of San Carlo (*see p72*) and Santa Cristina (*see p75*). **Amedeo di Castellamonte**, son of Carlo di Castellamonte, directed the expansion of Turin in the late 17th century and is responsible for the design of the architecturally uniform and much-celebrated via Po.

It was within this ordered framework of broad, straight streets and regular *piazze* that some of the most extraordinary works of late baroque architecture were realised. The three principal protagonists of this effort were Guarino Guarini, Filippo Juvarra and Bernardo Vittone (*see p25* **Masters of the baroque**).

THE 19TH-CENTURY CITY

Following the collapse of the Napoleonic empire, Turin once again began a project of expansion and building under the direction of the Savoy family. The completion of the grand neo-classical piazza Vittorio Veneto by **Giuseppe Frizzi** set the scale and tenor for the development of the 19th-century city. The arched portico framing the piazza, with its deep dark shadows and monumental scale, would later be a source of inspiration for the metaphysical artist De Chirico.

From 1861 to 1864 Turin was the capital of the newly unified Italy. Immediately following unification, the city's population exploded: French-style neighbourhoods with wide tree-lined boulevards were planned to meet the demand for accommodation. Few monumental government buildings and spaces were constructed due to the city's brief tenure as the national capital.

Other forces such as the rise of a wealthy and increasingly cosmopolitan bourgeoisie contributed to Turin's transformation in this period. In 1862 **Alessandro Antonelli** began work on what would become the symbol of the city, the spindly Mole Antonelliana (*see p77*). Begun as a synagogue, the structure was a major feat of engineering. Architects also turned to new building materials to create impressive spaces and forms. With its sweeping glass and iron window and gracious marble interior, Porta Nuova railway station (*see p71*) was at once a symbol of modern technology and a decorous entrance to the city. Glass and iron were also used by **Pietro Carrera** for the Galleria dell'industria subalpina (*see p69*), a subdued version of the arcades that were so fashionable in major European cities in the 19th century, the precursors of modern shopping malls.

CITY OF INDUSTRY AND THE ARRIVAL OF MODERNISM

In 1899 the automobile manufacturing company Fiat (Fabrica Italiana Automobili Torino) was founded and helped to usher in a new chapter in the architectural history of the city. Turin once again became a centre for innovation as the growth of industry created a new class of patrons. These patrons would embrace a new style of first design and later architecture known in Italy as *stile Liberty*. The name was inspired by the art nouveau textile designs that were (and are) a trademark of the Liberty department store in London.

It was the 1902 Exhibition of Decorative Arts in Turin, with its fanciful pavilions designed by **Raimondo D'Aronco** and **Annibale Rigotti**, that first introduced Italy and Turin to the organic forms of Liberty. D'Aronco was the principal designer and drew on buildings he had seen in Turkey and Austria to create temporary exhibition pavilions. The Casa D'Aronco (via Petrarca 44) adjacent to the Parco del Valentino (*see p80*), site of the 1902 exhibition, is the only trace of D'Aronco's contribution to Turin; its heavily projecting

Giugiaro's **Atrium**. See p65.

gable roof recalls forms that the architect would have seen while working in Istanbul.

The decorative potential of *stile Liberty* can be seen throughout the city in early factory buildings, shops and residences. A profusion of Liberty buildings can be found in neighbourhoods such as La Crocetta (*see p67*). Cafés that catered to the cosmopolitan tastes of the growing bourgeoisie – such as the sumptuous Bar Mulassano (*see p111*) by **Antonio Vandone di Cortemilia** and the Confetteria Baratti e Milano (*see p111*) by **Giulio Casanova** and **Edoardo Rubino** – also embraced this new vocabulary.

Piero Fenoglio is the best-known practitioner of *stile Liberty* in Turin and his Palazzina Scott (corso Giovanni Lanza 57) and Casa Fenoglio-La Fleur (via Principe d'Acaja 11), both of 1902, are impressive examples. The flowing stonework and ironwork, inventive window treatments and interest in organic forms are all characteristic of his work from this period. The Casa Fenoglio takes full advantage of its corner site with a projecting bay window and a glass and iron cornice. The Palazzina Scott occupies a more sylvan setting on the far side of the River Po and its elaborately framed windows provide views over the river and city beyond.

In sharp contrast to the decorative excesses of the Liberty Style, the Fiat factory at Lingotto (*see p86*) by engineer **Giacomo Matteo Trucco** announces a new functional direction that much of modern architecture was to pursue in the years following World War I. The otherwise unassuming block contains a soaring heliocoidal ramp that carried cars from the factory floor to the kilometre-long (half-mile) test track on the roof. The relationship between function and architecture demonstrated here was a source of inspiration for an entire generation of architects, including **Le Corbusier** who visited the factory and published photos of the project in his many books on architecture.

Turin played an important role in the development of modernism in Italy. Architect Giuseppe Pagano's first major work, the Palazzo Gualino (corso Vittorio Emanuele II 8), offices for the industrialist and art dealer of the same name, is one of the earliest examples in Italy of rationalism, a design aesthetic that favoured a rational or functional architecture that often included features such as horizontal windows, flat roofs, new materials and minimal decoration. The austerity of the Palazzo's main façade and the horizontally oriented windows were considered truly scandalous when they were first unveiled in 1930. Pagano later moved to Milan where he collaborated with Eduardo Persico on the influential architecture journal *Casabella*.

The rise of the Fascist regime in the 1920s and '30s brought a series of architectural and urban initiatives to Turin and left an unmistakeable mark on the city. The austere and massive classicism of via Roma is the work of **Marcello Piacentini**, Mussolini's favourite architect. Throughout the city, new schools, markets, athletics complexes and party headquarters brought much-needed infrastructure to the population and provided a constant reminder of the new political order. Architecture of this period escapes easy classification, but the effort to integrate elements of architectural modernism and monumentality is a theme that can be found repeatedly. One example is the wholesale fruit and vegetable market on piazza Galimberti by **Umberto Cuzzi**. The scale of the central tower and overall symmetry of the complex give it monumentality while the curved face of the tower, the windows and the prominent placement of a clock are all clear references to modern design.

In the 1920s and '30s Turin was a centre of innovation in Italian painting and sculpture. The Futurist movement, which advocated a complete break from the past, found an important spokesperson in **Filia** (real name Luigi Colombo) who founded the Turin Futurist group in 1923 and later participated in the advancement of Aeropittura – a second phase of Futurism that sought to translate the perceptual experiences made possible by flight into painting. In sharp contrast to the Futurist movement, which, to varying degrees, supported Fascism, **I Sei di Torino** looked for an alternative line of research. **Carlo Levi** is the best-known member of the group and the muted colours and everyday subject matter of his 1929 painting *Aria* are representative of his work in these years. Carlo Levi was later exiled to southern Italy for his anti-Fascist activities; this experience would later be captured in his book *Christ Stopped at Eboli*. Turin was also home for many years to **Felice Casorati** who was loosely associated with I Sei di Torino and likewise rejected the break with the past advocated by Futurism.

POST-WAR AND CONTEMPORARY TURIN

Post-war reconstruction and expansion in Turin, not unlike the rest of Italy, were driven by necessity and by a desire to break with the painful reminders of the immediate past. In the 1950s a young generation of architects took the lead and proposed an alternative to both Rationalism and the monumentality of the Fascist regime. The stock exchange (via San Francesco da Paola 28) by **Roberto Gabetti** and **Aimaro Orgelia Isola**, students of **Carlo Mollino**, was one of the first buildings to propose a solution and immediately attracted the attention of critics inside and outside of Italy. The massive rusticated base borrows from the architectural language of the Italian palazzo but is executed in a wholly new fashion and paired with contemporary forms and materials. Likewise, the charming and eclectic Erasmus Bottega (via Gaudenzio Ferrari 11), designed as a residence and antiquarian bookshop, is likewise at once engaged with history and thoroughly modern. The work of Gabetti and Isola, along with that of other architects pursuing a similar line of research, is sometimes referred to as *neo-Liberty*.

Exhibitions have continued to play an important role in Turin's history. The post-war period witnessed the construction of several permanent exhibition spaces. In the Padiglione Giovanni Agnelli & C (*see p85*) engineer **Pier Luigi Nervi** resorts to his favourite building material – reinforced concrete – to create soaring interior spaces uncluttered by vertical supports. Further along the Po is **Annibale** and **Giorgio Rigotti**'s remarkable Palazzo delle Mostre (aka *'La Vela'; see p85*).

More recently, the Fiat complex at Lingotto has been subject to renovations and expansions to designs by **Renzo Piano**, including a glass bubble meeting room perched atop the building at the centre of the aforementioned test track. Opposite the glass bubble is a floating steel box topped by a 'flying carpet' in which a portion of the Agnelli art collection (*see p88*) is displayed.

The arrival of the 2006 Winter Olympics has once again ushered in a major, concentrated building effort in the city. Umberto Cuzzi's wholesale fruit and vegetable market will be restored by **Gae Aulenti** to serve as the Olympic Village. The Olympics will also bring new buildings such as a speed skating rink (the Oval) near the Lingotto and a new hockey stadium near piazza d'Armi. Already operative is Atrium (*see p228* **Atrium**), a glass, wood and steel structure by Giorgetto Giugiaro where the city dispenses tourist and Olympic information in piazza Solferino. The Stazione Porta Susa will become the city's principal station and will be expanded and modernised to a plan by **Arep Studio**. In piazza della Repubblica, a zinc-roofed glass pavilion by Massimiliano Fuksas will replace the old clothing market (*see p120* **Bargain hunting**). Other ongoing projects – such as the development of a new underground network – continue to offer new solutions to the problems facing Turin in the 21st century.

Piedmont is food heaven, from cheeses...

Piedmont & Food

Turin is a food connoisseur's paradise: gorgonzola, truffles and, er, Nutella, are just some of the region's specialities.

If the EU were to divide territories by culinary cultures instead of political borders, it could create a new state where Piedmont lies. It may insult both the French and the (other) Italians, but there's no denying that dishes here typically involve both the boot country's embrace of good ingredients and a Gallic love of embellishment.

Egg-rich pastas, bathed in melted butter, provide a subtle backdrop for Alba's heady white truffle. Frog's legs are a local delicacy, often served with risotto; magnanimous applications of *maionese* improve the simplest salads and meats marinate in robust wines. Cheeses are a course unto themselves. Even coffee is treated to an extra flourish when layered with melted chocolate and hot milk.

Piedmont is also famed for the quality of its chocolate, which has been produced – and perfected – here since the 17th century.

Yet somehow over-indulgence doesn't find its way to the table. Food is revered here with an enlightened balance of appreciation and pleasure. That said, see 'E' for exhaustion.

AN A-Z OF PIEDMONTESE DELIGHTS

Agnolotti

This crescent-shaped stuffed ravioli, Piedmont's pasta of choice, is filled with anything from spinach to brains and often served with ragù or creamy fondue sauces. Look for the succulent, smallish *agnolotti del plin*, especially when served in silky broth.

Arneis

A once-forgotten, now-popular white grape of Piedmont used to make light wines in Roero and the Langhe (*see pp192-9*). A good accompaniment to *antipasti*. Production is limited, so take advantage while you're here.

Asti

Home to Spumante, the famously silly bubbly wine slurped with pink birthday cakes. Less known is the fragrant semi-sweet Moscato d'Asti (*see p32* **Regional wines**), a popular dessert wine with local connoisseurs, and the distinguished Barbera d'Asti.

... to salami...

Baci di Cherasco

Bite-sized chocolate clusters, filled with hazelnuts, from the town of Cherasco, which is known for its divine dark chocolate and snails (*see below,* lumache).

Bagna Cauda (*Bagna Caôda*)

A warm bath for dipping boiled or raw vegetables into. An aromatic mixture of olive oil and butter, anchovies, garlic and sometimes milk or cream, it's popular here but probably originated in neighbouring Liguria where there are olives and anchovies, unlike in colder, land-locked Piedmont.

Bettelmatt

This fontina-like cheese gives particular meaning to terroir: in Piedmont it's characterised by the *mutellina,* a herb that dairy cows graze on in a single pasture of the Val d'Ossola area.

Bicerìn

Bicerìn tastes as elegant as the chandeliered 19th-century Turin cafés where it gained popularity look. A warm, layered drink of melted chocolate, coffee and milk.

Bollito misto

Every Italian region has its take on boiled meats; the Piedmont version is a carnivore's delight on a platter, including up to (or more than) seven different types of meat accompanied by as many sauces.

Cardo (or *gobbo*)

The cardoon is a long slender vegetable that looks like celery and tastes of artichoke. Cardone is a broth made with cardoons, meat and cheese.

Cioccolato

Nostradamus knew that Turin was a chocolate lover's paradise when he came here to write his treatise on the historical confection. Today you can cross the city in chocolate steps, sampling some of the finest dark stuff the Continent has to offer. Look for **Peyrano** (*see p126*), **Pfatish** and **Gobino** (*see p126*) brands.

DOCG

Denominazione di origine controllata e garantita is the classification that identifies many of Italy's top wines. Piedmont's long history of protected viticulture has produced many high-status wines rated DOCG, including Barolo, Barbaresco, Moscato d'Asti and Gattinara (*see p32* **Regional wines**).

E...

... is for exhaustion, so pace yourself – and your stomach – in this land of plenty.

Ferrero

Ferrero began as a humble sweet shop in Alba. Today, still owned by the Ferrero clan, it's one of the world's biggest candy manufacturers, churning out Rocher, Tictacs, Nutella (*see p194* **Middle-aged spread**) and other tooth-rotters.

Fonduta

Piedmontese cheese fondue, usually made with fontina, is often a showcase for the area's pride and joy, the white truffle; a luscious combination.

Frogs

Frogs live in the rice paddies and their crunchy little legs are a local delicacy. The creatures are most often served, appropriately, with risotto.

Gianduja

This dreamy combination of chocolate creamed with hazel-nuts is named for Turin's *Commedia dell'arte* character (*see p137* **Gianduja**) who wore a three-horned hat – still the shape of most *gianduiotti* chocolates.

Grissini

In most restaurants in Italy you'll be given a basket of hard bread and a few industrially made breadsticks. In Turin, home of the bread-stick, you'll get delicious fresh *grissini*, made by local bakers.

Gorgonzola

The northern Italian cheese, at once creamy and sharp and striated with green and blue ribbons of mould.

Krumiri

If you ordered one of these before 1878, you got a liqueur. Today you'll get a plain, crunchy biscuit. In 19th-century Piedmont, one Domenico

In Context

Slow and steady

Newly arrived in Italy, the insatiably hungry giant named Fast Food hauled his substantial girth across the country. French fry in one hand, burger in the other, he enlarged people in his own image along the way.

When he stopped to rest at the base of the Spanish Steps in Rome, a snail appeared and tried to shoo him away: '*Via!*' it cried. The giant reached down to crush it, but the mollusc stood firm. A crowd gathered to watch the altercation. The snail, a pacifist by nature, turned away from the giant and spoke to the congregation. 'Put down your buckets of transfat, your heaped platters of fried, freakish chicken, your colossal containers of contaminated fish, and follow me – to Piedmont.' On his back he carried a sign: 'Slow Food: A movement for the protection of the right to taste'.

The **Slow Food** movement began in the mid 1980s when a group of left-leaning journalists in the small Piedmont city of Bra, south of Turin, learned that McDonald's planned to open shop in the heart of Rome. They gathered at their neighbourhood *osteria* – where else? – to create a manifesto that celebrates conviviality, promotes local, seasonal ingredients and counters 'the degrading effects of Fast Food'.

A dynamic non-profit organisation still based in Bra, Slow Food – like any good cook – understands the importance of timing. After a successful start at home, it went international in 1989 just as foodies en masse sprouted organic consciences.

Fifteen years later, Fast Food has produced an overweight population almost as numerous as the world's undernourished, while Slow Food has embraced 70,000 card-carrying members from America to Asia. The movement has been criticised as an exclusive gastronomic cabal, but its fearless leader Carlo Petrini and his colleagues work hard to offer more than just *tagliarini* tossed with trendy values.

An annual awards programme honours and subsidises those who work on the front line of protecting biodiversity of foods in Italy and, increasingly, further afield. The Ark of Taste defends endangered foods, and the Presidia programme builds bottom-line marketplaces to ensure a continued demand for those products.

At the heart of the organisation's worldwide presence are the volunteers who open local chapters, or *convivia*, and work with their members to create events that promote good things to eat, food issues, artists of the fields and the movement itself.

For the traveller in Italy, it's hard to miss. You can attend events year-round, visit the 32 *Città Slow* (Slow cities, so-called for their promise of well-being) and expand your mind and stomach at the biennial **Salone del Gusto** in Turin (the world's largest non-industrial food fair; *see p134*).

If you really seek full foody immersion, you can enrol in Slow Food's **Università di scienze gastronomiche**; at €19,000 a year for lessons, half-board, materials and health-care, it's certainly not cheap. But it's the price you pay for attending the world's first 'Academy of Taste'.

Snails, anyone?

Slow Food

Via Mendicità Istruita 14, Bra (0172 419 611/fax 0172 421293/www.slowfood.com).

Rossi needed a snack after a customary evening of tippling Krumiri, and so made biscuits and named them after his favourite grog. Rossi's brand is still made from the original recipe.

Lavazza

Turin's biggest coffee-roasting company, opened in 1895 by Luigi Lavazza, has been instrumental in getting the locals hooked on caffeine. You can buy the super-charged jo in most supermarkets and visit the Lavazza café (*see p113,* San Tommaso 10).

Lumache

A crop of snails is cultivated in the Cherasco area and tirelessly promoted by the town's mayor. In addition to the butter and garlic treatment, the mollusc of Piedmont is served in a sauce of garlic, tomatoes and olive oil.

Marmellata

The cherries, apples, summer berries and other fruits of Piedmont make for excellent preserves, especially those from Cuneo, an area also known for its quality chestnuts and chestnut spread.

Miele

Honey is one of the many delights of this region still defined by small agricultural enterprises, where you find delightful oddities such as rhododendron, dandelion and fir honeys.

Morra

Tucked in behind the streets of fancy food shops in the heart of Alba, Tartufi Morra (piazza Pertinace 3, 0173 366 271, www.tartufalba.com) is one of the smelliest, finest places to buy the prized white truffles

Regional wines

Some 80 per cent – the highest concentration in Italy – of the wines produced in the Piedmont region boast DOCG status, a guarantee that you'll find more or less consistent quality in the tremendous selection that ranges from the robust and chewy tannins of an aged **Barolo** to the sprightly effervescence of the white **Moscato d'Asti**. In between, there are wines of all ilks to complement the region's similarly impressive and varied cuisine.

Piedmont ranks fourth among Italian regions in terms of total production, but only Tuscany rivals it for sheer quality. The region's main wine-producing areas are located south and south-east of Turin in the provinces of Cuneo, Alessandra and Asti (*see pp184-91*), whose namesake sweet bubbly **Asti spumante** (which cork dorks dismiss with contempt) propels this province to the top ranks of wine-producing areas in Italy. Probably a better bet is to try the low-alcohol (generally four to six per cent) **Moscato d'Asti**, the de rigeur dessert wine of choice for discerning *piemontesi*.

Among the still whites, crisp cortese-based **Gavi** wines go well with seafood, and the fruity arneis and light favorita varieties make for good sipping brews, especially on days when you can't face up to the mighty reds that are the region's pride and joy.

The nebbiolo grape is the noble and wily ingredient that in the right hands is transformed into **Barolo**, **Barbaresco**, **Gattinara** and **Ghemme** wines. Ageing

and terroir account for this versatile fruit's expressiveness, rivalled only by pinot noir in its chameleon-like talents.

Barolo is a full-bodied, complex and tannic wine that mellows beautifully with time. Feisty in its youth, with mouth-puckering astringency, it requires a minimum three years of ageing. A rivalry exists between old-school winemakers and contemporary vintners who are making Barolo much more approachable at an earlier age. Still, this supremely structured wine has legs to last decades in a bottle. It has a velvety texture and intense aroma of berries and spices.

Barbaresco, which is also made in the scenic Langhe hills surrounding Alba (*see pp192-9*), is typically lighter-bodied and at its best between five and ten years of age.

For everyday drinking, the barbera grape does solid service, earning it the 'people's wine' moniker. It comes in many different varieties, from lightly fizzy to medium-bodied, which can lead to some confusion for the customer but generally doesn't disappoint. It's also affordable.

For sipping your way through the vast array of Piedmont wines, visit one – or all – of the ten publicly run wine cellars dotted throughout wine country (see www.enotecadel piemonte.it for addresses and information). *Enoteche* (off-licences) often specialise in the immediate vicinity's offerings: from one town to the next a completely different set of wine labels may materialise to bewilder and whet the appetite. *Cin cin.*

or the many pastes made from black truffles (also under its label, TartufAlba). Advice straight from one of the owners is to eat the white ones fresh and take home black ones in various preserved forms. Morra is credited with bringing the white truffle to the attention of the world's rich and famous in the 1930s and '40s – and it's never looked back.

Nebbiolo

Piedmont's noblest grape is named for the fog – *nebbia* – that transforms the region's expanse of vineyards into melancholy scenes that would make any sensitive soul weep for beauty – especially if they've sampled a glass or two of an aged Barolo from, say, vintner Paolo Scavino or Alexander Gaja. The versatile fruit is also the basis of Barbaresco, Gattinara and Ghemme wines.

Nocciole

Short, bushy hazel-nut trees cover the region's bucolic countryside. Look for the *Tonda gentile delle Langhe*, the region's top filbert. Also try the light *torta nocciola*, made with hazel-nuts, flour, eggs and butter.

Nutella

See p194 **Middle-aged spread**.

Oca alla piemontese

Goose preserved in fat – a local interpretation of the French *confit d'oie*.

Paniscia novarese

This sturdy risotto dish made with fresh beans is named for the rice-producing area of Novara that borders Lombardy.

Paste di Meliga

Slightly tangy butter cookies made with cornmeal. Typical to Piedmont, where they're sometimes served with *zabaione*.

Peperoni di Carmagnola

Peppers of Carmagnola are a local variety, sweet and delicious and available in some restaurants or in season in the region's food shops and markets.

Porta Palazzo

A large percentage of Turin's immigrant population – not to mention the locals – gathers at the market (*see p120* **Bargain hunting**) by this ancient city gate to find fine and rare foods. Anyone looking to experience the city's mosaic of food cultures should definitely drop in.

Quixotic

A word, if a single one will do, to describe Carlo Petrini, founder of Slow Food (*see p31* **Slow and steady**), fearless leader and visionary who hails from Bra and has been a household name

... and truffles.

in the region ever since he began penning his unabashed columns for *La Stampa*, Turin's daily newspaper.

Raschera

One of a multitude of fabulous local cheeses, this combines cow, goat and sheep's milk and comes from the high pastures of Monferrato (*see p187*).

Rice

See p181 **Piedmont paddies**.

Ris e riondele

A subtle dish of rice cooked with mallow leaves and milk. Just one example of a dish inspired by the region's rice production. (*See p181* **Piedmont paddies**.)

Robiola di Roccaverano

Another local cheese, this one is delicate and sweet. Often kept in oil.

Salone del Gusto

A singularly tasty event, this immense food fair takes place biennially at Turin's snazzy Lingotto convention centre (*see also p134*).

Savoia

The wealth and cultural influences brought to the region by its Savoy ruling family of French, Italian and Swiss origins certainly contributed to the tradition of fine foods in Piedmont. Duke Emanuele Filiberto patronised the production of chocolate in Turin in the late 16th century. Foods bearing the once-royal name are oddly commonplace: *savoiardi* or ladyfinger biscuits and savoia (a rather bland cheese much like Bel Paese).

Tajarin

If you're worried about cholesterol, you're in the wrong part of Italy, especially if the local fresh pasta proves too tempting to resist. At two dozen egg yolks per kilo of flour, the local take on *tagliolini* (a long, thin noodle) generously offers an average of two-and-a-half egg yolks per serving and is usually saturated with melted butter. A perfect accompaniment to *tartufi bianchi* (*see p198* **Truffle facts**).

Tartufo d'Alba

These dirty little treasures inspire people the world over to travel to Alba to smell, sample, swallow – *experience* – the deliciously complex tuber known as *Tuber magnatum Pico*. White truffles, which resist cultivation and grow in the wilds under oak, poplars and willows, are harvested each autumn. In spite of a fragrance so fierce you could use it as a weapon, the flavour vanishes if the fungus is cooked. (*See p198* **Truffle facts**.)

Toma piemontese

This category of mountain cheeses made from cow's milk, or from a mix of cow's and goat's milk, ranges widely in age, texture and taste.

Vermouth

See p122 **No Carpano, no party**.

Vitello tonnato

Another sumptuous Piedmont creation combining mayonnaise, this time in a whipped sauce, with tuna and capers, served over slices of cold roast veal. Also known as *vitel tonné*.

Year-round

Food and wine festivities continue throughout the seasons in Piedmont (*see pp132-4 and pp168-70*), whether it's a celebration of the apple harvest in early autumn or the making of a particular cheese in spring. Several local wines, including Asti and Barolo, are honoured with their own festivals.

Zabaione (or zabaglione)

Egg yolks, sugar and Marsala wine from Sicily are combined to make a frothy dessert or, in Piedmont, a rich beverage. Zabaione was originally invented at the Florentine court, but it's been a popular dessert here long enough to be considered a regional tradition. Occasionally it's served as a sauce for game.

Cioccolato

Turin's love affair with chocolate might be better described as an obsession, and chocoholics can only be grateful for it.

How many other cities can claim to have regulated the price of a beloved chocolate drink – the *bicerìn*, that artful blend of chocolate, coffee and milk that's a Turin café standard – so that it could be enjoyed by everyone, regardless of social class? Notch one up to Turin, which defied inflation and from the mid 19th century to 1913 fixed the price of the staple morning pick-me-up at 15 cents.

The Turin PR machine likes to stress Turin's role as a chocolate pioneer, glossing over hundreds of years of Mayan and Aztec culture and the fact that it had been available in Spain since the 16th century. But Turin did have a hand in creating new treats.

Chocolate, as with many other delicious edibles, was first officially acknowledged by a 1678 ducal decree that authorised and regulated production of the liquid drink. Only 100 years later did the chocolate bar

come to be and since then family-run businesses have been perfecting ways to consume the cocoa bean.

In 1826 a local company, Caffarel, purchased a machine that allowed it to churn out 320 kilograms of chocolate a day and a mini-industrial revolution began. Chocolate moved from the realm of the Savoy court to within the grasp of the bourgeoisie. Caffarel – which is still going strong – must also be thanked for the *gianduiotto*, a blend of chocolate, sugar and local hazelnuts, named after Turin's *Commedia dell'arte* mask Gianduja (*see p137* **Gianduja**). In its cream form, *gianduiotto* became the popular Nutella (*see p194* **Middle-aged spread**), produced by Ferrero. Novi is another important Piedmontese industrial chocolate maker.

Even with mass production going strong, Turin has not abandoned its handmade chocolate tradition, and several family-run shops – like **Guido Gobino** (*see p126*), **Stratta** (*see p127*) and **Peyrano** (*see p126*) – are famous for their specialities.

Where to Stay

Where to Stay 36

Features

Where to Stay

The choice of places to stay in Turin may not be overwhelming, but all tastes and budgets are catered to.

The stylish **Boston**. See p38.

If you go to Turin with romantic ideas about charming *Room with a View*-type places to stay, you'll be disappointed. The hotel scene is geared to a business clientele: functionality takes precedence over personality. There are a few exceptions to this rather bleak outlook, however, and they are listed below.

Once you've accepted that, hotel-wise, this is not Florence, Rome or Venice, the advantages begin to emerge. The most obvious of these are the very reasonable prices. A room in a central four-star hotel in high season will cost roughly half as much as a similar room in any of the aforementioned cities. Low season and weekend rates represent an even greater bargain.

Then there is the refreshing lack of tourists: you may easily find yourself the only tourist –

nay, foreigner – in your hotel, especially off-season. The almost universal *disponibilità* (helpfulness) of hotel staff, from manager to chamber maid, is remarkable: these people are clearly not jaded by a constant stream of demanding foreign visitors with more money than manners. The downside of this, however, is that *torinesi* hoteliers have had little reason in the past to arm themselves with more than a smattering of English, so communication in smaller places may be a struggle.

This is all set to change for the 2006 Winter Olympics (*see p214* **Olympic challenge**), for which just about every bed in the city and environs had already been snapped up as this guide went to press.

PRICES

The prices given below show the range from the cheapest room in low season to the most expensive room in high season. This being a business town, high season rates are applied during trade fairs and on weekdays. Low season in Turin means most of July, August, December and January, with even lower rates being applied at weekends throughout the year. These can be as much as 50 per cent less than the maximum rate: choose your dates carefully and you'll find tremendous bargains. Unless otherwise stated, prices include en suite bathroom and breakfast. Most hotels will put an extra bed in a double room for a fee (up to 30 per cent extra); many will provide baby cots, usually for free.

For hotel booking agencies, *see p228* **Atrium**. To book a room in a B&B – where standards vary wildly – try the **Bed and Breakfast Service agency** (via dei Mille 23, Centro, 011 812 3675, fax 011 814 0861, www.bed-breakfast.it).

STAR RATINGS AND FACILITIES

The majority of the hotels listed in this chapter are three-stars or more. This is because most of Turin's one- and two-stars are grim; and with the sort of money that you would spend on a very basic room in Venice or Florence you will be able to afford comparative luxury in this city.

Be aware, though, that star ratings are awarded according to facilities on offer and don't in any way reflect the level of service or ambience. In Turin, there are enormous discrepancies within each category. The Hotel

Victoria (*see p43*), for example, has three stars but could easily have a fourth in terms of its overall standards of comfort, while the San Giors (again, three stars; *see p38*) is quite spartan; both, though, have the phone, TV, en suite bathrooms etc required for this category. The difference is reflected in the price.

Most hotels have their best and worst rooms and these will probably vary in price. If you don't like the room you've been given, you have a right to refuse it and ask to see another. Rooms within the same hotel often vary considerably in terms of size and shape, amount of natural light, type of furnishings, style of bathroom and whether or not there is a terrace or balcony. Prices are determined by all of the above.

A fair number of hotels in Turin have their own parking facilities, but these are rarely free. Those that don't will usually have some kind of arrangement with a private (and probably expensive) garage nearby. The alternative is to find your own street parking (*see also p219*).

Most hotels listed here have no-smoking rooms, but these are not always respected. Facilities for the disabled are getting better, thanks to laws requiring accessible bedrooms and bathrooms. If in doubt, check first.

Piazza Castello

Moderate

Chelsea

Via XX Settembre 79E (011 436 0100/fax 011 436 3141/www.hotelchelsea.it). Bus 27, 57, 63/ tram 4. **Rates** €75-€110 single; €95-€145 double. **Credit** AmEx, DC, MC, V. **Map** p242 C3.
The main attractions of this 15-room hotel are its location, just west of piazza Castello (*see pp52-9*), and the inviting-looking restaurant downstairs, serving *cucina pugliese* from the heel of the Italian boot. Hotel guests can eat here for a modest supplement to their room rate. The modern bedrooms are nothing to write home about, but are perfectly comfortable, well equipped and clean. There's cheap private parking. **Hotel services** *Bar. Conference facilities. Parking (extra charge). Restaurant.* **Room services** *Air-conditioning. Hairdryer. Minibar. Safe. TV.*

Quadrilatero

Moderate

Ai Savoia

Via del Carmine 1B (339 125 7711/www.infinito.it/ utenti/aisavoia). Bus 12, 36, 46, 49, 55, 56, 59, 67/tram 1, 10, 13. **Rates** €80-€110 double. **Credit** MC, V. **Map** p242 C2.
Roberto Pavone and his uncle run this B&B housed in a modest corner of the splendid 18th-century

Palazzo Saluzzo di Paesana (*see p76* **Cortili**) near piazza Savoia. The entrance and staircase are unremarkable, but step inside this little doll's house and you'll find elegant 18th-century plasterwork, original wooden ceilings and chandeliers. The three small bedrooms (theatrically named after Savoy kings and queens) are furnished with painted 19th-century French pieces and flowery fabrics. One of the rooms (Re Alberto) has a small balcony. The hushed ambience makes it a good bet for those who seek peace, not parties. **Hotel services** *Parking (extra charge).* **Room services** *Air-conditioning. Dataport. Hairdryer. Safe. TV.*

Dogana Vecchia

Via Corte d'Appello 4 (011 436 7272/fax 011 436 7194/www.hoteldoganavecchia.it). Bus 5, 56, 61/ tram 4. **Rates** €70-€88 single; €90-€105 double. **Credit** AmEx, DC, MC, V. **Map** p242 C3.
Situated on the spot where travellers once had to pay their toll to enter the city (today it's a stone's throw from the buzzing Quadrilatero romano, *see pp60-63*), the Dogana Vecchia has been a hotel since the 1700s and retains something of an 18th-century air. The entrance hall is elegant, with fine plasterwork and a sweeping staircase, while the enormous, faded

The best **Hotels**

For mountain views
Le Meridien Lingotto (*p45*).
Art+Tech (*p45*).
Artuà e Solferino (*p39*).
Accoglienza della Basilica di Superga (*p47*).
Ostello Torino (*p47*).

For fans of *The Italian Job*
Le Meridien Lingotto (*p45*).

For good grub
San Giors (*p38*).
Grand Hotel Sitea (*p42*).

For a breath of fresh air
Villa Sassi (*p47*).
Accoglienza della Basilica di Superga (*p47*).

For a bargain
Vinzaglio (*p42*).
Montevecchio (*p42*).

For that English chintzy feeling
Victoria (*p43*).

For feeling ecclesiastical
Accoglienza della Basilica di Superga (*p47*).

salon/breakfast room tells of a more genteel age. The bedrooms are decidedly spartan and some are disappointingly characterless; those with antique furniture are more attractive. Staff are exceptionally helpful.

Hotel services *Bar. Parking (extra charge).*
Room services *Hairdryer. Minibar. Phone. Safe. TV (satellite).*

Budget

San Giors

Via Borgo Dora 3 (011 521 1256/fax 011 436 0208). Bus 11, 12. **Rates** €50-€70 single; €70-€90 double. **Credit** AmEx, DC, V. **Map** p242 B3.

New management has spruced up the 14 value-for-money rooms in Turin's second-oldest hotel, which was once an inn at a staging point on the old Turin–Milan road. Today it is situated in the heart of the Borgo Dora area, a few steps from Europe's biggest market at Porta Palazzo (*see p120* **Bargain hunting**). It's officially a three-star, but the bedrooms, while very clean and with all the required facilities, are quite plain. On the ground floor the restaurant of the same name serves *piemontese* classics in a wonderfully retro atmosphere.

Hotel services *Bar. Parking. Restaurant.* **Room services** *Air-conditioning. Hairdryer. Minibar. Safe. TV.*

Cittadella

Expensive

Boston

Via Massena 70 (011 500 359/fax 011 599 358/ www.hotelbostontorino.it). Bus 12, 14, 63/tram 15. **Rates** €69-€134 single; €88-€220 double; €105-€230 suite. **Credit** AmEx, DC, MC, V. **Map** p244 B3.

One of the few really interesting hotels in Turin, the 90-room, four-star Boston occupies two adjacent buildings (one a fine example of *stile Liberty; see p27*) a 15-minute walk away from the train station. Once through the door, you are immediately confronted with its raison d'être: art. The ground-floor public rooms are filled with the owner's eclectic art collection (look out for works by Warhol and Lichtenstein among the mainly Italian artists), along with the odd ethnic object and one-off pieces of contemporary furniture including some fine examples of American deco. The stylish if rather cold bedrooms (most are quite small) are all different, decorated in strong colours with modern furniture (a few have art deco or oriental pieces) and ethnic wall hangings. The Boston is also one of the few hotels in Turin to boast a (small) garden.

Hotel services *Bar. Conference facilities. Fax. Garden. Laundry. Lift. Parking (extra charge).* **Room services** *Air-conditioning. Hairdryer. Minibar. Room service. Safe. TV (satellite).*

Turin Palace

Via Sacchi 8 (011 562 5511/fax 011 561 2187/ www.thi.it). Bus 11, 12/tram 1, 4. **Rates** €108-€225 single; €138-€277 double; €370 suite. **Credit** AmEx, DC, MC, V. **Map** p244 A3.

Another dependable four-star choice slap bang next to the station and under the same management as the Sitea (*see p43*). It has more of a sober, old-world feel (it was opened as a hotel in 1872) than its sister establishment, although the large expanses of marble in the reception hall and dreary colours in some of the bedrooms are rather depressing. On the ground floor is a vast, high-ceilinged salon looking on to a pretty patio, a vaguely chinoise-style bar and a formal restaurant. The bedrooms vary wildly; some are very dated while others are in elegant Empire style with posh marble bathrooms. Staff can be surly.

Making room(s)

As this guide goes to press, Turin boasts 9,188 hotel beds. And, people in the know report, pretty much all of them are booked from 10 to 26 February 2006. The 2006 Winter Olympics present the largest challenge that the city's hotel sector has ever faced, but steps are being taken to increase availability substantially.

Hotels-to-be include a five-star job in the city centre and another in the Lingotto complex (*see p45*). Less luxurious but promising more character is the project for the Complesso monumental di San Filippo, a 17th-century Oratorian convent attached to the church of San Filippo Neri (*see p75*); Spain's *paradores* and Portugal's *pousadas* are being taken as a model for the

transformation of what for decades has been used as a school.

For sports fans on tighter budgets, the city council is encouraging alternative forms of inexpensive accommodation, including bed and breakfast in private homes.

But time is tight for getting these structures and arrangements in place, and demand for what could be a limited number of rooms will likely be sky high. There's a possibility, therefore, that hoteliers will get greedy, pushing prices up dramatically. While regional laws require hotels to declare their intended rates about a year in advance, there's no guarantee that this will prevent price increases. Don't, whatever you do, expect bargains in the winter of 2006.

The **Conte Biancamano** has grand public rooms.

Hotel services *Bar. Conference facilities. Fax. Laundry. Lift. Parking (extra charge). Restaurant.* **Room services** *Air-conditioning. Hairdryer. Minibar. Room service. Safe. TV (satellite).*

Moderate

Artuà e Solferino

Via Brofferio 1-3 (011 561 3444/fax 011 562 2241/ www.hotelsolferino.it). Bus 5, 14, 29, 59, 64, 67/ tram 4. **Rates** €65-€80 single; €75-€120 double; €93-€133 triple; €104-€154 quad. **Credit** AmEx, DC, MC, V. **Map** p244 A3.

Just off wide, leafy corso Re Umberto and housed on the fourth floor of a grand palazzo, the cosy Solferino and adjacent Artuà (situated in the next-door palazzo) are run as one hotel by the Vottero family. The Solferino has a particularly delightful, old-fashioned atmosphere: white lace curtains in the breakfast room, old paintwork on the double doors and wooden floors in some of the ten modest but pretty bedrooms, all of which have views of the mountains. The entrance to the Artuà is via a fabulous wood and glass lift that creaks its way up to the top floor. The rooms are a bit larger than next door but the same old-fashioned cosiness prevails.

Hotel services *Fax. Lift. No-smoking rooms. Parking (extra charge).* **Room services** *Air-conditioning. Dataport. Hairdryer. Minibar. TV.*

City

Via Juvarra 25 (011 540 546/fax 011 548 188/ www.bestwestern.it). Bus 29, 46, 59, 72/tram 1, 10, 13. **Rates** €68-€105 single; €99-€149 double. **Credit** AmEx, DC, MC, V. **Map** p242 C2.

Don't be put off by the rather dingy-looking 1970s building that houses the four-star City, situated near the train station; inside is a stylish hotel, refreshingly different from the Turin norm and offering very competitive rates. Lighting and furnishings are modern (at times decidedly quirky), colour schemes are bold and there is some striking art on the walls. Many of the rooms (some of which have balconies) look on to a quiet garden.

Hotel services *Babysitting. Bar. Conference facilities. Fax. Laundry. Lift. Parking (extra charge). Restaurant.* **Room services** *Air-conditioning. Hairdryer. Minibar. Room service. Safe. TV (satellite).*

Conte Biancamano

Corso Vittorio Emanuele II 73 (011 562 3281/ fax 011 562 3789/www.hotelcontebiancamano.it). Bus 11, 65, 68/tram 1, 4, 9. **Rates** €75-€95 single; €95-€130 double; €120-€150 suite. **Credit** AmEx, DC, MC, V. **Map** p242 D3.

One of Turin's more appealing hotels, just west of the station, is situated on the second floor of an elegant old palazzo and is reached by a wonderful old wood and glass lift. The public rooms of the friendly, family-run Biancamano are quite grand, with elaborately decorated ceilings, chandeliers and heavily scented flower arrangements. The 24 comfortable bedrooms are plainer, but are carefully and individually decorated. Roberto and Laura Rivella are charming hosts, the place is spotless and prices are very reasonable.

Hotel services *Bar. Parking (extra charge). Safe.* **Room services** *Hairdryer. Minibar (some). Phone. Room service. TV.*

AB+
Living + restaurant

location	historical roman city centre
building	conserved medieval
accomodation	2 penthouse suites +
	1 tower house with rooftop terrace
interiors	designer furniture + luxury comforts
food + drinks	fine food restaurant + wine tasting +
	cocktail bar + whisky parlour
entertainment	visual sound gallery + live jazz performaces
business amenities	wireless connection + conference hall
publishing house	cluster magazine
website	www.progettocluster.com

via della basilica 13 - turin - italy
+39 0114338732
online reservation
reservations@progettocluster.com

Genova e Stazione

Via Sacchi 14B (011 562 9400/fax 011 562 9896/
www.albergogenova.it). Bus 63/tram 4, 9. **Rates**
€98-€135 single; €135-€190 double; €145-€202
triple; €196-€233 suite. **Credit** AmEx, DC, MC, V.
Map p244 A3.

Part of the Best Western chain and one of the most
expensive hotels in its category, the three-star
Genova (situated opposite the train station) has just
undergone lavish, rather heavy-handed renovation.
While not much remains of the original 1880 building inside, the occasional old parquet floor, painted
ceiling and some original stained glass add character. The grand reception area is dominated by mirrors, chandeliers and elegant plasterwork, while the
78 bedrooms are comfortable and well equipped;
they even have electric kettles (unusual for Italian
hotels). Those on the top floor have sloping beamed
ceilings and little balconies with rooftop views.
Hotel services *Bar. Conference facilities. Fax.*
Laundry. Lift. No-smoking rooms. Parking (extra
charge). **Room services** *Air-conditioning. Hairdryer.*
Minibar. Room service. Safe. TV (satellite).

Liberty

Via Pietro Micca 15 (011 562 8801/fax 011 562
8163/www.hotelliberty-torino.it). Bus 55, 56, 58,
72/tram 13. **Rates** €62-€90 single; €83-€124 double.
Credit AmEx, DC, MC, V. **Map** p242 C3.

Situated near the boutiques, bars and restaurants of
the Quadrilatero (*see pp60-63*), the Liberty occupies
the sunny top floor of a fin-de-siècle building and
has the endearing atmosphere of an elderly aunt's
house: old wood floors, pretty old-fashioned bedrooms (some huge) and original double doors painted in pale green. Two cosy little sitting rooms and a
breakfast/dining room (dinner set menu €20) fit the
picture perfectly. The top-floor attic rooms are more
modern in style; a pity.
Hotel services *Bar. Parking (extra charge).*
Restaurant. **Room services** *Air-conditioning.*
Hairdryer. TV (satellite).

La Maddalena

Via San Secondo 31 (tel/fax 011 591 267/www.iam-
maddalena.com). Bus 63/tram 4. **Rates** €70 single;
€120 double. **No credit cards. Map** p244 A3.

Maddalena Vitale's small but perfectly formed B&B
is part of her own home (an elegant third-floor apartment housed in a palazzo dating from the early
1900s) and is just a ten-minute walk from the station. Very few Italians come anywhere near to
understanding the concept of the British B&B, but
this place really is a home-from-home – with all the
pros and cons. The three bedrooms – a double with
a four-poster and two twins – are filled with
Maddalena's own furniture, books, family photos
and ornaments. Beds are made up with pretty linens
while the bathrooms are stacked with abundant
hand-embroidered towels. Breakfast (home-made
cakes, breads and jams, plus bacon and eggs if you
want) is served round a communal antique table in
the small, sunny dining room. Mirto, the house dog,

Step back in time at the **Liberty**.

is as friendly as his owner; this is a great place to
stay if you want something really homely.
Hotel services *Lift. No-smoking rooms. Parking*
(extra charge). **Room services** *Dataport. Hairdryer.*
Phone. TV.

Le Petit Hotel

Via San Francesco d'Assisi 21 (011 561 2626/
fax 011 562 2807/www.lepetithotel.it). Bus 12, 29,
55, 56, 59/tram 13. **Rates** €65-€90 single; €90-€132
double; €120-€177 triple. **Credit** AmEx, DC, MC, V.
Map p242 D3.

Although the name sounds promising, this
centrally located hotel has 80 modern, over-lit and
rather soulless rooms. On a positive note, however,
they are neat and clean and have good bathrooms.
There are also ten cheerful, newly converted self-
catering apartments sleeping between one and four
(minimum stay one week).
Hotel services *Babysitting. Laundry. Lift. Parking*
(extra charge). **Room services** *Air-conditioning.*
Hairdryer. Minibar. Safe. TV (satellite).

Roma e Rocca Cavour

Piazza Carlo Felice 60 (011 561 2772/fax 011
562 8137/www.romarocca.it). Bus 12, 33, 34, 47,
58, 64/tram 1, 4, 9. **Rates** €48-€84 single; €75-€102
double; €86-€113 triple; breakfast €7 extra. **Credit**
AmEx, DC, MC, V. **Map** p242 D3.

Cosy **La Maddalena** feels like a home from home. *See p41.*

This historic family-run hotel feels like it hasn't changed in decades, particularly in the public areas with their creaking parquet floors. Many of the rooms – some furnished in *stile Liberty (see p27)* – are fairly dated, too, although those on the fifth floor are newer and have sloping attic ceilings, air-conditioning and views over the city skyline. A renovation programme is under way.

Hotel services *Bar. Conference facilities. Fax. Laundry. Lift. Parking (extra charge). Safe.* **Room services** *Air-conditioning (some). Hairdryer. Minibar (some). Modem. TV (satellite).*

Budget

Bologna

Corso Vittorio Emanuele II 60 (011 562 0191/ fax 011 562 0193/www.hotelbolognasrl.it). Bus 58, 63/tram 4, 9. **Rates** €54-€60 single; €70-€85 double; €95-€100 triple. **Credit** AmEx, DC, MC, V. **Map** p242 D3.

Situated right next to Porta Nuova station, this hotel, which opened in 1899, does not look very promising; the old-fashioned lobby badly needs a facelift. However, the Marenco family, who have been running the place for over 50 years, are very friendly and an ongoing modernisation programme means that at least half the rooms have parquet floors, modern wood furniture, soft lighting and new bathrooms. No.68 is a huge family room with an elaborately painted ceiling and grand, rather faded, old furniture.

Hotel services *Fax. Laundry. Lift. No-smoking rooms. Parking (extra charge).* **Room services** *Air-conditioning (some). Hairdryer. TV (satellite).*

Montevecchio

Via Montevecchio 13 (011 562 0023/fax 011 562 3047/www.hotelmontevecchio.com). Bus 3, 12, 58, 63/tram 1, 4. **Rates** €60-€65 single; €75-€80 double. **Credit** AmEx, DC, MC, V. **Map** p244 A3.

The small, modest, but super-friendly Montevecchio is a short walk south of the station. The bright reception area is particularly welcoming and basic bedrooms have been cheered up by new paintwork, colourful bedcovers and framed posters.

Hotel services *Fax. Parking (extra charge).* **Room services** *Room service. TV.*

Vinzaglio

Corso Vinzaglio 12 (011 561 3793/fax 011 561 3894/www.albergovinzaglio.it). Bus 1, 55, 65/tram 10. **Rates** €28 single (no bath); €38 double (no bath); €49 double. **Credit** AmEx, MC, V. **Map** p242 C3.

This modest one-star hotel is housed on the third floor of a lumbering palazzo west of the station. It's well maintained, has a friendly atmosphere and is cheap at the price. All but two of the rooms have bathrooms. It's a bit out of the way, but the No.1 bus stops right outside and will get you to the station in five minutes.

Hotel services *Fax. Lift. Phone. Public parking nearby.* **Room services** *TV (satellite).*

Centro

Expensive

Grand Hotel Sitea

Via Carlo Alberto 35 (011 517 0171/fax 011 548 090/www.thi.it). Bus 61/tram 18. **Rates** €116-€190 single; €155-€255 double; €230-€300 suite. **Credit** AmEx, DC, MC, V. **Map** p242 D3.

This traditional hotel is not exciting but it is reliable and well placed for both the train station and the via Roma shops. Frequently the choice for visiting celebs, past guests include Muhammed Ali, Lou Reed and Barry White. Its 114 comfortable rooms and suites are decorated in fairly restrained Empire style with dark wood panelling, elegant fabrics and wallpapers and thick carpeting; smart bathrooms (some with jacuzzis) are done out in marble. The elegant Carignano (*see p102*) restaurant justly enjoys a good reputation for its creative take on traditional Piedmontese fare.

Hotel services *Babysitting. Bar. Conference facilities. Fax. Laundry. Lift. Parking (extra charge). Restaurant.* **Room services** *Air-conditioning. Dataport. Hairdryer. Minibar. Room service. Safe. TV (satellite).*

Moderate

Des Artistes

Via Principe Amedeo 21 (011 812 4416/fax 011 812 4466/www.desartisteshotel.it). Bus 56, 61, 68/tram 9, 15, 16, 18. **Rates** €85-€125 single; €115-€160 double. **Credit** AmEx, DC, MC, V. **Map** p243 C1.

The name of this 22-room hotel near piazza Vittorio Veneto promises something more interesting than the uninspiring reality. However, it's clean and comfortable, and dated colour schemes in the bedrooms are softened by good lighting. It is also extremely central and in an area full of bars and restaurants.

Hotel services *Babysitting. Bar. Fax. Laundry. Lift. No-smoking rooms. Parking (nearby garage, extra charge; free on street).* **Room services** *Air-conditioning. Hairdryer. Room service. TV (satellite).*

Due Mondi

Via Saluzzo 3 (011 650 5084/fax 011 669 9383/ www.hotelduemondi.it). Bus 52/tram 1. **Rates** €65-€115 single; €80-€140 double; €140-€180 suite. **Credit** AmEx, DC, MC, V. **Map** p245 A1.

The newly renovated Due Mondi is a smart, cosy little hotel just off corso Vittorio Emanuele and a short walk from the train station. It's at the upper end of the three-star category in terms of both facilities and prices, offering a restaurant, a comfortable sitting room with squidgy sofas and armchairs and several bedrooms with shower-saunas or jacuzzis. The rooms are decorated in strong colours with swathes of heavy, patterned fabrics. There are 15% discounts in December, January and August.

Hotel services *Babysitting. Bar. Laundry. Lift. Parking (extra charge). Restaurant.* **Room services** *Air-conditioning. Hairdryer. Minibar. Room service. Safe. TV (satellite).*

Hotel Genio

Corso Vittorio Emanuele II 47 (011 650 5771/fax 011 650 8264/www.hotelgenio.it). Bus 1, 33, 58, 61/tram 4, 9. **Rates** €108-€134 single; €155-€186 double; €230 suite. **Credit** AmEx, DC, MC, V. **Map** p243 D1.

A nice old-fashioned entrance is about all that remains of the original Hotel Genio. Occupying an entire block a stone's throw from the station, its 120 rooms (most of which have been recently redecorated) are pleasantly decked out in busy, co-ordinated fabrics. Some rooms feature draped bedheads and there are even a few four-posters, but grandeur comes at a price; rates are at the upper end of this category. The private garage is a plus for drivers.

Hotel services *Bar. Conference facilities. Lift. No-smoking rooms. Parking (extra charge).* **Room services** *Air-conditioning. Hairdryer. Minibar. Room service. Safe. TV (satellite).*

Starhotel Majestic

Corso Vittorio Emanuele II 54 (011 539 153/ fax 011 534 963/www.starhotels.com). Bus 33, 61/tram 1, 9. **Rates** €90-€140 single; €110-€170 double; €159-€399 executive double. **Credit** AmEx, DC, MC, V. **Map** p243 D1.

The combination of its convenient location close to Porta Nuova station, good facilities and prices for standard doubles at the bottom of the four-star bracket makes the Majestic popular with upmarket tour groups as well as with business clients who take advantage of the conference centre. The ground floor is occupied by a huge open-plan reception and seating area, at one end of which is the Circolo bar where the prize-winning barman mixes a mean cocktail. The bedrooms are wrapped around a quiet inner courtyard; those facing the street have quadruple glazing to block out the noise. The standard rooms, while good value, are rather dreary in spite of new carpets and fabrics; the superiors and suites are more attractive and have better facilities, including kettles, dressing gowns and slippers, TVs in the bathrooms and, in some rooms, jacuzzis.

Hotel services *Babysitting. Bar. Conference facilities. Dataport. Laundry. Lift. Parking (extra charge). Restaurant.* **Room services** *Air conditioning. CD player (in executive rooms). Kettles (in superiors & suites). Hairdryer. Minibar. Safe. TV (satellite).*

Victoria

Via Nino Costa 4 (011 561 1909/fax 011 561 1806/ www.hotelvictoria-torino.com). Bus 61, 68/tram 18. **Rates** €107-€130 single; €154-€173 double; €200 suite. **Credit** AmEx, DC, MC, V. **Map** p243 D1.

Occupying a rather nondescript 1950s building near piazza San Carlo, everybody's favourite hotel in Turin has a devoted following and is often fully booked. Inside, it's a cosy homage to slightly dated English chintzyness. In spite of the 100-odd bedrooms, it has the feel of a much smaller hotel. The reception hall and sitting areas on the ground floor include an open fire and a bar, while upstairs the spacious bedrooms (some with four-posters) are individually decorated with flowery wallpapers, floral and striped fabrics, painted friezes and some fine antique furniture. Top-floor rooms have big terraces and impressive mountain views. The sunny breakfast room overlooks a pleasant neighbouring

garden. A swimming pool, sauna and Turkish bath should be ready by early 2005.

Hotel services *Bar. Fax. Laundry. Lift. Parking (nearby garage, extra charge).* **Room services** *Air-conditioning (in all but standard rooms). Hairdryer. Minibar. Room service. Safe. TV (satellite).*

Budget

San Carlo

Piazza San Carlo 197 (011 562 7846/fax 011 538 653/www.albergosancarlo.it). Bus 56, 58/tram 4, 18. **Rates** €38 single (no bath); €55 single; €75 double; €90 triple. **Credit** MC, V. **Map** p242 C3.

Several of the rooms in this simple one-star hotel overlook beautiful piazza San Carlo (*see p69*). Although the vast doorway and entrance hall promise grandeur, the rooms are very basic and not all of them have bathrooms. The place is very clean, however, and not without character; there's the odd twinkling chandelier and a few pieces of antique furniture. The hotel doesn't serve breakfast, but that provides a good excuse to indulge in a cappuccino and pastry at the nearby Caffè San Carlo (*see p115*) or Caffè Torino (*see p116*).

Hotel services *Lift. Parking (extra charge). Safe.* **Room services** *Air-conditioning (in 4 rooms, extra charge). Fridge (some). Hairdryer. TV.*

Collina

Moderate

Crimea

Via Mentana 3 (011 660 4700/fax 011 660 4912/ www.hotelcrimea.it). Bus 52, 64/tram 9. **Rates** €95-€120 single; €100-€160 double; €105-€210 triple. **Credit** AmEx, DC, MC, V. **Map** p245 A3.

The Crimea (a three-star member of the Best Western chain) occupies a rather drab modern-ish building in a quiet residential neighbourhood just across the river from the Parco del Valentino (*see p80*). Bedrooms are decent and clean if unexciting, bathrooms are well equipped and there is a pleasant open sitting area on the ground floor. Prices are on the high side.

Hotel services *Bar. Conference facilities. Fax. Laundry. Lift. No-smoking rooms. Parking (garage, extra charge; free on street).* **Room services** *Air-conditioning. Hairdryer. Minibar. Room service. Safe. TV (satellite).*

Lingotto

Luxury

Le Meridien Art&Tech

Via Nizza 230 (011 664 2000/fax 011 664 2001/ www.lemeridien-lingotto.it). Bus 35/tram 1. **Rates** €150-€310 single; €190-€410 double; €3,000 Lo Scrigno suite. **Credit** AmEx, DC, MC, V. **Map** p247 A2.

Industrial chic: **Le Meridien Lingotto.**

Opened in October 2003, the Renzo Piano-designed Art&Tech wing of the four-star Meridien-Lingotto (*see below*) was Turin's only five-star hotel at the time of this guide going to press. At the heart of the hotel is an immense, wood-panelled, glass-roofed central hall, which rises through the full height of the building. Three glass lifts (not for vertigo-sufferers) whizz up and down at great speed, offering a bird's-eye view of the bar and restaurant from the top floor. The 142 bedrooms are models of high-tech design with furniture and fittings by such illustrious names as Philippe Starck, Giò Ponti and Antonio Citterio. Each room has a plasma-screen TV, allergy-free carpets and bedding and a multi-jet power-shower in the bathroom. The panoramic jogging track (*see below* Meridien-Lingotto, also available to Art&Tech guests), which has views of the surrounding Alps, is handily close to the helipad if you fancy a run on arrival.

Hotel services *Babysitting. Bar. Conference facilities. Fax. Heliport. Laundry. Lift. No-smoking rooms. Parking. Restaurant.* **Room services** *Air-conditioning. Dataport. Hairdryer. Minibar. Room service. Safe. TV (satellite).*

Le Meridien Lingotto

Via Nizza 262 (011 664 2000/fax 011 664 2001/ www.lemeridien-lingotto.it). Bus 35/tram 1. **Rates** €110-€260 single; €125-€290 double; €300-€450 junior suite; €1,000 Presidential suite. **Credit** AmEx, DC, MC, V. **Map** p247 A2.

High tech at **Art+Tech**. *See p45.*

Designed by Renzo Piano and occupying part of the vast 1920s ex-Fiat Lingotto factory (*see p86*), Turin's Meridien is a stylish, understated hotel frequented mainly by a business crowd. The huge reception and sitting area on the ground floor is dominated by glass and lofty palms; a glass tunnel leads through the lush, tropical garden to one wing of bedrooms. Cool white sofas and armchairs provide a place to collapse while kilims add colour. Thanks to the original design of the building, which is said to have been much admired by Le Corbusier, the spacious bedrooms (with separate office areas) all have an entire wall in glass; try to secure one facing the mountains. The Torpedo restaurant (*see p106*), which is dominated by a vintage Fiat Torpedo, serves excellent food.

On the same site is a huge conference centre, a concert hall, an art gallery, a shopping mall, a food court and a cinema complex; guests are so well catered for they need never venture into town. On the roof is a heliport and a jogging track. The Meridien's critics complain that it is too far from the heart of things, but a regular bus service will drop you at the Porta Nuova train station in 15 minutes. While the rack rates are high, a weekend stay off-season can be a bargain.

Hotel services *Babysitting. Bar. Conference facilities. Fax. Heliport. Laundry. Lift. No-smoking rooms. Parking. Restaurant.* **Room services** *Air-conditioning. CD player. Dataport. Hairdryer. Minibar. Room service. Safe. TV (satellite).*

Suburbs

Expensive

Villa Sassi

Strada al Traforo di Pino 47, East (011 898 0556/ fax 011 898 0095/www.villasassi.com). Bus 61/ tram 15. **Rates** €185 single; €240 double; €280 suite. **Credit** AmEx, DC, MC, V. **Map** p241.

If you really want to steer clear of the centre of town and prefer the hills to the industrial sprawl of Lingotto and the Meridien (*see p45*), Villa Sassi is about your only decent option. Set in extensive grounds just below the basilica of Superga (*see p91*), it occupies what was once an aristocratic country residence. Behind the gracious pale yellow and white exterior, however, the inside is disappointing. The modernisation is now dated; the bedrooms, while perfectly adequate, are dull (try to book one of the top floor rooms, which are newer and more cheerful); and the whole place has a rather sad, shabby air to it in spite of some fine antiques. Its main business seems to come from the frequent weddings and other functions hosted in the huge, ugly banqueting hall.

Hotel services *Babysitting. Bar. Conference facilities. Fax. Garden. Laundry. Lift. No-smoking rooms. Parking. Restaurant.* **Room services** *Air-conditioning. Hairdryer. Minibar. Room service. Safe. TV (satellite).*

Shower&style at **Art&Tech**. *See p45.*

Budget

Ostello Torino

Via Alby 1, South-east (011 660 2939/fax 011 660 4445/www.ostellionline.org). Bus 52, 64. **Open** Feb-mid Dec. **Rates** €12 per person in dorm incl breakfast; €14-€17 per person in smaller rooms with bath; €8.50 meal. **Credit** MC, V. **Map** p241.

A couple of kilometres south-east of the city centre, across the Po and set among some gorgeous villas on a north-facing hillside, this 76-bed hostel occupies a modern building. Run by a young couple who have done their best to make things cheerful, the rooms are clean, quiet and sunny and sleep a maximum of six; there are a couple of four-bed family rooms with private bathrooms. Views of the mountains, particularly from the top floor, are stunning. Accommodation prices go up by €1.50 from mid October to mid April.

Services *Dataport. Garden. Parking. Restaurant. TV room. Vending machines. Washing machine.*

Camping

Camping Villa Rey

Strada Val San Martino Superiore 27, Suburbs: east (tel/fax 011 819 0117). Bus 61, then 54. **Open** year round. **Rates** Mid June-mid Sept €6 per person per night; €9/€10 per camper or caravan with/ without electric current; €4 per tent. Mid Sept-mid June €5 per person per night; €8/€9 per camper or caravan with/without electric current; €4 per tent. **Credit** MC, V. **Map** p241.

This family-run campsite is situated in the grounds of Villa Rey in the hills above the city not far from Superga. A No.61 bus from the station will get you there in 15 minutes. There are 114 pitches for tents, campers and caravans, plus showers, a restaurant and a supermarket. There's also a kids' playground.

Fondazione Torino Musei

GAM • Galleria d'Arte Moderna e Contemporanea

Museo d'Arte Antica e Palazzo Madama

Borgo e Rocca Medievale

CITTÀ DI TORINO

Sightseeing

Introduction

Turin has had a hard job shaking off its industrial image, but that's probably because its critics haven't visited in a while. They're in for a big surprise...

The rest of Italy has a problem with Turin. For them, this city is a Dickensian warren, its air poisoned by belching factory furnaces. They couldn't be more wrong.

The city earned this reputation when it was in the vanguard of the country's economic boom in the 1960s and '70s. But post-industrial Turin's factories have experienced the same downturn as much of Europe's heavy industry: many of the city's furnaces haven't been stoked for years. If this change has been bad for business it has been great for a *centro storico* that is unique. When the House of Savoy (*see p8* **The unstoppable Savoys**) made Turin its capital in the mid 16th century, this was little more than a medieval village on Roman foundations. The ruling dynasty set to work to create Europe's sole purpose-built unified-design capital. Scrubbed clean and restored over the past couple of decades, Turin is as splendid now as it was in its heyday. And its cultural life is once again worthy of a capital.

'Non può sbagliare!' (you can't go wrong!), confident Italian locals will tell hopelessly lost tourists. In Turin, with its regular grid-plan streets, it's likely to prove true.

Piazza Castello (*see p52*) is unquestionably the heart of the city, from which the rest of the *centro storico* radiates. But it's primarily a geographical and monumental heart, containing historical seats of temporal and spiritual power such as the **Palazzo Reale** (*see p54*) and the **Duomo** (*see p58*). The real life of the city goes on elsewhere.

Roman Turin – Augusta Taurinorum – stretched to the west of piazza Castello. The remains of a Roman theatre (*see p58*) serve as a reminder of this, as does the name – the **Quadrilatero romano** (*see p61*) – by which *torinesi* still call one of their city's liveliest

districts, packed with boutiques and bars. Also here is **Porta Palazzo** (*see p60*), Europe's largest open-air market.

Extensions to the Savoys' capital in the 1620s and 1660s respectively gave the city *vie* Roma and Po and their surrounding areas. This is the real **Centro** (*see pp69-80*) of Turin, with its shops, bars, eateries and museums. Porticoed, shop-lined via Roma stretches down to piazza San Carlo in baroque – then in Fascist – style to the Porta Nuova railway station. Along via Po, on the other hand, baroque porticos reach all the way to solemn piazza Vittorio Emanuele, with the River Po and the green, wealthy Collina (*see pp81-3*) district beyond.

The city spread west in the 18th and 19th centuries, along via Garibaldi, and then out towards what remained of the Cittadella (*see p66*), Turin's defence system. But its biggest sprawl came last century, when the presence here of auto maker Fiat (*see p21* **Whither Fiat?**) lured tens of thousands with the promise of employment, covering the area south of the city around its Lingotto (*see p86*) factory with industrial plants and jerry-built housing.

Peering down on it all is the city's best-known landmark, the 167-metre-high (548-foot) **Mole Antonelliana**. Now home to the **Museo nazionale del cinema** (*see p78*), the Mole has a glass lift that beams visitors up to the most spectacular view of the city and the Alps.

PRACTICALITIES

Turin is not subdivided into districts as such; areas tend to be called by the name of the nearest church or main thoroughfare.

Though Turin is Italy's car capital, the traffic situation hasn't changed much since the making of the 1969 cult classic *The Italian Job*. You might find it better to leave your vehicle at home. Its one-way systems are definitely better negotiated on foot, and even if the weather is foul, 18 kilometres (11 miles) of porticoed pavements will keep the rain off.

TICKETS & INFORMATION

For addresses of tourist information offices, *see p228* **Atrium**.

For information about museums and itineraries all over Turin and Piedmont, the toll-free number 800 329 329 operates from 9am-6pm daily.

Solemn monument: the **Gran Madre di Dio**. *See p82.*

In publicly owned museums and galleries, discounts apply to under-18s and over-60s from EU countries and many other countries with bilateral agreements; in some cases this means that admission is free, in others that you pay a reduced fee. You may also find that there are discounts for anyone with a valid student identity card or press card, or for members of a motoring organisation such as the AA or AAA; it pays to keep all your documents on you. The following multi-entrance tickets can substantially cut the cost of visiting central Turin's 40-odd museums and galleries and many others beyond:

Torino Card

(**Information** www.turismotorino.org).
This pass is valid for 48 hours (€15) or 72 hours (€17) and gives free access to 120 museums, monuments, castles, fortresses and royal residences in and around Turin. It also allows the holder free use of all urban public transport in Turin, of the lift to the top of the Mole Antonelliana (*see p77*), of the ferry service on the River Po (*see p218*) and of the Sassi-Superga railway (*see p91* La Cremagliera). It also offers reductions of up to 40% on theatre performances, concerts and guided visits. It can be purchased at Turismo Torino information points (*see p228* Atrium), at many Turin hotels, and at ACI (*see p219*).

Turin Piedmont Museum Card

This museum pass is valid for one calendar year and gives free and unlimited admission to perma-

nent collections in museums and galleries around the region, as well as to temporary exhibitions and activities organised by participating museums. It costs €40 (€25 for over-65s and under-26s in full time education). It also allows free admission to Artissima (*see p134*), the annual international exhibition of contemporary art in Turin. It can be purchased at Atrium (*see p228* **Atrium**), Teatro Regio (*see p156*) and the Salone della Stampa (via Roma 80, Centro, 011 563 817).

Blue Monday

In Turin, as in much of Italy, museums and galleries tend to close on Mondays, which is bad news for visitors who extend long-weekend trips to the beginning of the following week. Use your Monday morning for the following:
Market shopping
Markets at Porta Palazzo (*see p60*), piazza Benefica (*map p242 C1*), corso Palestro (*map p242 C2*) and La Crocetta (*see p67*) are all open on Monday mornings.
Churches
Almost all churches, basilicas and the Duomo (*see p58*) are open.
Palazzo Bricherasio
This contemporary art museum (*see p72*) is open during exhibitions.

Piazza Castello

The historic heart of Turin.

San Lorenzo. *See p53.*

Piazza Castello is the heart of Turin – not because it's particularly bustling or even a popular meeting point, but because it's the core around which the city has developed through the centuries and because many of the city's main thoroughfares set off from here.

It was at this strategic spot, between the rivers Po and Dora Riparia, that Romans followed the example of earlier populations and built a settlement – Augusta Taurinorum – in the 20s BC. As was their wont, Roman town planners conceived a rectangular area bounded by walls, sliced through by a rigid grid of perpendicular streets. There's little of the ancient left in this resoundingly baroque city, but it is on these foundations that the centre of Turin still stands today.

Piazza Castello & Palazzo Reale

Piazza Castello was given the shape it has today in the 1570s when the Savoy duke Emanuele Filiberto decided to shift his seat of power from across the Alps to Turin and make this largely medieval city his capital. Work

immediately got under way to transform the city: height, decoration, colours and aesthetic standards were all imposed by the rulers who were determined to upgrade the market town to a modern capital city.

The piazza is the result of efforts by three great architects: Ascanio Vitozzi kicked the process off by establishing a *'zona di comando'* – the ruling family's Palazzo Reale and the Duomo – in the north-west corner of the square in 1584; Amedeo di Castellamonte determined the overall structure of piazza Castello in 1649; and the baroque genius Filippo Juvarra added the finishing touches when he arrived in Turin in 1715. A make-over in 2000 gave the square a pedestrianised area complete with minimalist fountains and many park benches from which to appreciate the scenery.

Dominating and dwarfing the square is the double-faced **Palazzo Madama**, standing imposingly in its centre; inside is the **Museo civico di arte antica**. (Another more modern dominating feature, the ridiculously out-of-place Torre Littoria, dating back to 1933, pokes out above the baroque skyline to the south of the square; it was built in 1932 to a design by architect Armando Melis.) Nestling beneath the *portici* on the south side of the square are **Mulassano** and **Baratti & Milano** (for both, *see p111*), two of the city's most splendid cafés. On the east side of the piazza, the **Teatro Regio** (*see p156*) – a 1970s construction in glass and metal – is hidden (thankfully) behind what remains of the 18th-century theatre that burnt down in 1936. Continuing north, the **Archivio di stato** (state archives), **Armeria reale** (armoury) and glorious wood-panelled **Biblioteca reale** (royal library) lie to the north of Palazzo Madama.

In the north-west corner of piazza Castello, the piazzetta Reale is the gateway to the *'zona di comando'*. A solemn cast-iron fence by Pelagio Palagi (1835) replaced an earlier wall with a wooden pavilion; the pavilion once included a removable unit for displaying the Holy Shroud (*see p59* **Holy sheet**). The fence, with its ranks of cast-iron spears, has rhomboid lozenges with effigies of snake-haired Medusa, probably to ward off evil. Stout bronze columns shaped like cannon barrels decorated with festoons bear Carlo Alberto's name and the motto FERT (*see p56* **FERT?**), the mysterious acronym of the Savoys (*see p8* **The Unstoppable Savoys**). Flanking the entrance gate are statues of Castor and Pollux; these heavenly twins (the Gemini of the zodiac) are protectors of states and nations. This is one of Turin's key 'magic' spots (*see p66* **Hey Nostradamus!**). Closing the piazzetta Reale is the imposing façade of Palazzo Reale. Behind the palazzo lies the **Giardini Reali** (royal gardens), the entrance to which is usually from the courtyard of Palazzo Reale, but as this guide went to press was on the corner of viale 1° Maggio and viale Luzio, which despite its grand-sounding name is a narrow alley north-east of the Archivio di Stato.

Just outside the piazzetta railing, blending with the neighbouring buildings, the church of **San Lorenzo** (open 7.30am-noon, 4-7.30pm Mon-Fri; 9am-1pm, 4-7.30pm Sat, Sun) was begun in 1634 but not finished until 1680, after Guarino Guarini (*see p25* **Baroque protagonists**) had set an earlier unimpressive design to rights. The octagonal interior has a richly decorated high altar by Guarini.

Archivio di Stato

Piazza Castello 209 (011 540 382/toll-free 800 329 329). Bus 12, 27, 50, 51, 55, 56, 57, 61, 63/tram 11, 13, 15, 18. **Open** for exhibitions or research (*see p224*) only. **Map** p242 C3.
Carlo Emanuele III commissioned Filippo Juvarra to design the archives building, which was finished by 1734 along with the Segreterie di stato, the long stern wing connecting it to Palazzo Reale; once the offices of the ministers of the Kingdom of Sardinia and Piedmont, it is now the prefecture. Under the

porticos of the Segreterie di stato, plaques commemorate important figures and casualties of war. Students from the nearby university still stroke the finger of Christopher Columbus here to bring good luck in exams. The archive is located in six wide rooms furnished with cupboards stuffed with documents concerning Savoy territories and religious matters; it's one of the oldest examples in the world of a building designed with this specific purpose and still functioning as such. Occasional exhibitions and events allow a glimpse of the usually closed rooms; on these occasions the entrance is from piazza Mollino.

Armeria Reale

Piazza Castello 191 (011 543 889/toll-free 800 329 329). Bus 12, 27, 50, 51, 55, 56, 57, 61, 63/tram 11, 13, 15, 18. **Open** 1.30-7.30pm Tue, Thur; 8.30am-noon, 1.30-7.30pm Wed; 8.30am-noon Fri; 1.30-7.30pm Sat, Sun. **Admission** €4. **No credit cards**. **Map** p242 C3.
Note that the Armeria Reale will remain closed for restoration until September 2004, after which opening times may change.
The Savoy family weapons collection went on show for the first time in 1837 in this gallery frescoed by Francesco Beaumont – hence the name galleria del Beaumont – in the second half of the 18th century. The collection has grown over the years and today includes 57 complete suits of armour, Emanuele Filiberto's late 16th-century sword and the Sword of St Maurice, with its finely tooled sheath – used by the Savoys for investitures.

Biblioteca Reale

Piazza Castello 191 (011 543 855). Bus 12, 27, 50, 51, 55, 56, 57, 61, 63/tram 11, 13, 15, 18. **Open** 10am-5pm Tue-Sat. **Admission** free. **Map** p242 C3.
During the first half of the 19th century, Carlo Alberto converted a wood depot into a library. It now contains some 200,000 volumes, manuscripts, drawings, maps and photographs from the Savoy and Savoy-Carignano family collections. It has been open to the public ever since its establishment, as Carlo Alberto willed it. Pelagio Palagi's barrel-vaulted ceiling is impressive, suspended above the wooden scent of antiquity. Leonardo da Vinci's Codex on the flight of birds and self-portrait have been stored here since 1840; the self-portrait is occasionally exhibited here. The library sometimes stages art exhibitions, usually open to the public on Wednesdays and Sundays.

Giardini Reali

Viale Luzio. Bus 12, 27, 50, 51, 55, 56, 57, 61, 63/tram 11, 13, 15, 18. **Open** *Oct-May* 9am-5pm daily. *June-Sept* 8.30am-6.30pm daily. **Map** p242 C3.
The upper level of the gardens was designed in the late 17th century by André Le Nôtre, garden-maker to France's King Louis XIV. The gardens are run-down and the plants straggly, but the upper garden still retains a certain charm and Le Nôtre's use of symetrical elements to create wide perspectives –

flowerbeds near the premises and clusters of trees further away – is still discernable. At the centre of the gardens stands a fountain by Simone Martinez, nephew of architect Filippo Juvarra; swans pull a chariot carrying a buxom sea nymph who coyly watches a dance by the vigorous tritons arising from the sea blowing bugles.

Retrace your steps to exit from the upper levels and continue down viale dei Partigiani to reach the recently restored lower gardens, which are also accessible from corso San Maurizio and viale 1º Maggio. The gardens are charming, full of character and certainly worth a ramble; just be a little cautious if you opt for a moonlit stroll.

Palazzo Madama & Museo Civico di Arte Antica

Piazza Castello (011 442 9912). Bus 12, 27, 50, 51, 55, 56, 57, 61, 63/tram 11, 13, 15, 18. **Open** 10am-8pm Tue-Fri; 10am-11pm Sat; 10am-8pm Sun. **Admission** free. **Map** p242 C3.

Free tours are available of the restored parts of the palazzo; during the week you'll need to book. The Museo civico is closed for restoration until 2006.

Plonked in the middle of piazza Castello, Palazzo Madama is an incongruous jigsaw of very different historical periods. The foundations for a new fortress were laid in the 13th century over the Porta Decumana (the eastern Roman gate); remnants of the gate are visible (you can just walk in whenever the palazzo is open; a video explains what you're looking at) in the excavated area on the ground floor and in the towers incorporated in the medieval façade. This façade, facing via Po, is the result of

improvements commissioned between the 14th and 15th centuries by Princes Filippo and Ludovico d'Acaia. The castle underwent further transformations upon the arrival of Testa 'd fer (Iron-head, as Duke Emanuele Filiberto di Savoia was known).

The fortress's conversion into a palace got under way in the first half of the 17th century when *Madama reale* Marie Christine of France (*see p8*) chose it as her favourite residence; the open courtyard was covered to create a central hall. But it was *Madama reale* Marie Jeanne Battiste de Nemours who added the finishing touches with the help of Filippo Juvarra. Between 1718 and 1721 Juvarra designed the western façade, an ornamental avant-corps, whose main purpose was to lend an air of grandeur to the medieval castle. Juvarra's work met with harsh criticism, especially from essayist Francesco Milizia who described it as 'a façade without a building'. The palazzo's undeniable oddness is further enhanced nowadays by a boastful Fascist marble monument and hordes of skateboarders rehearsing freestyle jumps on the smooth grey marble outside. Step inside the palazzo for a glimpse of the Roman ruins and Juvarra's extraordinary staircase to the first floor.

Palazzo Reale

Piazzetta Reale (011 436 1455/fax 011 436 1484/ www.ambienteto.arti.beniculturali.it). Bus 12, 27, 50, 51, 55, 56, 57, 61, 63/tram 11, 13, 15, 18. **Open** *May-Sept* 8.30am-7.30pm Tue-Sun. *Oct-Apr* 9am-7.30pm Tue-Sun. Ticket office closes 6pm. **Admission** *Palazzo Reale* €6.50; *exhibitions* varies. **No credit cards. Map** p242 C3.

Palazzo Reale.

Palazzo Madama: an incongrous jigsaw. *See p54.*

Note that the Palazzo Reale can be visited only on half-hour guided tours in Italian, though the contents of each room are explained well on cards in English... if you're a quick reader. The tour often takes in the first floor only: check what's included when joining a tour group.

The stern façade of Palazzo Reale contrasts with interiors rich with stucco, gilt, frescoes, tapestries and decor that make it one of the city's most impressive baroque monuments. Begun in the first half of the 17th century, the palace was the official Savoy residence, designed to underscore the ruling family's idea of its own grandeur. It was built over the existing Palazzo del Vescovo (bishop's palace), bits of which are still visible at the eastern end of the ground floor. The Savoys ruled their kingdom from here until 1865, when, having become the reigning house of a newly united Italy, they were forced to up sticks and move to Florence, then Rome.

The palace's main façade (1658) by Carlo Morello is evenly dotted with windows and broken by a passage that leads beneath the palazzo and on to a cobbled courtyard on the far side of which the Giardini Reali (*see p53*) are visible but not accessible.

Leading up to the first floor is the grandiose **scalone**; this staircase was restyled in 1864 by united Italy's first king Vittorio Emanuele II and dedicated to his father Carlo Alberto. A plaque summons Italian artists to do their bit to make 'that place where the unification of Italy started' more solemn; and they did, despite the fact that weight limitations meant they had to add their artistic twiddles to the Scalone in papier-mâché rather than marble, a trick discovered only recently.

First floor

On the landing of the *piano nobile* (first floor) are works portraying episodes from Savoy family history, including one (west wall) of the marriage between Oddone di Savoia and Countess Adelaide, which brought Turin under Savoy control (*see p7*).

In the **Salone della guardia svizzera** – a cavernous space where the Savoys' Swiss mercenary guards would congregate – a frieze (1558) celebrates the legendary Saxon origins of the Savoy family. A refurbishment in 1834 by Pelagio Palagi gave the room a polychromatic fireplace, walls lined with green marble from Susa (*see p203*) and a wooden ceiling with a central painting portraying Amedeo VIII in the process of founding the order of the Santissima Annunziata, which replaced the original baroque vault. The broad canvas of *La battaglia di San Quintino* is by Palma il Giovane (1557).

The **Sala dei corazzieri** started life much larger, as a ballroom or a chapel, before Palagi reduced it to its present dimensions by raising the north wall. The 16 female figures in the vault represent key cities of the Savoy state; the tapestry (1695) showing water and earth by Philippe Behagle is part of an Elements series. Two 19th-century canvases face off across the room: Francesco Podesti's *Il giudizio di Salomone* and Francesco Hayez's painting of thirsty crusaders, *La sete patita dai primi crociati sotto Gerusalemme* – the latter a call to Carlo Alberto to quench the Italians' thirst for freedom by ridding the country of Austrian occupiers. The **Sala degli staffieri** was originally known as the Hall of Virtues because of Charles-Claude Dauphin's opus portraying Virtue subduing a chimera in the

Sightseeing

process of being crowned by Pallas (1662), which nestles in Carlo Morello's opulent baroque carved ceilings. The Gobelin tapestries (1746) depict scenes from the life of Don Quixote.

Following the Sala dei paggi is the **Sala del trono** (throne room), which was not used as such until 1831 when Carlo Alberto swapped a smaller, darker room at the back of the building for this more imposing one with windows overlooking piazza Castello and his subjects. In stark contrast with the intarsio floor are the Chinese-influenced Beauvais tapestries (early 18th century), testimony to the rage for all things Oriental at that time. Peace subdues Rage in Flemish painter Jean Miel's *Allegory of Peace* (1662) in the vault.

Important guests were received in the **Sala di udienza**, which may once have been the duchess's bedroom; adjoining it is a private chapel known as the Hall of Riddles because of its enigmatic symbols of love and conjugal fidelity. The decor here is by

FERT?

FERT, the motto of the House of Savoy (see p8 **The unstoppable Savoys**), is liberally dotted around Turin. But ask a local what it means, and you'll be met with a blank look. Even the experts are divided on the significance of the acronym... if, indeed, that's what it is.

Amedeo VII, *Il conte rosso* (the Red Count), is believed to have been the first Savoy to use FERT on his crest, some time around 1383.

Fortitudo Eius Rhodum Tenuit

His valour/strength saved Rhodes. This is the motto of the Order of the Annunziata, founded by Amedeo VI di Savoia in 1364. 'His' may refer to crusader Conte Amedeo V (1249-1323) or, possibly, to God.

Fides Est Regni Tutela

Faith is the protection of the kingdom.

Foedere Et Religione Tenemur

We will be kept together by the pact and by religion.

Foemina Erit Ruina Tua

Woman will be your ruin. Unlikely, this one, but popular lore holds that it relates to Vittorio Amedeo II's fiery relationship with a female member of the local aristocracy. Other interpretations say it's not an acronym at all but a corruption/use of *fertè* Old French for 'strength' *ferto* A coin introduced by Amedeo VI *fert* Latin for 'carry' or 'bear'.

Palagi, though the beautiful floor is dodgily attributed to Filippo Juvarra. In the **Sala del consiglio** are sanctimonious portraits of Savoys who passed away in an aura of sainthood. In his 1830s makeover, Palagi kept the baroque vault with Jean Miel's fresco of Hannibal asleep among the trees (*Sonno di Annibale fra gli alberi*) and the original walnut, elm, maple, mahogany and ebony floors.

The **Gabinetto cinese**, with its stunning lacquerwork designed by Juvarra, is another fine example of the early 18th-century chinoiserie craze. A door by Palagi separates the Gabinetto from the Queen's gallery in the eastern wing; organisational problems mean that the door is usually kept firmly shut, denying visitors the amazing view of the long gallery frescoed in the 18th century by Claudio Francesco Beaumont.

Carlo Alberto's *camera* (bedroom) is a small, bare affair – he had another grander one in his private apartments – with a camp bed for catnaps between meetings; nevertheless this tiny room was the only one in the palace with a terrace overlooking the gardens. It also houses Defendente Ferrari's *Madonna con il bambino* altarpiece (1523), given to him by St John Bosco. A short mirrored hall leads to the Sala della collezione, with an outstanding 17th-century gilt carved conch-vault with representations of day, night, years and eternity, and a fine specimen from the Savoys' precious collection of watches: a wall *pendule à placard* by Francesco Ladatte (1775). Note, too, the *sedia à la reine* with arm-rests attached to the back-rest only, to allow bulky dresses to be tucked neatly underneath.

The **Galleria di Daniel**, decorated by Daniel Seyter (c1690), connects the king's rooms to the queen's. Seyter's ceiling paintings show *The Apotheosis of a Hero* – namely Vittorio Amedeo II. Carlo Alberto turned it into a gallery of Piedmontese heroes with portraits of famous and saintly locals. The **Sala del caffè**, with its original 18th-century decor, contains 19th-century pieces of German china. En suite is the **Sala da pranzo** (banquet hall). The table is now set twice a year with two different sets of china and a forest of crystal.

The **Camera dell'alcova** was refurbished in 1662-3 on the occasion of Carlo Emanuele II's marriage to 15-year-old Francesca d'Orléans (note the French lily emblem). It was here that ruling Savoys enjoyed the *jus prima noctis* and Savoy heirs were born, under the scrutiny of courtiers whose job it was to make sure that marriages were consummated properly and that newborn heirs weren't swapped with illegitimate progeny.

The highly gilded **Sala del trono della regina** (queen's throne room) shines like a golden casket, especially after its recent renovation. The walls of the **Sala da ballo** (ballroom) are embellished with dancers in the style of Pompeii, where recent excavations had made all things ancient all the rage; 20 imposing white Corinthian columns encircle the room, which is dominated by Palagi's ceiling fresco of Olympus (1835-42).

The guided tour route ends at the foot of the magnificent **Scala delle forbici** (scissor staircase; 1720). An ingenious masterpiece by Filippo Juvarra, this stairway up to the second floor overcame problems of tight space and defied the rules of statics by casting its own incredible weight on the lateral walls. Under the first flight of steps Juvarra placed a medallion depicting a grotesque mask encircled by a snake's forked tongue, chopped by a pair of scissors… a message to those detractors who had predicted he would never complete the work.

Second floor

The palazzo's second floor is not always on show. At the head of Juvarra's staircase, the **Sala degli specchi** (hall of mirrors) hides a private altar made for Carlo Emanuele III and his wife Anna Cristina di Baviera: their initials are on the tapestry. Vittorio Emanuele II's office and bedroom overlook the piazza and have access to a pretty terrace. In the **Sala d'udienze del principe di Piemonte**, also known as the Sala delle cupolette, there is a painting of Carlo Emanuele II as a child, showing Palazzo Madama (*see p54*) as it was in 1640 before Juvarra's renovation in the background.

Teatro Regio

Piazza Castello 215 (011 881 5241). Bus 12, 27, 50, 51, 55, 56, 57, 61, 63/tram 11, 13, 15, 18. **Open** Guided tours only *Oct-July* 3pm Sat (rehearsals permitting; phone ahead to check). **Tours** €5. **Credit** AmEx, MC, V. **Map** p242 C3.
For information on performances, *see p156*.
Vittorio Amedeo II commissioned Benedetto Alfieri to design the royal theatre, which was completed in 1740, its façade blending into a unified whole with the Palazzo Reale offshoots. The original round theatre seated 1,500 people; the royal box was connected to the Palazzo Reale by a special corridor. Anyone in an evening suit could attend this democratic theatre which soon became a roaring social gathering place. Ladies improvised happenings in boxes, entertaining their guests with cakes and *marrons glacés*. In 1895 *La Bohème* premièred here under the baton of Arturo Toscanini. On 2 October 1936 a devastating fire caused irretrievable damage; World War II bombings dealt the death blow. The Regio as we see it today was designed and built by architects Carlo Mollino and Marcello Zavellani-Rossi between 1967 and 1973 when it was opened with Verdi's *Vespri siciliani*.

The Duomo & Roman Turin

In an oddly scrappy area west of the magnificent Renaissance Duomo, the little that remains of Augusta Taurinorum can be seen. Here, too, there are scant are vestiges of the medieval city.

A dingy passageway leads from the piazzetta Reale to piazza San Giovanni. Squint up beyond the Duomo (aka Cattedrale di San Giovanni)

The renaissance **Duomo**. *See p58.*

towards the **Cappella della Santa Sindone** (*see p59* **Holy sheet**)… it's the one view you'll get these days of this masterpiece by Guarino Guarini, which has been *in restauro* since a devastating fire in 1997.

Facing the cathedral is the appalling **Palazzaccio**; there's a strong lobby for its demolition but an equally weighty body of *nostalgici* who would like to see the area and the eyesore revamped.

Bordering the square to the south is the 17th-century **Palazzo Chiablese** (not open to the public), once the residence of the Chiablese branch of the Savoy family, and more recently home to the Museo Nazionale del Cinema (moved in 2000 to its current location in the Mole Antonelliana, *see p77*).

Heading west from the Duomo, the medieval **Casa Fossati Rayneri**, one of Turin's few medieval houses, stands on the corner of via IV Marzo and via Porta Palatina. Its brick façade frames the doorways of interesting shops on the ground floor and the rectangular windows topped with terracotta decoration on the upper floors. Beyond, pretty largo IV Marzo widens out, its tree-lined centre surrounded by low buildings. Further south, the churches of **Corpus Domini** (1603; open 7.30-11.30am, 3-6pm daily) and **Santo Spirito** (1765; open

Little remains of the **Teatro Romano**.

9.30-11.30am Mon-Sat) stand apse by apse, Corpus Domini's entrance being on piazza Corpus Domini and Santo Spirito's on via Porta Palatina. **Santissima Trinità** (open noon-5pm Tue, Wed, Fri; 8am-5pm Sat; 9.30-12.30am, 5.30-7.30pm Sun) – another work, c1598, by Ascanio Vitozzi who is buried there – is on the corner of via Garibaldi and via XX Settembre.

North from the Duomo along via XX Settembre, a fence encloses what remains of the **Teatro Romano**, probably dating from the first century BC though enlarged later; further north still, the well-preserved **Porta Palatina**, with its twin 16-sided towers, was Roman Turin's northern gate, dating from the first century AD. Opposite the gate, the **Museo di Antichità** contains bits and pieaces from the ancient city.

West of the Porta Palatina, the **Basilica dei Santi Maurizio e Lazzaro** – better known as the Basilica Mauriziana – stands by the southern entrance to the somewhat shabby **Galleria Umberto I**, a once-opulent early 19th-century shopping mall that has fallen on hard times. Opposite the church, the **Farmacia Anglesio** (via Milano 11, open 9am-12.30pm, 3.30-7pm Mon-Sat) is a rare example of an 18th-century pharmacy.

Basilica dei Santi Maurizio e Lazzaro

Via Milano 20 (011 436 1026). Bus 12, 27, 50, 51, 55, 56, 57, 61, 63/tram 11, 13, 15, 18. **Open** 8.15am-12.30pm Mon-Fri, Sun; 8.15am-6.30pm Sat. **Map** p242 C3.

An earlier (1572) centrally planned oratory was replaced in 1678 by the current church, which was then enlarged in 1772. Significant changes to the façade began in 1828 and continued until 1834: a neo-classical design by Carlo Bernardo Mosca (1834) includes heads of animals such as bulls – symbol of the town, a reminder that this block belongs to the municipality – lions and dogs, symbol of the Dominican order. (This symbol originates from a dubious interpretation of the Latin word *Domenicanes* – dogs of the Lord.

Corpus Domini

Piazza Corpus Domini (011 436 6025). Bus 12, 27, 50, 51, 55, 56, 57, 61, 63/tram 11, 13, 15, 18. **Open** 7.30-11.30am, 3-6pm daily. **Map** p242 C3.

In the mid 15th century a French soldier heading for Turin stole a chalice and a consecrated host along his route and brought it to the city. When he reached the spot where this church now stands, the host flew out of the plunderer's pocket and into the air and stayed there until the bishop of Turin ordered it down again. The miracle is depicted in all its glory in the vault and on the altarpiece. The chalice is in the Duomo (*see below*) where it is used to celebrate mass on Maundy Thursday. A church was not built here until 1603 when city authorities commissioned Ascanio Vitozzi to commemorate the miracle. The interior was decked out in red and black marble in 1752 to a design by Benedetto Alfieri.

Duomo

Piazza San Giovanni (011 436 1540). Bus 12, 27, 50, 51, 55, 56, 57, 61, 63/tram 11, 13, 15, 18. **Open** 7am-12.30pm, 3-7pm Mon-Sat; 8am-12.30pm, 3-7pm Sun. **Map** p242 C3.

Dedicated to Turin's patron saint, John the Baptist, the Duomo was built in 1491-8 to plans by architect Meo del Caprino. It stands on the site of three third-fourth-century churches and is Turin's only major example of Renaissance architecture.

The very symmetrical 15th-century façade is decorated with bas-reliefs in white Chianocco marble sculpted by Meo and assistants, framing elegant 18th-century portals.

Inside, an austere nave is flanked by two aisles that expand into chapels scooped out later from the thick lateral walls. The Last Supper above the main door is a 19th-century replica on wood commissioned by King Carlo Alberto.

The side chapels lining the aisles were decorated at different times by Turin's leading families and guilds; in the second chapel on the right is a beautiful polyptych by Giovanni Martino Spanzotti and Defendente Ferrari with stories of Saints Crispin and Crispinian (1504), patron saints of cobblers, commissioned by the Shoemakers' Guild.

In the right arm of the transept is an imposing gilded wood organ with elements dating back to 1567; it was extended and upgraded in 1874 and beautifully restored in 1973.

At the far end of the central nave stands Guarino Guarini's Cappella della Sacra Sindone (Holy Shroud chapel, *see below* **Holy sheet**) in black marble made even more lugubrious by the white marble nave. The black marble was expressly chosen by Guarini, who lined the chapel's entrance with the same material, to symbolise mourning. The chapel has been closed since a fire in 1997; so as not to disappoint visitors, there's a copy (one third smaller than the original) on the north side of the Duomo and a full-sized copy in San Lorenzo (*see p53*).

Museo di Antichità

Via XX Settembre 88C (011 521 2251). Bus 12, 27, 50, 51, 55, 56, 57, 61, 63/tram 11, 13, 15, 18. **Open** 9am-7pm Tue-Sun. **Admission** €4; €2 concessions. **No credit cards.** Map p242 B3.

Housed in the 18th-century orangerie of Palazzo Reale (*see p54*), this collection of statues, bronzes and tools dating from prehistory to the Barbarians, was begun by Duke Emanuele Filiberto (1572) and enriched over the centuries with objects from excavations carried out all over Piedmont. Since a make-over in 1989, when new exhibition space was added, parts of the Roman theatre (*see p58*) have been incorporated into the museum. There are free guided tours (in Italian only) on Sundays.

Holy sheet

The Sacra Sindone is a piece of linen measuring 4.34 metres by 1.9 metres (14 feet by six feet), clearly imprinted with the image of a man who appears to have suffered crucifixion. It has been in Turin since 1578; its whereabouts can be traced back to the mid 14th century. Beyond that, no record exists. Whether what believers insist was Jesus' winding sheet is a miraculous relic or an outright fraud remains a mystery. The Church sticks to its guns; the scientific community expresses its doubts; and visitors and pilgrims from all over the world just look and wonder.

Some of the Shroud's lengthy peregrinations have been reconstructed: legend recounts that it was brought to Europe from the Holy Land by a crusader in the 14th century; it certainly found its way into the hands of a French nobleman who donated it to the House of Savoy in the 15th century. When the Savoys moved their capital from Chambéry to Turin in the mid 16th century, the Shroud – symbol of divine approval for their absolutist rule – came too.

This venerated scrap of linen has a way of attracting fires. Its first scorching took place shortly before it left Chambéry; on that occasion it was saved from certain destruction at the very last minute. Again, in 1997, a brave fireman hacked his way to it just in time as fire ripped through the Cappella della Sacra Sindone (*see below*), which suffered devastating damage. The rescue was described in the local press as a miracle... with no inverted commas.

Microscopic examination, chemical analysis and carbon dating have so far failed to solve the riddle of the Shroud. Until they do,

experts, clerics and out-and-out cranks will continue to debate the issue at national and international Congresses of Sindonology.

Cappella della Sacra Sindone

Squeezed between Palazzo Reale (*see p54*) and the Duomo (*see p58*), the Cappella della Sacra Sindone can only be seen from outside (it has been closed since the 1997 fire) by peering up from piazza San Giovanni to the ornate dome. If the site seems a touch obscure for holding a relic of this importance, think again: it is situated strategically and symbolically at the nerve centre, the hinge between spiritual power (the Duomo) and the might of the Savoys (the palace): the ultimate symbol of the Savoys' divine right to rule.

Ascanio Vitozzi was commissioned to design a chapel for the Shroud adjoining the palace. Work, supervised by Carlo di Castellamonte, started in 1611 but was interrupted by war in 1624 and resumed some 30 years later by Bernardino Quadri who completed the first level of the chapel. In the original plan, the chapel's dome was to be higher than that of the Duomo but Quadri's design had made no allowance for the immense weight of the cupola. The problem was resolved in 1666 by Guarino Guarini who created a *trompe l'oeil* effect: light entering through large windows in the drum and smaller openings in the dome made the structure seem higher than it is, producing an effect of exceptional lightness. At the centre of the chapel is the altar by Ignazio Bertola (1694) that frames the silver casket that used to contain the Holy Shroud, which is now housed at the far end of the north nave in the Duomo.

Il Quadrilatero

Get lost in a maze of magnificent churches and sprawling markets.

Sightseeing

Stretching west from the city's '*zona di comando*' (*see p52*) is an area encompassing Turin's buzzing ethnic quarter, its bohemian backstreets and the hard core of its popular religious devotion.

Porta Palazzo, Borgo Dora & the Quadrilatero romano

Strictly speaking, Porta Palazzo is an anonymous opening on the northern side of piazza della Repubblica. But with Turin's typical disregard for toponymy (*see p61* **Toponymy**), the name now applies to the pungent, multi-hued market that fills the piazza every morning (*see p120* **Bargain hunting**), its exuberant, inexpensive contents being snapped up by everyone from *madamin* – the pernickety ladies of Turin's *alta borghesia* – to immigrants of all types, and trendy singleton

professionals. So overwhelming is this largest market in Europe in Turin's largest square, that you might never notice that baroque genius Filippo Juvarra was responsible for the layout of the piazza and of nearby via Milano.

Bustling and welcoming as it seems, this was once considered a dangerous area, and the sinister faces hanging out in sleazy bars on the square's north-western side show that some threat still lurks: after dark you might want to steer clear. But the inexorable advance of the wily developer means that this area, like the Quadrilatero romano (*see p61*) itself, will soon become the epitome of chic.

A case in point is Borgo Dora – a street and a quarter north-west of piazza della Repubblica and west of corso Giulio Cesare – which, like the Quadrilatero romano ten years ago, is well on its way to gentrification, with some great eateries already dotted around its alleyways (*see p97*). It's also home to a weekly antiques

Antiques and garbage at **Il Gran Balon**. *See p61*.

Toponymy

A KEY TO STREET NAMES

Thanks to the Romans and their grid plan, Turin is an easy town to get round. In theory. But beware that if you ask a local for directions, you run the risk of getting hopelessly lost. The *torinesi* don't call their *vie* and *piazze* by their official names. Why they don't is unclear. Just file it under the eccentricities of this city and bear in mind the following key to street names.

Il Quadrilatero

Corso Giulio Cesare is simply **corso Giulio** (and not to be confused with via Giulio, *map p242 B2*).
Corso Regina Margherita becomes **corso Regina**.

Cittadella

Corso Duca degli Abruzzi is **corso Duca**.
Corso Vittorio Emanuele II is **corso Vittorio**.

Centro

Corso Massimo d'Azeglio is **corso Massimo** (not to be confused with via San Massimo, *map p243 D1*).
Corso XI Febbraio is just **corso undici**.
Piazza Carlo Emanuele II is universally known as **piazza Carlina** (allegedly a snipe at Carlo Emanuele's camp leanings).
Piazza Vittorio Veneto is shortened to **piazza Vittorio** (few locals know that the Vittorio in question is not Vittorio Emanuele II).
Via Madama Cristina is **via Madama**.
Via Principe Amedeo is **via Principe**.

La Collina

Piazza della Gran Madre di Dio is simply **piazza Gran Madre**.

Lingotto

Corso Unione Sovietica is known as **corso Unione**.

market (*see p120* **Bargain hunting**) that expands every second Sunday of the month into **Il Gran Balon**, a massive flea market with the very best antiques and the very worst garbage.

West of Borgo Dora, narrow, dusty via del Cottolengo flanks the Piccola Casa della Divina Provvidenza, a vast complex of hospitals and schools for the poor and sick, better known as Cottolengo after its founder Giuseppe Benedetto Cottolengo. Further along the road is Maria Santissima Ausiliatrice (open 6am-noon, 2.30-7pm daily), a 19th-century church with a neo-Palladian façade that houses the remains of St John Bosco buried inside, and which plays a major social role in the surrounding neighbourhood.

Back (south-east) across corso Regina Margherita there's a piece of Roman masonry on the corner of via della Consolata and via Giulio: this square construction with a polygonal inner room is part of one of the corner towers that marked where city streets met the defensive walls.

In piazza della Consolata, **La Consolata** – Turin's favourite church and officially called Madonna della Consolata – is a masterpiece of the baroque by Guarino Guarini with additions by Filippo Juvarra. Outside, the forbidding Romanesque structure is all that remains of the 11th-century church of Sant'Andrea: part of the tower, and a section of the apse. The tiny café opposite is one of Turin's obligatory stopovers: Al Bicerin (*see p112*).

South and east from here, centring on piazza Emanuele Filiberto and via Sant'Agostino, is the area known as Il Quadrilatero romano. In fact only a small section of Roman Turin, this run-down area was occupied in the 1950s and '60s by immigrants from southern Italy, a poverty-stricken ghetto shunned by upright *torinesi*. All that changed just over a decade ago when its potential was spotted by far-sighted architects who have transformed it into the city's trendiest area, with soaring property prices to match. Designer boutiques (*see p123*), interior decor shops, restaurants (*see p97*) and nightspots sprout regularly. In the eastern fringes, where *vie* San Domenico and Milano meet, **San Domenico** is Turin's sole Gothic church.

To the north of Porta Palazzo the **Fondazione italiana per la fotografia** has recently moved into impressive new premises (*see p142* **Light show**).

La Consolata

Piazza della Consolata (011 436 3235/toll-free 800 329 329). Bus 52, 60, 67. **Open** 6.30am-7.30pm daily. **Map** p242 C2.
In the 11th century a church was built on this spot by devotees of the cult of Mary the Comforter (Madonna della Consolata), and dedicated to St Andrew. Now only fragments, including the bell tower, remain of the Romanesque church of Sant'Andrea. The first sweeping changes were made in 1678, when *Madama reale* Marie Jeanne Battiste de Nemours (*see p12*) commissioned Guarino Guarini to transform the church. Further extensions

Turin's best-loved church, **La Consolata**. *See p61.*

were made over ensuing years by Filippo Juvarra (1715-29). Between 1899 and 1904 Carlo Ceppi enriched the interior with polychrome marble, stucco work and bronze decorations.

A neo-classical portico leads to the aula di Sant'Andrea, an elliptical space with a vault frescoed by Mattia Bortoloni in the early 18th century. To the right is the richly decorated chapel of Nostra Signora delle Grazie, situated in what was the apse of the 11th-century church. Beyond the aula di Sant'Andrea is the sanctuary, consisting of a hexagonal oratory by Guarino Guarini with a lofty, frescoed dome. On the magnificent altar, designed by Juvarra, is the miraculous Hodegetria Madonna, a 15th-century copy of an icon in Santa Maria del Popolo in Rome. In the corridor to the right, thousands of ex-voto paintings and objects of all descriptions line the wall in a touching testimony to the faith placed by locals in Mary's comforting powers, which are celebrated annually in a procession on 20 June. On the largest cupola, you can still glimpse a cannon ball from the 1706 French siege.

San Domenico

Via San Domenico (011 521 7971). Bus 12, 50, 52, 60, 67/tram 4. **Open** 7am-noon, 4-6.30pm daily. **Map** p242 C3.

Always referred to as Turin's 'only Gothic church', San Domenico was built for the Dominican order early in the 14th century, but was in fact largely rebuilt in 1776. The 18th-century building stuck closely to the original plan, however. The simple

brick three-part façade has a high gable, a rose window and a series of pinnacles. The interior is laid out with a nave and two aisles, supporting ribbed cross vaults in the corners. At the left of the aisle is the Capella della Madonna delle Grazie, which boasts the city's only 14th-century frescoes, attributed to the so-called Maestro di San Domenico. The church's floor – lower than the street level outside – testifies to the age of the building.

Along via Garibaldi to piazza Statuto

Straight-as-a-die via Garibaldi was a major thoroughfare in Roman Turin and remains that way today. There's nothing particularly elegant about the shops that line this pedestrian precinct, but there's a comfortingly down-home feeling about the crowds that throng here, especially for the evening *vasca* (stroll – '*vasca*', which more usually means 'lengths' done in a swimming pool). This artery links the heart of the ancient city to the fruits of the third and final historical expansion – that overseen by Filippo Juvarra in the early 18th century.

South along via Milano, piazza Palazzo di Città stands where the Roman forum once was. In medieval times it was home to a busy food market, where tooth-pullers and second-rate actors would also gather to practise their trades and arts. Continuing the square's long tradition as fruit and vegetable market, stalls set up here on the first Sunday of the month, though – sign of the times – the produce is thoroughly organic and accompanied by handicrafts. At the centre (and known as *Il fermacarte* – the paperweight), the sword-wielding statue is of *Il conte verde* (the green count) Amedeo VI di Savoia, champion of a 14th-century crusade, immortalised in 1853 by Pelagio Palagi. The imposing building on the western side is the city hall.

To the south, today's via Garibaldi – straightened up and with its unified façades added in 1736 – follows the decumanus of the ancient town. Some two metres (seven feet) under today's road, Roman paving stones and remains of the drainage system have been found. Now, as – presumably – then, this is where locals stroll and window-shop of an evening; these days, it claims to be Europe's longest pedestrianised street.

As you follow suit, dodging shoppers and peering at window displays, you run the risk of missing several baroque churches along your route unless you look up and spot their cupolas. **Santissimi Martiri** is one of the largest churches along via Garibaldi and one of the most sumptuous in the city.

Off via Garibaldi (north) on via della Consolata, Palazzo Saluzzo di Paesana (No.1 bis; *see also p76* **Cortili**) was designed by Gian Giacomo Plantery between 1715 and 1722 for Count Saluzzo di Paesana. The second entrance on the west side of the courtyard was shut up, allegedly because Vittorio Amedeo II was offended by the opulence flaunted by the count, rivalling that of the king himself. Just beyond, piazza Savoia dates back to the first half of the 18th century. At that time, the buildings surrounding piazza Savoia were the residences of Turin's aristocracy; now they're offices and private flats. The obelisk was placed at the centre of the square in the 1850s to celebrate a law curtailing the power of the clergy; the names carved on it are those of the 800 municipalities that provided funds to build it. Beneath the obelisk are buried suitably secular symbols of the city: a packet of *grissini* (breadsticks), a bottle of Barbera wine and a copy of the local newspaper that announced drafting of the legislation.

From piazza Savoia, via del Carmine runs west parallel to via Garibaldi; at No.3 is the church of **Madonna del Carmine**, Juvarra's last effort before his death in 1736. Beyond, at the junction with via Valdocco, are the Quartieri militari, dwellings for the military designed by Juvarra as part of Vittorio Amedeo II's westward expansion of the city in 1716-30.

Two blocks to the north, the **Museo della Sindone** (Shroud museum, via San Domenico 28, www.sindone.it, open 9am-noon, 3-7pm daily, admission €5.50, concessions €4.50) will prove interesting only to those with a burning passion for the relic (*see also p59* **Holy sheet**).

Via Garibaldi finishes at piazza Statuto, which was designed by Giuseppe Bollati in 1864. The piazza was built to commemorate the Statuto Albertino, the liberal-ish constitution granted to the Kingdom of Sardinia-Piedmont in 1848 by monarch Carlo Alberto. When the Savoys moved on to occupy the Italian throne, this remained in force as the constitution of united Italy until 1946 when the current republican one was approved. A British company, the Italian Building Society, was commissioned to construct this red and white square surrounded by porticos; it went bankrupt, however, leaving a long-unfinished piazza and the long-lingering nickname of '*piazza degli inglesi*'.

Madonna del Carmine

Via del Carmine 3 (011 436 9525). Bus 12, 29, 36, 46, 49, 50, 52, 59, 60, 65, 67/tram 1, 4, 13. **Open** 7.30-11.30am, 3.30-7.15pm Mon-Sat; 9am-12.30pm Sun. **Map** p242 C2.

The church was designed for the Carmelite order by Filippo Juvarra in 1732 and completed in 1741; the façade, by Carlo Patarelli, was added in 1872. A single nave has side-chapels topped with lunettes. Juvarra died on a trip to Madrid, before this church was completed. The church's official name is Madonna di Monte Carmelo after the name of the mountain in the Holy Land where Jerusalem's patriarch bestowed the Carmelite rule upon a group of monks. The chiesa del Carmine suffered severe damage in World War II air strikes, so much so that there were plans to demolish it; in the end it was restored, but much of its Juvarrian charm vanished. Today the church is a focal point for Turin's Romanian community; mass is said in Romanian each Sunday.

Santissimi Martiri

Via Garibaldi 25 (011 562 2581). Bus 12, 29, 36, 46, 49, 50, 52, 59, 60, 65, 67/tram 1, 4, 13. **Open** 8am-noon, 4.30-7pm daily. **Map** p242 C3.

The exterior of this massive church is astonishing: the huge white baroque façade contrasts with its stern side brick wall. The church is dedicated to martyrs Solutor, Adventor and Octavius, first patron saints of Turin. It was built in 1577 for the Jesuits to a design by Pellegrino Tibaldi. The church has a single nave embellished with marbles, stuccoes and bronze. The high altar is attributed to Filippo Juvarra. The stone at the foot of the large pillars supporting the presbytery is the one on which the little-known St Solutor met his end. In the oldest chapel there's a painting of St Paul by Federico Zuccari (1607) and a 17th-century bronze statue of St Francis Xavier by Giuseppe Riva.

Sightseeing

Cittadella

One of Turin's less visually striking quarters is nonetheless home to
a burgeoning arts scene and a few dark secrets...

Via Pietro Micca branches off west from piazza
Castello (*see p52*) to a quieter and altogether
more staidly *torinese* part of town. Yes, there
are shops and markets and outbreaks of bustle
here and there. But there is certainly none of
the ethnic-mix colour of Porta Palazzo (*see p60*),
and the elegance and neatness of buildings
lining the *vie* and *piazze* here convey a real
feeling of *torinesità* – civilised, predictable
and impervious to the various types of
'contamination' to which any modern city is
prone. This comes to a head in the south-west,
in the exclusive, wealthy, beautiful but
somewhat soulless Crocetta district.

The whole area centres around the Mastio
della Cittadella, all that remains of the 16th-
century fortress that stood up repeatedly to
attack and siege.

From via Pietro Micca
to Porta Susa

This area to the west of the baroque centre is
the result of a project for 'clearing unhealthy,
run-down districts' – ie anything old and with

a bit of character – drawn up by a commission
of engineers whose agenda included very
straight, wide streets and much pomposity.
Reconstruction work was carried out to plans
by architects Gaetano Lombardi, Carlo Promis
and Count Cesare Alberico Balbiano di Viale
between 1885 and 1915. These were years when
the Universal Exhibition (*see also p27*) brought
new decorative ideas to Turin, and when brisk
trade with the rest of Europe was filling the
pockets of a new merchant class eager to make
their mark on the architectural fabric of the city
in a way that would rival the *palazzi* of the
aristocratic establishment.

Via Pietro Micca can be immediately spotted
on a map as one of only two roads (the other is
via Po, *see p75*) in the centre that don't follow
the regular grid pattern; along one side of the
street are porticos, under which bars and low-
cost clothes shops nestle.

Via Pietro Micca ends in piazza Solferino,
laid out in 1860 on the site of the former hay
and wood market and now home to Giorgetto
Giugiaro's high-concept Atrium pavilion where
the city dispenses tourist and Winter Olympics

Fontana angelica. *See p65.*

Sympathy for the devil

Commissioned by Count Carlo Truchi di Levaldigi, court architect Amedeo di Castellamonte designed a palazzo at via Alfieri 15 (*map p242 D3*) which was completed in 1675. Two gates from the palazzo's courtyard opened on to streets on opposite sides, making it a handy shortcut for the local populace. Annoyed by this state of affairs, the count had them both closed. For the one facing on to the main street, he had a magnificent wooden door carved in Paris, and,

when it was ready, had his new acquisition hung under the cover of darkness. Maybe it was only pique on the part of surprised locals that caused this door to become known immediately as the *porta del diau* ('devil's door' in Piedmontese dialect). But it was a diabolical coincidence that, in 1738, the palazzo became home to the *Real Casa dei Tarocchi* where the House of Savoy had its playing and tarot cards printed. And the tarot card depicting the devil is number 15.

information (*see p228* **Atrium**); the cost of these two *gianduiotto*-chocolate-shaped (*see p34* ***Cioccolata***) structures shocked many *torinesi*, especially as their fate after the 2006 Winter Olympics remains unclear. In the semicircular space at the north of the square stands the **Fontana angelica** (1930) by Giovanni Riva. The fountain was much appreciated by the city's Fascist authorities, and you can see why: the neo-classical figures that adorn it have the kind of bulging-muscle physiques that any good Blackshirt would have desired. The figures represent the four seasons, and the whole fountain is wrapped in masonic symbolism. Esoterics consider the fountain another of Turin's 'magic' spots (*see p66* **Hey Nostradamus!**), the *Porta dell'Infinito* (the door to the infinite).

The monument to Ferdinando di Genova, Vittorio Emanuele II's brother, that stands in the piazza's central reserve is by Alfonso Balzico (1863-70); the anatomical detail is so precise that it gave rise to rumours of unseemly dissections by the artist to get the hang of muscle movements. On the west side of the square is the **Teatro Alfieri** (*see p156*), which used to be a true hippodrome – with shows on horseback – and now stages light comedies.

East off the northern end of the square, via Santa Teresa leads east to the church of the same name and to the **Museo della marionetta** (*see p137*) with its wonderful collection of puppets and miniature scenery. Via Cernaia, on the other hand, heads west towards Porta Susa station.

Leading north from via Cernaia are streets (via Mercanti, via Botero, via San Dalmazzo) full of eateries, wine bars and shops. Cutting across them parallel to via Cernaia, via Monte di Pietà becomes via Santa Maria, where the 18th-century church of **Santa Maria di Piazza** (*see p66* **Hey Nostradamus!**; open 7.30am-12.45pm, 3-7pm daily) is located. At

Museo Civico Pietro Micca. *See p66*.

Walk Hey Nostradamus!

Futuristic design and high-concept make-overs may be a characteristic of 21st-century Turin, but they mask something murkier and more ancient. Turin, Lyon and Prague, esoterics will tell you, mark the corners of the white magic triangle; Turin, San Francisco and London those of the black magic triangle. All of which makes this city a magic force to be reckoned with.

Tales of magic surround Turin's foundation myth: it was strong energy streams, the story goes, that persuaded Egyptian prince Pheriton Siue Pheaton (aka Feto or Eridanus, son of the sun and the goddess Isis) to build a settlement here in the pincer grip of the River Po (associated variously with the sun and male nature) and the River Dora Riparia (female nature).

An astrolabe in **piazza Statuto** (*see p62*) recalls that the 45th parallel passes nearby. For Romans, the west was the bad end of town: where the sun sets, where light meets darkness and good, evil. Roman Turin didn't get much more westerly than where piazza Statuto now stands. This, then, is the black heart of Turin, the *vallis occisorum* where executions and burials took place. The necropolis may have stretched as far as **corso Francia** (*map p242 C1*). The gallows stood in this square until the French moved it in the early 19th century to *'l rondò dla forca* (the gallows roundabout, where via Cigna now meets corso Regina Margherita, *map p242 B2*). Moreover, the main access to Turin's sewerage system – considered the *Porta dell'Inferno*, the gate of hell – is in piazza Statuto.

Two thirds of the way along via Garibaldi, via Sant'Agostino leads north into the Quadrilatero romano (*see p61*) and dark, narrow, sinister-feeling **via Bonelli**, which was once home to Turin's executioners, who were stationed at No.2.

South of via Garibaldi in via Santa Maria stands the church of **Santa Maria di Piazza** (*see p66*); inside, local chronicles say, is a portrait from the life of the Madonna, painted by St Luke – a powerful force for good. In a house nearby, a black veil said to once belong to the Blessed Virgin herself is jealously guarded.

In nearby **piazza Solferino** (*see p64*), the **Fontana angelica** is a mysterious spot, full of odd allegories and masonic symbolism.

---

the end of this road is the **Giardino della Cittadella** – more car park with some skimpy trees than gardens – and the adjoining piazza Arbarello, which is, likewise, little more than a car park when it's not fulfilling its traditional role as rallying point for demonstrations.

Due south, at the junction of via Cernaia and corso Galileo Ferraris, the Mastio (main gate) della Cittadella is all that remains of a much larger 16th-century defensive system; it now houses the **Museo nazionale dell'artiglieria**.

Via Cernaia continues west to Porta Susa station. Shortly before reaching the station, via Guicciardini leads (south) to the **Museo civico Pietro Micca** beneath which a labyrinth of galleries was part of the Cittadella, and the location of much historic derring-do (*see p7* **Pietro Micca**).

Museo Civico Pietro Micca

Via Guicciardini 7A (011 546 317/ www.comune.torino.it/musei). Bus 1, 10, 52, 55, 56, 59, 65. **Open** 9am-7pm Tue-Sun. Tours of tunnels depart every 35 mins from 9.35am-12.05pm; every hr from 1.20-6.20pm. **Admission** *Museum & tunnels tour* €3; €2 concessions. **No credit cards**. Map p242 C2.

This tiny museum is dedicated to the achievements of Pietro Micca (*see p7* **Pietro Micca**). Built in 1961, on the centenary of Italian unification, the museum contains documents and artefacts relating to the 1706 siege in which Pietro Micca lost his life, plus a fascinating model of 18th-century Turin. But the real interest here lies underground, in the kilometres of 17th-century countermine tunnels that extended beneath the Cittadella (*see below*).

Museo Nazionale dell'Artiglieria & Cittadella

Corso Galileo Ferraris (011 562 9223). Bus 5, 14, 29, 50, 55, 56, 58, 59, 67, 72/tram 13. Closed as this guide went to press, due to reopen in Sept 2004. Map p242 C2.

Savoy Duke Emanuele Filiberto – known as *Testa 'd fer* (Iron-head), for his genius in military strategy – had little time for frippery when he first made Turin the capital of the family dominions in the mid-16th century. With the French high-handedly trying to lay claim to much of Italian territory, it was fortifications that were foremost in his mind, and for that reason, he focused his building activities on a fortress known as the Cittadella (1564-66). Engineers Francesco Orologi and Francesco Paciotto da Urbino came up with the plan for a pentagonal stronghold, which stretched roughly from today's corso Galileo

Believers say it's *La Porta dell'Infinito* (the gate to the infinite): in the space between the two male figures is a rectangle representing a threshold... to an unknown dimension beyond the pillars of Hercules; a *caverna luminosa* where the solutions to alchemical mysteries that control the world are held. Don't bother trying to enter: the profane don't stand a chance.

Somewhere in **piazza Castello** (*see p52*) – experts disagree over the exact spot – is the white heart of Turin. Its magic value owes much, naturally, to the presence of the Holy Shroud (*see p59* **Holy sheet**). In this mysterious scrap of linen the four elements are contained: earth (it began life as a flax plant); water and wind (it was blown over the seas from the Holy Land); and fire, which has failed several times to destroy it. These days the Shroud is rarely given an airing; in the past, it was suspended in a special glass case for display during royal weddings and victory celebrations.

The space between the statues of Castor and Pollux, at the grille between Palazzo Reale and piazza Castello proper, is one of Turin's most magical spots. The heavenly twins are said to represent the opposing poles that dominate existence; they stand guard here where the sacred and diabolic meet.

The Savoys were as caught up in their city's mysteries as any of their subjects. In the basement of **Palazzo Madama** (*see p54*), it's said, Emanuele Filiberto whipped up potions with famous wizards and attempted to turn base metal into gold.

Down via Po and across the river, the **Gran Madre di Dio** church (*see p81*), some believers claim, stands on or near the spot where the Holy Grail lies concealed. This pompous neo-classical temple seems to have been conceived with occult symbolism in mind. On 24 June – the summer solstice and the feast of Turin's patron St John – the sun hits the top of the church's façade at noon exactly. The two statue groups in front of the main entrance, adepts say, are linked to the prophecies of Nostradamus (1503-66) who spent some time in Turin, though his house north-west of the city centre has been bulldozed to make way for a park. Nostradamus was a familiar figure at the court of hyper-superstitious Emanuele Filiberto, and predicted the birth of his son.

Ferraris to Porta Susa station. Housing some 3,000 soldiers, the Cittadella survived three fearsome sieges (1640, 1706 and 1799) but fell before an onslaught by property developers in 1856 when it was considered an obsolete pile hampering the city's spread westwards. All that remains of the Cittadella now is the *mastio* (main gate), which was restored in 1893 by Roberto Braida, but already in 1733 it had been made into a museum, making it one of the world's oldest. On the ground and first floors are flags, great cannons and mortars, and Italian firearms. In the round third-floor room is a collection of exhibits from the colonial wars (1870-1933). A statue of gallant Pietro Micca (*see p7* **Pietro Micca**) stands out front.

Santa Teresa

Via Santa Teresa 5 (011 538 278). Bus 5, 11, 12, 14, 27, 29, 50, 55, 56, 57, 58, 59, 63, 67, 72, 92/tram 4, 13. **Open** 7.30am-noon, 3.30-6pm daily. **Map** p242 C3.
This church was commissioned in 1642 by Marie Christine of France, the first *Madama reale* (queen mother regent), whose ashes are kept in the first chapel on the right. Note the chapels in the transepts, designed by the baroque genius Filippo Juvarra in 1730-33. The neo-classical façade was added in 1764 by Carlo Filippo Aliberti.

GAM & the Crocetta

Wide corso Ferraris shoots south from via Cernaia to piazza Vittorio Emanuele II where a statue of the (very short) man himself peers down from a very tall pillar. Around the pedestal are engraved the names of battles won (and lost) during Vittorio Emanuele II's reign.

Located just beyond the piazza is the **Galleria civica d'arte moderna e contemporanea** (GAM), a modern structure, surrounded by bamboo, where the city's extensive collection of 19th- and 20th-century art is housed.

Between corso Vittorio and corso Rosselli, the Crocetta (little cross) district is a web of broad and narrower streets flanked by some of the city's most expensive real estate, including a few mid 19th-century blocks, some extremely pretty *stile Liberty* (*see p231* **Glossary**) villas and a great number of self-important carbon-copy early 20th-century blocks of immense dullness. The district is livened up every morning when less well-to-do fashion victims flock to via Marco Polo, corso De Gasperi, via Lamarmora and vicolo Crocetta where an open-air cheap-and-chic clothes market takes place.

Stile Liberty details in **La Crocetta**. *See p67*.

South of corso Einaudi at via Marco Polo 8 stands the church of the **Beata Vergine delle Grazie** (1588; open 7.30am-6.30pm daily), which houses a fresco by the school of Tintoretto (some attribute it to Palma il Giovane but this is dodgy to say the least) depicting the Madonna della Croce (Our Lady of the Cross) – from whence the name of the district. That's one story; another says the name derives from the crosses on the habits of the Trinitarian friars who lived in the church's adjoining monastery.

The **Fondazione Sandretto Re Rebaudengo** stages temporary exhibitions of contemporary art, plus conferences, debates and concerts; it's located south-west of the Crocetta.

See also p143 **Art on Track**.

Galleria Civica d'Arte Moderna e Contemporanea (GAM)

Via Magenta 31 (011 562 9911/www.gamtorino.it). Bus 5, 33, 52, 58, 64, 67, 68/tram 1, 9. **Open** 9am-7pm Tue, Wed, Fri, Sat; 9am-11pm Thur; 9am-8pm Sun. **Admission** €5.50; €3 concessions. **No credit cards**. Map p242 D2.

A low, grey, purpose-built 1950s structure houses a municipal collection numbering some 20,000 artworks from the 18th to the 20th centuries, some 600 of which are usually on show. Note, however, that occasionally the permanent collection is removed from the exhibition spaces to stage temporary shows. A good audio guide is available in English.

A core collection of Piedmontese pieces has been extended in recent years with acquisitions of works by international artists. Among 19th-century Piedmontese artists shown here are Eleuterio Pagliano (*San Luigi Gonzaga*, 1851), Andrea Gastaldi (Portrait of Pietro Micca, 1858, much loved locally; *see also p7* **Pietro Micca**), Giacomo Grosso (*La nuda*, 1896), Medardo Rosso (*Donna con bambino*, 1886) and Giuseppe Pellizza da Volpedo (*Lo specchio della vita*, 1898). Other Italians featured include Francesco Hayez (Portrait of Carolina Zucchi, 1825), plus a collection of sculptures by Antonio Canova and Carlo Marocchetti (*see p75* **Carlo Marocchetti** among others.

On the second floor developments in Piedmontese art in the 20th century are charted and compared to those in the rest of Italy and further afield. The *avanguardie torinesi* – Giacomo Balla, Felice Carena and Felice Casorati – are pitted against the likes of Amedeo Modigliani, Filippo De Pisis, Giorgio De Chirico, Otto Dix, Max Ernst, Alberto Savinio, Lucio Fontana, Paul Klee and Fernand Léger.

Fondazione Sandretto Re Rebaudengo

Via Modane 16 (011 1983 1600/www.fondsrr.org). Bus 55. **Open** noon-8pm Tue, Wed, Fri-Sun; 1-11pm Thur. **Admission** €5; €3 concessions; free 8-11pm Thur. **No credit cards**. Map p244 B1.

This striking 3,500sq m (37,600sq ft) space designed by Claudio Silvestrin and James Hardwick is located in Quartiere San Paolo, a tough, run-down area littered with abandoned factory spaces – a sad sign of the city's industrial decline. An odd place, then, for such an ambitious project, which is gradually, however, overcoming local hostility and a host of teething problems to become a point of reference for contemporary art in the city. The Fondazione's huge spaces are used for a host of events ranging from art and photography exhibitions to concerts. There's a classy bar and restaurant too.

Il Centro

Where it's all happening.

Uniformly elegant **piazza San Carlo**.

A cursory glance at a map of Turin might suggest that piazza Castello (*see p52*) is the city centre. Historically and geographically speaking, it is. But '*centro*' to a *torinese* has different connotations. The fulcrum of shopping, drinking, working and playing lies elsewhere, along buzzing *vie* Roma and Po and in the regular grid of streets sandwiched between.

If orderly baroquedominates in this area, it's not the whole story. Dotted around are neo-classical hiccoughs and an outbreak of rationalism as via Roma heads towards Porta Nuova station; there's the curvaceous (**Palazzo Carignano**, *see p72*) and the plain bizarre (**Mole Antonelliana**, *see p77*), plus galleries and museums catering to every taste. And when you can take no more, the **Parco del Valentino** (*see p80*) offers a breath of almost-country air and river views.

Via Roma & the Contrada Nuova

The first extension/modernisation of Turin after it was promoted to capital of the Savoy duchy took place south from the '*zona di comando*' (*see p52*) along what is now via Roma (originally via Nuova). The medieval fabric and two sets of Roman walls were razed to make way, in the 1620s, for a broad main drag of extraordinary uniformity. In the area bordering on to this artery – the Contrada Nuova – were the homes of the wealthy and the aristocracy.

The 17th-century section of via Roma ends at **piazza San Carlo**, designed by Carlo di Castellamonte. The southern end of via Roma, joining piazza San Carlo to Porta Nuova railway station, is an equally imposing – though very different in spirit – rationalist effort (1933-7) by *Il Duce*'s favourite architect Marcello Piacentini; today its porticos, with their designer boutiques, lure well-heeled purchasers and slavering window-shoppers. At the southern end of via Roma, piazza Carlo Felice was completed in 1823 by architects Gaetano Lombardi, Giuseppe Frizzi and Carlo Promis.

Leading out of the south-east corner of piazza Castello (*see p52*), the **Galleria subalpina** (officially the Galleria dell'Industria subalpina) was designed in 1873 by Pietro Carrera; it's an elegant short cut, once the haunt of bons vivants who frequented the café-chantant on the corner where the Cinema Romano now

Rigidly Rationalist
piazza CLN. *See p71.*

stands. At the arcade's southern end **piazza Carlo Alberto** is small by Turin standards, closed in on its east side by the **Biblioteca nazionale** (*see p224*) where once stood the stables of Palazzo Carignano, and to the west by the neo-classical rear façade of the palazzo itself.

Circumnavigate the massive bulk of this palazzo to **piazza Carignano**. Peaceful and elegant, the piazza's eastern side is occupied entirely by the curvaceous brick walls of Palazzo Carignano, now home to the **Museo del Risorgimento**, with the historic **Teatro Carignano** (*see p157*) opposite. Also facing the palazzo, the **Ristorante il Cambio** (*see p101*) was the favourite haunt of statesman Camillo Cavour (*see p10*), while in the far south corner of the square is **Pepino** (*see p118*), another historic venue whose home-made ice-creams are a habit few can kick.

A block to the south in via dell'Academia delle Scienze is the extraordinary **Museo Egizio** with its collection of mummies and, in the same palazzo, the **Galleria Sabauda** where the Savoy art collection is on display.

Opposite the gallery, on the corner of bustling via Maria Vittoria, stands the church of **San Filippo Neri**. Concealed behind the façades of via Maria Vittoria are some exquisite courtyards (*see p76*). South from the Museo Egizio in via Lagrange is **Palazzo Bricherasio** where the Fiat car giant saw the light of day in 1899.

Heading west along via Maria Vittoria will bring you to **piazza San Carlo**, its long façades the striking result of the Savoys' uniformity dictates. Built between 1640 and 1650 to a plan by Carlo di Castellamonte, it was adjusted by Benedetto Alfieri in 1769, when, for static reasons, the original slim twin pillars supporting the porticos were bulked out, to the detriment of proportions and light and shade effects. In 1864, when it was announced that the capital of newly united Italy was to be shifted to Florence, piazza San Carlo was stained with the blood of 200 people killed or injured in an outpouring of rage. The piazza was severely damaged in World War II air raids but painstakingly rebuilt in post-war years.

Off the north-west corner of piazza San Carlo stands the T-shaped **Galleria San Federico**, designed in 1856 by Barnaba Panizza. This gorgeous arcade once hosted the offices of the *La Stampa* newspaper; it's now home to designer shops and top-class boutiques. Its vaults also shelter the **Lux**, once Italy's largest cinema and a rare example of art deco style that has survived the make-over into a modern multiplex. In the 19th century, when it was still called Galleria Natta, the spot where the cinema stands today was the site of Caffè La Meridiana, a favourite haunt of artists and writers, including Edmondo De Amicis.

The equestrian monument of Emanuele Filiberto di Savoia has stood at the centre of the piazza since 1838; commissioned by his

Before reaching piazza Carlo Felice, nip east along **via Cavour**: a plaque at No.8 indicates the family home of statesman Count Camillo Benso di Cavour (*see p10* **The four horsemen of the Risorgimento**); Palazzo Cavour is now used for temporary exhibitions.

Piazza Carlo Felice is named after the last true-blue Savoy: the childless Carlo Felice's successor was his nephew Carlo Alberto, a Savoia-Soissons-Carignano. Until recently a sorry spectacle with wretched gardens at its centre, it is, at the time of writing, a sorry spectacle with a wretched building site at its centre, dominated by an ugly 2006 Winter Olympics logo. Overlooking the chaos is the **Porta Nuova railway station**, a ground-breaking creation in glass and iron when it was built in 1861-8.

Galleria Sabauda

Via Accademia delle Scienze 6 (011 547 440). Bus 12, 27, 50, 51, 55, 56, 57, 63/tram 4, 13, 15, 18. **Open** *8.30am-2pm Tue, Fri-Sun; 2-7.30pm Wed; 10am-7.30pm Thur.* **Admission** (tickets from Museo Egizio ticket office, *see below*) *Galleria & Museo Egizio* €8; *Galleria only* €4; €2 concessions. **No credit cards. Map** p242 C3.

Upstairs from the Museo Egizio (*see below*), the Galleria Sabauda holds a collection of canvases from the Savoy family collection. From 1832 they were exhibited in Palazzo Madama (*see p54*) then transferred here in 1865. Though the collection has been beefed up over the years by acquisitions and donations, many of the older masters met sorry ends: Carlo Emanuele III had 40 paintings on mythological subjects burned because he thought them lascivious and sinful; in 14 years of Napoleonic occupation 350 sculptures and paintings disappeared and not all of the booty was returned. There is much in here that you'll find yourself rushing by, but watch out for fine works by Jan van Eyck (*St Francis Receiving the Stygmata*) and Hans Memling (*The Passion*), a Madonna and Child by Fra Angelico and some mighty self-glorifying portraits of the host family.

Museo Egizio

Via Accademia delle Scienze 6 (011 561 7776). Bus 12, 27, 50, 51, 55, 56, 57, 63/tram 4, 13, 15, 18. **Open** *8.30am-7.30pm daily.* **Admission** *Museo & Galleria Sabauda (see above)* €8; *Museo only* €6.50; €3 concessions. **Credit** MC, V. **Map** p242 C3.

The biggest collection of Egyptian artefacts this side of Cairo is housed in what was built as a Jesuit-run school for noble offspring and has a suitably boarding school air about its corridors and ex-dormitories. In the 18th century the building passed into the hands of the Academy of Sciences. Today the museum holds some 30,000 pieces, a collection that was started in the 17th century when the Savoys began dabbling in Egyptian oddments.

A slow-moving revamp has left the museum with an incongruous mix of new and old display styles, and with an awkward route through the rooms,

descendant Carlo Alberto, the statue was cast in Paris by Carlo Marocchetti (*see p75* **Marocchetti**) and portrays the duke sheathing his sword after the victory of St Quentin in 1557; the armour worn by the rider of what locals refer to as the *caval d'brons* (bronze horse) is a faithful reproduction of a suit kept in the **Armeria reale** (*see p53*).

Guarding the south side of piazza San Carlo are the striking *chiese gemelle* (twin churches) of **Santa Cristina** and **San Carlo**, both begun in the first half of the 17th century, then completed later.

Nestled under the west porticos of the piazza at No.144 is **Palazzo Turinetti di Pertengo**, housing the historic Caffè Torino (*see p116*); grinding your heel on the genitals of the bronze bull on the pavement outside apparently brings good luck. This café was the first in Turin to get gas lighting, in 1832. On the same side of the piazza is the Caffè San Carlo (*see p116*). On the eastern side is the chocaholic's dream-emporium the **Confetteria Stratta** (*see p127*), unaltered since it opened in 1836. (*See also p34* **Cioccolata**.)

Beyond piazza San Carlo, via Roma becomes a gleaming white corridor, furiously fascist in style yet exuding a solidity and neatness that inspire admiration. Back to back with piazza San Carlo, Marcello Piacentini's **piazza CLN** (Comitato di Liberazione Nazionale) is guarded on opposite sides by two marble fountains representing the rivers Po and Dora.

which from the ground floor leads to the underground level, then up again to the ground floor and finally to the first floor.

The shiny-new first room on the ground floor, reopened in 2000, displays various vases and household objects dated between 6,000 and 3,500 BC, and a reconstructed tomb from the fourth millennium BC. In an adjoining room is a copy of the Rosetta Stone (the original has been in London's British Museum since 1802).

The route continues to the underground section, dedicated to three archaeological sites: Qau el Kebir, Assiut and Gebelein. Here, too, is a segment of Turin's Roman wall, unearthed during renovation. The itinerary continues in the two statue-filled rooms on the ground floor where the original core of the collection is kept – a hoard that in 1824 Carlo Felice bought from Bernardino Drovetti, who had taken advantage of his post as French consul in Cairo to put together the world's largest collection of antiquities. The black basalt statue of Ramses II, located in the first of the two statuary halls, is considered one of the pinnacles of Egyptian art.

It's a time-machine leap on to the first floor with its old-fashioned displays of tightly wrapped mummies and their gaudily painted sarcophagi languishing in dusty glass coffins, accompanied by knick-knacks in equally dusty showcases. There's the tomb of the architect Kha and his bride with complete funeral kit, furniture and perfectly preserved garlic included, from Deir el Medina.

On weekdays, your concentration is likely to be disturbed by overexcited school groups; lack of staff means rooms are often closed without notice.

Palazzo Bricherasio

Via Lagrange 20 (011 571 181/www.palazzo bricherasio.it). Bus 12, 27, 50, 51, 55, 56, 57, 61, 63/tram 4, 13, 15, 18. **Open** 2.30-7.30pm Mon; 9.30am-7.30pm Tue, Wed, Sun; 9.30am-10.30pm Thur-Sat. **Admission** €6.50; €4.50 concessions. **No credit cards. Map** p242 C3.

On 11 July 1899 a document setting up the Fabbrica Italiana Automobili Torino (Fiat) was signed in this palazzo; a copy (the original belongs to the Fiat-owning Agnelli family) of Lorenzo Delleani's painting showing the founders signing it is displayed on the first floor (not always open to visitors). In 1999 the palazzo became a private contemporary art museum hosting important exhibitions.

Palazzo Carignano & Museo del Risorgimento

Via Accademia delle Scienze 5 (011 562 1147). Bus 12, 27, 50, 51, 55, 56, 57, 61, 63/tram 4, 13, 15, 18. **Open** 9am-7pm Tue-Sun. **Admission** *Museum* €5; €3.50 concessions. **No credit cards. Map** p242 C3.

This extraordinarily curvy red-brick palazzo was designed by Guarino Guarini for Prince Emanuele Filiberto Carignano and constructed between 1679 and 1684. The building marks a totally new departure in the layout of Italian baroque palaces. So

detail-obsessed was Guarini that he had a brick kiln built behind the church of San Lorenzo (*see p53*) where he could bake bricks in whichever forms he pleased. For decorations, Guarini eschewed the usual putti and grotesque masks, preferring instead to draw on stories told by a certain Giovanni Niccolis di Brandizzo, who in 1665 joined a regiment recruited by Carignano to help the French fight Iroquois Indians who were threatening the French colony in Canada. Back in Italy in 1672, Brandizzo's reports enchanted the court. On to the façade of Palazzo Carignano went motifs based on Indian headgear. In 1864 an eastern wing was added by Giuseppe Bollati who respected Guarini's original design on the whole – note Guarini's favourite decoration, the star, repeated inside the courtyard – but branched out with a neo-classical façade looking east on to piazza Carlo Alberto. From the courtyard, the two different sections of the building are clearly recognisable: brown 17th-century brickwork sets off the bright red bricks of the 19th-century addition.

When Carlo Felice, the last of the true-blue Savoys, died in 1831 it was Carlo Alberto of the cadet Carignano line who took over the throne. Both he and Vittorio Emanuele II – who would later become united Italy's first monarch – were born here. In 1848 Carlo Alberto was forced to grant his country a liberal-ish constitution – the Statuto Albertino – which introduced a form of democracy in the realm. The *parlamento subalpino* held its first meetings in the palazzo's converted ballroom.

The ballroom-amphitheatre, where parliament sessions were held, is now preserved in all its recently restored glory in the **Museo del Risorgimento**, entered from the first floor of the palazzo. Drilled and grilled on the events of the glorious Risorgimento (*see p10*) at school, Italians approach this museum with knee-trembling awe. Anyone less steeped in Italian history may not find it quite so thrilling, but the huge collection does have a ramshackle charm. Coaches belonging to Cavour and Giuseppe Garibaldi parked on the landing of the *piano nobile* are interesting, and there's a documentary shown (in English) explaining some of the history you've missed, plus essential historical documents galore and a collection of weapons. In the beautiful red-velvet parliamentary chamber, the calendar still shows 1860 to recall the last meeting held there before completion of the new deputies' hall in the western section that was never used: by the time it had been completed, the capital had been transferred to Florence, from where it shifted definitively to Rome.

San Carlo Borromeo

Piazza San Carlo (011 562 0922). Bus 12, 27, 34, 35, 50, 51, 52, 61, 63, 64, 67, 68/tram 1, 4, 9, 15, 18. **Open** 7.10am-noon, 4-6.30pm Mon-Fri; 9am-1pm Sat, Sun. **Map** p242 D3.

On the façade of San Carlo, completed in 1834 by Ferdinando Caronesi, a relief depicts San Carlo Borromeo who, at the end of a bout of plague in Milan where he was bishop, swore he would walk

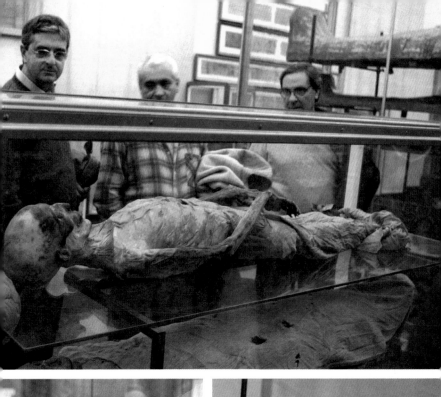

Museo Egizio. *See p71.*

to Chambéry to give thanks for deliverance in front of the Holy Shroud (*see p59* **Holy sheet**). Duke Emanuele Filiberto decided to make the bishop's stroll shorter by bringing the Shroud to Turin, promising to return it to Chambéry once the vow had been fulfilled. The Shroud, however, is still here. Inside, a painting over the high altar by Bernardino Quadri (1653) shows San Carlo venerating the piece of linen. On the west wall of the church, on the corner of via Alfieri, there's a poster-sized fresco reproduction of the Shroud, probably dating back to 1706.

Santa Cristina

Piazza San Carlo (011 539 281). Bus 12, 27, 34, 35, 50, 51, 52, 61, 63, 64, 67, 68/tram 1, 4, 9, 15, 18. **Open** 8am-12.45pm, 3-7pm daily. **Map** p242 D3.
A twin to the church of San Carlo across the way, Santa Cristina was commissioned by *Madama reale* Marie Christine of France (*see p9*) and designed by Carlo di Castellamonte, but not finished until 1715-18 when Filippo Juvarra gave it a Borromini-inspired façade with a very prominent Savoy coat of arms. The rather dull interior was extensively reworked in the 19th century. The *Allegories of the Theological and Natural Virtues* (1715-18) were sculpted by Carlo Tantardini.

San Filippo Neri

Via Maria Vittoria 5 (011 541 136/011 538 456). Bus 11, 12, 27, 50, 51, 55, 56, 57, 61, 63/tram 4, 13, 15, 18. **Open** 8am-noon, 5.30-7pm Mon-Sat; 10am-noon Sun. **Map** p242 C3.
This church and oratory was commissioned in the second half of the 17th century but, when the dome of that original plan collapsed, Filippo Juvarra came up with a more grandiose project in 1711. It took many years of hard labour to finish; at last on 26 May 1772 – the saint's feast day – the church was consecrated. The neo-classical façade was added later by architect Carlo Giuseppe Talucchi. External pomposity is in noticeable contrast to the dusty decadence of the lofty (31m/102ft high) single nave; wooden floors and a bare vaulted ceiling add a touch of simplicity, somehow enhancing its charm. The church's excellent acoustics mean it is best seen during a Settembre Musica concert (*see p157*).

Along via Po to piazza Vittorio Emanuele

Via Po, connecting piazza Castello to piazza Vittorio Veneto and the Po, is a much-frequented artery where trams clatter past a flawless succession of porticos; even the gaps between buildings where side-streets pass were porticoed over in 1819, to allow the Savoys and their subjects to move from the Palazzo Reale (*see p54*) to the river without getting their hair wet. Nowadays, *torinesi* take advantage of this royal whim to browse in pavement book stalls, sit in cafés and enjoy the best *gianduiotto* ice-cream in town at **Fiorio** (*see p117*).

The street is the result of Carlo Emanuele's expansion – the second major enlargement of the city – towards the east in 1670 to connect the *'zona di comando'* (*see p52*) with the old wooden bridge across the river. The new axis was revolutionary in that it was wide enough to allow three carriages to travel abreast. Instantly pin-pointable on a map as one of only two central streets (the other is via Pietro Micca, *see p64*) that don't follow the orthogonal street grid, via Po's layout was dictated by the already-existent church and convent of San Francesco da Paola.

Spreading around the axis is an area originally (though no longer) known as the *Contrada di Po*, where court architect Amedeo di Castellamonte drew up urban planning requirements, then saw to it that they were implemented: three-storey buildings overlook the street, uniformly painted.

At No.15 is the **Università** (courtyard always open). This seat of learning was established by Pope Benedict VIII in 1404 in Chieri, east of Turin, and finally came to rest in the city in 1566. Built in 1714 to a design by

Marocchetti

Carlo Marocchetti (1805-67) was born in Turin. He studied in Paris with the classicist François Joseph Bosio, then moved to Rome where he continued his studies at the Accademia di Francia (French Academy) until 1830. In 1848 he landed in London and exhibited in the Royal Academy, catching the eye of British patrons who would commission him to provide some of that city's best-known statues.

Despite his classical formation, his works are pure Romantic. This is particularly perceivable in his equestrian monuments – not only in the postures of his subjects, but also in subtle handling of mass and light effects. The statues of Emanuele Filiberto in piazza San Carlo in Turin and Richard the Lion-heart in front of the Houses of Parliament in London (1860) are his masterpieces. His Queen Victoria in Glasgow was well received by city elders but not popular with the public. Marocchetti's works were overwhelmingly monarchist, and unsubtle in their hero-worship of European royal families; if his patrons welcomed his extreme promotion of patriotism, the masses were less impressed.

Michelangelo Garove, the stunning university courtyard (wander in when the gates are open) is surrounded by a double loggia of pillars; the wrought-iron gate is by Filippo Juvarra.

Running parallel to via Po is narrower, quieter via Verdi where, at No.16, the **Museo della radio**'s collection of period radio and television sets can be visited by appointment only (011 812 6696).

To the east in via Montebello stands the city's most cumbersome monument, the **Mole Antonelliana**, with its uniquely spiky roof; designed – though never used – as a synagogue, the Mole now houses the **Museo nazionale del cinema**.

South of via Po, the **Pinacoteca dell'accademia Albertina delle belle arti** is home to a huge collection of historic prints, as well as (minor) old master paintings and sculptures. Further south again lies **piazza Carlo Emanuele II**, known by locals as piazza Carlina (*see p61* **Toponymy**). This pretty square has a French air about it. Surprisingly, for Turin, it lacks porticos; some of the surrounding *palazzi* have been restored while others are in various states of decay, giving the whole a bohemian look. Standing proud in the middle is Camillo Cavour (*see p10* **The four horsemen of the Risorgimento**). On the piazza's southern side is the church of **Santa Croce** (closed for restoration), built for the Augustinian order of nuns to a design by Filippo Juvarra in the early 18th century.

Back on via Po at No.45, the 17th-century church of the **Santissima Annunziata** (open 3.30-7.30pm Tue; 10am-noon, 3.30-7.30pm Wed-Fri; 10am-noon Sat) contains a clockwork crib, a

Walk *Cortili*

Behind the stern, strictly unified façades of Turin's baroque *palazzi*, individualism breaks out. Imported from Roman and from church architecture, the courtyards of baroque buildings became another reception 'room' and as such needed 'decor' that was a fitting indicator of the rank of the owners. With no urban planning strictures to follow, architects could run riot.

Today courtyards are the undisputed domain of the porter whose brief is to protect residents' privacy; discretion, therefore, is imperative on any tour of *cortili*.

Across the road from the church of San Filippo Neri (*see p75*), **Palazzo Asinari di San Marzano** (via Maria Vittoria 4) was designed for one of the city's oldest noble families by architect Michelangelo Garove in 1684. Now the headquarters of vermouth maker Carpano (*see p122* **No Carpano, no party**), it's closed to the public, but stick your head inside the charming courtyard with its spiralling pillars.

A peek through the main gate of **Palazzo Birago di Borgaro** (via Carlo Alberto 16) reveals a wonderful spectacle. The back wall was built to hide stables; in fact, until the 17th century, aristocratic dwellings had a smart courtyard (*cortile d'onore*) and a more homespun one (*cortile rustico*) where the stables were; steeper real estate prices in the 18th century meant only the richest could afford to be fussy, resulting in charmingly haphazard arrangements.

At via Bogino 9, **Palazzo Granari della Roccia** was built in the 1680s for Marco Antonio Graneri, scion of a rich noble family related to the House of Savoy. At the end of the *cortile* Granari created a small pleasure park divided into three parts and crossed by cobbled paths; there's not much of it left today, yet the remaining obelisks that divide the courtyard from the park offer a charming view. The palazzo is now home to the *Circolo degli artisti*.

Tack west across piazza Castello and along via Garibaldi for **Palazzo Scaglia di Verrua** (via Stampatori 4), to see Turin's only remaining example of a private 16th-century dwelling (albeit reworked in the 17th and 18th centuries). Many lovely frescoes adorn the façade. There are two courtyards: the one lavishly decorated is the palazzo's smart courtyard while the other, rich in green vegetation, dates back to the 18th century.

WIth an area of 5,000 square metres (53,760 square feet), the **Palazzo Saluzzo di Paesana** (via della Consolata 1bis) is by far the largest and one of the most impressive of Turin's private 18th-century palaces, built between 1715 and 1722 by Gian Giacomo Plantery for Count Saluzzo di Paesana. Its back façade faces via Bligny, and the main doors are permanently shut. Allegedly, King Vittorio Amedeo II was offended by the count's presumption: only the king was allowed two symmetrical accesses to his palace. In the courtyard, between the two porches at first-floor level, look out for two French cannon balls that have been stuck in the wall since the 1799 siege.

favourite with locals. At No.55, the **Fondazione Accorsi** is a treasure trove of mainly 18th-century knick-knacks.

Via Po ends in the magnificent piazza Vittorio Veneto, with a view beyond to the **Gran Madre** church (*see p81*) and the green Collina (*see p81*). Metaphysical painter Giorgio De Chirico found piazza Vittorio fascinating and made it a recurring image in his odd and disturbing works. You can see why. Baroque as it seems, the piazza was not created until 1825 when architect Giuseppe Frizzi came up with a design for *palazzi* and porticos that would present a unified, symmetrical whole despite a drop of 11 metres (36 feet) from the square's north-west to its south-east extremities. Though some of the square's grandeur is diminished by hordes of parked cars, large swathes of the 35,000-square-metre (376,344-square-foot) surface have been pedestrianed, and colonised by cafés and wine bars.

The **Museo regionale delle scienze naturali** (natural history museum) lies a few blocks south, near the formal **Aiuola Balbi** gardens and piazza Cavour, with its replica of an English Romantic landscape. Nearby, tiny leafy **piazza Maria Teresa** is a prosperous alternative to the elite neighbourhood on the Collina (*see p81*).

Pointy heap: **Mole Antonelliana**.

Fondazione Accorsi – Museo delle Arti Decorative

Via Po 55 (011 812 9116/www.fondazioneaccorsi.it). Bus 15, 30, 53, 55, 56, 61, 70/tram 13, 16. **Open** 10am-8pm Tue, Wed, Fri, Sun; 10am-11pm Thur. **Admission** €6.50; €5 concessions. **No credit cards.** Map p243 C1.

This museum opened in 1999, funded by a generous legacy left by antiques dealer Pietro Accorsi. The 27 rooms hold thousands of rarities, mostly from the 18th century, including a cabinet inlaid with precious woods, ivory and tortoiseshell made in 1738 by Pietro Piffetti, and Piedmontese silver artefacts such as a *rocaille* coffee pot by Giovanni Battista Carrroni, court taster from 1753 to 1778, bearing his engraved signature. Amid the paintings note the series of hunting scenes by Vittorio Amedeo Cignaroli (1739-1800). The foundation offers guided tours in English and a touch-tour for the blind. It is also an active promoter of exhibitions, conferences, concerts and history of art classes.

Mole Antonelliana

Via Montebello 20 (011 812 5658). Bus 15, 55, 56, 61, 68/tram 13, 16. **Open** 9am-7pm Tue-Sun; 9am-11pm Sat; ticket office closes 1hr earlier. **Admission** Lift €3.62; €2.58 concessions. **No credit cards.** Map p243 C1.

Mole means 'heap' and Alessandro Antonelli was the architect who designed this eye-catcher, commissioned by Turin's sizeable Jewish community after the liberal Statuto Albertino (*see p13*) made life easier for non-Christians in the Savoy realm. The site bought in 1859 was so small that only a very daring or very foolish architect would consider placing a major construction on it; in fact, Antonelli's was the only project entered for the competition and even he refused subsequently to reveal his original blueprint. Suffice to say that a first-draft structure of 47m (154ft) grew rapidly to its present 167m (530ft), under the alarmed gaze of the city elders. The cost of the Mole was such that the Jewish community abandoned the still-unfinished project ten years later. Disappointed, they handed it over to the town council, which converted it into a memorial to King Vittorio Emanuele II.

Antonelli died in 1888, before the Savoy symbol – a winged genius, star over his head, spear in his right hand, palm of victory in his left – was placed on top of the heap. Early in the 20th century he was knocked off his pinnacle by a hurricane and replaced, for safety's sake, with a star (the statue is now on display inside the Mole). Something of a dead weight on municipal hands, the Mole was used briefly as the Risorgimento museum (moved in 1931 to Palazzo Carignano, *see p72*). Nowadays it contains the wonderful **Museo nazionale del cinema**. The original brick, iron and stone of the spire was swept away by a tornado in 1953, after which the burghers of Turin all chipped in to have the city's symbol rebuilt… in reinforced concrete. No longer the tallest brick building in the world, it remains the tallest museum.

Utterly inauthentic: the **Borgo Medioevale.** *See p80.*

Experience vertigo with a trip in the lift through the cinema museum and up to the viewing platform 85m (279ft) high up on the spire of the building. The panorama over the city and out across the Alps is simply breathtaking.

Museo Nazionale del Cinema

Via Montebello 20 (011 812 5658/www.museo nazionaledelcinema.it). Bus 15, 55, 56, 61, 68/ tram 13, 16. **Open** 9am-7pm Tue-Sun; 9am-11pm Sat; ticket office closes 1hr earlier. **Admission** €5.20; €4.20 concessions. **No credit cards**. **Map** p243 C1.

Local collector and media historian Maria Adriana Prolo began piecing together a cinema-related collection in the 1940s. It was later displayed in Palazzo Chiablese (*p57*) near piazza Castello, but when that palazzo was closed in 1983 for security reasons, the museum remained homeless until 2000 when the collection was moved to its current location inside the distinctive Mole Antonelliana (*see p77*). It's now an overwhelming exhibit of models of film sets, documents, antique movie cameras, film snippets and stills, distributed over five levels. It's a three-stage experience: the section called *Archeologia del cinema* recounts the birth of film-making; the *Sala del tempio* (temple room) has ten themed 'chapels' dedicated to horror, sci-fi, film in Turin and so on; the *Macchina del cinema*, on the other hand, covers all aspects of filmmaking, from sound effects to photography to instantly recognisable props from legends and classics of the big screen – the great director Federico Fellini's hat and scarf, Lawrence of Arabia's kaftan, Alien suits from the Ridley Scott creepie and heaps more. On the ground floor is a well-stocked bookshop and a snazzy *aperitivo* bar.

Museo Regionale di Scienze Naturali

Via Giolitti 36 (011 4320 7332/www.regione. piemonte.it/museoscienzenaturali). Bus 15, 55, 56, 61/tram 13, 16. **Open** 10am-7pm Mon, Wed-Sun; ticket office closes 1hr earlier. **Admission** €5; €2.50 concessions. **No credit cards**. **Map** p243 D1.

Housed in what was once the Ospedale Maggiore di San Giovanni Battista – a 1680 creation by court architect Amedeo di Castellamonte – this natural history museum is of the academic, hands-off variety. Still, there's a certain old-fashioned charm to its presentation of vast butterfly and insect collections. Botany, mineralogy, palaeontology and zoology are covered exhaustively. A massive whale's skeleton is always the highlight for small visitors.

Pinacoteca dell'Accademia Albertina di Belle Arti

Via Accademia Albertina 8 (011 817 7862). Bus 15, 55, 56, 61, 68/tram 13, 16. **Open** 9am-1pm, 3-7pm Tue-Sun. **Admission** €4; €2.60 concessions. **No credit cards**. **Map** p243 C1.

There are some 300 paintings, drawings and sculptures in this august academy established in 1678. Particularly outstanding are the 60 *cartoni* – full-sized preparatory sketches – done by local artist Gaudenzio Ferrari in the 16th century. On the façade, note the gable festooned with the Savoys' coat of arms held by two lions, a work added by sculptor Giacomo Spalla in the 1820s.

By the Po

Note that the stretch of river between Ponte Vittorio Emanuele I, past Torino Esposizioni (*see p80*) and down to Moncalieri (*see p93*), is

Walk In the footsteps of Cavour

Were Camillo Benso, conte di Cavour (*see p10* **The four horsemen of the Risorgimento**), the statesman credited as being the linchpin of Italian unification, to take a stroll down memory lane to his old Turin haunts, he'd find that, apart from improved lighting, things hadn't changed much in the last 150 years.

Every city, village and hamlet in Italy has at least one avenue, piazza or side-street named after the Piedmontese statesman. In Turin there was a Palazzo Cavour (*see p71*) long before Camillo talked world leaders into changing the face of Europe. Our itinerary starts there, where Camillo was born on 10 October 1810, and died in 1861. In this palazzo in the street of the same name, the moderate political daily, *Il Risorgimento* published Cavour's visions for Italy between 1847 and 1852.

Near the palazzo stands the church of **Madonna degli Angeli**, the Franciscan parish church frequented by the Cavour family. Cavour's funeral was held in this church, despite the fact that he'd been excommunicated for wresting territory from under the Church's control.

On nearby piazza San Carlo, the **Confetteria Stratta** (*see p127*) has been soothing *torinesi* sweet-teeth since 1836. Even a quick glance at its front window goes a long way to explaining Cavour's distinctive girth. Stratta did the catering for the receptions at the foreign ministry during Turin's brief spell as capital of Italy in 1861-4. The count was foreign minister. Stratta also catered for lavish private receptions at Camillo's request, causing many altercations with his older brother Gustavo, a staunchly Catholic widower who strongly disapproved of conspicuous consumption.

Inside the same building as the Confetteria Stratta – the 17th-century **Palazzo Isnardi di Caraglio** – is the Whist Society that Cavour founded as Turin's snooty answer to London's private clubs; it's still going strong. In a merger in 1948 with the Philharmonic Academy, the clique got bigger but no less exclusive. Admission to the society's grand rooms is strictly for members only.

Any paying patron is welcome, on the other hand, at the **Ristorante del Cambio** (*see p101*), conveniently situated in front of Palazzo Carignano (*see p72*), the site of the first Italian parliament. Here Cavour ate many a lunch during his political career, sitting at a table (now marked with a plaque) from which he could see his secretary motioning to him from across the square if he was needed back at the ranch.

Palazzo Carignano, a grandiose baroque palace designed by Guarino Guarini in 1679, was first the home of a cadet branch of Savoys and then, from 1848, the seat of the *parlamento subalpino*; since 1934 it has housed the **Museo del Risorgimento**. Among the museum's highlights is a careful reconstruction of the office in the foreign ministry occupied by Cavour from 1852 to 1859.

All great men deserve a great monument, and Cavour got his after his death on 6 June 1861, a few months after the proclamation of the Kingdom of Italy. The imposing neo-classical work in **piazza Carlo Emanuele II** (*see p76*) by Sienese sculptor Giovanni Duprè was inaugurated in 1873 to a mixed reception. The reliefs around the base pay homage to Cavour's political brilliance, while the marble groups represent Independence, Politics, Law and Duty.

Nearby via Po is a clutter of cafés and shops. Like other cafés in Turin, the **Fiorio** (*see p117*) was a popular hangout for politicians talking shop in comfort. It remains a Turinese drawing room today, though its patrons are more likely to be discussing broadband reception than waging war on Austria. Lobbying was so heated here that King Carlo Alberto demanded daily reports of café gossip. It was here that Cavour founded the Whist Society, squatting on the low, plush red velvet chairs in what is now the no-smoking room.

It's not possible to visit the **Segretaria di stato** (*see p53*), the long four-storey building connected to the Palazzo Reale (*see p54*); Cavour had his ministerial offices here, enabling him to brainstorm with the king in secrecy. Also off-limits is the **Palazzo di Città** (*see p62*), still the City Hall 153 years after Cavour sat as a city councillor and began to stretch his law-making muscles.

In piazza della Consolata is **Al Bicerìn** (*see p112*), the coffee house where Camillo was an assiduous patron and where the trademark coffee-chocolate concoction will restore your flagging energy after a walk in Cavour's footsteps.

plied by river boats. For information, *see p218*. The Murazzi embankments flanking the river and its corniche above (corso Cairoli) run parallel towards Parco del Valentino, providing a delightful promenade and a view of the statue of Giuseppe Garibaldi, 'Hero of the Two Worlds' (*see p10* **The four horsemen of the Risorgimento**). Designed by Carlo Bernardo Mosca between 1830 and 1835, these riverside bastions are Turin's vanity fair, where on summer nights *tutto-Torino* comes to party.

Ponte Umberto I marks the northern edge of the **Parco del Valentino**, a green lung of 450,000 square metres (4.8 million square feet), a mecca for locals who flock to picnic on the grass, stroll off a day's office-anxiety, jog or cycle along its criss-crossing tracks. It's no less frequented after dark (but if you venture there, do remember to keep your wits about you), especially in summer when the hangouts – former rowing clubs, now popular nightlife venues – at the water's edge provide a welcome refuge from the fug of the centre.

The park was first conceived in 1630 by Carlo di Castellamonte and was a work in progress until the 1660s. It was not until early in the 19th century, however, that the Valentino took on its current appearance, thanks to French architect Jean-Pierre Barillet-Deschamps who 'naturalised' it, providing looping paths, artificial slopes and woods.

At the heart of the park is the **Castello del Valentino** (closed to the public), an imposing pile dating back to the 16th century. Bought by Emanuele Filiberto di Savoia in 1564, it became the seat of the ducal court. In time it passed to *Madama reale* Marie Christine who had it extended and renovated. When these major works had been completed, it became the Savoys' riverside delight, looking out over the Po from deep within the park's rich vegetation.

The castle's glory was short-lived. After Marie Christine's death it was left to rot until 1858 when architects Domenico Ferri and Luigi Tonta were commissioned to revamp it. It became the seat of the university's architecture faculty, and still serves the same purpose for the *Politecnico di Torino* (Turin Polytechnic).

On the north side of the Castello del Valentino is the **Orto botanico** (botanical garden). Further south is the fairy-tale **Borgo medioevale**.

Towards the southern end of the park, where it approaches Ponte Principessa Isabella, is the **Fontana dei Dodici Mesi** designed by Carlo Ceppi in 1898 to celebrate 50 years of the Statuto Albertino (*see p13*). The 12 statues encircling the fountain represent the 12 months; the four central statues represent Turin's rivers, and the four seasons.

West of the fountain is **Torino Esposizioni** (corso Massimo d'Azeglio 15), a trade fair complex that has seen better days. Built between 1938 and 1950, it has a central exhibition space (1948) by engineer Pier Luigi Nervi in his favourite cast concrete, visitable only during shows.

Borgo Medioevale

Viale Virgilio 106 (011 443 1701). Bus 45, 46, 52, 64/tram 9, 16. **Open** *Apr-Sept* 9am-8pm daily. *Oct-Mar* 9am-7pm daily. **Admission** *Borgo* free. *Rocca* €3; €2 concessions. **No credit cards**. **Map** p245 A1.

This quaint medieval outcrop has everything you'd expect to find in a 15th-century Piedmontese village: a drawbridge, narrow winding alleyways and ye olde workshoppes. In fact, it's an out-and-out fake, built for Turin's 1884 Expo by architects Giuseppe Giacosa and Alfredo d'Andrade. Inside the village is La rocca (the castle), a faithful copy of a 15th-century castle decorated with frescoes copied from other medieval castles around Piedmont and the neighbouring Val d'Aosta region.

Orto Botanico

Viale Mattioli 25 (011 661 2447). Bus 45, 46, 52, 64/tram 9, 16. **Open** 9am-1pm, 3-7pm Sat, Sun. **Admission** €3; €1.50 concessions. **No credit cards**. **Map** p245 A1.

Created in 1729 to grow *semplici* (simples) for making medicine, Turin's tiny botanical garden has some rare species and a herbarium containing 700,000 specimens. Furthermore, inside the *orto botanico* there is a *giardino roccioso* containing the most important Alpine species.

Under cover

There's little opportunity for singin' in the rain in Turin, where 18 kilometres (11 miles) of *portici* (plural of *portico* in Italian) provide shelter from adverse weather conditions, thanks to the whims of spoilt monarchs and ingenious architects. Though built in different epochs and as part of different development projects, the *portici* seem to form a unified whole and are clearly a city hallmark. Today the *portici* not only keep rain off heads but provide cover for all kinds of activity and entertainment, from sitting at pavement tables outside historic cafés, to shopping and riffling through second-hand books along via Po. Besides via Po, covered walkways run down via Roma and through piazza San Carlo, along via Pietro Micca, via Cernaia and as far as Porta Susa railway station, and all along the northern side of corso Vittorio Emanuele.

La Collina

Turin's green and lofty heights.

The mighty green ridge rising from the eastern bank of the River Po provides a natural boundary to the city. Exploited for defence purposes by the Romans then neglected for centuries, this rise has now blossomed into Turin's most elite quarter. If the view from piazza Vittorio Veneto (*see p77*) doesn't quell your curiosity, hop on a bus (though truthfully a car would help here) and discover why Turin has nothing to envy Tuscany.

Gran Madre & Borgo Po

Ponte Vittorio Emanuele I crosses the river from piazza Vittorio (*see p77*). Commissioned by Napoleon (there are 88 French coins and a silver tape-measure buried beneath its foundations) and designed by Claude-Joseph La Ramée-Pertinchamp in 1810, it affords a view of the long embankments – the Murazzi (*see p80*) – on the western bank. Looking west across the bridge towards the city centre, the distinguished **Gran Madre di Dio** church with its cupola inspired by Rome's Pantheon is as much a symbol of the city as the **Mole Antonelliana** (*see p77*). Clustered around are the lush and leafy houses of well-heeled *torinesi*, in Borgo Po.

Borgo Po was once the name of the walled area stretching from piazza Castello (*see p52*) to the Po, an area razed in 1536. That district was rebuilt in elegant fashion in the 1660s, while the hilly land across the river – considered too far from the '*zona di comando*' (*see p52*) by the city's rich and powerful – remained the domain of poor country folk. Nothing much changed until the old wooden bridge was replaced by what is now **Ponte Vittorio Emanuele I**: a new suburb arose on the eastern side of the river and assumed the name of razed Borgo Po.

By the early 20th century Borgo Po had become what it is today: the most exclusive area in town, with beautiful detached houses and *stile Liberty* villas concealed in leafy gardens looking loftily down over the city centre. As you'd expect with residents of this ilk, it's a pretty area, with smart boutiques, quality bread shops and prime wineries – an altogether more exclusive scene than you'll experience on the opposite bank. Below, traffic screams along corso Casale towards the motorways. Between road and river lies **Parco Michelotti**, once home to the zoo, which closed in the mid 1980s. Now it's the site of **Experimenta** (*see p137*), an interactive science museum: it's not quite a theme park but it is a fine place to get your children jumping down holes, climbing up poles and pushing buttons. There's also a playground and a municipal library. South-east of the Gran Madre, via Villa della Regina leads up to the **Villa della Regina** itself, a 17th-century palace in scenic parkland (closed for restoration as this guide went to press).

Gran Madre di Dio

Piazza Gran Madre di Dio (011 819 3572). Bus 55, 56, 61/tram 13. **Open** *7.30am-noon, 4-7pm daily.* **Map** *p243 D2.*

Following the Congress of Vienna in 1815 the Turin's ruling Savoy family returned to the city from exile with great pomp and ceremony. The

The best **Views**

Lingotto
(*See p86*)
Unquestionably Turin's coolest lookout, the former racing test track on top of the Lingotto building has high sides that obliterate the city, leaving only a sublime panorama of the Alps.

Mole Antonelliana
(*See p77*)
A glass lift whizzes you up to the top of this 167-metre (548-foot) needle for a 360-degree view from the terrace.

Museo Nazionale della Montagna Duca degli Abruzzi
(*See p82*)
Atop the Cappuccini hill, the museum's Vedetta Alpina viewing platform is simply breathtaking.

Superga
(*See p91*)
Some distance from the city centre, and topped by Juvarra's basilica, the panorama from the peak of this hill is the epitome of Italian loveliness.

Gran Madre di Dio. *See p81.*

1618. Later, from 1723 to 1729, Filippo Juvarra was given the job of renovating the villa, giving it the form we see today. It was here that the learned cardinal met with members of the Accademia dei Solinghi for debates on philosophical and mathematical matters; this little coterie soon developed an anti-French agenda, becoming a busy hub for reactionary plots.

Later in the 17th century it became the official residence of Anne d'Orléans, Vittorio Amedeo II's wife, hence the name Villa della Regina, the queen's villa. The villa derives much of its charm from its layout: scenic parkland descends over several levels, all with a magnificent view over the city. It is now a UNESCO World Heritage Site. The villa suffered bomb damage in 1942 and has been *in restauro* ever since, though it is due to open to the public in 2005, partly as a museum with routes around the elegant rooms of the villa's *piano nobile* and gardens and partly as a regional archive with documentation on restoration taking place in Piedmont.

Santa Maria del Monte & Monte dei Cappuccini

A 15-minute walk separates piazza Gran Madre from Monte dei Cappuccini. There are three good reasons to induce you to take a brisk hike up to its top: the breathtaking view (if you have any breath left that is), the **Santa Maria del Monte** church and the **Museo della Montagna**. A funicular railway built in 1888 once made the journey much easier but unfortunately it was bombed during the war and was never restored. Now via Giardino loops around the Cappuccini hilltop, providing access to the summit.

To reach the bushy heart of the Collina, just keep climbing. This is an area of sweeping parkland: on the Colle della Maddalena are the **Parco della Maddalena** and **Parco della rimembranza**, created in memory of those *torinesi* who died in World War I, and further to the south towards **Moncalieri** (*see p93*) is **Parco Europa** (bus 47). It's a tortuous drive up a twisty road, but the views out across the eastern side of the ridge make it worthwhile.

glorious homecoming of Vittorio Emanuele I was celebrated with the erection of a solemn monument dedicated to the Gran Madre di Dio (great mother of God). The church was designed by Ferdinando Bonsignore, who modelled this stern temple (1827-31) on the Pantheon in Rome and raised its circular bulk on a podium so as to make it visible from piazza Castello (*see p52*). A wide staircase (made famous internationally when three Mini Coopers bumped down it in the cult movie *The Italian Job*) leads to the six-columned pronaos. Above the gable, the town council is portrayed praying in front of the Virgin Mary. The neo-classical statues inside are by Carlo Finelli, a pupil of Antonio Canova. Between 1933 and 1940, an ossuary was added, to a design by Giovanni Ricci, to hold bones of soldiers who fell in World War I, and then World War II. Local lore has provided this forbidding church with a slew of legends: some say it stands over an ancient temple to Isis; others argue that the Holy Grail is hidden hereabouts. But whichever story they choose to believe, everyone agrees that it's a very magic spot (*see p66* **Hey Nostradamus!**).

Villa della Regina
Strada Santa Margherita 40 (011 819 5035).
Bus 53, 55, 56, 66. Closed for restoration at the time of writing; due to reopen in 2005. **Map** p243 D3.
A semicircular garden precedes this magnificent palace designed by Ascanio Vitozzi as the sumptuous dwelling of Cardinal Maurizio di Savoia, Vittorio Amedeo I's brother. Construction work began in

Museo Nazionale della Montagna Duca degli Abruzzi
Via Giardino 39 (011 660 4104/fax 011 660 4622/ www.museomontagna.org). Bus 53, 55, 56, 66.
Open 9am-7pm daily; ticket office closes 6pm.
Admission €5; €3.50 concessions. **Map** p243 D2.
Luigi di Savoia (1873-1942), duke of Abruzzi, had little time for courtly power-politics, preferring the more rarified air of high mountain ranges. He even took part in the first Italian expedition to K2, though he was forced to abandon the climb; he did, however, bring back an important collection of photographs and detailed maps of the area. It is

fitting, then, that the Club alpino italiano (CAI), which was founded in Turin in 1863, should have dedicated this museum housed in the Capuchin convent to the mountain-loving royal.

The museum is organised over three levels: the ground floor is dedicated to the natural Alpine environment, with descriptions and pictures of vegetation and a host of anthropological facts. On the second floor is a collection of important mementoes and trophies of the many great expeditions upon which the duke embarked; for all but the most passionate botanists and mountaineers, the third floor is the high point of the museum: the Vedetta Alpina with its spectacular view of the Alps from Monviso (*see p201*) to Monte Rosa.

Santa Maria del Monte

Via Giardino 35 (011 660 4414). Bus 53. **Open** 8.40am-noon, 3-7.30pm daily. **Map** p243 D2.

The church of Santa Maria del Monte stands 248m (814ft) above sea level on a strategic hummock where the Romans set up an outpost. Conceived in 1584 as the church of the adjoining (still-active) Capuchin convent – which, incidentally, gives this hill its name – it was not consecrated until 1656. This lapse of time gave architects such as Ascanio Vitozzi and Carlo di Castellamonte time to impose their very different styles on different parts of the centrally planned building. The statue of the Madonna at the centre of the square outside was erected in 1960 by pious Fiat workers.

Collina's countess

Virginia Oldoini came from an aristocratic Ligurian family. In 1854, at the age of 17, she was married off to Count Francesco Verasis di Castiglione, equerry to Turin's King Carlo Alberto. Her father bought the young couple a fine palace next door to that of statesman Count Camillo Cavour (*see p10*). Her neighbour's politics proved far more interesting to this highly intelligent and exquisitely beautiful lady than marital bliss, however. And when Cavour found he needed something more subtly persuasive than an official ambassador to send to Paris to convince Napoleon III to back the Italian states in their struggle to rid the peninsula of the hated Austrian occupiers, it was to the countess that he turned.

Cavour instructed Virginia to succeed 'by all means you deem necessary'. And so she did. By 1857 she was rumoured to be Napoleon III's lover. Her deeds, real or imaginary, became the stuff of romance and legend, which she enthusiastically fomented. But legend has a way of turning sour, and the stories surrounding Turin's 'ambassadress' became gradually more hostile as the Parisian court turned against her. Late one night, it was reported, the French ruler barely survived an assassination attempt as he made his way to Virginia's apartment. Rumour blamed Virginia for the attack, and she was warmly invited to leave Paris.

Back in Turin, this Mata Hari was no longer the darling of a Risorgimento set that had no wish to let it be known that part of their success was due to the wiles of *La divina Castiglione*, as Virginia was known (by those too polite to use her other nickname, *La vulva d'oro del Risorgimento*). Rejected, the beauty

took to modelling for artists and photographers, a pastime she enjoyed until 1867 as she shuttled back and forth between Turin and Paris. These pictures of the stunning Virginia in her prime contrast sadly with those she had taken after 1893; aged and withered, and probably suffering from mental disorders, the former beauty lived in her secluded house high on Turin's Collina. She died in Paris in 1899 and there her body has remained.

Lingotto

A beguiling landscape of post-industrial decline and architectural regeneration.

For most of the 20th century, all of Turin *was* Fiat town. But the pulsing heart of the car-making empire was south of the city centre, in districts called Lingotto, Millefonti, Italia 61 and Mirafiori. Never beautiful, these areas thrived, and bristled with startling examples of industrial architecture. The buildings are still there, in various states of renaissance or sorry decay; but with the exception of the Lingotto plant itself – where Fiat set up its first production line – with its shops, cinemas, snazzy hotels and top-ranking restaurants, an air of post-industrial wasteland hangs over much of the rest, a symbol in bricks and mortar of Turin's industrial decline.

Corso Massimo d'Azeglio skirts the Parco del Valentino (*see p80*) and Torino Esposizioni

(*see p80*), before crossing corso Dante. In this road, at No.102, stands the first ever Fiat factory, a *stile Liberty* building designed by Alfredo Premoli (1904-6).

Corso D'Azeglio becomes corso Dogliotti as it passes the daunting premises of the Molinette hospital complex. This area between the River Po and the railway tracks is called **Millefonti** (a thousand springs). It was the abundance of water that induced Duke Carlo Emanuele I to commission Carlo di Castellamonte to build a hunting lodge here in the 16th century with splendid gardens; unfortunately nothing remains of it today. Well outside the boundaries of the old city, Millefonti was an agricultural area; one of the large farms here – La Molinetta – was to give its name to the

The **Museo dell'automobile**.
See p88.

hospital. The high road to Nice and the sea
passed through here. Beyond the hospital,
the riverside road changes name again, to
corso Unità d'Italia.

At No.40 is the **Museo dell'automobile**.
Although desperately in need of a revamp, this
museum contains one of the world's greatest
collections of cars.

Between corso Unità d'Italia and the parallel
via Ventimiglia lies **Italia 61**, a district built
to house celebrations for the centenary of
Italian unification. Architect Nello Renacco
came up with plans for a park in which
pavilions set in open spaces would host the
various centenary exhibitions. The **Palazzo
delle Mostre** (via Ventimiglia 145; 1959-61)
by Annibale and Giorgio Rigotti is also known
as Palazzo Vela (the sail); this was the hub of
the 1961 expo, and will soon be at the centre of
attention again when it becomes the Palavela
ice skating rink for the 2006 Winter Olympics
(*see p214* **Olympic challenge**).

To the south stands the **Palazzo del
Lavoro** (1959-61) by Pier Luigi Nervi, in
this engineer's favourite medium, cast concrete.
Sixteen massive pillars support a structure of
skylights and slatted blinds. Temporary
exhibitions and trade fairs are still held here.
Down by the river is the International Labour
Organisation's (ILO) training centre, a campus-
like affair offering vocational training for
developing-world professionals and technicians.
Further south, facing the river, stand Nello
Renacco's now-unused **Padiglioni delle
regioni** (1960-61) exhibition spaces and the
monorail – a state-of-the-art transport system
when it was inaugurated for the 1961 expo
but now defunct; part of the track's southern
stretches and terminal stations are still visible.

A couple of blocks west of Italia 61 in via
Nizza, the **Lingotto complex** was Fiat's
second factory. Built in 1923, it contained Fiat's
first American-style assembly line. (To get here
more quickly take via Nizza along the eastern
side of Porta Nuova railway station, *see p71*.)

Stretching to the south is the district called
Mirafiori. Looking at the run-down, high-
rise residential blocks and sprawling industrial
plants here today, it's difficult to imagine
this as a magnificent flower-filled park fed
by innumerable springs. In 1586 Carlo
Emanuele turned again to his court architect
Carlo di Castellamonte to have a palace
designed for a newly purchased plot of land
on the east bank of the Sangone river, just
before it merges into the River Po. The
Castello di Mirafiori ('look at the flowers')
was never completed; frequent flooding over
the years forced it to be abandoned. Today no
trace of the palace remains.

Ramp inside the **Lingotto** factory.
See p86.

Both part of the Fiat-owning Agnelli family's
(*see p21* **Whither Fiat?**) Grand Plan, Lingotto
and Mirafiori served very different purposes.
Lingotto was to the Agnellis what piazza
Castello (*see pp52-9*) had been to Turin's other
ruling family, the Savoys: the '*zona di
comando*', where fates were decided, decisions
taken and orders imparted to the straggling
plants and Fiat dormitories in Mirafiori.
Conceived as an American-style assembly
line factory in the second decade of the 20th
century, the revamped Lingotto nowadays
resembles an American-style shopping mall…
though this massive retail, dining and hotel
complex also boasts a rooftop racetrack, a
helicopter landing pad and a small collection
of old masters in the **Pinacoteca Giovanni
e Marella Agnelli**. Out in Mirafiori, on the
other hand, the make-over is more slow-moving,
but the eyesore high-rises are gradually being
demolished to make room for more attractive
residential accommodation.

Olympic venues

Over 2,500 athletes, as many officials and up to 10,000 journalists are expected to flood into Piedmont for the 2006 Winter Olympics, from 10 to 26 February 2006. The city of Turin is gearing up for the Games with six new and restored structures for hosting the events concentrated to the south of the city centre.

A **Villaggio Olimpico** to host up to 2,500 athletes is being constructed around the old **Mercati generali** wholesale fruit and vegetable market (see p28); the market itself will host a press centre and services for Olympic guests. The 700 lodgings in the Olympic Village will become residential accommodation after the 2006 event.

By the railway tracks to the west of the Lingotto complex (see p86), a new skating rink called the Oval will play host to speed skating races. The **Palazzo delle Mostre** (aka Palavela, see p85) will become a 9,000-seat venue for figure skating. Pier Luigi Nervi's **Padiglione Giovanni Agnelli** in Torino Esposizione (see p80) will host ice hockey matches, as will a new structure – the 12,500-seat **Palasport Olimpico** – which is going up in the Stadio Comunale area. After 2006 this latter complex will become a multipupose venue. A new training rink further south on corso Tazzoli, on the other hand, will continue to serve as the city's ice arena after 2006.

Lingotto

Via Nizza 280. Bus 35/tram 1, 18. **Open** *Shopping mall* noon-10pm Mon; 10am-10pm Tue-Sun. **Map** p245 D1

The Lingotto complex was designed between 1914 and 1916 by architect Giacomo Mattè Trucco, and was inspired by Ford's ground-breaking assembly line plant at Highland Park, near Detroit. In this one complex, the Fiat company brought together production and management in what was universally considered Europe's most efficient factory for the mass production of motor vehicles, using methods of unequalled efficiency. Two parallel buildings, each 500m (1,640 feet) long, were joined at various points by office towers, which created a series of internal courtyards. More efficient production meant more white collar staff, and extra office space had to be added to the north of the building in 1922. The general manager's department moved here the following year. In 1925 a northern ramp joining all the floors was designed and the following year the southern ramp was added; it was up this that cars were taken to the rooftop test track.

With production booming at Lingotto, agricultural workers left Piedmont's fields and headed for the Big Smoke, provoking a first disastrous building boom that put paid to the rural area to the south of the city. But soon even Lingotto was unable to cope with the demand for Fiat cars. By the time the Mirafiori factory – a massive 3,000,000sq m of production space – opened nearby in 1939, Lingotto seemed obsolete: its assembly lines on different floors made it uneconomical; even the rooftop test track — designed for unthinkable speeds of up to 90kph – was not up to the new generation of faster-moving vehicles. (Amazingly, high-speed tests were carried out in via Nizza before the morning rush hour, until the new track at Mirafiori was completed.) Already before World War II there was talk of decom-

missioning Lingotto; but production continued there, with thousands of workers employed, until 1982.

In 1986, the first stage of the Lingotto make-over – overseen by architect Renzo Piano – got under way, with the conversion of the press rooms into exhibition pavilions, inaugurated in 1992 with a display of American art.

In 1994 Claudio Abbado conducted the Berlin Philharmonic for the first concert in the 2,000-seat auditorium dedicated to Giovanni Agnelli (1866-1945), founder of Fiat. Piano worked with Helmut Muller to get the acoustics just right: a false ceiling can be moved up and down by 6m (20ft) to make sure the sound is perfect, whether this cherrywood-lined space is being used for concerts or conventions.

By 1996 Piano had worked his magic on the roof of the old factory. Overlooking the 1km (half mile) test track – which is as much a symbol of the city as the Mole Antonelliana (see p77) or the Gran Madre church (see p81) – are playful yet functional spaces known as *la bolla* (the bubble; 1994) and *lo scrigno* (the casket, opened 2002; see also p88 Pinacoteca Giovanni e Marella Agnelli). The curved glass sides of the bubble have a system of blinds that automatically follow the sun. Right outside, Agnelli's helipad, built in 1993, can be used by anyone who prefers this mode of transport, but you'll need to call ahead for permission (011 664 4111) before landing.

The Otto Gallery, an American-style shopping mall, opened in the north wing in 2002 with some 90 shops spread over an area of 20,000sq m (215,000sq ft). In three internal courtyards, restaurants and snack bars have outside tables that can be covered with sliding glass roofs if Turin's weather misbehaves. In case all this seems too good to leave, Piano also came up with hotels inside the complex, including the Art+Tech (see p45) and the Meridien (see p45), the two halves of which are linked by a glass corridor through a forest of palm and olive trees,

La bolla on the **Lingotto** factory.

Shopping at the **Lingotto**.

The revamped **Lingotto complex**. *See p86.*

magnolias, bamboo and other exotic species planted in the northernmost courtyard. The test track on the roof is now mainly pedestrianised and a wonderful place for a bird's-eye view of Turin and the surrounding countryside (*see p81* **The best Views**), but there is also car access to the chic rooftop La Pista restaurant (*see p106*).

Museo dell'Automobile

Corso Unità d'Italia 40 (011 677 666/www. museoauto.org). Bus 34, 35, 45, 74/tram 1, 18. **Open** 10am-6.30pm Tue-Sat; 10am-10pm Thur; 10am-8.30pm Sun. **Admission** €5.50; €4 concessions. **Credit** MC, V. **Map** p245 D1.

The three-storey building overlooking the River Po that houses the car museum was designed by Amedeo Albertini between 1958 and 1960 and is a gem of modern architecture – although in its current state of disrepair you could be forgiven for failing to notice this. Inside you'll find a well-stocked library, a document and photograph archive and over 170 classic vintage cars.

The very earliest models are on the first floor, including a very tall 1854 Steam Landau, 1920 Temperino and elegant 1926 Scat Ceirano. On the second floor are sports cars from between the two World Wars, including a collection of vintage Ferraris and Alfa Romeo racing models. Also here is the 500 Topolino, Fiat's first car for the masses, and a much posher Isotta Fraschini (1929) used in the film classic *Sunset Boulevard*; the initials ND – for Norma Desmond, the ageing, half-mad forgotten star played by Gloria Swanson – can be seen on the back doors.

On the haphazardly organised ground floor is a photograph gallery with fascinating scenes of Italian life and lifestyle in the 1950s and '60s, but you'll have to squint hard to see them in the poor lighting.

Pinacoteca Giovanni e Marella Agnelli

Via Nizza 230 (011 006 2713). Bus 35/tram 1, 18. **Open** 9am-7pm Tue-Sun. **Admission** €4; €2.50 concessions. **No credit cards. Map** p245 D1.

Before visiting the Pinacoteca (art gallery), it's well worth taking a look at it from outside. To do so, you'll have to make your way to the rooftop racetrack of the Lingotto, where the Pinacoteca sits like a casket (and, indeed, *lo scrigno* – the casket – is how it's often referred to) plonked on the roof. Inside, architect Renzo Piano has given the gallery a minimalist treatment in wood and glass, with the glass ceiling providing the main light source for the fifth-floor Agnelli collection. When the gallery opened to much fanfare in 2002, many people argued that the 25 pieces displayed here were a disappointingly small slice of the vast Agnelli treasure trove. There's nothing particularly challenging, art-wise, but there's no getting away from the fact that there are some minor gems here, including Giacomo Balla's *Velocità astratta* (1913), six Venetian landscapes by Canaletto, two landscapes of Dresden by Bernardo Bellotto, *La Négresse* by Manet, *La Baigneuse Blonde* by Renoir, six pictures by Matisse, Picasso's *L'Hétaïre* and a *Nue Couchée* by Modigliani.

Temporary exhibitions are often staged on the lower floors of the Pinacoteca.

The Suburbs

You don't have to travel far out of Turin to see the Savoys' impressive legacy of grand country estates.

As you pass through the randomly scattered high-rises, sprawling supermarkets and grimy, run-down factories of Turin's polluted suburbs, you'll be hard pressed to believe that the city's outer reaches conceal anything worth visiting. But the urban blight does come to an end, opening out suddenly and unexpectedly into beautiful countryside and dreamy village landscapes with some astounding royal country residences set in magnificent estates (*see p92* **Crown of delights**).

North

Venaria Reale

For most *torinesi*, Venaria is synonymous with the temple to football, the **Stadio delle Alpi** (*see p162*), or failing that with light industry, poisonous air and some very ugly buildings. Yet this is the unlikely setting for one of the largest nature reserves in the Po valley, the **Parco regionale La Mandria**. The park's 6,750 hectares (16,679 acres) contain deer, boar, birds galore, walking and cycling tracks and the 18th-century **Castello della Mandria**. Far grander still than this glorified hunting lodge is the nearby **Castello della Venaria Reale**.

Castello della Mandria & Parco Regionale La Mandria

Parco Regionale La Mandria *Via Carlo Emanuele II 256 (011 499 332/www.parks.it/ parco.mandria). Bus 72.* **Open** *Mar-Sept* 8am-8pm daily. *Oct-Feb* 8am-5pm daily. **Admission** free. **Map** p241.
Castello della Mandria *Via Carlo Emanuele II 256 (011 499 3322). Bus 72 then 1km walk through park.* **Open** guided visits 10.30am, 11.30am, 2.30pm, 3.30pm Sun; by appointment at other times. **Admission** €6; €3 concessions. **No credit cards**.
Mandria means 'herd' and this huge estate to the north of Turin was where horses were bred for the Savoys and their cavalry from the 18th century. A nature reserve since 1978, La Mandria is home to one of the largest remaining stretches of the glorious deciduous forests that once covered much of the (now denuded) Po valley. Inside the park, the Castello della Mandria was built in 1702 and later extended by Filippo Juvarra, but didn't really come into its own until the mid 19th century when Vittorio Emanuele II had the crumbling building patched up and used it for dallying with la Bella Rusìn (*see below* **La Bela**

Rusìn). As this guide went to press major restoration work was under way in the park and in the Castello della Venaria Reale.

Castello Reggia Venaria Reale

Piazza della Repubblica 4 (011 459 3675/ www.lavenaria.it). Bus 11, 72, then 1km walk. **Open** 9-11.30am, 2.30-5pm daily. **Admission** €3 (guide included). **No credit cards**. **Map** p241.

La Bela Rusìn

Though he became king of Sardinia-Piedmont in 1849 and king of Italy in 1861, Vittorio Emanuele II preferred horses, hunting and women to court life and regal glamour. His philandering was legendary, his illegitimate children numerous. But one woman managed to capture his errant heart in a love affair that lasted a lifetime. Rosa Vercellana – also known as *La Bela Rusìn*, pretty Rosy – was a curvaceous 14-year-old peasant girl when Vittorio Emanuele took a fancy to her in April 1848 and had her virtually kidnapped. Vittorio Emanuele's wife Maria Adelaide was none too happy when Rosa gave birth to Vittoria eight months later. She was still more furious in 1858 when the king's relationship with Rusìn – who in the meantime had given the king a son, Emanuele Alberto – became common knowledge. The king kept his mistress in various royal residences. At Stupinigi (*see p93*) he lodged her in a cottage at the far end of the park where Vittorio Emanuele could drop by between hunts. La Bizzarria – a folly that was allegedly built for Rosa – is in the grounds of La Mandria (*see p89*). The couple also holed up at Fontanafredda, near Serralunga d'Alba (*see p198*), another of the king's happy hunting grounds. Their son Emanuele Alberto turned this estate into a winery. Vittorio Emanuele ignored the advice of his outraged ministers and made Rosy countess of Mirafiori, marrying her in a civil ceremony after the death of Maria Adelaide and living with her at the Castello della Mandria.

Ghost with a *grissino*

On dark nights, a figure swathed in a black cloak haunts the grounds of the Castello della Venaria Reale. With its left hand, it steadies a rearing steed; in its right it carries a gold candlestick. Get close enough, however, and it becomes clear that what's illuminating this spectre – the ghost of Vittorio Amedeo II – is not a candle but a flaming breadstick. Racked by a recurring form of gastroenteritis that would have led to certain death, the young duke was placed under the care of court doctor Don Baldo Pecchio in around 1675. The wise physician identified badly cooked bread as his patient's problem and prescribed thin sticks of twice-baked bread to ensure that any germs in the dough were destroyed. So the *grissino* was born. The once-sickly Vittorio Amedeo turned into a strapping young man, ousted his mother *Madama reale* Marie Jeanne-Baptiste from her regent's role and was upgraded from duke to king in 1713.

At the time of writing, extensive ongoing renovation work meant that only the courtyard, Diana's gallery, the stables and the *citroniera* were visitable.

The Savoy's hunting estate at Venaria (from the Latin *venatio*; hunt) was dedicated to the goddess Diana, its full name being Castello della Venaria Reale-Palazzo di Diana, regina delle cacce (palace of Diana, goddess of hunting). More often than not, it's just called La Reggia. Commissioned by Carlo Emanuele II in the mid 17th century, the Castello, its spectacular gardens (no longer in existence) and surrounding Mandria park (*see p89*) were designed by Amedeo di Castellamonte, who also ran up the en suite *borgo* (hamlet) in just three years.

Castellamonte's palace was built around two courtyards, with the huge Salone di Diana at its core. To the south-west were the stables, the kennels, the *citroniera* where lemon trees from the gardens were placed to protect them from winter frosts, the deer park and, overlooking the Borgo, the chapel of San Rocco. French troops destroyed part of the estate in 1693, providing an opportunity for refurbishment. In 1699-1713 Michelangelo Garove came up with a grandiose project for Vittorio Amedeo II but only the south-western part was completed before the architect's death in 1713. The castle as we see it today is almost entirely by Filippo Juvarra who took over the project in 1716. He revamped the courtyard facing the Borgo, emphasising this new space by raising the gallery and opening it towards the outside with a series of wide windows. Between 1717 and 1722 Juvarra completed the church of Sant'Uberto, a Greek cross structure with circular chapels on the diagonals (similar to Superga, *see p90*); in 1721 he added another structure at the far south-east end of the palace containing the Scuderia grande (large stables) and another *citroniera*. When Juvarra died in 1736, Benedetto Alfieri was appointed in his place. In 1751 work began on the long L-shaped gallery between Sant'Uberto and Garove's pavilion towards the Borgo. Between 1754 and 1755 Alfieri added a smaller gallery connecting the church to the *citroniera*. The buildings behind Sant'Uberto date from 1757 and were used as coach houses. Surrounding the castle was a spectacular park dotted with pavilions, lakes, fountains and over 300 statues.

The Salone di Diana is undoubtedly the Reggia's most impressive room; though hunting canvases by Jean Miel from the room's walls are now kept in Palazzo Madama (*see p54*), his frescoes from 1663 are still visible on the ceiling. In the Sala delle cacce, the Gabinetti delle cacce and the Sala dei templi are frescoes by Giovanni Andrea Casella, Giovanni Paolo and Giovanni Antonio Recchi.

For many years, this estate known as '*il Versailles del Piemonte*' was the chief delight of the Savoy court, which would round off hunting expeditions here with feasts and parties. Plundered by French troops in 1693 and 1706 but restored by the Savoys, its popularity plummetted after 1729 when Juvarra turned his attention to the Palazzina della Caccia at Stupinigi (*see p93*). More damage was done during the Napoleonic occupation of Piedmont in the early 19th century; Vittorio Emanuele II preferred the humbler Castello della Mandria (*see p89*). Used as a barracks during World War II, the Reggia's few bits of remaining furniture were burnt as firewood in the cold winter of 1942.

Today the palace is at the centre of one of Europe's biggest restoration projects, financed by local, state and EU funds. Yet no one is sure what will become of this massive pile. Plans to shift the Museo Egizio (*see p71*) here were shelved; a Savoy 'experience'-cum-theme park linking the Reggia, the Castello della Mandria and the park has been mooted. Other plans circulating include one to make the stables into Piedmont's answer to the Fiat-owned Palazzo Grassi in Venice – a prestigious venue for high-profile, pack-'em-in themed art and history exhibitions. The original artworks from the Salone di Diana are expected to be brought back. The church of Sant'Uberto may become a concert venue, and the Manica lunga (long gallery) is expected to house a restaurant. Other plans include a museum on Savoy court life, and a museum of Mediterranean history. All of which, management says, would attract a million visitors a year making the 'Versailles of Piedmont' a self-financing proposition.

Sightseeing

East

Superga

High on the ridge of hills east of Turin stands one of the city's architectural jewels, the **basilica di Superga**, which bears the unequivocal signature of baroque genius Filippo Juvarra.

Basilica di Superga

Strada della Basilica di Superga 73 (011 899 7456). Bus 79/Sassi-Superga railway (see right **La Cremagliera***). Open Basilica 9am-noon, 3-6pm daily. Cupola & Savoy tombs Apr-Sept 9.30am-noon, 3-6pm Mon-Fri; 9.30am-7pm Sat; 1-7pm Sun. Oct-Mar 9.30am-noon, 3-5pm Mon-Fri; 9.30am-6.15pm Sat; 3-6.15pm Sun.* **Admission** *Cupola & Savoy tombs* €5; €2 concessions; free under-12s. **No credit cards. Map** p241.

In 1706, on the eve of a make-or-break battle against the French, Duke Vittorio Amedeo II promised the Virgin Mary a major architectural tribute if she helped the Savoy army to victory. She did. Ten years later work began on construction of this basilica perched in a commanding position on a hill east of the city. Building materials were taken from a quarry at the foot of the hill, a spot ever since known as Sassi (stones); the rack railway to Superga departs from there.

La Cremagliera

The rack railway known as La Cremagliera climbs 3,100 metres (10,200 feet) up from Sassi in Turin's northern suburbs to the magnificent basilica at Superga (*see left*), an 18-minute ride that provides superb views over the city and surrounding countryside. The railway was installed in 1934, replacing an earlier cable car. Two 'carriages' – one with glass in its windows and one very drafty one without – shuttle up and down. At the top there are well-marked walking tracks through the **Parco naturale della Collina di Superga**, as well as the basilica itself.

Information *011 899 7511/581 1900. Bus 61/tram 15 to the Sassi terminus.* **Open** *9am-noon, 2-8pm Mon, Wed-Fri; 7pm-midnight Tue; 9am-8pm Sat, Sun.* **Tickets** *Mon-Fri* €1.55 *single;* €3.10 *return. Sat & Sun* €2.58 *single;* €4.13 *return. Free with Torino Card, Carta Musei, Abbonamento Musei (see p51).* Services depart from Sassi on the hour and from Superga on the half hour.

Arguably the greatest – and certainly the most prominent – work by Sicilian architect Filippo Juvarra, the basilica has a mighty pronaos supported by eight Corinthian columns in front of a cylindrical structure surmounted by a cupola 65m (213ft) high. Flanking the church are symmetrical bell towers.

To the left of the main entrance, a staircase leads down to an underground space, designed by Juvarra's pupil and nephew Francesco Martinez, containing the tombs of Carlo Alberto, Vittorio Amedeo II and Carlo Emanuele III (Vittorio Emanuele II is in the Pantheon in Rome).

Over the high altar, a marble relief by Bernardino Cametti shows the battle of 1706. In the left transept is a chapel commemorating Vittorio Amedeo's vow. To reach the dome (entrance to the right of the main door), be prepared for the hundreds of steps.

Off the cloister is the Sala dei papi, with portraits of all 240 popes, from St Peter to John Paul II. Also accessible from the cloister is the Museo del Grande Torino, a museum commemorating the local football team killed in a plane crash here in 1949 (*see p161* **Il Grande Toro**).

Chieri

Chieri was founded by the Romans but boomed in the 11th century when the locals turned their hand to manufacturing textiles. Still a bustling place, Chieri has a quaint red-brick medieval *centro storico* and churches galore. The history

Juvarra's **basilica di Superga**.

Crown of delights

It was court architect Amedeo di Castella-monte who in 1674 coined the phrase *Corona di delizie* (crown of delights) for the palaces that the House of Savoy was embellishing around its capital at Turin. But the decision to ring the city with Savoy possessions was symbolic and strategic too – an iron curtain, in the rulers' eyes, as much as a ring of pleasure.

Their exposed position meant that these great palaces – **Venaria-La Mandria** (*see p89*), **Moncalieri** (*see p93*), **Stupinigi** (*see p93*) and **Rivoli** (*see p94*), as well as others that have since disappeared, such as the Castello di Mirafiori (*see p85*) – were particularly open to attack by invading forces, causing building work to come to a halt on some, while others were gradually largely abandoned. In 1997 UNESCO made the *Corona di delizie* a World Heritage Site.

Other further-flung jewels in the Savoy crown include the **Castello Ducale** at Agliè to the north of the city and the **Castello di Racconigi** to the south.

Only 18 of the Castello Ducale's 300-plus rooms are visitable but these are sufficient to give a feel for the splendid lifestyle enjoyed in this castle. The place as we see it today is the result of reworking over the centuries of a 13th-century castle. The great Salone da ballo (ballroom) is lavishly frescoed and stuccoed, while the Sala dei monumenti archeologici has a a precious collection of Etruscan, Greek and Roman objects. Outside are 32 hectares (79 acres) of English-style landscaped garden. The monumental fountain was designed by the Collino brothers in the 1770s.

The castle at Racconigi has its origins in the 11th century. Successive Savoys worked on the structure; but it was Carlo Alberto who was fondest of all of this castle: between 1825 and 1847 he bought up adjoining properties and demolished anything in the way of his own extension, planned by Pelagio Palagi. Once the palace was up to royal scratch, it became the stage for major events such as the wedding reception for Vittorio Emanuele II and the much-betrayed Maria Adelaide (*see p89* **La Bela Rusìn**) in 1842, and the birth of King Umberto II. In 1820 the park was given its current romantic wilderness look by German landscapist Xavier Kurten. Dotted around the grounds are a Swiss chalet (1890), a Merlin's cave with a Doric temple and a Russian dacha that is to become a library.

Castello Ducale d'Agliè

Piazza Castello 2, Agliè (0124 330 102). Bus SATTI (toll-free 800 019 152) operates infrequent services from via Fiocchetto 23. **Open** 8.30am-6.30pm Tue-Sun. **Admission** €4; €2 concessions. **No credit cards**. **Map** p240.

Castello di Racconigi

Piazza Carlo Alberto, Racconigi (0172 84005). On the Turin-Cuneo railway line. **Open** 8.30am-6.30pm Tue-Sun. **Admission** €5; €2.50 concessions. **No credit cards**. **Map** p241. Bicycle rental in the park costs €2.50 per day for adults and €1.50 for children. A 50-seater train (operates 11am-6pm Tue-Fri, tickets €2) does a 5km tour of the grounds of the palace.

---

of fabric making is explained in the **Museo del tessile**. Just outside Chieri in Pessione, the **Museo Martini di storia dell'enologia** charts another local industry, wine production. Bus 30 from piazza Vittorio goes to Chieri.

Duomo

Piazza Duomo 1 (011 947 1667). **Open** 7.30-11.30am, 3-6pm Tue-Sun. **Map** p241. Chieri's cathedral is dedicated to Santa Maria della Scala (the ladder – *scala* – was one of the symbols of Christ's Passion) and is one of Piedmont's most impressive 15th-century buildings. The brick and terracotta façade has a tall stone Gothic pediment decorated with vegetation motifs, and surmounted by spires. The bell tower and the baptistery may date from an earlier Romanesque church on this site.

Recent excavations revealed a stretch of Roman wall three metres below the church.

Museo del Tessile

Via G Demaria 10 (011 942 7421). **Open** by appointment only. **Admission** free. **Map** p241. Housed in the rooms of the former Santa Chiara convent this museum displays typical tools of the textile trade: dyeing devices, cotton spinning and weaving machinery.

Museo Martini di Storia dell'Enologia

Azienda Martini & Rossi, piazza Luigi Rossi 2, frazione Pessione (011 941 9217). **Open** 2-5pm Tue-Fri; 9am-noon, 2-5pm Sat, Sun. Closed Aug. **Admission** free. **Map** p241.

Palazzina di Caccia di Stupinigi: the Savoys' hunting hideaway. *See p94.*

This museum is located in the cellar of a late 18th-century palace that housed the first Martini & Rossi factory. Documents, Roman glass tokens and a grape harvest cart are among the items used to chart the history of wine making.

San Domenico
Via San Domenico 1 (011 940 3911). **Open** 8.30am-noon, 5.30-6.30pm Mon-Thur, Sat, Sun. **Map** p241.
At the end of Chieri's main drag, via Vittorio Emanuele, the Gothic church of San Domenico is a remarkable example of 15th-century Piedmontese architecture with an impressive Gothic portal. The bell tower dates from 1381.

South

Moncalieri

Overshadowed by a forbidding Castello, this spawling modern town on the plain south-east of Turin has a *centro storico* paved with blocks of porphyry. Walls surrounded the town until 1785, when all the defences save the main gate, now known as *l'arco*, were knocked down. From this arch, via San Martino climbs to piazza Vittorio Emanuele with its *portici*. In the piazza is the rather dull 18th-century church of **San Francesco** (open 7.30am-noon, 3-7pm daily) and **Santa Maria della Scala** (open 8am-12.30pm, 3-7pm daily), a 13th- to 14th-century Lombard-Gothic church with a painted terracotta *Pietà* dating from the 15th century in the first chapel on the left. Off the piazza, at via Real Collegio 28, is the **Real Collegio** (not open to the public) where scions of Turin's noble families were once sent to study. An antiques market fills the streets leading to the piazza on the first Sunday of every month.

Bus lines 35, 40, 45, 67, 80, 81, 83 go to Moncalieri from Turin.

Castello di Moncalieri
Piazza Baden Baden 4 (011 640 2883). **Open** guided visits depart every 45mins from 9.30am-6.30pm Thur, Sat, Sun. **Admission** €2. **No credit cards. Map** p241.
Work began in 1619 to transform this 15th-century fortress into a fine baroque castle, and continued through much of the 18th century. Despite its size, few rooms are visitable (much of the castle is occupied by the Carabinieri police), but grand apartments done out for King Vittorio Emanuele II, his wife Queen Maria Adelaide and their grand-daughter Maria Letizia are on show.

Stupinigi

Despite its proximity to Turin, no town ever grew up around Stupinigi, home to Filippo Juvarra's Palazzina di Caccia. Corso Unione Sovietica leads straight as a die from the city centre to the *palazzina*. Once this was a tree-lined route to the Savoy kings' favourite hunting lodge. Now it's an uninspiring succession of apartment blocks and factories. As the road nears the baroque hunting lodge it passes houses designed by Filippo Juvarra for agricultural labourers employed on the Stupinigi reserve; the houses are now private but their inhabitants are still closely linked with the land.

Palazzina di Caccia di Stupinigi

Piazza Principe Amedeo 7, Stupinigi (011 358 1220/www.mauriziano.it). Bus 41. **Open** *Oct-Mar* 9.30am-5pm Tue-Sun. *Apr-Sept* 10am-6pm Tue-Sun. Ticket office closes 1hr earlier. **Admission** €6.20; €5.20 concessions. **No credit cards.** **Map** p241.

The statue of a deer atop the cupola of this extraordinary structure designed by Filippo Juvarra in 1729 is a clear sign of what the *palazzina* was for. Vittorio Amedeo II would hunt here at least twice a week, and subsequent Savoys continued using the building for sumptuous ceremonies and parties. Under Napoleonic occupation in the early 19th century, the *palazzina* was the residence of Napoleon's sister Paolina and his viceroy, Paolina's husband Camillo Borghese. In 1919 the building became state property and it now houses the **Museo dell'ammobiliamento artistico** furniture museum.

Vittorio Amedeo II was Grand Master of the Order of St Maurice, a knightly religious order founded in the 16th century dedicated to caring for the sick. It was on a huge stretch of wooded land belonging to this order that the king ordered Juvarra to design a hunting lodge. The Sicilian architect came up with a plan inspired by the order's symbol, the cross of St Andrew: four diagonal wings branch off from an eliptical central ballroom.

The copper deer by Francesco Ladatte placed on the roof in 1766 has since been replaced by a wrought-iron copy; the original now graces the ticket office.

Not all the 18th-century furniture on show here is from the *palazzina*; many pieces have been brought from other Savoy residences. And much of the collection went missing in February 2004 when burglars swiped an estimated €10 million worth.

The route starts in the library, where there's a collection of pale blue lacquered furniture from 1740. The Sala da gioco (gaming room) has panels by Christian Wehrlin, a Viennese painter who worked at Stupinigi from 1763 to 1766. Paolina Bonaparte had Turin's first marble bath tub installed in her Saletta degli specchi (mirror room). Scenes from 18th-century Chinese life are depicted on the rice-paper wallpaper in the Salette cinesi (Chinese rooms). In one of the bedrooms in the eastern wing was a prie-dieu (1748-50) by local artisan Pietro Piffetti inlaid with mother of pearl, ivory and tortoiseshell (part of the stolen works).

In the east wing four large canvases by Vittorio Amedeo Cignaroli (1772-78) show Stupinigi and the Castello di Mirafiori (see p85), which no longer exists.

The eliptical Salone centrale ballroom has an immense crystal chandelier, placed here in 1773 for Maria Teresa di Savoia's marriage to Count Filippo

d'Artois. On the walls are works by Giuseppe and Domenico Valeriani (completed in 1733). In the west wing and east wing respectively are the king's and queen's apartments, each with an antechamber, a dressing room, a bedroom and a drawing room. In the king's drawing room are beautiful carved wood mirrors (1790) by Giuseppe Maria Bonzanigo. The walls of the queen's apartment are lined with silk with matching silk-upholstered furniture. Carlo Felice's apartment in the west wing has two drawing rooms and two bedrooms; the highlight is the *comoda*, an armchair-like commode. The Napoleonic and 19th-century collections were closed for restoration as this guide went to press.

At the front of the *palazzina* are geometric parterres designed in 1740 by Francesco Bernard; at the rear there is an English-style wilderness. Carlo

A nature reserve surrounds the *palazzina*, with great avenues flanked by towering trees. Tracts of forest conceal hares, foxes, weasels and white storks. A cycle track runs inside the regional park of Stupinigi.

West

Rivoli

Corso Francia, formerly the via delle Gallie, is the old road heading west from Turin to France. The medieval town of Rivoli, dominated by its castle, is 13 kilometres (eight miles) along it.

Castello di Rivoli

Piazza Mafalda di Savoia (011 956 5222/ www.castellodirivoli.org). Bus 36/frequent shuttle service from piazza Castello Sat & Sun (€3 return). **Open** 10am-9pm Tue-Thur; 10am-9pm Fri-Sun. **Admission** €6.50; €4.50 concessions; under-10s free. **Credit** AmEx, MC, V. **Map** p241.

An 11th-century fortress here passed under Savoy control in the 13th century. After moving his capital to Turin in 1559, Emanuele Filiberto began a long process of transforming the fortress into a ducal dwelling, a process worked on over the centuries by a *Who's Who* of great architects – most notably Filippo Juvarra – but which was never completed. Today the castle is a startling mix of the old and the very, very new; this is especially apparent in the Manica lunga (long gallery) begun in the 17th century and finally 'finished' in 1998.

Since 1984 the castle has been home to Turin's contemporary art gallery. The 400-odd works of the permanent collection are displayed against reworked historical backdrops but are shifted about regularly. In the Sala degli stemmi, with its geometrical patterned walls and its medieval well in the centre of the floor, is Charles Ray's *Revolution Counter-Revolution* (1990). From the beautiful stuccoed ceiling of the Sala degli stucchi hangs Maurizio Cattelan's *Novecento*, a stuffed horse. Other artists represented here include Sandro Chia, Frank O Gehry, Rebecca Horn, Joseph Kosuth and Sol Lewitt. The museum also organises major temporary exhibitions.

Eat, Drink, Shop

Restaurants

Eating out in Turin is not for the faint-hearted: Piedmontese fare is rich and hearty and portions tend to be more than ample.

Turin is often maligned as a city of indifferent cuisine, but this reflects an inferiority complex rather than a real state of affairs. While it is true that the best Piedmontese restaurants are in the provinces rather than in the capital and that once-famous places such as the legendary Balbo have closed in recent years, there's still a wide choice of excellent eateries, at prices lower than those of Milan, Venice or Florence and without the tourist traps found in so much of Italy. The trend here recently has been towards a levelling-out of prices, so a set menu in one of the classier spots can cost little more than a basic meal in a trattoria.

WHAT TO EAT

Though more than half of Turin's population hails from other regions of Italy – particularly Veneto and the South – there are surprisingly few good Italian regional restaurants, with the exception of *pizzerie* and the classic old-fashioned Tuscans. So a good meal out in Turin will mean either traditional Piedmontese cooking (some of the best and most varied in Italy, *see pp29-34*) or modern Italian and, in the best restaurants, a combination of the two. This means joy for carnivores in particular, although you will find plenty of fish. The lack of a coastline is no drawback, as the best fish in Italy tends to come by fast transport from the Adriatic or the South. Antipasti, pasta and risotto dishes, not to mention excellent Piedmontese cheeses (*see p107* **Not meat**), ensure that vegetarians will not go hungry.

WHERE TO EAT

The restaurants reviewed in this chapter are obviously just a small selection of what's on offer. Newly fashionable areas such as the Quadrilatero (*see pp60-63*) and the Murazzi (*see p80*) are packed with restaurants and wine bars, but they tend to open, close and change hands with alarming frequency. Consequently, apart from the odd old favourite such as **Tre Galline** (*see p97*), it is difficult to recommend anything here; however, you can always play it by ear and follow the crowds – there are plenty of fun places, and you might just get lucky as far as quality is concerned.

Another restaurant-packed part of town is the Collina (*see pp81-3*) and several of the better places are mentioned here.

If you're in Turin on business, your hosts will no doubt take you to some of the business favourites… and very pleasant they can be on a summer evening, but often the cooking tends to be decidedly boring.

PRACTICALITIES

The *torinesi* are slightly more hostile towards restaurant-going children than most other Italians but all but the smartest places won't make their disapproval too obvious.

For each restaurant we give an average price based on a *primo* (first course, usually pasta or risotto), main course, and *contorno* (side dish) or dessert. You may just opt for a bowl of pasta and a vegetable dish, in which case you'll pay less. The opening times in our listings refer to the times when the kitchen is open, that is when you can order cooked food; many restaurants will stay open well after this time as diners drain their bottles of wine and finish their grappa.

Time warp: **Trattoria Valenza**. *See p97*.

Many visitors to Turin never make it to a restaurant, having fallen at the first (*aperitivo-hour*) hurdle (*see p116* **Aperitivi** **galore**). Note that many of the establishments listed in our Cafés & Bars chapter (*see pp109-18*) also serve anything from snacks to slap-up meals.

For an explanation of Italian food terms and dishes, *see also p98* **Understanding the menu** *and pp29-34*.

Quadrilatero

Restaurants

Savoia

Via Corte d'Appello 13 (011 436 2288). Bus 50, 51, 52, 60. **Meals served** noon-2pm, 8-10pm Mon-Fri; 8-10pm Sat. Closed 2wks Aug. **Average** €30. **Credit** AmEx, DC, MC, V. **Map** p242 C2.

An elegant restaurant in a fine building on the edge of the fashionable Quadrilatero romano, the Savoia offers a consistently higher standard of cooking than you will find in the newer restaurants nearby. There are four set menus: fish, vegetarian, traditional and (a great idea for most appetites) a small traditional at a reasonable €29 – or you can go à la carte. Memorable among the starters are *tuna tartare*. Piedmontese-style raw meat is also worthwhile, as are the rabbit salad and peppers in *bagna cauda* (garlic and anchovy sauce). Classic pasta dishes include *agnolotti* stuffed with *seirass* (Piedmontese ricotta) and there are delicious risottos according to the season. Main courses range from typical Piedmontese meat dishes to fish prepared in a southern Italian style, such as monkfish with aubergines – all accompanied by a larger selection of vegetables than is common in Piedmont. You can find good cheese and desserts, as well as a considerable and fairly priced wine list.

Trattoria Valenza

Via Borgo Dora 39 (011 521 3914). Bus 11. **Meals served** noon-2.30pm, 8-10pm Mon-Sat. **Average** €25. **No credit cards. Map** p242 B3.

Situated just a stone's throw from the colourful Mercato del Balon (*see p120* **Bargain hunting**) antiques/flea market, and in one of the most down-home areas of the city, the atmospheric, family-run Trattoria Valenza – like some of its clients – seems to be caught in a time warp. The dark, low-ceilinged, wood panelled interior is crowded with assorted memorabilia, old paintings and prints, clocks and old-fashioned ceramics. The menu offers no-fuss, authentic local dishes, with *bagna cauda*, marinated anchovies, *vitello tonnato*, *agnolotti* and gnocchi. The *bollito misto* (mixed boiled meats) and *cotecchino* (stuffed pig's trotters) come with sauerkraut, and excellent tripe is served with white beans. There is no wine list to speak of, but the house reds on tap are decent and cheap. While no bargain, a meal here offers a genuine taste of old Turin.

Best for fish: **Mare Nostrum.** See p102.

Tre Galline

Via Bellezia 37 (011 436 6553/www.3galline.it). Bus 3, 4, 11, 12, 16, 50, 51, 57, 63. **Meals served** 7.45-11pm Mon; 12.45-2pm, 7.45-11pm Tue-Sat. **Average** €32. **Credit** AmEx, DC, MC, V. **Map** p242 C3.

This is one of the oldest restaurants in Turin and a lively place to sample traditional Piedmontese food. Modernisation has not spoilt the character of the place, but try and get a table in the cosier wood-panelled room. Each night of the week a local speciality is on offer; from Wednesday to Saturday choose from the great trolley laden with mixed boiled meats (it's one of only two restaurants left in the city to serve *bollito misto* in this way); on Saturday experience *bagna cauda alla piemontese* in all its glory. Otherwise many regional dishes (both familiar and obscure) are here: ravioli stuffed with donkey meat, *tagliolini* with wild boar sauce, pumpkin risotto, snails, kid stewed with chestnuts and mackerel cooked in milk. Regional cheeses, from gorgonzola to robiola and toma varieties, are served from another vast trolley. The wine list is ample and honestly priced.

Understanding the menu

Reading the menu
Pasti meals; **prima colazione** breakfast; **pranzo** lunch; **cena** supper; **uno spuntino** a snack.

Antipasti – hors-d'oeuvres
Acciughe al verde anchovies in green sauce; **alici marinate** marinated anchovies; **antipasto di mare** seafood hors-d'oeuvres; **antipasto misto** mixed hors-d'oeuvres (usually includes cold cuts); **bresaola** dry-cured beef; **bruschetta** toast with garlic, oil and optional tomatoes; **peperoni con bagna cauda** peppers in a garlic and anchovy sauce; **prosciutto cotto/crudo/con melone** cured ham/raw (Parma) ham/ham with melon; **tomini elettrici** little cheeses served with spicy sauce; **vitello tonnato** veal in a tuna mayonnaise.

Pasta & rice
agnolotti similar to ravioli but meat-filled; **orecchiette** pasta discs, often served with a broccoli sauce; **ravioli ricotta e spinaci** ravioli stuffed with cottage cheese and spinach, often served with **burro e salvia** (butter and sage); **tajarin** long flat egg pasta strips; **pasta e fagioli** thick bean and pasta soup. **Toppings: all'amatriciana** with tomato, chilli, onion and sausage; **all'arrabbiata** with tomato and chilli; **alla carbonara** with bacon, egg, parmesan; **al pesto** with a sauce of pine nuts, pecorino and basil; **al pomodoro fresco** with fresh, raw tomatoes; **al ragù 'bolognese'** (a term not used by Italians), ie with minced meat and tomatoes; **al sugo** with puréed cooked tomatoes; **alle vongole** with clams (usually in *bianco*, without tomatoes).

Risotto (usually made with meat stock) **alla milanese** with saffron; **ai funghi** with mushrooms; **al nero di seppia** with cuttlefish ink.

Carne – meat
agnello lamb; **capra, capretto** goat, kid; **coniglio** rabbit; **lardo** fatty bacon; **maiale** pork; **manzo** beef; **pancetta** similar to bacon; **pollo** chicken; **prosciutto cotto, prosciutto crudo** 'cooked' ham, Parma ham; **tacchino** turkey; **vitello, vitellone** veal. **Offal: cervello** brain; **lingua** tongue; **nervetti** strips of cartilage; **fegato** liver; **rognoni** kidneys; **trippa** tripe; **finanziera** a mixed dish of chicken livers, cock's combs and sweetbreads in a rich vinegar-based sauce.

Piatti di carne – meat dishes
bollito con salsa verde boiled meat with parsley in vinegar sauce; **brasato al Barolo** braised beef in a rich wine sauce; **carpaccio** paper-thin slices of cured beef; **carne cruda** or **carne all'albese** raw veal either finely chopped or thinly sliced served with oil and lemon; **ossobuco** beef shins with marrow jelly; **rognoni trifolati** stir-fried chopped kidneys, usually with mushrooms; **salsicce** sausages; **spezzatino** casseroled meat; **spiedini** anything on a spit; **fritto misto alla piemontese** a mixture of breaded and fried veal, chicken, pork, liver, brains and other offal, courgettes and other vegetables, apple, semolina and amaretto biscuits.

Formaggi – cheeses
(*See also* p107 **Not meat**)
gorgonzola strong blue cheese, in creamy (**dolce**) or crumbly (**piccante**) varieties; **parmigiano** parmesan; **ricotta** crumbly white

---

Enoteche & wine bars
See p112 **Tre Galli**.

Pizzerie
See p101 **Gennaro Esposito**.

Cittadella

Restaurants

Torricelli
Via Torricelli 51 (011 599 814). Bus 10, 12.
Meals served 7.30-10.30pm Mon; 12.30-2.30pm,

7.30-10.30pm Tue-Sat. Closed Aug. **Average** €30. **Credit** AmEx, DC, MC, V. **Map** p244 B2.
This is a long-established restaurant in the elegant, well-heeled residential Crocetta district (*see p67*). The decor is rather depressing, but the place redeems itself in summer when there's a pleasant area with tables on the pavement outside. The food, moreover, is consistently good. Departing from a solid Piedmontese base, this retaurant also serves good fish and more creative dishes. The set menu at €38 is vast. The à la carte menu varies from season to season – and day to day, in the case of fish – depending what's in the market. Starters could include Jerusalem artichoke tart or poultry salad; pasta dishes range from *agnolotti del plin* to the

cheese, often used in desserts; **stracchino** creamy, soft white cheese; **fontina** rich mountain cheese.

Pesce – fish

alici, acciughe anchovies; **baccalà** salt cod; **branzino, spigola** sea bass; **cernia** grouper; **merluzzo** cod; **pesce San Pietro** John Dory; **pesce spada** swordfish; **razza** skate or thornback ray; **rombo** turbot; **salmone** salmon; **sarago, dentice, marmora, orata** all bream of various kinds; **sarde, sardine** sardines; **sogliola** sole; **tonno** tuna; **trota** trout.

Frutti di mare – seafood

astice, aragosta lobster, spiny lobster; **calamari, calamaretti** squid, baby squid; **cozze** mussels; **crostacei** shellfish; **gamberi, gamberetti** shrimps, prawns; **granchio** crab; **mazzancolle** king prawns; **moscardini** baby curled octopus; **ostriche** oysters; **polipo, polpo** octopus; **seppie, seppiette, seppioline** cuttlefish; **telline** wedge shells (small clams); **totani** baby flying squid; **vongole** clams.

Verdura/il contorno – vegetables/the side dish

aglio garlic; **asparagi** asparagus; **basilico** basil; **bietole rosse** beetroot; **broccoli** broccoli; **broccoletti** tiny broccoli sprigs, cooked with the leaves; **carciofi** artichokes; **cardi** cardoons; **carote** carrots; **cavolfiore** cauliflower; **cetriolo** cucumber; **cicoria** green leaf vegetable, resembling dandelion; **cipolle** onions; **fagioli** haricot or borlotti beans; **fagiolini** green beans; **fave** broad beans; **funghi** mushrooms; **funghi porcini boletus** mushrooms; **indivia** endive; **insalata** salad; **lattuga** lettuce; **melanzane**

aubergine; **patate** potatoes; **peperoncino** chilli; **peperoni** peppers; **piselli** peas; **pomodori** tomatoes; **porri** leeks; **prezzemolo** parsley; **radicchio** bitter purple lettuce; **rughetta, rucola** rocket; **scalogno** shallots; **sedano** celery; **spinaci** spinach; **verza** cabbage; **zucchine** courgettes.

Dolci/il dessert – desserts

bunet or **bonet** a rich chocolate or coffee crème caramel; **gelato** ice-cream; **montebianco** cream, meringue and maron glacé; **panna cotta** a very thick, blancmange-like cream, often served with chocolate (**cioccolata**) or wild berry (**frutti di bosco**) sauce; **sorbetto** sorbet; **tiramisù** mascarpone and coffee sponge; **torta di mele** apple flan; **millefoglie** flaky pastry cake; **zabaione** or **zabaglione** a cream of egg yolks, sugar and Marsala or Moscato wine.

Pizza

calzone a doubled-over pizza, usually filled with cheese, tomato and ham; **capricciosa** ham, hard-boiled or fried egg, artichokes and olives; **funghi** mushrooms; **marinara** plain tomato, sometimes with anchovies; **margherita** tomato and mozzarella; **napoli, napoletana** tomato, anchovy and sometimes mozzarella; **quattro formaggi** four cheeses; **quattro stagioni** mozzarella, artichoke, egg, mushrooms.

Pizzeria extras

bruschetta coarse toast with raw garlic rubbed into it and oil on top, and usually diced raw tomatoes; **crostini** slices of toast, usually with a grilled cheese and anchovy topping; **olive ascolane** deep-fried battered olives stuffed with sausage meat.

Ligurian *trofie* with red mullet sauce; main courses from stuffed capon with chestnuts to turbot with apples and onions or monkfish medallions. There is a well-stocked cheese trolley with plenty of local specialities and good desserts to follow. The wine list covers the whole of Italy, with a page featuring bargain bottles.

Enoteche & wine bars

L'Ostu

Via Colombo 63 (011 596 798). Bus 10, 12. **Meals served** noon-2.30pm, 8-11.30pm Mon-Sat. Closed Aug. **Average** €20. **Credit** MC, V. **Map** p242 B2.

This is not the place for a gourmet dinner, but it is one of the few real old-style *osterie* (*piola* in the local dialect) left in Turin. It also acts as a wine shop and bar – with an extremely varied clientele – but there is a non-smoking dining room at the back, as well as tables inside the wine shop. You can eat anything from a snack to a full meal – the antipasti include salami and *lardo* (fatty bacon), anchovies and tongue with green sauce plus a number of *torte salate* – flans with potatoes and gorgonzola, leeks or artichokes. The most interesting first courses are *agnolotti* in a wine sauce; the second courses are almost meat-based and not particularly exciting. The choice of wines is ample – you can choose from the list or just select your bottle from the shelves.

Eat, Drink, Shop

The "Babette" restaurant and the wine tower.

architects: alessandro armando_matteo casalegno   executor: gruppo SAE srl

Walking between *Piazza S. Carlo* and *Piazza Solferino* along the road named *via Alfieri*, you will reach the magnificent XVII century *Palazzo Lascaris di Ventimiglia*, seat of the Regional Government of Piemonte, at present. In front of it, in the *Palazzo Valperga di Masino*, there is the "Babette" restaurant, an essential stage for those who want to enjoy the taste of great wines and precious dishes. The "Babette" restaurant has been made in the rooms of the XVIII century palace, using the ground floor with an intermediate floor and the basement. All the interiors have been organized on different levels, connecting the spaces by opening new passages in the walls through footbridges. If you chance to have dinner or lunch at the "Babette", you will find out some unpredictable interior spaces and, at the same time, a restaurant conceived as a plain and elegant place. Descending in the basement through the staircase that opens in a single volume the three floors along 10 metres of height a steel *cor-ten* wall will welcome you in the inner room. A rising corridor opens a high and narrow passage in the metallic surface, and leads you at the *torre del vino* (wine tower). Once arrived on the threshold of this wine cellar, the room suddenly lights up and reveals a six thousands wine bottles-tower, 5 metres high, whose lower half part is visible behind your feet: the entrance is, in fact, 2,5 metres higher than the floor of the cellar; this will let you to float around the bottles of wine, even before to have chosen yours, among the six thousands "jewels" of the *torre del vino*.

Ristorante cantina *Babette*, via Alfieri 18, 10121 Torino
Tel. 0039011547882
On Saturday lunch closed;

Pizzerie

Amici Miei
Corso Vittorio Emanuele II 94 (011 506 9961).
Bus 9, 68. **Meals served** noon-2.30pm, 7pm-
midnight Mon-Fri; 7.30pm-12.30am Sat, Sun.
Average €15. **Credit** MC, V. **Map** p242 D2.
There are two branches of this pizzeria, one near
the GAM modern art gallery (*see p68*) and the other
near via Nizza. Both are quite roomy, so finding a
table is not usually a problem. The via Valperga
branch has some tables outside in summer. They
both offer good Neapolitan-style pizzas and *calzoni*
– the deep-fried *calzone fritto* is delicious, if not
exactly light, while the usual range of *pizze* includes
a good *alla diavola* (with spicy sausage). Focaccia
with raw ham, *lardo* (fatty bacon) or fresh tomato
and basil makes a good (if huge) starter. Round off
your meal with a typical Neapolitan dessert: *pastiera*
(a rich tart with cereals and dried fruit) or *zeppole*
(a sort of doughnut). There's a selection of wines at
reasonable prices.
Other location: Via Valperga di Caluso 5, Lingotto
(011 650 2851). **Map** p247 A2.

Gennaro Esposito
Corso Vinzaglio 17 (011 531 925). Bus 1, 10, 55,
65. **Meals served** 12.15-2.30pm, 7.15pm-midnight
Mon-Fri; 7.15pm-midnight Sat. Closed 2wks Aug,
2wks Dec. **Average** €12. **No credit cards**.
Map p242 C2.
This pizzeria has two branches – the small original
one in via Passalacqua, just off piazza Statuto, and
the larger new one in corso Vinzaglio, which in
summer also has a number of tables outside under
the arcades. The look in both is strictly Neapolitan.
This is not the place for a leisurely meal – customer
turnover is brisk – but the pizzas are excellent and
authentically Neapolitan in style. Particularly tasty
are pizza with buffalo mozzarella and fresh tomato
and pizza with sausage and *friarielli* (a typically
southern green leaf vegetable). There is also a selection of antipasti, pasta and fish dishes from the
menu and daily specials chalked up on a blackboard.
Other locations: Via Passalacqua 1G, Quadrilatero
(011 535 905). **Map** p242 C2.

Centro

Restaurants

Del Cambio
Piazza Carignano 2 (011 546 690). Bus 13, 15, 18,
55, 56, 61. **Meals served** 12.30-2.30pm, 8-10.30pm
Mon-Sat. Closed 1wk Aug; 1wk Jan. **Average** €70.
Credit AmEx, DC, MC, V. **Map** p242 C3.
The Cambio is the most famous restaurant in Turin;
Cavour (*see p10* **The four horsemen of the**
Risorgimento), the father of united Italy, used to
eat here every day. It has kept its 19th-century feel,
with lashings of red velvet and antique mirrors, and
large numbers of efficient waiters. The food is

The best Restaurants

Restaurants

For traditional atmosphere
Osteria Antiche Sere (*p107*), Dai Saletta
(*p103*).

For Piedmontese cuisine
Del Cambio (*p101*), Tre Galline (*p97*).

For a summer evening
I Birilli (*p105*), La Taverna di Frà Fiusch
(*p108*), Con Calma (*p107*).

For fish
Mare Nostrum (*p102*).

For a romantic evening
Locanda Mongreno (*p107*), Hosteria
La Vallée (*p102*).

For local colour and character
Trattoria Valenza (*p97*), L'Ostu (*p99*).

For pizza
Gennaro Esposito (*p101*).

For creative modern cuisine
La Pista (*p106*), Al Garamond (*p101*).

fortunately lighter than the decor, but very much
within the Piedmontese tradition, including dishes
that are not always easy to find like *finanziera* (poultry offal in a rich sauce, here served as a starter),
risotto al Barolo, *fritto misto* (the Piedmontese version is not fish, but various meats, vegetables and
fruit, amaretti biscuits and semolina). In addition,
there are less unusual Piedmontese meat dishes like
brasato al Barolo, raw meat and steaks. There's also
fish and cheese, if you don't want meat. The vast
national and international wine list is particularly
strong on Piedmontese reds – generally speaking,
the cheaper wines offer less value for money. There
are tables outside on the piazza in summer.

Al Garamond
Via Pomba 14 (011 812 2781). Bus 9, 18, 52,
67, 61, 68. **Meals served** 12.30-2.30pm, 8-10.30pm
Mon-Fri; 8-10.30pm Sat. Closed Aug. **Average** €45.
Credit AmEx, MC, V. **Map** p242 C3.
Elegant, quiet and centrally located, the Garamond
offers what some feel is the best food in Turin.
Moreover, the €40 set menus – either fish or meat –
consisting of a pre-antipasto, two starters, a pasta,
a main course and dessert are excellent value,
though you can also eat à la carte. The home-made
bread is excellent, while the menu offers both traditional and creative dishes, largely based on seasonal produce with frequent changes. In local style you
could find a Jerusalem artichoke flan with anchovy
sauce, while fish carpaccio with foie gras is more

Eat, Drink, Shop

international in flavour. The desserts are decidedly moreish, but don't forget to leave room for the exquisite petits fours. The wine list is ample, with more than the usual selection of Piedmontese varieties; particularly interesting are the less well-known Italian wines at good prices, and some wonderful dessert wines by the glass.

Hosteria La Vallée

Via Provana 3B (011 812 1788). Bus 68/tram 16. **Meals served** noon-2pm, 8-10.30pm Mon-Fri; 8-10.30pm Sat. Closed Aug. **Average** €45. **Credit** DC, MC, V. **Map** p243 D1.

In a quiet street by the gardens of piazza Cavour (*see p77*), this is a good place for a restful, high quality meal. The dining room with its vaulted ceiling offers plenty of space between tables, while decor and service are decidedly superior to your everyday *osteria*. The menu includes dishes inspired by the cuisine of the Piedmontese mountain valleys, such as *insalata di testina* (calf's head salad), and classics like *risotto al nebbiolo* and donkey meat *agnolotti*. However, it also serves more creative dishes (*piccione al nido* – pigeon in a nest of various ingredients) and fish, including pasta with a red mullet and saffron sauce and an excellent tuna châteaubriand. At lunchtime there's a menu offering outstanding value: €4 for pasta and €6 for main courses. The wine list is ample, but pricey by local standards.

Mare Nostrum

Via Matteo Pescatore 16 (011 839 4543). Bus 55, 56, 61/tram 13, 15, 16. **Meals served** 8-10.30pm. Mon-Sat. Closed 2wks Aug, 2wks Dec. **Average** €50. **Credit** AmEx, DC, MC, V. **Map** p243 C1.

Probably the best fish restaurant in Turin, Mare Nostrum is in a quiet street near piazza Vittorio Veneto (*see p77*). There are three rooms with smoking and non-smoking sections, all attractively furnished. The menu offers only fish and varies according to what the market has to offer that day. You can start with the mixed antipasti – tiny dishes of, for example, marinated anchovies, sea snails in a spicy sauce, baby squid marinated in wine and swordfish *involtini*. For the first course there is a choice of four or five pasta dishes; *spaghetti alla chitarra* with fish ragù is recommended. The main courses always include a deliciously light *fritto di paranza* (mixed grill), oven-cooked fish and, when in season, *moleche* (soft-shell crabs). The wine list is all white and features some excellent labels from southern Italy and Sicily.

Ponte Vecchio

Via San Francesco da Paola 41 (011 835 100). Bus 9, 18, 52, 67, 68. **Meals served** 7.45-10.45pm Tue; 12.45-2pm, 7.45-10.45pm Wed-Sun. **Average** €25. **Credit** DC, MC, V. **Map** p243 D1.

This traditional Tuscan restaurant a few minutes from Porta Nuova station offers reliably – if not excitingly – good food at fair prices. The menu includes both meat and fish and varies according to the season. Among the antipasti are *olive all'ascolana* (stuffed and deep fried olives) and *crostini di fegatini* (hot chicken liver pâté on toast), a Tuscan speciality. In late summer and autumn you'll find excellent and reasonably priced mushrooms, both as a base for risotto or pasta sauce and fried, grilled, stewed or raw as a main course. All year round there is a good selection of pasta as well as soups such as *pasta e fagioli*. Other main courses are Florentine steak, rabbit, and kidneys stewed with onions. Vegetable side dishes are served separately, so if you want, you can skip the meat. The wine list concentrates on Tuscan wines (at a reasonable mark-up), but includes plenty from other Italian regions.

Ristorante Carignano of the Grand Hotel Sitea

Via Carlo Alberto 35 (011 517 0171). Bus 61/tram 18. **Meals served** 7.30-10.15pm Sat; 12.30-2.15pm, 7.30-10.15pm Mon-Fri, Sun. **Average** €40. **Credit** AmEx, DC, MC, V. **Map** p242 C3.

The elegant Carignano is a restaurant for grown-ups, the sort of place you'd hope to be taken by a well-heeled uncle. It's not stuffy, but the uniformed service is of the co-ordinated silver-cloche-lifting variety and soft classical music sets the mood. The

La Pista. *See p106.*

food itself is very good indeed. All things considered, prices are surprisingly reasonable, especially the five-course *ménu degustazione* at €42 including wines. The menu features both Piedmontese classics and more creative (but not overly fussy) 'modern Italian' dishes: rich calf liver pâté flavoured with cognac and served with a tart redcurrant sauce, delicate carpaccio of salmon and turbot, and flavoursome goose ragù. Rack of lamb is stuffed with a whole black truffle, while thinly sliced duck breast is enhanced by a richly reduced balsamic sauce. Desserts are visually spectacular and delicious; try the semi-molten chocolate soufflé. The wine list is comprehensive with prices starting at a very reasonable €11. Try the delicious, full-bodied Barbera d'Asti Superiore 2001 Cipressi dalla Court at €20.

Dai Saletta

Via Belfiore 37 (011 668 7867). Bus 1, 34, 35/ tram 16. **Meals served** 12.30-2pm, 8-10pm Mon-Sat. Closed Aug. **Average** €25. **Credit** AmEx, DC, MC, V. **Map** p254 A1.

A real family trattoria, Dai Saletta offers simple Piedmontese food at very competitive prices with friendly service and cheerful checked tablecloths.

Unusually, it's strictly a non-smoking restaurant. The *antipasto rustico della casa* (mixed starters) features salami of various types and *lardo* (fatty bacon), as well as Russian salad, anchovies in green sauce, stuffed vegetables and *vitello tonnato*. First courses include *agnolotti* with the classic roast meat sauce, fresh pasta and seasonal risottos. Main courses are meat-based, with the house speciality a supremely tender version of the Piedmontese classic *brasato al Barolo*, as well as duck, and rabbit with prunes and lamb. Vegetable side dishes should be ordered separately. There is a small selection of Piedmontese cheese and typical desserts like *bonet* (a chocolate pudding) and *panna cotta*. The wine list, mainly Piedmontese, is remarkably good value, with several bottles at €7 or €8.

Sotto La Mole

Via Montebello 9 (011 817 9398). Bus 13, 15, 55, 56, 61/tram 16. **Meals served** 12.30-2pm, 7.45-11pm Mon, Thur-Sat; 12.30-2pm Sun. **Average** €28. **Credit** MC, V. **Map** p243 C1.

This popular restaurant is situated 'Under the Mole' just opposite the entrance to the Museo nazionale del cinema (*see p78*); it serves classic *piemontese*

Con Calma. *See p107.*

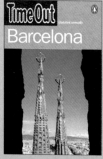 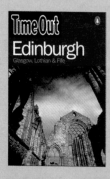 

 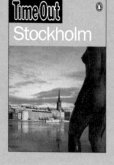 

dishes (with the odd variation) in a brick-vaulted room. The reworking of a familiar antipasto comes in the form of a *bavarese* of sweet peppers served in a puddle of creamy anchovy sauce. If this is too rich (it may come back to haunt you), there is a bright orange pumpkin soup served with goat's cheese. *Primi* include a hefty risotto with Barbera and *salsiccia* while *tajarin* are served with peppers and courgettes (in season). The *finanziera alla piemontese* is a labour-intensive stew of cock's combs, heart, testicles and the like, but if you don't do offal, there is rabbit cooked in a rich *nebbiolo* sauce or rack of lamb with a herb crust. Leave room for some excellent local cheeses or a delicious dessert; the dark chocolate *giandujot* is a good bet.

Enoteche & winebars

Cave du Jour

Corso San Maurizio 69bis/G (011 836 145/ www.cavedujour.com). Tram 16. **Meals served** 7.30-11pm Mon-Sat. Closed 3wks Aug, 1wk Jan. **Average** €25. **Credit** DC, MC, V. **Map** p243 C2.
Situated near the Po, this *ristorante-enoteca* is the baby of young chef Dario Milano, whose interesting menu of Italian regional dishes and excellent wine list represent great value for money. The ambience in the modern, functional room with its exposed brick and bright yellow paintwork is pleasant and relaxed (too much so in terms of service). The likes of the Eagles provide the background sound, and the food, although not entirely consistent, is generally very good. The menu changes daily but features fresh seasonal produce worked into a series of nicely presented and obviously cooked-on-the-spot dishes: *gallantine* of guinea fowl in balsamic vinegar (delicious), red mullet fillets in a tangy, Sicilian-style tomato, caper and black olive sauce, squid risotto, *agnolotti del plin, filetto di fassano* (overcooked and dull) and loin of pork in a mustard sauce. The wine list has an interesting 'bin ends' section that offers a 25% discount on selected labels.

Le Vitel Etonné

Via San Francesco da Paola 4 (011 812 4621/ www.leviteletonne.com). Bus 13, 18, 15, 55, 56, 61. **Meals served** 12.30-2.30pm, 8.30-10.30pm Mon, Tue, Thur-Sat; 12.30-2.30pm Wed, Sun. **Average** €20. **Credit** AmEx, DC, MC, V. **Map** p243 D1.
This very central *vineria*, only a couple of minutes from piazza Castello (*see p52*), is a charming place for a glass of wine with a bit of *salumi*, but also for a light lunch or even a complete dinner; it is also open until late. The premises are small and cosy (and non-smoking) with an attractive tiled floor and a spiral staircase going down to the wine cellar. The menu is short and varies from day to day. As its name suggests, *vitello tonnato* is always to be had, while the other starters can include raw meat and vegetable options. There's fresh pasta and hearty cereal-based soups. Rather than the meat or fish main courses you might prefer some of the excellent

Not pasta

Despite a large foreign community, there are few good ethnic restaurants (and many that should be given a very wide berth) in Turin. Since most visitors stop over here only briefly, we haven't listed any. However, if you simply can't face another bowl of pasta or risotto, you could try one of the following.

Reasonable Chinese restaurants include **King Hua** (corso Racconigi 30bis, Suburbs: west, 011 331 967) and **Via della Seta** (corso Casale 162, Collina, 011 819 0557). **Gandhi** (corso Regio Parco 24, Suburbs: north, 011 247 0643) is probably the best Indian, while **Wasabi** (corso Ferrucci 72, Suburbs: west, 011 447 3812) and **Kiki** (via della Rocca 39G, Centro, 011 835 084) have genuine Japanese food. **Arcadia** (Galleria Subalpina, Piazza Castello, 011 561 3898) is a mainly Italian restaurant that does reasonable sushi and tempura. The Kurdish **Kirkuk Caffè** (via Carlo Alberto 16bisA, Centro, 011 530 657) is an island of tranquillity in the heart of the city.

local cheeses, such as *robiola di Roccaverano*. There is an interesting selection of wines by the glass – for instance a fine Verdicchio at only €2 – as well as a good choice of bottles, again reasonably priced.

La Collina

Restaurants

I Birilli

Strada Val San Martino 6F (011 819 0567/ www.birilli.com). Bus 56. **Meals served** *June-Sept* 12.30-2.30pm, 7.30-10.30pm daily. *Oct-May* 12.30-2.30pm, 7.30-10.30pm Mon-Sat. **Average** €30. **Credit** AmEx, DC, MC, V. **Map** off p243 C2.
This restaurant, at the foot of the Collina (*see pp81-3*) on the right bank of the Po, has a predominantly young clientele. The walls are covered with photos of film stars, while in summer you can eat outside in a delightful vine-covered courtyard. The food is a mixture of modern-creative and traditional Piedmontese cooking. There are two set menus, one fish and the other meat, including different wines with each course for about €35. However, you can eat as much or as little as you like. The starters, including a good *vitello tonnato*, come in considerable helpings. The house speciality is the pasta dish *birilli alla birilli*, short pasta in a creamy tomato and cheese sauce, and among the best main courses are

Eat, Drink, Shop

Hang out with the locals at **Antiche Sere**. *See p107.*

lamb and tuna steak – which are quite enough in themselves for a summer lunch. The wine list covers all of Italy, ranging from everyday bottles at reasonable prices to the top end.

Restaurants

La Pista

Via Nizza 262 (on foot) or 294 (by car) (011 631 3523). Bus 1, 18, 35. **Meals served** 12.30-3pm, 7.30-11pm Mon, Wed-Sun. Closed 3wks Aug. **Average** €50. **Credit** AmEx, DC, MC, V. **Map** p247 A2
This new restaurant right on top of the Lingotto centre (*see p86*) takes its name from the rooftop car test track (*pista*). If you arrive by car, you'll go up the spiral ramp – a gem of industrial architecture. In summer you can eat on the terrace, which gives you a magnificent view of the city, La Collina and the Alps in the background. The menu won't let you down either: traditional (€45), fish (€55), or à la carte

dishes, ranging from traditional Piedmontese *bue stracotto* (beef stew) to starters like *millefeuille* of *ombrina* (fish) with leeks and olives, and main courses of *scaloppa di foie gras* served with a complex fruit sauce. Cheeses are provided by Parola of Saluzzo – a world-class cheese merchant – while desserts and petits fours can be accompanied by a glass from an amazingly long dessert wine list – in addition to the normal wine list offering a vast choice at not excessive prices.

Torpedo at the Meridien-Lingotto

Via Nizza 262 (011 664 2714). Bus 1, 18 , 35. **Meals served** 12.30-2.30pm, 7.30-10.30pm daily. **Average** €30. **Credit** AmEx, DC, MC. V. **Map** p247 A2.
The industrial area of Lingotto is a bit of a culinary desert, with one exception: the Torpedo at the Meridien hotel (*see p45*). A splendid vintage Fiat Torpedo dominates the calm, comfortable restaurant, a reminder that you are eating in a former car plant. Tables are set out along a glass wall and look over the lush, tropical garden where there are more tables in the summer. The food is modern

and inventive drawing on both Piedmontese and Mediterranean flavours: sautéd baby squid with ginger and chilli, *tortino* of pumpkin and ricotta with a chestnut sauce, tagliolini with spinach and pine nuts in a saffron sauce; grilled swordfish with aubergine and anchovies; and rack of lamb with a grainy mustard crust and sweet-and-sour peppers. Part of the à la carte menu highlights particular seasonal flavours (pumpkin and chestnuts in December, for example) and changes monthly. There is also a daily set menu: €28 for two courses plus dessert or €34 for three.

Pizzerie

See p101 **Amici Miei**.

Suburbs

Restaurants

See also p108 **Fratelli La Cozza**.

Con Calma

Strada Comunale del Cartman 59 (011 898 0229). **Bus 54, 61**. **Meals served** 8-10.30pm Tue-Sat; 1-2.30pm, 8-10.30pm Sun. **Average** €28. **Credit** AmEx, DC, MC, V. **Map** p241.
This delightful restaurant is just a short trip into the hills near Superga (*see p91*). Occupying an old, yellow-painted village house with several additions, it is rustic and cosy inside with bright kilims on brick floors and warm lighting. The food – carefully prepared and presented Piedmontese fare – suits the ambience. The generous plate of *antipasti misti* (including a delicious Jerusalem artichoke *sformato* in a cheese fondue) is enough for two, while among the *primi* (all pasta is home-made) are such familiar dishes as *agnolotti*. There are variations,

too: *risotto alla Barbera* with carp, leek and potato ravioli served with mackerel and cherry tomatoes, *lepre* (hare) stew flavoured with juniper and grappa, and perch with tomatoes and saffron. Save room for the chocolate fondue, a shockingly sinful way to end a meal. The well-priced wine list is almost entirely made up of regional labels; the lively house Barbera d'Asti is good and cheap.

Locanda Mongreno

Strada Comunale Mongreno 50 (011 898 0417). **Bus 15, 61, 68**. **Meals served** 8.15-10.30pm Tue-Sun. Closed 2wks Jan, 2wks Sept. **Average** €55. **Credit** AmEx, MC, V. **Map** p241.
This is a fashionable, if not cheap, restaurant in the hills of Turin, albeit not too far from the centre. From outside it looks like an *osteria*, but the decor is distinctly stylish and the young waiters are very professional. The cooking is modern-creative in style – there are set menus of various size on offer, the most expensive of which includes sushi – but you can also eat à la carte. The selection of breads and focaccia baked on the premises is particularly notable and includes interesting little pre-starter nibbles. There are also more traditional Piedmontese dishes, like *agnolotti* or risotto, but reinterpreted in a lighter style and with more Mediterranean ingredients, like mozzarella and top-quality olive oil. Meat courses (the lamb is especially good) can be followed by light but chocolatey desserts or a selection of cheeses. The wine selection is good.

Osteria Antiche Sere

Via Cenischia 9 (011 385 4347). **Bus 55, 68**. **Meals served** 8-10pm Mon-Sat. Closed Aug, 2wks Dec-Jan. **Average** €25. **No credit cards**. **Map** p241.
This traditional *osteria* with wooden tables and period photos is well outside the city centre and not easy to find, but worth the trek. Given its popularity,

Eat, Drink, Shop

Not meat

Piedmontese food is heavily meat-oriented, but meat-shunners shouldn't despair: the region has the widest selection of good cheeses in Italy. Local favourites include **gorgonzola** – both creamy *dolce* and crumbly *piccante* – as well as many other less familiar taste sensations. **Caprini** are small goat's cheeses which may be fresh and soft (*fresco*) or mature (*stagionato*) and hard with a stronger flavour. The term **robiola** covers a number of cheeses from the southern Langhe (*see p194*): **robiola di bossolasco** is soft and delicate, **robiola del bek** is similar to camembert, while those from Lesegno and Murazzano become rich and creamy as they mature. **Seirass del fen** is a type of ricotta that is matured in hay – delicious both on its

own and as a filling for ravioli. **Paglierina** is a small, round, flat cheese, which is rich and creamy. The mountain valleys (*see pp206-214*) are home to varieties of **toma**, which are usually large round cheeses, matured for six months or more. Commonly found are **toma di Lanzo** or **toma di Valchiusella**. **Murianengo** is a strong blue cheese, while both **bettelmatt** (from a valley near the border with Switzerland) and **castelmagno** (from a valley in the south-west of Piedmont) are matured at length and are rare and expensive, but worth trying if you find them.

Restaurants with good cheese selections: **La Pista** (*p106*), **La Taverna di Frà Fiusch** (*p108*), **Torricelli** (*p98*) and **Le Vitel Etonné** (*p105*).

Cosy **La Taverna di Frà Fiusch**.

Pizzas (and mussels) at **Fratelli La Cozza**.

booking is advisable. The service is exceptionally friendly and the food good Piedmontese fare. The choice isn't vast, but freshness is guaranteed. Dishes vary according to the season, but salami, *tomini al verde* or *elettrici* (small goat's cheeses in a parsley-based or spicy red sauce) and vegetable flans are always top quality. The first courses include *tajarin* and, if you're lucky, *paniscia*, a type of risotto from the north of Piedmont. The main courses are meat-based, the speciality being *stinco di maiale* (pork shin bone). There is a fair cheese selection for non-meat eaters, while the desserts are simple but good, the *zabaione* in particular. You will find a good and reasonably priced selection of wines, especially Piedmontese reds. In winter finish off with *zuccherini* – sugar cubes preserved in pure alcohol with coffee beans and lemon rind. Dogs, oddly, are welcome.

La Taverna di Frà Fiusch

Via Beria 32, Revigliasco, Moncalieri (011 860 8224). **Meals served** 8-11.30pm Tue-Fri; 12.30-2.30pm, 8-11.30pm Sat, Sun. Closed 2wks Sept. **Average** €30. **Credit** AmEx, MC, V. **Map** p241.
This restaurant is outside Turin's city boundaries, in the main street of the pretty village of Revigliasco on the other side of the Collina (*see pp81-3*). There are four small rooms: two downstairs with a wood fire in winter, and two upstairs including a veranda with a magnificent view over the surrounding countryside. The menu is very much in the Piedmontese tradition: mixed antipasti with peppers in anchovy and garlic sauce, Russian salad and vegetable flans with fondue, pasta dishes including excellent *agnolotti del plin*, various *risotti* and *tajarin*,

while main courses feature rabbit and pork shin bone. There is a vast selection of high-quality cheese and traditional desserts. On Fridays you'll find a beautifully cooked *fritto misto alla piemontese* – two large platters with all the classic meat, offal, vegetables and sweets (so go easy on anything else). Wines are reasonably priced, with a wide selection from Piedmont and the rest of Italy. The kitchen will stay open later than the times given above if you book ahead.

Pizzerie

Fratelli La Cozza

Corso Regio Parco 39 (011 859 900/www. lacozza.com). Bus 77/tram 18, 68. **Meals served** 12.30-2.30pm, 7.30-11.30pm daily. **Average** *Restaurant* €25; *Pizzeria* €11. **Credit** AmEx, DC, MC, V. **Map** p243 B1.
Just in case you don't understand the name, there are molluscs all over the huge 'Mussel Brothers' Neapolitan pizzeria and restaurant, housed in an ex-warehouse in the north-east corner of the city. The decor is wacky: a bright red pizza delivery van, giant plastic vegetables mounted on bare brick walls, fairy lights and an oversized chandelier. Groups are seated at one of the round tables at street level, but if you are after a table for two, try and secure one of those on the balcony with its view of the action below. In spite of three sittings for dinner, there's always a long queue waiting to be fed pizzas (no better than decent), pasta (ditto) and, of course, mussels in various guises. So don't expect a great, or particularly cheap, meal; but that's not really the point of this place: it's entertaining and a good choice for a fun, noisy night out.

Cafés & Bars

The rituals of coffee-drinking and *aperitivi* are taken very seriously in Turin.

Maybe it's because of the grey, foggy winter weather and the snow so shiver-inducingly visible on the surrounding Alps, but the *torinesi* were among the first Italians to discover the pleasure of a cup of strong coffee or a steaming chocolate sipped in warm, intimate surroundings.

Indeed, café society here has a long and glorious tradition, going back to the days of Savoy rule when liberal-intellectual conspirators hatched plots against absolutist tyrants and foreign occupiers in the smoky comfort of these establishments. The locals are very proud of their historic coffee houses, some of them looking now exactly as they did two centuries ago and still offering the same impeccable service. There's no denying that sitting in baroque splendour adds a little something to indulging in the pleasure of a cappuccino accompanied by a mouth-watering pastry.

Coffee-making is considered an art in Turin and has been perfected over time by local artisans producing and roasting their own particular blends of coffee in-house. One of these – a Signor Luigi Lavazza – opened his little shop here a century ago and went on to conquer the world with his own brand of beans.

In Turin – like the rest of Italy – a *caffè* is also a bar serving alcoholic beverages, and can double up as a *pasticceria* (cakes), *gelateria* (ice-cream) or *latteria* (dairy products).

But there are certain features that set *torinesi* cafés and bars apart. Chocolate and pastries, for example, are taken particularly seriously here and have a long and glorious history. Swiss chocolate makers came to Turin to learn their art in the 18th century. The local *pasticcini* (mini-pâtisserie) are a delight for both eyes and palate.

Turin's bars are also big on food: at lunchtime, cafés may serve anything from simple *tramezzini* (sandwiches) to three-course meals accompanied by a glass of wine. And the food aspect resumes at around 7pm, when the locals begin their *aperitivo*-hour grazing ritual (*see p116* **Aperitivi galore**).

Cafés' edible delights are often on display and available all day, but don't be fooled: *torinese* etiquette demands that you indulge at very specific times. Breakfast consists of a cappuccino or *caffè* (espresso) with a *brioche* (croissant), usually consumed at the counter.

Caffè Elena. *See p115.*

If you don't want to be treated with withering contempt or simple pity, don't ask for a cappuccino after 11am, and restrict your cake consumption to teatime. If it's ice-cream you're after (only after lunch, *please*), seek out a *produzione artigianale* sign: this means that the ice-cream has been whipped up on the premises.

The end of *aperitivi* is when many bars pull down their shutters, but some new-style places remain open into the early hours of the morning. Despite the ubiquitous presence of historic cafés in Turin, a good number of trendy design-led venues have flown in the face of tradition, especially in the areas around piazza Vittorio Veneto (Centro) and piazza Emanuele Filiberto (Quadrilatero).

Be aware that in Turin, as all over Italy, there's a premium to be paid for sitting down both inside and – even more wallet-threateningly – outside. For the privilege of being served at a pavement table, expect to pay twice as much as you would standing at the counter; it's not always the case, but if in doubt, ask. The

Eat, Drink, Shop

Mulassano.
See p111.

upside of this is that your outlay entitles you to as unhurried a sit-down as you like; bring those postcards for a leisurely writing session.

Turin has, to date, remained largely untouched by mass tourism. The unofficial 'tourist-tax' rip-off you find yourself paying in, say, Venice, does not really exist here. You can be pretty sure you'll be treated as a local and get the same value for money.

Piazza Castello

Coffee & cakes

Abrate
Via Po 10 (011 812 2206). Bus 33, 55, 61/tram 13, 15, 18. **Open** *June-Sept* 7am-8.30pm Mon-Sat. *Oct-May* 7am-8.30pm daily. Closed 2wks July. **Credit** MC, V. **Map** p242 C3.
This lovely wood-panelled café-bar, formerly a bakery dating from 1866, is warm and inviting. Renovated for the first time in the 1950s, it was further refurbished in 2002 when the original vaulted brick ceilings were exposed and the flooring stripped back to reveal the 17th-century pavement of via Po. There's a comfortable dining area and a kitchen producing light meals.

Baratti & Milano
Piazza Castello 27 (011 440 7138). Bus 11, 12, 27, 55, 57, 61, 63/tram 4, 13, 15, 18. **Open** 8am-9pm Tue-Sun. **Credit** AmEx, DC, MC, V. **Map** p242 C3.

A Turin institution and long-time supplier to the Savoy royal family, Baratti & Milano has been in business since 1873, and very little has changed since then. Indeed, the large tearoom overlooking the Galleria subalpina (*see p69*) looks straight out of a movie set with its late 19th-century decor. Order a hot chocolate and some of the delicious miniature pastries from the counter, take a seat by the large window and feel like royalty. The pastries, cakes and chocolate assortments – to eat in or take away – are exquisite. Don't miss the *bignole* (sweet glazed pastry cases filled with fresh cream in a selection of flavours) or chocolate and hazel-nut Gianduja in either of its manifestations: as a small triangular chocolate or a spreadable cream in a jar (a far cry from Nutella, *see p194* **Middle-aged spread**, its modern industrial counterpart).

Mulassano
Piazza Castello 15 (011 547 990). Bus 11, 12, 27, 55, 57, 61, 63/tram 4, 13, 15, 18. **Open** 7.30am-9pm daily. **Credit** AmEx, MC, V. **Map** p242 C3.
Mulassano serves excellent coffee, tea and a small selection of pastries in its glorious wood-panelled interior. But it's best known for the quality and variety of its *tramezzini* (sandwiches) and even lays claim (along with many other establishments around Italy) to having been the first place to have put fillings between two thin slices of bread in the 1920s. In the summer, enjoy (but be prepared to pay over the odds for) a table outside under the lovely porticos of the piazza Castello.

Caffè, cappuccino, *zabaione* and *bicerìn*

Italian coffee enjoys a worldwide reputation and Turin is one of the best cities in the country to sample it. As well as all the usual variations there are some indulgent local specialities.

Caffè Espresso.

Cappuccino You know that one!

Caffè americano Very diluted espresso in a large cup.

Caffè corretto Espresso with a drop of spirits, usually grappa but you can specify.

Caffè con panna Espresso with sweet whipped cream.

Caffè freddo Iced coffee.

Caffè macchiato Espresso with a drop of milk.

Caffè latte A cappuccino with less coffee and more milk (don't ask for a *latte*... unless you want a glass of cold milk).

Latte macchiato Hot milk with a just a drop of coffee.

Cioccolato caldo Hot chocolate, usually so thick in Turin that a teaspoon can stand in it.

Zabaione A *torinese* classic, made with egg yolk, sugar and sweet Marsala (or, occasionally, Moscato) wine. Prescribed since the 17th century to enhance sexual performance.

Bicerìn Piedmontese for *bicchierino* (small glass), this is a small glass of espresso, hot chocolate and cream. Supposedly invented in the 18th century in Fiorio (*see p117*), it's best sampled today at Al Bicerìn (*see p112*).

Marocchino Slightly less calorific than *bicerìn*, with coffee, hot chocolate and skimmed milk.

Tè If tea is your tipple, choose from the bar's 'selection' box where possible (the standard brew may be dreadful). If you take milk, ask for it *con latte*, otherwise it'll arrive with lemon on the side. *Tè freddo* (*al limone* or *alla pesca* – peach flavoured) is refreshing in summer but is rarely home-made nowadays.

Moroccan delight: **Hafa Café**. *See p113*.

Wine & food

Caffè Roberto

Via Po 5 (011 817 7665). Bus 33, 55, 61/tram 13, 15, 18. **Open** 7.30am-10pm Tue-Sun. Closed 2wks Aug. **Credit** DC, MC, V. **Map** p242 C3.
Located under the porticos on via Po, this café's sumptuous *aperitivo* buffet attracts large crowds. You can serve yourself to hot and cold nibbles or be served at tables inside and out. There's a good selection of wines and a fresh seasonal fruit-based *aperitivo della casa* to which the bartender adds a suitable alcohol upon request: try the pineapple rum or strawberry *spumante*.

Caffè Rossini

Corso Regina Margherita 80E (011 521 4105). Bus 68/tram 3, 16, 18. **Open** *June-Sept* 10.30am-3.30am Mon-Sat. *Oct-May* 7.30am-3.30am Mon-Sat; 6pm-2am Sun. Closed Aug. **Credit** MC, V. **Map** p242 B3.
A popular venue with a late 20s/early 30s crowd, the Rossini is much frequented for its *aperitivi* and late opening times. At weekends, you'll have to fight for space, but this contributes to its particular smoky atmosphere. Occupying two storeys on a corner site overlooking the River Dora, during the day it's a cosy location for watching the locals go about their business through the huge windows that surround the bar. If you're feeling peckish, breakfast and lunch are served.

Wonderbar

Via San Francesco d'Assisi 2B (011 561 8424). Bus 50, 51/tram 4. **Open** 7.30am-7.30pm Mon-Thur, Sat; 7.30am-11.30pm Fri. Closed 2wks Aug. **No credit cards**. **Map** p242 C3.
Creative 1960s decor makes this place a favourite with a late 20s, alternative clientele, especially on Friday nights when the bar stays open late with live music or DJs. During the day it serves a good selection of lunches from panini (filled rolls) to fresh salads and pasta dishes. A themed *aperitivo* buffet is served from 7pm. Opens on Sundays in December.

Quadrilatero

Coffee & cakes

Al Bicerìn

Piazza della Consolata 5 (011 436 9325/ www.bicerin.it). Bus 50, 51, 52, 60, 67. **Open** 8.30am-7.30pm Mon, Tue, Thur, Fri; 8.30am-1pm, 3.30-7.30pm Sat, Sun. Closed Aug. **No credit cards**. **Map** p242 C2.
However short your stopover in Turin, don't miss Al Bicerin. This tiny gem was founded in 1763, and it's not difficult to picture gentlemen in powdered wigs and silk stockings among the marble tables and mirror-lined walls. Situated in a delightful square opposite the church of La Consolata (*see p61*), the café also has outside tables at which to sip a *zabaione* or a *bicerin* (*see p111* **Caffè**, cappuccino, *zabaione* and *bicerin*) in its purest form, accompanied by one of the delicious homemade pastries. Try to avoid Sunday afternoons, when the wait for a table can be interminable.

Barolino Cocchi

Via Bonelli 16C (011 436 7245). Bus 11, 12, 19, 27, 50, 57, 63/tram 3, 4. **Open** 9am-8pm Mon-Sat. **No credit cards**. **Map** p242 C3.
This little bar, in an 18th-century palazzo designed by the baroque genius Filippo Juvarra, consists of one elegant circular room with a frescoed dome ceiling, in which to sip your morning coffee or your *aperitivo*. The bar specialises in vermouth-based *aperitivi* and also serves Barolo *chinato*, a tipple made from Barolo wine, quinine extracts, rhubarb roots and gentian. There are tiny tartines and pasta nibbles to accompany your drinks.

Wine & food

Il Bacaro

Piazza della Consolata 3F (011 436 9064/ www.bacaropanevino.com). Bus 50, 51, 52, 60, 67. **Open** noon-3pm, 6pm-2am Tue-Sun. Closed 2wks Aug. **Credit** AmEx, DC, MC, V. **Map** p242 C2.
This cosy wine bar located on two floors overlooking the lovely piazza della Consolata specialises in Venetian cuisine for lunch and dinner, but it's also a terrific place for a swanky *aperitivo* or a glass of wine from its impressive list. The prices are a little

on the high side, but the service and choice make up for this. There's outside seating in the summer, in a quiet, romantic spot.

Hafa Café
Via Sant'Agostino 23C (011 436 7091). Bus 11, 12, 19, 27, 50, 57, 63/tram 3, 4. **Open** 11am-2am Tue-Sun. **Credit** MC, V. **Map** p242 C3.
Step through the door of this Moroccan-inspired café and you'll be assailed by an Aladdin's cave of smells and visual delights. The deep red hues and sandal-wood incense radiate an atmosphere of calm and relaxation. Sit down at the low tables where you can order from a large selection of teas, spiced Arabian coffees, cocktails and French or Italian wines. Mahgreb specialities are served at lunch and *aperitivi* start at 7pm. And you can take home a slice of the ambience: there's a shop attached selling exotic furniture and objects.

Pastis
Piazza Emanuele Filiberto 9B (011 521 1085/ www.associazioneazimut.it). Bus 11, 12, 19, 27, 50, 57, 63/tram 3, 4. **Open** *Mar-Oct* 9am-2am Mon-Sat. *Nov-Feb* 9am-3pm, 6pm-2am Tue-Sat; 6pm-2am Sun. Closed 2wks Dec-Jan. **No credit cards.** **Map** p242 C3.
With its decor harking back to the 1950s, this café-restaurant situated in one of Turin's trendiest *piazze* is ideal for lunchtimes when you can choose from a selection of Piedmontese wines to wash down some of the locally inspired cuisine. The bar hosts frequent exhibitions, thus attracting an arty clientele. In the summer months tables outside on the piazza make Pastis even more of a crowd-pleaser.

Tre Galli
Via Sant'Agostino 25 (011 521 6027/fax 011 521 7114/www.3galli.com). Bus 11, 12, 19, 27, 50, 57, 63/tram 3, 4. **Open** noon-2.30pm, 6pm-2am Mon-Sat. Closed 2wks Jan. **Credit** AmEx, MC, V. **Map** p242 C3.
One of the first places to open in this recently trendified area of the city, Tre Galli offers a wide selection of wines to be enjoyed with cured meats and cheese platters. Large windows add to the open atmosphere and allow you to see and be seen by the beautiful people. There is a large outside seating area on the pedestrianised street, which is perfect for your summer afternoon 'al fresco'.

Cittadella

Coffee & cakes

Caffè Norman
Via Pietro Micca 22 (011 540 854). Bus 55, 72/ tram 13. **Open** 8am-1am Mon-Thur, Sun; 8am Fri-1am Sun. **Credit** DC, MC, V. **Map** p242 C3.
Overlooking the beautiful piazza Solferino, Caffè Norman is sumptuously decorated with lashings of marble and polished wood. It has been doing business for several decades and the level of service and quality have remained consistently high. Come here for a relaxing breakfast, a chic lunch or to dip into the large cocktail buffet as part of the *aperitivo* ritual and you won't be disappointed. Note this café's unusual Friday and Saturday opening times.

Platti
Corso Vittorio Emanuele II 72 (011 506 9056/ www.platti.it). Bus 5, 14, 33, 50, 59, 67/tram 4, 15. **Open** 7.30am-9pm daily. **Credit** AmEx, DC, MC, V. **Map** p242 D3.
Since 1870, Turin's upper classes have been coming here to socialise and enjoy the many delicacies on display. The tradition continues and Platti, with its glorious Liberty (art nouveau) interior, remains a stomping ground for the *alta borghesia*. Whatever your rung on the social ladder, there's nothing stopping you from sampling Platti's vast *aperitivo* buffet… just be careful not to spill your drink on anyone's fur coat. In the summer, you can relax (at a price) at one of the tables under the porticos.

San Tommaso 10
Via San Tommaso 10 (011 534 201/www.lavazza.it). Bus 55/tram 13, 15. **Open** *Café-bar* 8am-7pm Mon-Sat. *Restaurant* noon-2.30pm, 8-10.30pm Mon-Sat. Closed 1wk Jan, Aug. **Credit** AmEx, DC, MC, V. **Map** p242 C3.
A recent addition to Turin's café scene, this is the official showcase of Turin's internationally renowned coffee brand Lavazza. Located in the heart

Sumptuous buffet: **Caffè Roberto**. *See p112.*

Turin
surprises you

Turin surprises you. Always.
With a rich calendar of events, with the exciting
show of the Winter Olympic Games in 2006
and with a cultural wealth that can't be
missed: the Egyptian Museum, the National
Cinema Museum, the GAM–Gallery of Modern
and Contemporary Art, the Museum of
Contemporary Art of the Rivoli Castle.
Let yourself be surprised.

Turin is easy with...

- Torino Card: your pass for
  more than 120 museums in
  Turin and Piedmont
- Week-end a Torino: special
  prices for an unforgettable
  weekend
- TurismoBus Torino: the touris
  bus for visiting the city at you
  own pace; you can get on an
  off at any stop.

i For information:
Turismo Torino
Ph. +39 0118185011
info@turismotorino.org
www.turismotorino.org

of the city centre, this mishmash of old and modern decor verges on tacky... which doesn't stop it from being wildly popular and chic. As you'd expect, the selection of coffees is excellent with some unusual touches such as hazel-nut or almond flavours. The food is also palatable if pricey: try the *gamberi fritti in camicia di patate* (fried prawns in potato jacket) or the fresh pasta made on the premises. For the complete experience choose from the extensive wine list from Italy and France.

Testa
Corso Re Umberto 56 (011 599 775). Bus 11, 12/ tram 15. **Open** 7am-8.15pm Mon-Sat. Closed 2wks Aug, 1wk Dec. **No credit cards. Map** p244 A3.
Once a simple *latteria* (dairy shop), Testa was refurbished and transformed into a café a few years ago, but still manages to maintain a down-home neighbourhood feel. Many of the local stalwarts who can't conceive of a day starting without a cappuccino here have been frequenting the place since they were in short trousers. But customers also come from much further afield for some of the best home-made ice-cream in town, and Testa's famous hot chocolate with whipped cream in the winter.

Ice-cream
See also above **Testa.**

Caffè Miretti
Corso Matteotti 5 (011 533 687). Bus 27, 57, 59/ tram 4, 15. **Open** 7am-1.30am Tue-Sat; 8am-2am Sun. Closed 1wk Aug. **Credit** AmEx, DC, MC, V. **Map** p242 D3.
Not far from Porta Nuove railway station, this luxurious little café-*gelateria* offers some of the most delicious ice-cream in town. Enjoy it sitting inside the comfortable baroque-style surroundings or take it away in a *coppetta* or cone. It also serves excellent coffee, cappuccino, teas and a good selection of fine sweet pastries. And it's all freshly made on the premises.

 The best *Aperitivi*

Bar Nazionale
See p115.

Caffè Norman
See p113.

Caffè Roberto
See p112.

Caffè Rossini
See p112.

Platti
See p113.

Coffee & cakes
See also p117 **Fiorio.**

Caffè Elena
Piazza Vittorio Veneto 5 (011 812 3341). Bus 30, 53, 55, 61, 70/tram 13, 15, 16. **Open** 8.30am-midnight Mon, Tue, Thur, Sun; 8.30am-1am Fri, Sat. Closed 1wk Aug. **No credit cards. Map** p243 C1.
A long-time favourite with students, intellectuals and would-be-bohemians from the nearby literature faculty. Nietzsche made this his favourite café during his sojourn in Turin. This establishment's old-world charm will entice you to spend a moment of relaxation savouring a good *bicerin* (*see p111* **Caffè**, cappuccino, *zabaione* and *bicerìn*) or a glass of wine at *aperitivo* time. Like all the other cafés in this piazza, there's outdoor seating in summer and (thanks to gas heaters) in winter too. Stays open an hour later in summer.

Café Flora
Piazza Vittorio Veneto 24 (011 817 1530). Bus 30, 53, 55, 61, 70/tram 13, 15, 16. **Open** 2pm-3am Tue-Fri; noon-3am Sat; 10am-3am Sun. Closed 2wks Aug, 2wks Dec-Jan. **No credit cards. Map** p243 C1.
Flora was here on the now super-trendy piazza Vittorio long before any of the recent slew of design-driven bars elbowed their way in. The warm, cosy atmosphere and its corner location overlooking the piazza and the Po make Café Flora a popular choice with locals. Foreign students flock here, too, to read the café's array of European newspapers. This mixed clientele sips cocktails until the early hours, not to mention *aperitivi* earlier in the evening.

Caffè Nuovo Nazionale
Via Accademia Albertina 1 (011 882 140). Bus 33, 55, 61/tram 13, 15, 18. **Open** 7am-midnight Mon-Sat. Closed 2wks Aug. **No credit cards. Map** p243 C1.
The 1950s decor of this corner bar, with its curved metal counter and neon sign over the door, makes it look like it's straight out of a Fellini film. The trendy retro atmosphere – authentic, not reconstituted – makes the Nazionale a favourite with students from the nearby art college. Large windows and a prime location – it overlooks via Po – mean this delightful little bar is perfect for sitting and watching the world go by. There are appetising panini (filled rolls) and *tramezzini* (sandwiches) at lunchtime; even better, come here for *aperitivi* and try your luck with the card trick – if you split the pack on the counter and get the joker, your drink is on the house.

Caffè San Carlo
Piazza San Carlo 156 (011 532 586). Bus 11, 12, 27, 57, 58, 63, 65, 72/tram 4, 15. **Open** 8am-midnight Mon-Thur, Sun; 8am-1am Fri, Sat. **Credit** AmEx, MC, V. **Map** p242 C3.

Eat, Drink, Shop

A Turin institution, the San Carlo impresses with its regal atmosphere and a definite sense that it has remained unchanged for centuries. Renowned for being the first café in Italy to install gas lighting in 1832, the San Carlo prides itself on the superior quality of its food and drinks – even the bread is home-made. The service is highly professional and sitting at an outside table observing this splendid baroque piazza is a real (though pricey) treat.

Caffè Torino

Piazza San Carlo 204 (011 545 118/www. caffetorino.com). Bus 11, 12, 27, 57, 58, 63, 65, 72/tram 4, 15. **Open** 7.30am-1am daily. **Credit** AmEx, DC, MC, V. **Map** p242 C3.
The Torino pips its neighbour San Carlo at the post for early-morning opening and otherwise shares the same prestigious setting and lengthy history. With its top-class service, it's a perfect place to take a break from your retail exercises in the shopping core of the city; refuel with its remarkable pastries and cakes. Quality like this clearly comes at a price, but sipping a coffee at one of the tables outside under the porticos of the piazza is a very special experience.

Wine & food

Café des Arts

Via Principe Amedeo 33F (011 882 212). Bus 33, 55, 61/tram 13, 15, 18. **Open** 7.30am-10pm daily. Closed 2wks Aug. **No credit cards**. **Map** p243 C1.
Contemporary artwork and brightly coloured murals adorn the walls of this favourite student hangout. But you don't need to be 20-something to appreciate the welcoming, creative atmosphere of this café. The set home-made lunch costs just €10 with a glass of wine, good *aperitivi* are served from 6.30pm and there are themed dinners and live jazz once a week on a Thursday. The café's speciality is *marocchino* ('Moroccan' coffee) made with cream, cocoa and Nutella.

La Drogheria

Piazza Vittorio Veneto 18D (011 812 2414). Bus 30, 53, 55, 61, 70/tram 13, 15, 16. **Open** 11am-2am daily. **Credit** MC, V. **Map** p243 C1.
One of the most popular of the new bars on bustling piazza Vittorio, La Drogheria stands out from the high-design crowd thanks to a relaxed living-

Aperitivi galore

The Italian lifestyle is largely defined by what you eat and drink at particular times of the day, and nowhere is this more true than in Turin, where locals have added another, unmissable 'meal' to the traditional breakfast-lunch-dinner combo. The *aperitivo*, they'll tell you, has a specific function: alcoholic or not, but generally bitter-sweet in taste, it should be drunk shortly before dinner to enliven your taste buds and stimulate your appetite... which doesn't explain why these days it usually comes with a buffet so huge that dinner afterwards is quite out of the question.

The variety of *aperitivo* tipples is endless. Most bars have their own home-made mix, the *aperitivo della casa*: it pays to enquire into its contents before indulging.

Many traditionalists go for a glass of dry white wine – an Arneis, a Gavi or a bubbly Prosecco (*see p32* **Regional wines**). Others opt for a light Piedmontese red, like Grignolino or – if you're here in October-November when the new wine arrives – Novello.

Then there are the bitters, such as Aperol, which is light in alcohol (11 per cent), bright orange in colour, and is usually beautifully served in a glass with the rim encrusted in sugar. Sanbitter is similar but without alcohol, or you can go for a Campari (specify if you

want the real thing, rather than fizzy stuff – Campari soda – out of a little bottle). If you're feeling homesick, a *gin-tonica* is perfectly acceptable, but if you want to go native, then vermouth should be your choice (*see p122* **No Carpano, no party**). Have it straight, in a Martini cocktail, or in a Negroni: one third gin, one third Campari and one third of thoroughly *torinese* Punt e Mes. But restrict yourself to one or you may find yourself making your way to bed instead of the restaurant.

Aperitivi are, in theory, accompanied by nibbles in order to bridge the gap until dinner. But as bars cash in on the fact that *aperitivo* hour in Turin is now the most important moment in everyone's social diary, the nibbles on offer have been transformed into vast buffets. Around 7pm each evening, hungry, thirsty crowds throng to cafés all over the city searching for the biggest and best. There'll be everything from canapés, cured meats and salamis, cheese and grilled vegetables to little portions of risotto and fresh pasta. Buying a drink entitles you to sample any of the goods on offer, but remember – the bounty of the buffet will be reflected in the price you pay for your drink. Don't be shy: grab your plate and fill it with whatever you fancy... oh, and remember to cancel that restaurant reservation.

room-style interior replete with comfy sofas and armchairs in a variety of styles. It's large and rambling, but its twists and turns are bright and airy. Drop in to sample one of its creative panini or salads accompanied by the usual selection of coffees and teas. Lunchtime can be very chaotic as the large outside seating area overlooking the piazza fills up. The *aperitivi* are popular with a twentysomething clientele and drinks continue to be servd until late.

Refettorio
Via dei Mille 23D (011 887 422). Bus 68/tram 18.
Open 8.30am-9pm Mon-Sat. Closed 3wks Aug.
No credit cards. Map p245 D1.
Strongly recommended for lunchtimes, Al Refettorio (the Canteen) is an eat-in delicatessen with a wide variety of hot and cold foods of excellent quality on offer. The welcoming and friendly service – not to mention value for money – makes this café very popular with office workers in the area who drop by in the morning for cappuccino and a fresh croissant and at lunchtime for soup, salads or quiche.

Taberna Libraria
Via Bogino 5 (011 836 515). Bus 33, 55, 61/ tram 13, 15. **Open** 10am-9pm daily. **Credit** AmEx, MC, V. **Map** p243 C1.
If you are a book lover and a wine lover, you can indulge both your passions under one roof at this establishment. Taberna Libraria is exactly what the name says: a bookshop-tavern. Here you can have a glass of wine from the wide selection while browsing the shelves for your favourite food and wine review. The place has a modern look, provides tapas-style nibbles and has a small room for taking the weight off your feet at the back. It also sells local food and designer kitchenware.

Ice-cream

Fiorio
Via Po 8 (011 817 0612). Bus 33, 55, 61/tram 13, 15, 18. **Open** 8am-1am Tue-Thur, Sun; 8am-2am Fri, Sat. Closed 2wks Jan. **Credit** DC, MC, V.
Map p243 C1.
In Turin Fiorio is simply synonymous with ice-cream. Its cone with Gianduja and whipped cream is unforgettable. This café-*gelateria* has been in business since 1780 and maintains much of its original decor; particularly splendid is the marble counter of the main bar. Before Italian unification, when Turin was still the capital of the Kingdom of Piedmont, political decisions were made here rather than in the parliament. You can sit outside under the porticos and order one of its extravagant goblets or simply buy a cone and enjoy your stroll along busy via Po.

Pepino
Piazza Carignano 8 (011 542 009). Bus 33, 55, 61/tram 13, 15. **Open** 8am-midnight daily.
Credit AmEx, DC, MC, V. **Map** p242 C3.
This charming old-style café-*gelateria* is just over a century old. The home-made ice-cream is renowned

Caffè San Carlo. *See p116.*

all over Piedmont but Pepino is particularly famous for having invented the choc-ice, which in these parts is called a *pinguino* (penguin) and is quaintly served here in a frosted paper wrapping. In summer there's a pleasant outside seating area.

La Collina

Coffee & cakes

Antico Bar Pasticceria Maggiora

Corso Fiume 2 (011 660 4647). Bus 52, 64, 66, 70, 73. **Open** 7am-8pm Tue-Sun. Closed 2wks Aug. **No credit cards**. **Map** p245 A2.

This chic little bar-*pasticceria* is a favourite with students from the exclusive colleges dotted around the hill. But there's nothing pretentious about this place; the atmosphere is relaxed and the owners welcoming. The selection of pâtisserie to accompany your morning cappuccino is excellent and the home-made cakes are delicious; the lunch menu includes freshly made pasta. *Aperitivi* are served from 6.30pm when there's a choice of local cured meats to nibble with your wine.

Caffè Chantilly

Piazza Gran Madre di Dio 1 (011 819 0489). Bus 33, 55, 66, 73/tram 13. **Open** 7am-1.30am daily. **No credit cards**. **Map** p243 D2.

This café situated in the shadow of the Gran Madre church (*see p81*) makes the best ice-cream this side of the river. The decor is elegant and a tad formal but in tune with the highly professional service. Its cappuccino is one of the creamiest in the city, best enjoyed al fresco in the outside seating area, with a home-made pastry or slice of cake to top it off. In the evening it also serves *aperitivi* with a small but interesting buffet.

Gran Bar

Piazza Gran Madre di Dio 2 (011 813 0871). Bus 33, 55, 66, 73/tram 13. **Open** Apr-Oct 7am-2am daily. Nov-Mar 7am-2am Tue-Sun. Closed 2wks Jan. **No credit cards**. **Map** p243 D2.

There has been a café on these premises since 1845, but the recently renovated Gran Bar has now acquired ultra-modern minimalist decor. It's the traditional stomping ground of the well-heeled families living in the exclusive residential areas around the hill. With large picture windows facing on to the piazza, this is the place to be seen mingling with the rich and the beautiful. *Aperitivi* are served daily from 6.30pm to 9.30pm, with wine tasting each Thursday and a themed buffet each Tuesday. During the summer months you can sip your cocktail on the large terrace outside.

Wine & food

Enoteca Zacco-Dafarra

Via Monferrato 23 (011 839 9080). Bus 33, 55, 66, 73/tram 13. **Open** 8am-9pm Mon-Sat. Closed 2wks Aug. **Credit** AmEx, MC, V. **Map** p243 C2.

Brothers Roberto and Gabriele will welcome you into this cute café-wine bar (known to all as *Il Piolino*) with its friendly atmosphere and local clientele. Piedmontese vintage wines predominate in a wide-ranging wine list that also includes a good selection from the rest of the country: you can order by the bottle or by the glass starting at €1.90. At lunch, simple but tasty panini using the best local meats and cheeses are served.

Lingotto

Coffee & cakes

Officina 500A

Via Nizza 230C (011 667 7572). Bus 17/tram 1, 18. **Open** 8am-11pm daily. **Credit** DC, MC, V. **Map** p247 A2.

This café is located at the entrance to the vast Lingotto (*see p86*), once a Fiat factory, now a shopping complex. The decor is suitably post-industrial, with an old Fiat car that hangs from the ceiling and moves on a pulley. A perfect spot for a relaxing cappuccino with a pastry after a shopping spree, a pick-me-up lunch after a mad shopping spree or for an *aperitivo* with buffet after… you know what!

Ice-cream

Silvano Gelato d'altri Tempi

Via Nizza 142 (011 696 0647). Bus 17/tram 1, 18. **Open** 8am-midnight Mon-Fri, Sun. Closed 2wks Aug. **No credit cards**. **Map** p245 D1.

Silvano advertises his *gelato* as 'the ice-cream of a time gone by'. Certainly today it's the best home-made ice-cream in the area. This big *gelateria* can fulfil your desires in situ or takeaway. The list of flavours is endless and changes according to the fruits in season. Be prepared to queue during summer months, especially on Sunday afternoons.

The best Cakes

Antico Bar Pasticceria Maggiora
See left.

Baratti & Milano
See p111.

Caffè Miretti
See p115.

Caffè Norman
See p113.

Caffè Torino
See p116.

Shops & Services

Whether you're looking to top up your designer wardrobe, your antiques collection or your wine cellar, you're unlikely to leave Turin empty-handed.

There's a dignified air to this city's baroque centre where 18 kilometres (11 miles) of porticos keep the rain off your retail-focused head and the grid streetplan makes it easy to locate just the elegant shop you want. As a counterbalance, there's a fast-growing multi-ethnic area around piazza della Repubblica, home to Europe's biggest open-air market (*see p120* **Bargain hunting**).

Whatever you're looking for, piazza Castello is a good point of departure for discovering all that this imaginative city has to offer.

Set off south along glittering via Roma for bourgeois boutiques and celebrated confectioners. Or head west up via Garibaldi for the cheap 'n' cheerful buzz of Europe's longest pedestrian precinct. Via Milano leads north from via Garibaldi towards piazza della Repubblica; don't be afraid of venturing into the narrow backstreets en route – you'll be pleasantly surprised by clusters of artsy emporia on via Bonelli and via delle Orfane. Parallel to via Garibaldi, via Barbaroux has antiques shops, home design, jewellers and candle shops. To the east of piazza Madama, via Po and piazza Vittorio have arcades to protect you from rain and sun as you browse through their eclectic mix of antiques, second-hand book stalls and affordable fashion shops.

ETIQUETTE
Falso e cortese (polite but false) is how other Italians describe the *torinesi*. You may encounter this stuffiness in the more elite shopping haunts where the unspoken rule is don't enter unless you intend to purchase. Elsewhere, however, shop assistants are generally polite and helpful. Entering shops with a warm *buongiorno* and *posso dare un'occhiata?* (may I look around?) breaks the ice.

WHEN TO SHOP
Weekdays are the best bet for a less hectic shopping experience. The bigger the retail crush, the more pickpockets may be lurking: keep your money in an inside pocket or a bag worn slung around your neck and avoid using rucksacks or backpacks, especially in the markets, since it's difficult to keep tabs on wandering hands.

All shops once followed the standard 9.30am-1pm and 3.30-7.30pm Monday to Saturday

opening hours; many don't close for lunch nowadays, and some remain open until later in the evening and/or on Sundays. Food shops and small supermarkets generally close on Wednesday afternoons. Non-food shops close on Monday mornings. In December central shops competing for Christmas cash open every Sunday.

Antiques

The richly stocked antiques shops of via Maria Vittoria and via della Rocca bear witness to the *torinese* love of luxurious decor. Rare prints and maps can be found in the **Galleria subalpina** (*see p69*) and second-hand books along via Po.

Books & prints

Bourlot
Piazza San Carlo 183, Centro (011 537 405).
Bus 11, 12/tram 4. **Open** 3-7.30pm Mon; 9.30am-12.30pm, 3-7.30pm Tue-Sat. **Credit** AmEx, DC, MC, V. **Map** p242 C3.
Expensive and exclusive, Bourlot has been in the antique books market since 1848.

Galleria Gilibert
Galleria Subalpina 17-19, Piazza Castello (011 561 9225). Bus 11, 12, 55, 56, 63/tram 13, 15. **Open** 9.30am-12.30pm, 3.30-7.30pm Tue-Sat. **Credit** AmEx, DC, MC, V. **Map** p242 C3.
This charming shop located inside the splendid Galleria subalpina (*see p69*) has rare editions but is also a good place to find special presents at affordable prices. There's a section housing unique prints and old Alpine guidebooks too.

Libreria Antiquaria Pregliasco
Via Accademia Albertina 3bis, Centro (011 817 7114). Bus 68/tram 18. **Open** 3.30-7.30pm Mon; 9am-12.30pm, 3.30-7.30pm Tue-Fri; 9am-12.30pm Sat. **Credit** AmEx, DC, MC, V. **Map** p243 C1.
Pregliasco has been around since 1913 and sells works mainly on Piedmont and Turin. Choose from around 140 prints of regional landscapes.

Furniture

Alternariato
Piazza Vittorio Veneto 16B, Centro (011 882 384). Bus 55, 56, 61/tram 13, 15. **Open** 3.30-7.30pm Mon; 10.30am-7pm Tue-Sat. Closed Aug. **Credit** AmEx, DC, MC, V. **Map** p243 C1.

This collection of 20th-century memorabilia ranges from the traditional to the very far-out. Pay a visit if you're into watches.

Galleria Luigi Caretto

Via Maria Vittoria 10, Centro (011 537 274/ www.galleriacaretto.com). Tram 18. **Open** 9.45am-12.30pm, 4-7.30pm Tue-Sat. **No credit cards. Map** p243 C1.

One of the city's best-known shops, it could be mistaken for a private museum. The collection is extensive and includes a range of precious period antiques. Caretto also houses its own private art gallery specialising in Flemish and Dutch art from the 16th and 17th centuries.

See also p128 **Mondadori Multicenter**. Many bookshops around the centre have an English language section. For local history or literature, it's worth browsing through the second-hand bookstalls along via Po (north side).

Bargain hunting

Turin is well served with produce markets (open 7.30am-1pm Mon-Fri; 7.30am-7.30pm Sat) which are to be found dotted all over town. One-off markets selling local organically-grown produce and crafts are a frequent occurrence: check at the tourist office (*see p228* **Atrium**) for upcoming events.

PORTA PALAZZO

Straggling across the rather shabby baroque Piazza della Repubblica, Europe's largest open-air market is known locally as Porta Palazzo. Once it sold produce brought to town by local farmers; nowadays it reflects the neighbourhood's rich ethnic mix in a dazzling jumble of hues, smells and wares.

Since 1996, Porta Palazzo and its surrounding area has been at the centre of a vast urban renewal scheme entitled The Gate – Living Not Leaving (for information, see www.comune.torino.it/portapalazzo), financed to a large extent by the European Union. As well as innumerable schemes to improve infrastructure (such as the vehicle underpass beneath piazza della Repubblica), housing standards, unemployment and crime records, and trading conditions in the traditionally run-down Porta Palazzo and Borgo Dora areas (*see pp60-63*), there are exciting architectural projects including Massimiliano Fuksas' extravagant zinc-roofed glass structure that will replace the old clothing market building in the north-west quadrant of the square.

Entering piazza della Repubblica from via Milano, you'll find yourself swamped in flowers, confectionery and cheap or second-hand 'fashion'. Give clothes a thorough once-over before buying: check that the size corresponds to the label, the seams are intact and there are no permanent stains.

Feeling peckish? Keep to the right (east) of the piazza and feast your eyes on stalls laden with seasonal fruit and vegetables from every region of Italy. Also nestling on this side is an unexpected section of affordable lingerie, kids' clothes and economical household wares, as well as tiny cafés where stall holders and happy shoppers munch slabs of pizza or arancini (fried Sicilian rice-balls filled with ham), all costing a fraction of the price you'd pay elsewhere in the city.

The large building on this same side houses one of Porta Palazzo's three indoor markets. Enter through swing doors located on its west, east and north facades and wend your way through a pungent array of stalls. Salted anchovies, sun-dried tomatoes, capers and olives are sold in easy-to-carry containers perfect for taking a little bit of Italy home.

Further to the north, corso Regina Margherita slices through the market. Beyond stands the Antica Tettoia dell'Orologio, with a large clock (orologio) above its north-west entrance. There's an abundance of fresh meat and offal, plus bread, cheeses, fresh pasta and wines. For excellent freshly-sliced Italian ham and salami try stand number

Feltrinelli

Piazza Castello 19 (011 541 627). Bus 12, 27, 50, 51, 55, 56, 57, 61, 63/tram 11, 13, 15, 18. **Open** 9am-7.30pm Mon-Sat; 10am-1pm, 3.30-7.30pm Sun. **Credit** AmEx, DC, MC, V. **Map** p242 C3.
One of Turin's biggest book stores.
Other location: Via Roma 80, Centro (011 530 869).

Figuriamoci – La Libreria del Fumetto

Via San Massimo 2B, Centro (011 817 2662/ www.figuriamoci.it). Bus 55, 56/tram 13, 15.

Open 10am-1pm, 3-7.30pm Tue-Sat. Closed 3wks Aug. **No credit cards**. **Map** p243 C1.
Hundreds of comics line the walls here alongside posters, toys, DVDs and videos.

Hellas International Bookshop

Via Bertola 6, Centro (011 546 941/www.hellas.it). Bus 12, 72/tram 4. **Open** 3-7.30pm Mon; 10am-7.30pm Tue-Sat. Closed Aug. **Credit** MC, V. **Map** p242 C3.
Book-hunt at your leisure in this friendly shop while chatting to one of the ex-language teachers working here. Books in English on local history are on sale.

six... then head down the aisle and out the swing doors from here to the selling-ground of local farmers. Piero sells mouth-watering cheeses: join his dedicated customers and queue patiently for gooey *paglierina*, aged *tome* and fresh ricotta. His jovial neighbour Walter sells home-made salami and ham that are oven-cooked by his mother.

Another set of swing doors straight ahead leads to the household goods section, with its dazzling selection of pots, pans, glasses, knives, chopping boards and coffee makers. To avoid paying over the odds ask how much something costs (*quanto costa?*) before agreeing to buy it (*va bene*).

Outside the Antica Tettoia to the west is shoe paradise.

Catch the green light at corso Regina Margherita and head for the stocky white building in front of you for marine life galore. Roll up trailing trouser legs before entering: the floor tends to get slushy. Sea bass, king prawns, squid, eels, crab, mussels, sardines and fresh anchovies entice cautious housewives who scrutinise fish eyes and bodies for the slightest sign of doubtful freshness.

Give yourself a well-deserved break after completing your tour of Porta Palazzo by making for piazza Emanuele Filiberto and the café called **Pastis** (*see p113*) where they mix one of the best mojitos in Turin.

Mercato di Porta Palazzo

Piazza della Repubblica. Bus 11, 12, 52, 63/tram 3, 4, 16. **Open** 7.30am-1pm Mon-Fri; 7.30am-7.30pm Sat.

IL BALON

No weekend stopover in Turin would be complete without a browse through Il Balon, the flea market that rambles through the streets (via Mameli, via Borgo Dora, via Lanino, via Andreis etc)

north of piazza della Repubblica and west of corso Giulio Cesare towards the river Dora Riparia. There's a preponderance of cheap tack, and imitations are rife, but a patient rake may well turn up an authentic antique. Balon is mainly a second-hand and antique furniture market. But you'll also find stalls selling second-hand clothes, books, household goods, knick-knacks and memorabilia. Every second Sunday of the month the market explodes into the Gran Balon (aka Baloon), when 200 stall-holders from all over Piedmont and even from France descend on these streets. If you're not up to the noisy bartering, or afraid to pull your cash out of your pocket in what can seem a dodgy end of town, do your buying in one of the little antiques shops or restorers' workshops in via Borgo Dora. Then head for **Trattoria Valenza** (*see p97*) for the tastiest *pasta e fagioli* in town.

Il (Gran) Balon

(Information 011 436 9741/ www.comune.torino.it). Bus 11, 12. **Open** 7.30am-7.30pm every Sat; 7.30am-1pm 2nd Sun of each month.

Luxemburg International Bookshop
Via Cesare Battisti 7, Centro (011 540 370/
luxbooks@libero.it). Tram 18. **Open** 8am-7.30pm
daily. **Credit** AmEx, DC, MC, V. **Map** p242 C3.
On the ground floor is a multilingual newsagent and
an Italian bookshop. English novels are located on
the second floor. It also stocks a collection of gay,
lesbian and Jewish publications.

Mood Libri e Caffè
*Via Cesare Battisti 3E, Centro (011 566 0809/fax
011 518 4077/www.moodlibri.it). Tram 18.* **Open**
Bookshop 10am-9pm Mon-Sat. *Café* 8am-9pm Mon-
Sat. Closed 1wk Aug. **Credit** MC, V. **Map** p242 C3.
In this funky café-bookshop you can shop, munch,
read, sip a glass of red and relax.

Department stores

La Rinascente
*Via Lagrange 15-17, Centro (011 561 1577).
Tram 18.* **Open** 1-8.30pm Mon; 9.30am-8.30pm
Tue-Fri; 9.30am-9pm Sat. **Credit** AmEx, DC, MC, V.
Map p242 D3.

No Carpano, no party

The evergreen cocktail favourite vermouth
had humble origins beneath the arcades
of piazza Castello, according to local lore.

Recently arrived in Turin from his native
town of Biella (*see p174*) in the 18th
century, craftsman Antonio Carpano kept
himself warm with his favourite tipple –
moscato wine – fortified with bitter herbs.
Such concoctions had long been made
for medicinal purposes by monks who
used wormwood (*wermuth* in German,
hence the name); but the scions of Turin's
upper class who flocked to this workshop-
turned-drinking-den were clearly not
thinking of their health. Duke Vittorio
Amedeo III held it in such high esteem that
he declared vermouth the court *aperitivo*.

Carpano's name lives on in one of the
more 'authentic' vermouths on the market:
Carpano Punt e Mes (meaning one point
sweet and half a point bitter). A little later
the Cinzano brothers patented their own
version, while Messers Martini and Rossi
started brewing just outside the city at
Pessione. Today vermouth accounts for
25 per cent of the Italian wines and spirits
exported worldwide. **Parola** (*see p126*)
has a good selection.

Over three floors, the Rinascente houses fashion,
watches, tableware, jewellery and cosmetics.

UPIM
*Via Roma 305, Centro (011 544 957). Bus 11, 12,
63/tram 4.* **Open** 1-8pm Mon; 9.30am-8pm Tue-Sat.
Credit AmEx, DC, MC, V. **Map** p242 D3.
A low-priced department store that stocks clothes
for men, women and children, plus underwear,
cosmetics and homeware.

Fashion

The city centre caters for all tastes and
budgets but you should also take time out to
see what Turin's young fashion designers are
coming up with. Via Roma (*map p242 CD3*) is
the catwalk of the city, a grand affair lined
with designer shops.

Designer labels

Emporio Armani
*Via Bruno Buozzi 5, Centro (011 562 5977/
www.emporioarmani.com). Bus 11, 12, 63/tram
4.* **Open** 3.30-7.30pm Mon; 10.30am-7.30pm Tue-
Sat. Closed 1wk Aug. **Credit** AmEx, DC, MC, V.
Map p242 D3.
The service is impressive in this large boutique.

Hermès
*Via Roma 124, Centro (011 546 971). Bus 11, 12,
63/tram 4.* **Open** 3-7pm Mon; 10am-1.30pm, 2.30-7pm
Tue-Sat. **Credit** AmEx, DC, MC, V. **Map** p242 C3.
Gossip… the only Hermès boutique in Europe that
doesn't print 'Hermès' on the bags because *torinesi*
ladies prefer to keep their shopping habits secret.

Massanova
*Via Roma 365, Centro (011 544 516). Bus 11, 12,
63/tram 4.* **Open** 10am-1pm, 3-7.30pm Mon, Wed,
Fri, Sat; 10am-7.30pm Tue, Thur. Closed 1wk Aug.
Credit AmEx, DC, MC, V. **Map** p242 C3.
Shopping at Massanova is costly but the mix
of labels on sale – from Moschino to Alberta Ferretti
– raises your chances of finding something you like.
Other location: Via Pietro Micca 1, Centro (011 549
261). Map p242 C3.

Top Ten
Via Soleri 2, Centro (011 535 360). Tram 18.
Open 3-7.30pm Mon; 10am-7.30pm Tue-Sat. Closed
1wk Aug. **Credit** AmEx, DC, MC, V. **Map** p242 D3.
Torino's trendsetters shop here for all the top labels
including Yamamoto, Prada and DKNY.

Mid-range fashion

La Bottega di Fulgenzi
*Via dei Mercanti 15B, Centro (011 562 4843). Bus
55, 56/tram 13, 15.* **Open** 3-7.30pm Mon; 10am-
12.30pm, 3-7.30pm Tue-Sat. Closed Aug. **Credit**
AmEx, MC, V. **Map** p242 C3.

This shop sells top-quality men's shirts in all sizes or made to order. Prices can be steep so keep an eye out for the sales.

Scali Promo
Via Po 18, Centro (011 889 302). Bus 55, 61/ tram 13, 15. **Open** 3.30-7.30pm Mon; 10am-2pm, 3.30-7.30pm Tue, Wed; 10am-7.30pm Thur-Sat. **No credit cards. Map** p243 C1.
Affordable, funky fashion for women.

Kids' clothes

Prime Vanità
Via XX Settembre 56, Centro (011 532 828). Bus 11, 12, 55, 56/tram 13, 15. **Open** 1-7.30pm Mon; 10am-7.30pm Tue-Fri; 9.30am-12.30pm, 3.30-7.30pm Sat. Closed 1wk Aug. **Credit** AmEx, DC, MC, V. **Map** p242 C3.
Well-made children's clothes at honest prices.

New names

Many top young designers showcase their wares in **via Bonelli** in the Quadrilatero district (*see pp60-63*). There are currently four (with more to come) funky boutiques with amazing window displays featuring the ultimate in quirky stuff. Some stay open late on Fridays and Saturdays.

Autopsie Vestimentaire
Via Bonelli 6B, Quadrilatero (011 436 0641). Bus 11, 12, 63/tram 4. **Open** 3-7.30pm Mon-Thur; 3-7.30pm, 10.30pm-midnight Fri, Sat. **Credit** AmEx, DC, MC, V. **Map** p242 C3.
Owner Alice makes the eye-catching garments that hang from the ceiling of this shop. Off-the-peg clothing for men and women changes with the seasons, but don't be shy to ask for something custom-made.

Galleria Piás
Via Bonelli 11A, Quadrilatero (011 436 1579/ galleriapias@libero.it). Bus 11, 12, 63/tram 4. **Open** 11am-9pm Tue-Sat. Closed 3wks Aug. **Credit** MC, V. Map p242 C3
This 'gallery' hosts collections by up-and-coming fashion designers. Clothes and accessories for women and men co-exist with a host of *objets*.

Scout
Via Mazzini 1, Centro (011 533 000). Bus 55, 56/tram 13, 15. **Open** 3-7.30pm Mon; 9.30am-1pm, 3-7.30pm Tue-Sat. Closed 1wk Aug. **Credit** AmEx, DC, MC, V. **Map** p243 D1.
There's an oh-so-modern vibe in this micro-boutique with its unusual collection of clothes for women.

Serienumerica
Via Bonelli 4C, Quadrilatero (011 436 9644). Bus 11, 12, 63/tram 4. **Open** 3.30-8.30pm Mon; 11am-1pm, 3.30-8.30pm Tue-Thur; 11am-1pm, 3.30-8.30pm, 10.30pm-midnight Fri, Sat. Closed 3wks Aug. **Credit** MC, V. **Map** p242 C3.

Unusual *objets* and styles at **Galleria Piás.**

If you want to give Italian haute couture a miss, Fulgenzi has affordable, ethnic attire from India, Thailand and the Far East.

Oltre
Via Garibaldi 22, Centro (011 521 7454). Bus 55, 56/tram 13, 15. **Open** 3.30-7.30pm Mon; 9.30am-7.30pm Tue-Sat. **Credit** DC, MC, V. **Map** p242 C3.
Competitively priced women's fashion. The clothes are well cut and the staff are welcoming. Don't miss the fab selection of fashion accessories.

Poncif
Piazza Vittorio Veneto 5, Centro (011 817 3040). Bus 55, 56/tram 13, 15. **Open** 3.30-7.30pm Mon; 10am-1pm, 3.30-7.30pm Tue-Thur, Sat; 10am-7.30pm Fri. Closed 2wks Aug, 1wk Jan, 1wk Feb. **Credit** AmEx, DC, MC, V. **Map** p243 C1.
Minimalist chic for women.

Promod
Via Roma 315, Centro (011 543 069). Bus 11, 12/tram 4. **Open** noon-8pm Mon; 9.30am-8pm Tue-Sat. **Credit** AmEx, DC, MC, V. **Map** p242 D3.
High street fashion at its best. Promod also sells accessories and footwear.

Ruffatti
Via Accademia delle Scienze 4, Centro (011 562 9294). Tram 18. **Open** 3.30-7.30pm Mon; 10am-1pm, 3-7.30pm Tue-Fri; 10am-7.30pm Sat. Closed 2wks Aug. **Credit** AmEx, DC, MC, V. **Map** p242 C3.

Eat, Drink, Shop

Rosella Lavatelli and Maria De Ambrogio work together to create their one-off garments for women. It's defiantly not cheap: a jacket goes for around €300; however, the stylish bags and accessories are more affordable.

Walter Dang – Atelier Couture

Via Bonelli 15C, Quadrilatero (011 438 0094). Bus 11, 12, 63/tram 4. **Open** 10.30am-1.30pm, 3.30-8pm Tue-Sat; 10pm-midnight Fri, Sat. **Credit** AmEx, MC, V. **Map** p242 C3.

Walter is from Paris; his partner is Italian. One experiments with fabric, the other with tableware and interior design. Some truly wild items of clothing are countered by a considerably tamer casual range. Tops are priced from €75; an evening creation can go for €500.

Leather & shoes

Italians love good shoes, bags and belts, and will hunt for the prized seconds of famous brands in markets. In Turin, head for the market in **via Marco Polo** (tram 10, 16) in the Crocetta district (*see p67*) where the fight for a 60 per cent-off pair of Missonis calls for some polite but firm elbow work.

Arbiter

Piazza Carlo Felice 35, Centro (011 547 074). Bus 9, 67, 35/tram 4. **Open** 3-7.30pm Mon; 9.30am-7.30pm Tue-Sat. **Credit** AmEx, DC, MC, V. **Map** p242 D3.

This spacious shop sells a decent choice of bags, gloves, wallets and suitcases, with prices ranging from very cheap to expensive.

Baronio

Via Garibaldi 46, Quadrilatero (011 436 6388/ pbaronio@alma.it). Bus 36, 72, 10/tram 13. **Open** 3.15-7.30pm Mon; 9am-1pm, 3.30-7.30pm Wed, Fri, Sat. Closed 1wk Aug. **Credit** AmEx, DC, MC, V. **Map** p242 C3.

Leather bags, suitcases, briefcases and wallets from upmarket names such as The Bridge, Prima Classe, Mandarina Duck and Calvin Klein.

Bertolini & Borse

Piazza Vittorio Veneto 8-9, Centro (011 812 7273/ www.bertolinieborse.com). Bus 55, 56/tram 13, 15. **Open** 3.30-7.30pm Mon; 9.30am-1pm, 3.30-7.30pm Tue-Sat. **Credit** AmEx, DC, MC, V. **Map** p243 C1.

A favourite haunt of *torinesi* with a passion for well-made designs: a vast selection of shoes, hats, scarves, umbrellas and bags.

Contigo

Via Garibaldi 16, Quadrilatero (011 436 7072). Bus 55, 56/tram 13, 15. **Open** 3.30-7.30pm Mon; 9.30am-7.30pm Tue-Sat. **Credit** AmEx, DC, MC, V. **Map** p242 C3.

The cheery staff in this boutique are quick off the mark and will help you to choose from the in-vogue range of shoes and boots and the selective range of glamorous evening wear.

Il Pallino

Via Godetti 7, Centro (011 535 637/ www.ilpallino.com). Tram 18. **Open** 3.30-7.30pm Mon; 10am-2pm, 3.30-7.30pm Tue; 10am-7.30pm Wed, Thur, Fri; 10am-1pm, 3-7.30pm Sat. **Credit** AmEx, MC, V. **Map** p242 D3.

Downstairs from the unadorned first floor, where you'll find mostly uninteresting clothes, there's a large selection of well-priced designer shoes for men and women.

Taccomatto

Via Garibaldi 21, Quadrilatero (011 562 8210). Bus 55, 56/tram 13, 15. **Open** noon-7.30pm Mon; 9.30am-12.30pm, 3.30-7.30pm Tue-Fri; 9.30am-7.30pm Sat. Closed 3wks Aug. **Credit** AmEx, MC, V. **Map** p242 C3.

Extravagant and a bit dear, the shoes and boots for men and women in Taccomatto are ideal if you're looking for something unusual.

Food & drink

Supermarkets

You'll have to schlep to the outskirts of the city to find massive Auchan, Carrefour and GS supermarkets.

Dì per dì

Via Santa Teresa 19F, Centro (011 549 715). Bus 5, 14, 55, 56/tram 13, 15. **Open** 8.30am-8pm Mon, Tue, Thur-Sat; 8.30am-2pm Wed. **Credit** DC, MC, V. **Map** p243 D2.

Right in the heart of the city, this supermarket has all the usual fare plus fresh bread, fruit and veg. **Other location:** Via Maria Vittoria 11, Centro (011 883 115). Map p243 C1.

Shopville Le Gru

Via Crea 10, Suburbs: west (011 770 9665). Bus 17. **Open** 9am-10pm Mon-Sat; 9am-9pm 1st Sun of mth. **Credit** depends on shop. **Map** p241.

Turin's biggest shopping mall, replete with hypermarkets, is a 30-minute bus ride from the centre of town.

Local food & wine

Borgiattino

Corso Vinzaglio 29, Cittadella (011 562 9075). Tram 10. **Open** 8.30am-1pm, 4-7.30pm Mon, Tue, Thur-Sat. Closed Aug. **Credit** AmEx, V. **Map** p242 C2.

The Borgiattino family has been selling fine cheeses from this shop since 1927. Dino, the friendly owner, always slices a sliver for you to sample. Try the toma or robiola cheeses from Piedmont's Alpine valleys. **Other location:** Via Cernaia, Cittadella (011 535 237).

Casa del Barolo

Via Andrea Doria 7, Centro (011 532 038). Tram 18. **Open** 3-7.30pm Mon; 9am-12.30pm, 3-7.30pm Tue-Sat. **Credit** AmEx, DC, MC, V. Closed 3wks Aug. **Map** p242 D3.

Eat, Drink, Shop

Pralines and candies at **Stratta**.

Just off piazza San Carlo, Casa del Barolo is more a gourmet boutique than a wine shop, with its soft lighting and pale wooden shelves. Select a bottle of Barolo and a local gastronomic delight for reminiscing over your holiday when you get back home.

Parola

Corso Vittorio Emanuele II 76A, Cittadella (011 544 939). Bus 9, 68. **Open** 3-7.30pm Mon; 9am-1pm, 3-7.30pm Tue-Wed; 9am-7.30pm Thur-Fri; 9am-1pm, 3-7.30pm Sat. Closed 2wks Aug. **No credit cards.** **Map** p242 D3.
There has been a wine shop here since 1890; excellent for first-rate Italian and international wines and grappa. Staff will arrange for international delivery.

Steffanone

Via Maria Vittoria 2, Centro (011 546 737/ www.steffanone.com). Bus 68/tram 15. **Open** 8.30am-1pm, 4-7.30pm Mon, Tue; 8.30am-1pm Wed; 8.30am-7.30 pm Thur-Sat. Closed 1wk Aug. **Credit** AmEx, DC, MC, V. **Map** p242 C3.
A huge variety of specialist produce: fine wine, quality olive oil, aged balsamic vinegar, cheese, foie gras, caviar, white truffles and raw ham.

Cakes & confectionery

Some of Europe's best chocolate has long been made in Turin by family-run businesses. (*See p34* **Cioccolato**).

Gerla

Corso Vittorio Emanuele II 88, Cittadella (011 545 422). Bus 9, 68. **Open** 9am-7.30pm Tue-Sat; 8.30am-1pm Sun. Closed 1wk Aug. **Credit** AmEx, MC, V. **Map** p242 D3.
This small but exquisitely decorated cake shop brims with local delicacies such as marrons glacés and innovative creations such as chocolate 'salami'. The famous chocolate and hazel-nut *torta sabauda* is divine with afternoon tea.
Other location: Via Principi d'Acaja 12, Suburbs: west (011 434 2821).

Gertosio

Via Lagrange 34, Centro (011 562 1942). Bus 68/tram 15. **Open** 8am-7.30pm Tue-Sat; 8am-1pm Sun. Closed 1wk Aug. **Credit** AmEx, MC, V. **Map** p242 C3.
Divine mini-choux pastries and 50 mouth-watering varieties of praline chocolate.

Guido Gobino

Via Cagliari 15B, Suburbs: north (011 247 6245/ www.guidogobino.it). Bus 68. **Open** 8.30am-12.30pm, 2.30-6pm Mon-Fri; 8.30am-12.30pm Sat. **Credit** MC, V. **Map** p243 B1
Best known among chocolate afficionados for inventing the *turinot* – a mini-*gianduiotto* (*see p34*) – Gobino is currently one of the highest-rated chocolatiers in Turin.

Peyrano

Corso Vittorio Emanuele II 76, Cittadella (011 538 765/www.peyrano.com). Bus 9, 68. **Open** 9.30am-8pm Tue-Sat; 9.30am-1pm Sun. **Credit** MC, V. **Map** p242 D3.
Ready to spend? Enter the Peyrano family confectioners: 90 different types of chocolate plus great biscuits and pastries… overshadowed by unbearably complacent staff. Don't let them put you off though. If you can only try one thing, make it the Alpine: mini-cups of hazel-nut milk chocolate with liqueur filling, made to a jealously guarded secret recipe.

Stratta

Piazza San Carlo 191, Centro (011 547 920). Bus 11, 12, 63/tram 4, 18. **Open** 3-7.30pm Mon; 9.30am-7.30pm Tue-Sat. **Credit** AmEx, DC, MC, V. **Map** p242 C3.
The beautiful shop windows of this old shop – it first opened in 1836 – reveal a fine display of candies, sweets, chocolates, pralines, marrons glacés and candied fruit set amidt precious crystal and wood.

Healthfood

A&G di Claudia Avonti

Via Bertola 26B, Cittadella (011 544 652). Bus 11,12/tram 4. **Open** 1-7.30pm Mon; 10am-2.30pm, 4-7.30pm Tue-Sat. Closed 2wks Aug. **Credit** AmEx, MC, V. **Map** p242 C2.
This shop sells a wide assortment of fresh organic fruit and vegetables, as well as sugar-free sweets, bread and tofu.

Eat, Drink, Shop

Sesamo Macrobiotica

Via Berthollet 4, Centro (011 650 3874). Tram 18. **Open** 9.30am-7.30pm Mon, Tue, Thur-Sat; 9.30am-1.30pm Wed. **Credit** MC, V. **Map** p245 A1.
Sesamo attracts a young, health-conscious crowd. It is also a deli and sells some wholesome takeaway meals at very affordable prices.

Gifts & houseware

De Carlo

Via Cesare Battisti 5, Centro (011 561 3378/ www.decarlo.org). Tram 18. **Open** 3-7pm Mon; 9.30am-1pm, 3-7.30pm Tue, Wed, Fri, Sat; 9.30am-7.30pm Thur. **Credit** AmEx, MC, V. **Map** p242 C2.
This rather pricey shop has a great selection of kitchen and tableware as well as top-quality shaving equipment. Wine glasses, espresso cups, copper pans and chopping boards in abundance.

Luigi Conterno di Colenghi

Piazza Solferino 3, Centro (011 562 2550). Bus 5, 14. **Open** 3.30-7.30pm Mon; 9am-12.30pm, 3.30-7.30pm Tue-Sat. Closed Aug. **No credit cards.** **Map** p242 C3.
Conterno's has been producing beautiful hand-finished candles since 1795.

Tendenze

Corso Vittorio Emanuele II 74, Cittadella (011 517 2591/www.tendenzetorino.it). Bus 9, 14, 68. **Open** 3.30-7.30pm Mon; 9.30am-1pm, 3.30-7.30pm Wed, Fri, Sat; 9.30am-7.30pm Tue, Thur. Closed 1wk Aug. **Credit** AmEx, MC, V. **Map** p242 C3.
An amusing choice of 'design' objects and gadgets.

Valentina

Piazza Vittorio Veneto 12C, Centro (011 882 076). Bus 55, 56, 61/tram 13, 15. **Open** 9am-12.30pm, 2.30-6.30pm Tue-Fri; 9am-noon Sat. Closed 2wks Aug. **No credit cards.** **Map** p243 C1.
Exquisite antique glass lamps, bowls and containers. Purchases are artfully gift-wrapped by the staff.

Jewellery & watches

Cosimo di Lilla – Gioielli Imprevedibili

Via dei Mercanti 15C, Centro (011 562 7680/ www.cosimodililla.com). Bus 55, 56/tram 13, 15. **Open** 9am-12.30pm, 3-7.30pm Tue-Sat. Closed 2wks Aug. **Credit** AmEx, DC, MC, V. **Map** p242 C3.
The creations of this intriguing jeweller are indeed *imprevedibili* (unpredictable) and combine real craftsmanship with precious materials.

Gioielleria Fasano

Via Roma 325, Centro (011 530 225). Bus 11, 12, 63/tram 4. **Open** 9.30am-1pm, 3.30-7.30pm Tue-Sat. Closed Aug. **Credit** AmEx, DC, MC, V. **Map** p242 C3.
Fasano is a distinguished jeweller specialising in gold and precious gems. It may be hard to get in the door if you're not sporting just the 'right' look.

Blue Spirit & Blue Watch

Piazza Castello 60 & 66, Piazza Castello (011 562 0404). Bus 11, 12, 55/tram 13, 15. **Open** 3-7.30pm Mon; 10am-7.30pm Tue-Sat. **Credit** AmEx, MC, V. **Map** p242 C3.
This fashion jeweller has a second shop (next door) dealing in watches.

Gold and precious gems at **Gioielleria Fasano**.

Music

Les Yper Sound
Via Rossini 14, Centro (011 812 0152). Bus 68.
Open 3-7.30pm Mon; 10am-7.30pm Tue-Fri; 10am-1pm, 3-7.30pm Sat. Closed Aug. **Credit** MC, V.
Map p243 C1.
This shop sells new and used LPs and CDs. There are frequent prize finds, particulalry prog, psychedelic and vinyl from the 1960s and '70s, although all musical tastes are catered to.

Mondadori Multicenter
Via Monte di Pietà 2, Centro (011 577 8811/ www.informatica.mondadori.com). Bus 11, 12, 63/tram 13, 15, 4. **Open** 9.30am-8pm Mon-Sat; 10am-8pm Sun. **Credit** AmEx, DC, MC, V.
Map p242 C3.
Three floors bursting with CDs, bestsellers, computers, mobile phones, DVDs, video cameras and much more. There's a play area for children and an internet point.

Ricordi Mediastore
Piazza CLN 251, Centro (011 562 0830). Tram 18.
Open 9am-7.30pm Mon-Sat; 10am-1pm, 3.30-7.30pm Sun. **Credit** AmEx, DC, MC, V. **Map** p242 D3.
Music-lovers will enjoy the buzz in Ricordi. The young, helpful staff will point you in the right direction; the huge selecion includes chart hits, jazz, blues, soul and rock. There's a ticket agency in the store selling tickets for concerts and events of all descriptions all over the country.

Rock & Folk
Via Bogino 4, Centro (011 839 4542). Bus 55, 56, 61/tram 13, 15. **Open** 3.30-7.30pm Mon; 9.30am-2pm, 3.30-7.30pm Tue-Sat. **Credit** DC, MC, V.
Map p243 C1.
Turin's biggest but also most expensive specialised music store. Two shops are right next door to each other: one sells CDs and videos, the other vinyl.

Perfumes and cosmetics

Douglas
Via Roma 95, Centro (011 539 917/www.douglas.it). Bus 11, 12, 63/tram 4. **Open** 3-7.30pm Mon; 9.30am-7.30pm Tue-Sat. **Credit** AmEx, DC, MC, V. **Map** p242 C3.
A mecca of special offers. Deep plastic tubs full of discounted perfume and cosmetics flank the entrance.

La Recolte
Via Cosmo 9, Collina (011 8193049). Bus 53, 56, 61, 66/tram 13. **Open** 3.30-7.30pm Mon; 9am-12.30pm, 3.30-7.30pm Tue-Sat. Closed 3wks Aug.
No credit cards. Map p243 C2.
A qualified herbalist, Mariarosa Panizzolo will give friendly advice on herbal remedies and prepare them for you. Shop for natural cosmetics, anti-ageing creams, Bach remedies, ointments for ailments such as stiff joints, and pure wax candles.

Services

Beauty, hair & health
Italian hairdressers are generally open on Saturdays but shut on Mondays. All but the trendiest places will do your hair without an appointment; for famous snippers you'll have to book and wait.

Blue Sun
Piazza Cavour 6, Centro (011 547 077). Tram 18.
Open 2-8pm Mon; 9.30am-8pm Tue-Sat. Closed 1wk Aug. **Credit** AmEx, DC, MC, V. **Map** p243 D1.
Blue Sun offers waxing, a variety of beauty treatments and a solarium.

Forbie
Piazza Castello 83, Piazza Castello (011 545 161). Bus 11, 12, 55/tram 13, 15. **Open** 2-7.30pm Mon, Wed; 10am-7.30pm Tue, Thur; 10am-9pm Fri, Sat. Closed 1wk Aug. **Credit** MC, V. **Map** p242 C3.
Cheap prices (€12 for a wash and blow-dry) plus rapid service. Note its particular opening hours.

Franco Curletto
Corso Francesco Ferrucci 34A, Suburbs: west (011 433 6000). Bus 9. **Open** 8am-6pm Tue-Sat.
Credit AmEx, DC, MC, V. **Map** p244 A1.
Super-stylish unisex hair boutique. Said to be one of Italy's best for scissor skills, the Franco experience will set you back a few euros if you manage to get an appointment.

L'Oasi
Piazza Statuto 5, Cittadella (011 544 587). Bus 55, 56/tram 1, 10. **Open** 9am-7pm Tue-Sat. **Credit** MC, V. **Map** p242 C2.
Solarium, aromatherapy, anti-stress, firming and toning massages, pedicures and manicures for men and women.

Fax & photocopying

FUSA
Via Monte di Pietà 16, Centro (011 538 498/ 011 562 9205). Bus 55, 56/tram 13, 15. **Open** 9am-12.30pm, 3-7pm Mon-Fri. Closed 2wks Aug.
No credit cards. Map p242 C3.
Fax, photocopying and couriers, plus a selection of software and stationery.

Laundry & dry-cleaning

Billandi
Via della Misericordia 6, Cittadella (011 562 1866). Bus 67. **Open** 9am-7.30pm Mon-Sat. Closed 3wks Aug. **No credit cards. Map** p242 C2.
If you're feeling decadent opt for this upmarket dry cleaners: garments are treated to perfection, wrapped in perfumed paper and delivered to the customer for a hefty sum.

Eat, Drink, Shop

Blue Surf

Piazza della Repubblica 1D, Quadrilatero (011 521 7925). Bus 11, 12, 63/tram 3, 4, 16. **Open** 9am-7.30pm daily. **No credit cards.** **Map** p242 B3.
You might have to wait a bit for your turn but this self-service laundrette is conveniently central. €3.50 for a 7kg wash, € 6 for a 16kg wash and €3.50 to spin dry.

Opticians

Grand Optical

Via Arcivescovado 1, Centro (011 440 7496). Bus 11, 12, 58/tram 4. **Open** 3.30-7.30pm Mon; 9.30am-7.30pm Tue-Sat. **Credit** AmEx, MC, V. **Map** p242 D3.
The efficient staff at Grand Optical will carry out minor repairs to glasses free of charge or replace broken lenses (if in stock) within one hour. The shop can also make up a pair of prescription glasses in the same day.

Salmoiraghi & Viganò

Via Roma 33, Centro (011 562 9062/ www.salmoiraghivigano.it). Bus 11, 12/tram 4. **Open** 3.30-7.30pm Mon; 9.30am-7.30pm Tue-Sat. **Credit** AmEx, DC, MC, V. **Map** p242 D3.
Minor adjustments are done at no cost and replacement lenses priced from €40 can supplied within 24 hours.

Pharmacies

When closed, all pharmacies have *farmacie aperte/farmacie di turno* notices pinned up outside telling you where the nearest open shop is. For further information check www.farmapiemonte.org.

Carlo Felice

Piazza Carlo Felice 63, Centro (011 547 626). Bus 35/tram 18. **Open** 9am-12.30pm, 3-7.30pm Mon-Sat. Closed 3wks Aug. Closed Aug. **Credit** AmEx, MC, V. **Map** p242 D3.
Staff at this pharmacy are attentive, ready to listen and speak English.

Farmacia Centrale del Dottor Santomartino

Via Roma 24, Centro (011 562 8018). Bus 11, 12/tram 4. **Open** 9am-12.45pm, 3.15-7.30pm Mon-Sat. **Credit** AmEx, MC,V. **Map** p242 D3.
This pharmacy is convenient because of its central location but staff can be very unfriendly.

Farmacia Degli Stemmi

Via Po 31, Centro (011 817 3027). Bus 55, 56/ tram 13,15. **Open** 9am-1pm, 3-7.30pm daily. **No credit cards.** **Map** p243 C1.
One of Turin's oldest pharmacies, Degli Stemmi stocks many homeopathic remedies. Even if you're not suffering from an ailment pay a visit just to see the original wooden furnishings.

Photo developers

24-hour developing is more common than one-hour service so time it wisely if you're impatient to see your snaps while still on holiday.

Europhoto

Piazza Carlo Felice 23, Centro (011 562 9452). Bus 35/tram 18. **Open** 3-7.30pm Mon; 9am-7.30pm Tue-Sat. **Credit** AmEx, DC, MC, V. **Map** p242 D3.
Photos are developed in 24 hours; you can also shop for cameras, eyewear, GPS toys, suitcases and mobile phones.

Rapid Foto

Via XX Settembre 1, Centro (011 546 085). Bus 11, 12, 63/tram 4. **Open** 9am-6.30pm Mon-Fri. **No credit cards.** **Map** p242 C3.
Your photos will be developed in 23 minutes. Services include instant ID photographs, enlargements and reprints.

Ticket agents

See p128 **Ricordi Mediastore** and *p228* **Atrium**.

Travel agents

BoPa

Stazione di Porta Nuova, Centro (011 534 663). Bus 5, 12, 14, 33, 34, 35, 50, 52, 57, 59, 63, 64, 65, 67//tram 4, 9, 15, 18. **Open** 8am-7.30pm Mon-Fri; 9am-4.30pm Sat, Sun. **Credit** AmEx, DC, MC, V. **Map** p242 D3.
This agency inside the main train station handles railway tickets, hotel reservations, shuttles to Turin and Milan airports, international bus lines and Interrail. You can also book airline tickets, holidays and tours.

Cit Viaggi

Piazza San Carlo 205, Centro (011 562 5652/ www.citonline.com). Tram 18. **Open** 9am-1pm, 2.30-6.30pm Mon-Fri; 9am-1pm Sat. **Credit** AmEx, DC, MC, V. **Map** p242 C3.
Cruises, hotel bookings, car hire, airline and railway tickets.

Last Minute Tour Torino

Via Pietro Micca 20, Cittadella (011 532 022/ toll-free 800 133 331/www.lastminutetour.com). Bus 55, 56/tram 13, 15. **Open** 9.30am-7.30pm Mon-Sat. **Credit** AmEx, V. **Map** p242 C3.
The database has anything from last-minute short breaks in Italy to package deals.

Rive Gauche Viaggi

Via Cernaia 18, Cittadella (011 562 7688/ www.rivegauche.it). Bus 55, 56/tram 13, 15. **Open** 9am-12.30pm, 3-7.30pm Mon-Fri. **Credit** AmEx, DC, MC, V. **Map** p242 C2.
Rive Gauche always has special offers that can also be booked online.

Eat, Drink, Shop

The Italian Job

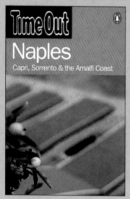

Available from all good bookshops
and at www.timeout.com/shop

Arts & Entertainment

Features

Festivals & Events

Whether you're a culture buff, a party animal or just love good food,
Turin's calendar of events has something for everyone.

For events outside Turin, *see p168* **Piedmont By Season**. For national holidays, *see p230* **When to go**. For jazz and blues festivals, *see p150*. For the Torino Settembre Musica festival, *see p156*.

While all trace of the lavish festivities, masquerades, jousting tournaments, balls and pageants that were so much a part of life under the Savoys (*see p10* **The unstoppable Savoys**) have virtually disappeared, Turin's long and fruitful relationship with music and the theatre remains a driving force in its programme of annual festivities. Also featuring large in today's events are celebrations of the city as cradle of culture (film) and industry (cars), not to mention its long-running dedication to seriously good food and truly excellent wine.

Spring

Festa della Donna
Date 8 Mar.
International Women's Day is celebrated with a sprig of mimosa being given to every woman by family, friends, employers, shops, restaurants… plus theatre concessions, debates, exhibitions etc.

Giornate FAI
Fondo per l'Ambiente Italiano (FAI), via F Dellala 32. **Information** 011 530 979/www. fondoambiente.it. **Date** 1 weekend in Mar or Apr.
For just one weekend each year the non-profit FAI organisation persuades private owners and institutions to open the doors to historic properties that are generally kept under lock and key. Guided tours are given to huge numbers of visitors.

Turin Marathon
Information 011 663 1231/www.turinmarathon.it. **Date** Apr.
This international event attracts vast crowds of both runners and cheering public over its 42km course, which winds through the city, along the river and out into the suburbs, finishing in the central Parco del Valentino (*see p80*). For the slightly less fit, there's the *Stratorino*, a 12km fun-run around the centre of town held in May (information: www.joyfulpromo.it/stra).

Settimana dei Beni Culturali
Information toll-free 800 991 199/ www.beniculturali.it. **Date** usually spring.

All public museums and monuments are open free of charge for Cultural Heritage Week and many normally closed properties open specially for the occasion.

Da Sodoma a Hollywood – Turin International Gay and Lesbian Film Festival
Teatro Nuovo, corso Massimo d'Azeglio 17, Lingotto. Bus 45, 67/tram 9, 16. **Information** 011 534 888/www.turinglfilmfestival.com. **Date** Apr. **Map** p245 C1.
Started in 1981, this festival has gone from strength to strength to become one of the most highly acclaimed of its type in Europe (*see p141*).

Primo Maggio
Piazza San Carlo, Centro. Tram 15. **Date** 1 May. **Map** p242 C3.
This public holiday is celebrated by trade unions with processions converging for the main demonstration in piazza San Carlo. Afterwards participants traditionally disperse to the countryside for long, winey lunches.

Fiera Internazionale del Libro
Lingotto Fiere, via Nizza 280, Lingotto. Bus 35/tram 1, 18. **Information** 011 518 4268/ www.fieralibro.it. **Open** 10am-11pm. **Date** early May. **Admission** €7; €18 day pass; student concessions. **No credit cards. Map** p247 A2.
This book fair is a high point in the cultural calendar of Turin, attracting vast crowds. For five days you can visit the stands of more than 1,000 publishers, purchase every sort of book, seek out the smallest and least-known presses, attend meetings and signings with important international authors, take part in furious debates about the thorny question of paper versus net, or attend conferences on all aspects of publishing.

Torino e Oltre
Ticket office AtriumCittà, piazza Solferino, Cittadella. Tram 15. **Information** 011 443 9040/ toll-free 800 015 475/ www.torinocultura.it. **Open** 11am-6pm Mon-Sat though subject to change. **Tickets** €1.80-€6. **Date** May-June, Sept-Nov. **No credit cards. Map** p242 C3.
Held in spring and autumn, these guided tours (given in Italian only) in and around Turin reveal the historical, artistic and architectural heritage of this city founded by the Romans. This event offers myriad different itineraries and visits, led by experts and volunteer guides from the city's cultural associations. It recently added a modern art itinerary.

Luci d'artista. *See p134.*

Summer

Experimenta

Parco Michelotti, corso Casale 15, Collina. Bus 61, 75/tram 3. **Information** 011 819 0403/toll-free 800 329 329/www.experimenta.to.it. **Open** *June-mid Sept* 4pm-midnight Tue-Fri; 3pm-midnight Sat; 10am-8pm Sun. *Mid Sept-1st wk of Nov* 3-8pm Tue-Sat; 10am-8pm Sun. **Admission** €6.50; €4 under-6s. **No credit cards. Map** p243 B3.

A fun, hands-on way to discover the scientific aspects of the city and the world we live in. Themes vary annually. *See also p137.*

Processione della Consolata

Chiesa della Consolata, piazza della Consolata, Quadrilatero. Bus 52, 60. **Information** 011 436 3235. **Date** 20 June. **Map** p242 C2.

A prayer-fest in preceding days culminates in the procession of the Madonna, accompanied by huge torch-bearing crowds of believers (and non-believers) that leave the basilica of the Consolata (*see p61*), Turin's religious core, after dusk to wind through the narrow streets of the old city.

Festa di San Giovanni

Murazzi, piazza Vittorio Veneto, Centro. Bus 55, 56, 61/tram 13, 15, 16. **Date** 24 June. **Map** p243 D1-C2.

The city shuts down to celebrate its patron St John with various events throughout the day, culminat-

ing in spectacular fireworks after dark on the river bank and bridge by piazza Vittorio – a vestige of lavish 17th-century firework displays.

Chicobum Festival

Parco Chico Mendes, via Carolina, Borgaro Torinese. **Information** 011 819 4347/www.barrumba.com.

Held slightly out of town (you'll need your own transport to get there), this mainly rock music event is one of the city's important summer music festivals, featuring famous and not-so-famous Italian groups, plus internationally known bands on the main stage. Past festivals have seen artists like Alanis Morissette and Subsonica. As well as concerts, the festival offers many clubbing opportunities: dance nights organised by Xplosiva (*see p148*) feature top electro and house DJs (Coccoluto, Jeff Miles etc).

Rowing regattas

River Po, between bridges Vittorio Emanuele I & Isabella. **Information** www.canottaggiopiemonte.it. **Date** summer. **Map** p243, p245.

Turin boasts a number of historic rowing clubs and various regattas are organised annually.

Traffic Torino Free Festival

Parco delle Pellerina. **Information** toll-free 800 015 475/www.extrafestival.com. **Date** July. **Admission** varies with event. **No credit cards. Map** p241.

Arts & Entertainment

festival of Turin; ·ous city associations, ·afestival manages to ·st bands – Massive Brothers have been ·ay alongside up-and-·so dance displays, ·hts' in clubs around ·r-known DJs.

Rivelazioni Barocche

Various (baroque) venues. **Information** SPABA, via Napione 2, 011 817 7178/toll-free 800 329 329/ www.piemonte-emozioni.it. Tram 15. **Open** *Office* 3-6pm Mon, Wed-Fri; 10am-noon Tue. **Date** mid Aug-Nov. **Map** p243 C2.

Free, expertly guided visits to the city's baroque monuments and buildings, many of which are usually closed to the public.

Autumn

Torino Settembre Musica

Various venues. **Information** www.comune. torino.it/settembremusica. **Date** Sept.

A classical music festival that attracts major performers like Vladimir Ashkenazy, Salvatore Accardo and Uto Ughi. It also includes work by contemporary composers and, since 1997, ethnic music from Africa, China, the Himalayas and Java. (*See also* p156 **Torino Settembre Musica**.)

Identità e Differenza

Various venues. **Information** toll-free 800 015 475/ www.comune.torino.it/cultura/intercultura. **Date** Sept-Oct.

A festival of inter-racial culture to showcase the art, traditions and gastronomy of Turin's now multiracial population.

Salone del Gusto

Lingotto Fiere, via Nizza 230, Lingotto. **Bus** 35/tram 1, 18. **Information** 011 562 3309/ 436 731/www.slowfood.it/www.lingottofiere.it. **Open** 11am-1pm. **Date** Oct (even years only). **Admission** €18. **Credit** AmEx, DC, MC, V. **Map** p247 A2.

A must for all foodies everywhere. Organised by Slow Food (*see* p31 **Slow and steady**) and the regional council, this event celebrates great food and enjoyable eating. Thousands of stands from all over Italy – and further afield – provide tastes of regional specialities.

Torino Film Festival

Pathè Multiplex, via Nizza 230, Lingotto. Bus 35/tram 2, 18. **Information** 011 562 3309/ www.torinofilmfest.org. **Date** Nov. **Admission** variety of passes from €5-€60; €6.50 daytime showings; €9 evening showings. **No credit cards. Map** p247 A2.

The most important film festival in Italy after Venice, the Turin event specialises in young film-makers, avant-garde cinema, non-European

film production and fascinating in-depth retrospectives. It has made its mark on the international film circuit too (*see* p141).

Artissima

Lingotto Fiere, via Nizza 260, Lingotto. **Bus** 35/tram 1, 18. **Information** 011 546 284/ www.artissima.it. **Date** Nov. **Admission** €9. **Credit** AmEx, DC, MC, V. **Map** p247 A2.

An internationally respected fair of contemporary art hosting stands of at least 180 galleries from all over the world that display the most recent tendencies in modern art. Alongside renowned galleries, there are special sections for new galleries and young artists.

Winter

Luci d'Artista

Monuments, squares & streets throughout the city. **Information** 011 535 181/www.torinoarte contemporanea.it. **Date** Nov-Jan.

In the winter months the city of Turin is lit up with art installations in light by world-acclaimed Italian – and now also international – artists. Christmas lights with a definite difference, they make a wonderful change from the usual baubles.

Turin Christmas Street Fair

For two weeks in December Turin's Christmas market takes place in the Cortile de Maglio, in the suitably atmospheric Borgo Dora. Every year there's a different theme, expounded by vendors from all over the country.

Natale & Santo Stefano

The city closes down over the Christmas period as the *torinesi* move en masse to their mountain houses, preferring white snowy surroundings for their traditional Christmas (*Natale*) dish of *agnolotti* and a little light skiing to recover on Boxing Day (Santo Stefano).

Capodanno

Piazza San Carlo, Centro. **Bus** 12, 27, 50, 51, 55, 56, 57, 61, 63/tram 11, 13, 15, 18. **Map** p242 C3.

Those *torinesi* who decamped to the mountains for Christmas might well return to the city for New Year's Eve and the open-air concert organised by City Hall in the most beautiful piazza in the city, or for an evening of feasting at *cenoni* (banquets) at city restaurants. Others will make the reverse trip to eat their New Year good-luck plate of *lenticchie e cotecchino* (lentils and pig's trotter) on the ski slopes amid the *fiaccolate* – torch-lit ski processions.

CiccolaTO

Throughout central Turin. **Information** 011 442 2369/www.cioccola-to.com. **Date** last wk Feb-mid March.

Chocolate gets its sticky fingers into events all around town, from tastings to literary encounters to photography exhibitions, in diverse indoor and outdoor venues including clubs, restaurants and historic buildings.

Children

From car museums to puppet shows, there's loads to keep kids busy in Turin.

Not only is Turin surprisingly green, it's also remarkably small-user-friendly, thanks to dedicated work by the local council and cultural associations, which have spearheaded a host of extracurricular activities for schools and are now, with the 2006 Winter Olympics approaching, creating an avalanche of child-related initiatives on the slopes (*see pp206-14*).

Other Italians consider the *torinesi* reserved and driven by an almost Calvinistic sense of order and duty. This parlays into a most un-Italian resistance to children being present in grown-up situations. In smarter restaurants, alarmed waiters will pointedly whisk knives, forks, plates and glasses out of the reach of childish fingers; humbler establishments will do their best to make the whole family welcome.

A hard core of tried-and-tested museums (many of which organise special activities for children), adventure playgrounds and theme parks make this once-industrial city a fun place

to visit. If their appeal doesn't do the trick, there is always the persuasive power of Turin's delicious chocolate (*see p34* **Cioccolata**). And remember, if you happen to be here immediately pre-Lent, get your child a Carnevale (mardi gras) costume and let them join the dressing-up fun.

For further information on child-oriented events, look in the kids' section of *Torino Sette*, the supplement that comes with Friday's *La Stampa*. It's in Italian, but easy to follow.

TRANSPORT

Turin's city centre is small enough to cover on foot and 18 kilometres (11 miles) of covered *portici* mean that this is an option whatever the weather conditions. A number of pedestrianised *piazze* – including piazza Castello (*see pp52-9*), with its geyser-like fountains bubbling up from beneath the paving stones to the delight of every child – and the longest pedestrian promenade in Europe along via Garibaldi (*see p62*) make walking even more pleasant.

Bus and tram services are frequent, but often crowded; hopping on is often an ordeal with a pushchair. Toddlers and obviously pregnant women will courteously be offered a seat. Children under a metre high travel free. Above that, you need to get a full-price ticket for them (*see also p217*).

When your offspring refuses to take another step, you could do worse than putting him/her on one of the heavy trams that trundle at a donkey's pace through the majestic streets. The No.13 is perfect for this. From piazza Statuto it grinds down to piazza Castello – where, if the weather is hot, you might consider a splash in the aforementioned fountains – then continues down via Po to piazza Vittorio Veneto (*see p77*), in recent years the unlikely stage for snowboarding championships in winter, when a colossal ski jump is constructed and snow machines are brought in to smother everything in the fluffy, white raw material. Crossing the river, you should have (fog permitting) a splendid view of Monviso (*see p201*) on your right in the distance. The tram ride terminates across the river in piazza Gran Madre di Dio, conveniently close to Experimenta (*see p137*).

Italian cars (and their drivers) are to children what Captain Hook is to Peter Pan. The best place to see them up close is in the Museo dell'automobile (*see p88*).

Arts & Entertainment

Let your children share in **Carnevale** fun. *See p135.*

Sightseeing

Mummified Egyptian royalty and their pets and faithfully reconstructed tombs in the **Museo Egizio** (*see p71*) are guaranteed to grip your children's imaginations. Across the street inside curvy Palazzo Carignano, the **Museo del Risorgimento** (*see p72*) documents the birth of united Italy in an extensive collection of pikes, axes and other implements for doing away with your enemy, as well as a collection of portraits including a fine one of Giuseppe Garibaldi (*see p10* **The four horsemen of the Risorgimento**) – of biscuit fame.

Chances of catching a glimpse of the Turin Shroud (*see p59* **Holy sheet**) are slim; even the Cappella della Sacra Sindone (Holy Shroud chapel) has been off-limits since a fire in April 1997. But the history of this mysterious scrap of linen is charted in the **Museo della Sindone** (*see p63*). Nearby, the **Consolata** church (*see p61*) is one of Turin's most impressive, with its luscious, overpowering interior; a room to the right of the altar is packed with tragi-comic ex-voto pictures, a storyboard for a macabre action movie.

The tallest building in the city, the Mole Antonelliana (*see p77*) is home to the **Museo nazionale del cinema**. There are magic lanterns, Indonesian shadow puppets and optical wizardry, plus examples of the latest film and animation techniques. The upper galleries contain sets and props from famous films or genres: Dracula's teeth, Bogart's cigarettes, King Kong's fur. For a bird's-eye view of the city and its dramatic surroundings, take the lift to the viewing platform.

A punishing day's sightseeing in the centre can be broken up with a picnic (pick up the wherewithal at the Porta Palazzo market, *see p120* **Bargain hunting**) or an ice-cream in the Giardini Reali (*see p53*) where there's a stunning fountain of Triton with sea-nymphs: how many weird and wonderful carved animals can your offspring spot?

A trip out to the **Lingotto** (*see p86*) is an adventure with an altogether different flavour. Whizz round the banked curves of the ex-Fiat factory's rooftop test track, the ideal setting for impromptu running races. Back on the ground, the **Museo dell'automobile** (*see p88*) is full of sleek and stylish models that rolled off the Fiat production line when dazzling chrome and leather upholstery were the norm.

For a bit of post-industry green, head for the **Parco del Valentino** (*see p80*), which is criss-crossed by paths that can be negotiated on bikes. (For bike rental, *see p220*.) The **Borgo Medioevale** (medieval village) by the riverside is in fact a 19th-century fake, but its 'authentic' drawbridge and medieval trappings always appeal to children. After your exertions, drift back up to the centre on a river boat (*see p218*). In summer, the **Museo Pietro Micca** (*see p66*) offers respite from the scorching sun with its extensive network of cool, creepy brick-lined passages beneath the city streets.

If you have any energy left at all at sunset, treat your kids to a tour of Magic Turin. **Somewhere Tours** (011 668 0580/ www.somewhere.it) will lead you (in English on request; tickets €18) into the darker recesses of the city: discover dark angels, dragons, ghouls and things a-plenty that go bump in the night.

Entertainment

See also p158 **Alfa Teatro**; *p159* **Teatro Agnelli**; *p159* **Teatro Araldo**.

Experimenta

Parco Michelotti, corso Casale 15, Collina (toll-free 800 329 329/www.experimenta.to.it). Bus 30, 61, 75/tram 3. **Open** *June-mid Sept* 4pm-midnight Tue-Fri; 3pm-midnight Sat; 10am-8pm Sun. *Mid Sept-1st wk Nov* 3-8pm Tue-Sat; 10am-8pm Sun. **Admission** €6.50; €4 under-6s. **No credit cards. Map** p243 B3.
Each summer, the ex-zoo turns into a science park. The theme changes yearly, but old favourites keep coming back: cycle from one tree to another on a tightrope suspended 12m (40ft) above the ground; feel the pull of gravity in the penguin enclosure; and shake hands with one of the robots designed to assemble Fiat cars.

Books

Willy Beck's *Bambini alla scoperta di Torino* (Fratelli Palombi; no English version) brilliantly unveils some of the mysteries of the city, its museums and monuments from a kid's point of view.

The **Libreria Hellas** (*see p120*) stocks the best selection of children's books in English.

Babysitters & childcare

Higher-range hotels have their own babysitting services, and all but the most basic hotels will arrange a babysitter for you.

Spoonny

Via Barbaroux 37-39, Quadrilatero (011 545 438/ www.spoonny.com). Bus 56, 60/tram 13. **Open** 3.30-10.30pm Tue-Fri; 9.30am-11pm Sat, Sun. **Credit** DC, MC, V. **Map** p242 C3.
The colourful restaurant at Spoonny provides a playful setting in which to tuck into alien fillets, crocodile sandwiches and a glass of jungle juice. The cheerful space also includes rooms for safe (and supervised) romping and a small cinema. Park junior here if you feel like popping back to try on that nice pair of shoes you saw earlier. Prices depend on services requested.

Gianduja

All self-respecting Italian cities have their own particular stock character from the *Commedia dell'arte* theatre tradition. Venice has Pantaleone, Bergamo has Arlecchino (Harlequin), Naples has Pulcinella (the forerunner of Punch), Rome has the lying braggart Rugantino. And Turin has Gianduja.

With his big red nose, pigeon chest and three-pointed hat, Gianduja pops up at local carnivals, village fêtes and wherever there is an unattended *boccale* (flagon of wine). Though the children love to be frightened by his drunken outbursts, best delivered in the local dialect, they soon gather round when he dishes out little *gianduiotti* chocolates.

Free puppet shows are often put on in the Giardini Reali (*see p53*) in summer, when miniature versions of best-loved operas are performed on scaled-down stages complete with elaborately painted backdrops, full musical score and complex scene changes

Compagnia Marionette Grilli

Teatro Alfa, via Casalborgone 16, Collina (011 819 7350/www.marionettegrilli.com). Bus 30, 61. **Open** Box Office 11am-1pm Sun.

Shows 4.15pm Sun. **Tickets** €6; €4 under-12s. **No credit cards. Map** p243 C3.
Every Sunday afternoon from November to February the curtain goes up on an ever-changing world of mystery and magic with visiting puppeteers from as far afield as St Petersburg and Cuba. Wraps come off some of the in-house collection of 8,500 puppets before and after the performance. From May to September Sunday afternoon performances are staged free in the Borgo Medioevale (*see p80*) at 4.15pm.

Museo della Marionetta

Via Santa Teresa 5, Cittadella (011 530 238). Bus 55, 72/tram 4, 13. **Open** by appointment only 9am-1pm Mon-Fri. **Admission** *Museum* €2.60. **Shows** €5-€6. **No credit cards. Map** p242 C3.
The Museo della Marionetta (puppet museum) contains a collection of more than 5,000 hand and string puppets, theatres and costumes brought together by the Lupi puppeteering family during the 18th and 19th centuries. Special performances bring to life some of these beautiful exhibits (*see p157*).

Film

Turin was the birthplace of Italian cinema, and nearly a century on the city's passion for film hasn't waned.

Turin has the highest proportion of cinema screens to inhabitants of any Italian city, an indication of the importance attributed to film from the earliest days of cinema by the city and its keen movie-going public. Turin was Italy's leading film-producing centre until Rome's Cinecittà stole the limelight in the late 1930s (*see p140* **Trail blazing**). But thanks to the **Museo nazionale del cinema** (*see p78*) and to the Film Commission Torino Piemonte (www.filmcommtorinopiemonte.it), Turin's long-running connection with cinema has not been lost; the city and region still provide the backdrop for films, TV dramas and soaps.

The vast Museo nazionale del cinema collection has been beautifully and imaginatively sited inside the unique **Mole Antonelliana**: in its 3,200 square metres (34,400 square feet) it contains 7,000 films, 9,000 cinema-related objects, 200 magic lanterns, 200,000 original film posters and much more – including a very smart café with outside seating.

The Film Commission is a non-profit organisation backed by City Hall and the regional council, which promotes Turin and Piedmont as a location for national and international film and television productions;

it also supports the local cinema industry. The Commission offers an across-the-board service for production companies, helping to procure all necessary filming permits, equipment, actors and studios, and offers assistance during filming too. It was also involved in the conversion of the former FERT studios on corso Lombardia (*see p140* **Trail blazing**) into a Virtual Reality and Multimedia Park (www.vrmmo.it) – a production and post-production centre equipped with all the most advanced digital technology.

Turin also hosts several annual film festivals (*see p132 and p134*), including the **Torino Film Festival**, Italy's largest after Venice, and an ever more highly regarded date on the international festival calendar.

The growth of modern multiplexes in suburban shopping malls has sounded the death knell for some of Turin's beautiful historic cinemas; the art deco **Lux** lost its fight against closure as this guide went to press. To survive, a few have been converted into miniplexes;

In Italy the dubber reigns supreme. You will only get to see films in English haphazardly at film festivals or at the once-weekly screenings entitled 'The Stand In' at the **Cinema Nazionale** (via Pomba 7, Centro, 011 812 4173)

Museo nazionale del cinema. See p78.

On location

With the gradual eclipse of its film industry after World War II, Turin continued to feature as a cinematic location. Arcaded via Po has been the backdrop for many films, from Antonioni's *Le Amiche* (*The Girl Friends*, 1955) to Gianni Amelio's *Così ridevano* (*So They Laughed*, 1998). Via Po was just one of the *torinesi* locations used in *The Italian Job* (*pictured*), Peter Collinson's madcap 1969 car caper, starring Michael Caine and Raf Vallone, in which a gridlocked city centre provides the scene for a memorable payroll heist, with Minis racing around the test track on the roof of the Fiat Lingotto factory (*see p86*), down the steps of the Gran Madre church (*see p81*) and under those via Po arcades. (Turin was apparently chosen over more recognisable Italian destinations because it was the only city whose authorities were prepared to allow such temporary desecration of its monuments.) The hills behind the city are associated with the horror maestro Dario Argento: both *Profondo Rosso* (*Deep Red*, 1975) and *Nonhosonno* (*I'm Not Sleepy*, 2000) are set in the villas of La Collina (*see pp81-3*). Luigi Comencini's successful comedy thriller *La donna della domenica* (*The Sunday Woman*, 1975), with Marcello Mastroianni and Jean-Louis Trintignant, played out between another hillside villa, elegant corso Cairoli and Turin's Balon flea market (*see p120* **Bargain hunting**). The Savoy residences of Palazzo Reale (*see p54*), Castello del Valentino

(*see p80*) and Stupinigi (*see p93*) were used for exterior shots in King Vidor's megabuck epic *War and Peace* (1956), which also saw massed armies facing off in the Piedmontese countryside for the first time in almost a century. More recently, Mimmo Calopresti's dark post-terrorist drama *La Second Volta* (*Second Time*, 1995), starring Nanni Moretti, made good use of the gloomy architectural anomie of the industrial suburbs around corso Unità d'Italia. Calopresti's second film, *La parola amore esiste* (1998), also set in the city, starred another cinematic *torinese*, actress Valeria Bruni Tedeschi, sister of model and Jagger girl Carla Bruni. Calopresti is one of a new generation of Turin-based filmmakers, which also includes Marco Ponti – whose generational comedy *Santa Maradona* (2001) showed a Turin of student pads and late-night clubs – and Giulio Base. Location shooting in the city is now facilitated by the Film Commission Torino Piemonte, one of the most active in Italy, which offers tax breaks for local and international productions – like Tom Tykwer's *Heaven* (2001), a morality tale based on an unfinished script by Krzysztof Kieslowski, starring Cate Blanchett and Giovanni Ribisi, which pans out between Turin and Tuscany. The latest film to be set in the city, Davide Ferrario's *Dopo Mezzanotte* (*After Midnight*, 2004), is a meta-cinematic love story involving a night-watchman who works in the Museo nazionale del cinema (*see p78*).

Arts & Entertainment

Trail blazing

The Italian cinema industry was born in Turin. It was here, in the years just before World War I, that the first historical 'colossals' were shot and the first Italian divas were discovered. It was only in the 1930s that the city's title of Italian film capital was wrested away by Rome's celebrated Cinecittà studios.

In 1908 photographer Arturo Ambrosio founded the Società Anonima Ambrosio, Turin's first moving picture company. His first production, *Gli ultimi giorni di Pompei* (*The Last Days of Pompei*, 1908) was also the first Italian film to achieve a degree of international success. In the same year, a rival production company, Itala Film, was established by entrepreneurs Carlo Sciamengo and Giovanni Pastrone. Comedy was a strong point at first: Itala's much-loved *Cretinetti* (*Little Cretins*) films, starring (and in some cases directed by) French knockabout actor André Deed, were soon answered by Ambrosio's *Tontolini* (*Little Dimwits*) series. But it was the historical 'colossal' that would bookmark a place for Turin in histories of world cinema. In 1912 Pastrone directed *La caduta di Troia* (*The Fall of Troy*), which made a name for Itala abroad, especially in America, where the film was a box office hit and greatly influenced the development of Hollywood historical epics

such as *Intolerance*. But it was Pastrone's next project, the melodramatic and decadent Carthage-set epic *Cabiria* (1916), co-scripted by literary lion Gabriele D'Annunzio, that really made history. The *Cleopatra* of its time, this three-hour epic with its improbable operatic storyline was longer, more expensive and more technically innovative than any European film up to that time. Pastrone used a moving camera mounted on a new type of dolly that he had invented and patented, and he even experimented with a rudimentary form of colour, tinting the final print in no fewer than 12 separate shades.

Turin's place as an important centre of the industry was consolidated by the birth in 1919 of FERT, an independent studio and production facility that was most active between the wars but that finally closed down only in the early 1970s. It was responsible for introducing the co-production system in the 1950s, and counted among its collaborators Federico Fellini, veteran producer Franco Cristaldi and Michelangelo Antonioni, whose FERT-produced *Cronaca di un'amore* (*Story of a Love Affair*, 1950), was shot in the streets of Turin. The old FERT studios have been resurrected recently as the headquarters of the Virtual Reality and Multimedia Park (*see p138*).

on Tuesdays at 6.45pm and 9.30pm from November to April. A full season's membership costs €50 to view recent (but not all that recent) blockbusters in English.

Elsewhere, regular 90-minute films are generally shown at 4.30pm, 6.30pm, 8.30pm and 10.30pm. Cinema tickets range from €6.50 to €7.50, with reductions all day Monday.

The small selection of cinemas below are all in the centre, show the latest releases and are either historic names or have recently been refurbished.

Art house, independent and other films that never hit the big screen are shown in 14 *cinema d'essai* (art house cinemas) affiliated to the national AIACE film club (Galleria Subalpina 30, Centro, www.arpet.it/aiaceto, open 3.30-6.30pm Mon-Fri), which has had its headquarters in Turin since 1968. AIACE membership (€11.50 from the main office) gives you a 30 per cent discount on tickets at affiliated cinemas, which are listed in the local press.

Cinemas

Ambrosio
Corso Vittorio Emanuele II 52, Centro (011 547 007). Bus 9, 52, 67, 68/tram 18. **Tickets** €6.75. **No credit cards. Map** p242 D3.
Since being renovated, this miniplex offers three screens, each with surround sound and seats for about 400. Very central, it shows all the latest releases. Popular with young cinema-goers.

Massimo
Via Verdi 18, Centro (011 812 5606). Bus 55, 56, 61/tram 13, 15. **Tickets** €6.50. **No credit cards. Map** p243 C1.
This recently revamped miniplex is linked to the nearby Museo nazionale del cinema (*see p78*). Its three screens show the latest releases as well as film classics associated with Museo retrospectives and art house productions.

Pathè
Via Nizza 230, Lingotto (011 667 7856). Bus 1, 35/tram 18. **Tickets** €7.50. **No credit cards. Map** p245 D3.

The Pathè is the largest cinema in Turin, with 11 screens. Designed by architect Renzo Piano, this cinema is a recent addition to the multifarious offerings inside the Lingotto complex (*see p86*). Slick and well organised, the Pathè also offers the advantage of being able to slip out and do a bit of shopping in the mall if the mainly mainstream fare on offer here proves not to be to your liking.

Reposi
Via XX Settembre 15, Centro (011 531 400).
Bus 11, 12/tram 4, 15. **Tickets** €7. **No credit cards. Map** p242 C3.
This five-screen cinema, along with the Massimo (*see p140*), used to host the Torino Film Festival (*see p133*). Today it screens all the major recent releases.

Romano
Galleria Subalpina, Centro (011 562 0145). Bus 55, 56, 61/tram 13, 15. **Tickets** €6.50. **No credit cards. Map** p242 C3.
Set in the beautiful Galleria Subalpina (*see p69*) in the very centre of town, this cinema has recently been converted into three small theatres and shows major box office hits.

Pathè.
See p140.

Festival Cinema delle Donne
Festival information *corso Raffaello 5, Centro (011 440 7801/www.festivalcinemadelledonne.com). Bus 67/tram 9, 16.* **Open** 9am-6.30pm Mon-Fri.
Map p245 B1.
Festival venue *Teatro Nuovo, corso Massimo d'Azeglio 17, Lingotto (011 650 0200). Bus 67/tram 9, 16.* **Dates** usually early Mar; in 2004 changed to Oct. **Tickets** €5.50. **No credit cards.**
Map p245 C1.
The only Italian festival dedicated entirely to women celebrated its tenth edition in 2003. All the productions screened here are directed by women and come from all over the world.

Torino Film Festival
Festival information *via Monte di Pietà 1, Cittadella (011 562 3309/www.torinofilmfest.org). Bus 51, 56/tram 4.* **Open** 9.30am-6.30pm Mon-Fri.
Map p242 C3.
Festival venue *Pathè, via Nizza 230, Lingotto (011 667 7856/www.torinofilmfest.org). Bus 1, 35/tram 18.* **Dates** Nov. **Tickets** variety of passes €5-€60; €6.50 daytime showings; €9 evening showings. **No credit cards. Map** p245 D1.
Italy's largest film festival after Venice has recently shifted its venue to the 11-screen Pathè multiplex (*see p140*). The festival started its life as a showcase for young directors, and was seen as a breeding ground for new talent. Nowadays it attracts bigger names too, but up-and-coming talent is still given plenty of space, as are productions from developing countries.

Turin International Gay & Lesbian Film Festival
Festival information *piazza San Carlo 161, Centro (011 534 888/www.turinglfilmfestival.com). Tram 15.* **Open** 9am-6pm Mon-Fri. **Map** p242 C3.
Festival venue *Teatro Nuovo, corso Massimo D'Azeglio 17, Lingotto (011 650 0200). Bus 67/tram 9, 16.* **Dates** Apr. **Tickets** €5.50. **No credit cards. Map** p245 C1.
Since it started in 1991 this festival has progressively assumed great importance on the Italian film scene, presenting films that would otherwise never be shown in Italy. The artists who enter their films come from all over the world.

Sottodiciotto Film Festival
Festival information: *AIACE Torino, Galleria Subalpina 30, Centro (011 538 9862/www.arpnet.it/aiaceto).* **Open** 3.30-6.30pm Mon-Fri.
Festival venue: *Cinema Massimo, via Verdi 18, Centro (011 812 5605) and other venues. Bus 55, 56, 61/tram 13, 15.* **Dates** Nov-Dec. **Tickets** free.
Map p243 C1.
A festival of films organised by AIACE for, about and by young people, the Sottodiciotto Film Festival is particular in that it gives space to young artists and directors under the age of 18. Often schools take part in the event as well.

Arts & Entertainment

Galleries

The number of public art spaces and independent galleries in Turin is growing apace, putting the city back at the forefront of Italy's modern art scene.

Amid the frenzy of refurbishment and regeneration projects under way in the run-up to the 2006 Winter Olympics, Turin is focusing hard on modern and contemporary art.

The city is no newcomer on this scene. In the late 1960s Turin was the birthplace of Arte Povera, a term coined by art critic and curator Germano Celant in 1967. His pioneering texts and a series of key exhibitions provided a collective identity for a number of young Italian artists, the leaders of which (Mario Merz, Michelangelo Pistoletto, Gilberto Zorio, Giuseppe Penone) were *torinesi* born and bred. Gallery owner Gian Enzo Sperone (who had already brought the likes of Pop Art and conceptual art to the Italian public's attention) spotted the potential of Arte Povera, displaying it in his cutting-edge Galleria Sperone that operated first in Turin in the 1960s, moving afterwards to Rome and New York.

Today Turin is once again attracting young, go-getting artists and gallery owners, who are creating a vibrant new art scene. Along with high-profile spaces (*see also* 144 **The shock of the new**) such as the **Castello di Rivoli** (*see p94*) and the Claudio Silvestrin-designed **Fondazione Sandretto Re Rebaudengo** (*see p68*), a host of small independent galleries have also opened in recent years. And council-sponsored art is taking to the streets; *see p143* **Art on track**.

Quadrilatero

Paolo Tonin
Via San Tommaso 6 (011 1971 0514/ www.toningallery.com). Bus 11, 12, 55, 56, 72/tram 4. **Open** 10.30am-12.30pm, 3.30-7.30pm Mon-Fri. **No credit cards. Map** p242 C3.
Tonin opened in 1974 and today concentrates mainly on emerging international artists, although occasional works by the likes of Mario Merz, Carol Rama, Alghiero Boetti, Man Ray and others reappear at the gallery.

Cittadella

Gas Art Gallery
Corso Vittorio Emanuele II 90 (011 1970 0031/ www.gasart.it/gallery). Bus 68/tram 9. **Open** 3-8pm Tue-Sat. **Credit** MC, V. **Map** p242 D2.

Light show

The **Fondazione italiana per la fotografia**, which opened in new, larger premises in the Ponte Mosca district north of Porta Palazzo (*see p60*) in March 2004, grew out of a photo museum opened in the 1980s. For many years the Fondazione has promoted high-level exhibitions and the **Biennale internazionale della fotografia** event; but with its move, the Fondazione plans a significant increase in its activities, including much larger, longer exhibitions both in via La Salle – where two major shows are scheduled each year – and in major venues around the Piedmont region.

Also in the new premises, the reorganised library will offer a more user-friendly service to the public, while archive and cataloguing activities will be stepped up, as will the programme of lectures and courses. The Fondazione's photo-restoration unit is located in via Locana 14. The move to this far-from-central area of town brings the Fondazione's headquarters close to the **Progetto Ponte Mosca**, a city- and region-funded urban renewal project for this run-down area that, it is hoped, will go the way of the Quadrilatero romano (*see pp60-3*) and become a trendy cultural hub. A multi-functional, multi-ethnic **Centro per la produzione e diffusione culturale** was scheduled to open on a vast tract of land between corso Giulio Cesare, lungodora Firenze, via Aosta and corso Brescia by 2006.

Fondazione Italiana per la Fotografia
Via La Salle 17 (011 544 132). Bus 12, 50, 63/tram 4, 18. **Admission** varies according to exhibition. **No credit cards. Map** p242 B3.

The owner of this gallery has a background in advertising and it shows in the way he has created an experimental space for high-tech and graphically enhanced artistic projects.

Galleria Mazzoleni Arte Moderna

Piazza Solferino 2 (011 534 473/
www.mazzoleniarte.it). Bus 5, 14, 29, 50, 59/
tram 13. **Open** 10am-12.30pm, 4-7.30pm Tue-Sun.
No credit cards. **Map** p242 C3.
Founded in the 1960s, Galleria Mazzoleni specialises in modern art, presenting work by many of the Italian greats including Alberto Burri, Felice Casorati and Ugo Nespolo.

Centro

Carbone.to

Via dei Mille 38 (011 839 5911/www.carbone.to).
Bus 68/tram 16. **Open** 4-7.30pm Tue-Sat.
No credit cards. **Map** p243 D1.
Carbone has given support to many young Italian artists over the years and works principally with contemporary painters from Italy and abroad. Artists represented here include Laura Viale, Maurizio Vetrugno and Francesco Lauretta.

41 Artecontemporanea

Via Mazzini 41 (011 812 9544/www.41arte
contemporanea.com). Bus 18, 61, 67, 68/tram 18.
Open 4-7.30pm Tue-Sat. **No credit cards**.
Map p243 D1.
Up-and-coming *torinesi* artists are often shown at this gallery alongside leading international talent and the more established Italians like Luigi Mainolfi and Aldo Mondino.

Giampiero Biasutti Arte Moderna e Contemporanea

Via della Rocca 6B (011 814 1099/
www.galleriabiasutti.com). Bus 52/tram 16.
Open 10.30am-12.30pm, 3.30-7.30pm Tue-Sat.
No credit cards. **Map** p243 D1.
A wide selection of great Italian artists from the 1900s including Sironi, Soffici, De Pisis and Cassinari can be seen in the halls of Biasutti's gallery, along with some post-war key international artists like Soldati, Sutherland, Ernst, Rotella and Schifano.

Guido Costa Projects

Via Mazzini 24 (011 815 4113/guidocosta@
libero.it). Bus 52, 68/tram 16. **Open** 11am-1pm, 3-7pm Mon-Sat. **No credit cards**. **Map** p243 D1.
The gallery concentrates almost exclusively on new American art, with a particularly strong emphasis on photography.

In Arco

Piazza Vittorio Veneto 1-3 (011 812 2927). Bus 55, 56, 61/tram 13, 15. **Open** 10am-12.30pm, 4-7.30pm Tue-Sat. **No credit cards**. **Map** p243 C1.
This space inside a courtyard exhibits young Italian artists and specialises in painting.

Art on track

The Spina centrale (the central spine – or, more prosaically, the Passante ferroviario, the railway bypass) is a key element in Turin's ongoing urban redevelopment plan and a fine opportunity to demonstrate the city's dedication to contemporary art.

Where tracks once sliced through the urban fabric – from largo Orbassano in the south (*Map p244 C2*) to the clearway to Caselle airport in the north (*Map p241*) – the railway is being sunk below ground level and replaced with a tree-lined road, cycle track, dedicated public transport lanes and islands of contemporary sculpture.

Of 11 planned artworks, only two had been unveiled when this guide went to press: Mario Merz's *Fontana* and Giuseppe Pennone's *Giardino di Cefalonia a Corfù*, both in corso Lione. Other pieces to be added as building work progresses include works by Giovanni Anselmo, Pier Kirkeby, Jannis Kounellis, Luigi Mainolfi, Giuio Paolini, Walter Pilcher, Michelangelo Pistoletto, Ulrich Rückriem and Gilberto Zorio.

Lose yourself in **Galleria Maze**. *See p144.*

The shock of the new

Turin's baroque façades conceal examples of modern and contemporary art – from substantial collections of Arte Povera from the 1960s and '70s to exhibitions of the very latest from around the world – that are as impressive as they are unexpected. Still more examples can be found in purpose-built (or purpose-refurbished) containers.

Some of Turin's more traditional galleries host exhibitions of modern art alongside their permanent collections. Temporary shows at the **Palazzo Bricherasio** (see p70) have ranged from the Impressionists to Salvador Dalí and Christo. **Palazzo Cavour** (see p71), with its spacious rooms and halls, is more dedicated and suited to modern art.

Perched on the roof of the old Lingotto Fiat factory (see p86), the **Pinacoteca Giovanni e Marella Agnelli** (see p88) is home to a small collection that includes Matisse, Picasso, Manet and Renoir.

The **Galleria civica d'arte moderna e contemporanea** (**GAM**, see p68) is a modern structure that houses an excellent, predominantly Italian collection of work from the 18th century to the present day, providing a clear overview of Arte Povera and other modern Italian art movements.

The seriously contemporary **Fondazione Sandretto Re Rebaudengo** (see p68) opened in 2002. Designed by minimalist architect Claudio Silvestrin and located in an ex-industrial area of the city, the new space is a light, flexible structure that has changing exhibitions of the latest in contemporary art. Films, talks, music, theatre and dance are organised parallel to all the main exhibitions.

The **Società promotrice delle belle arte** (Castello del Valentino, viale Balsamo Crivelli 11, 011 669 2545), in the pleasant surroundings of Parco del Valentino (see p80), has regularly changing exhibitions of modern and temporary Italian artists.

The **Fondazione italiana per la fotografia** (see p142 **Light show**) hosts exhibitions of reportage and projects by world-renowned photographers, as well as organising the **Biennale internazionale della fotografia**.

Outside the city, the **Castello di Rivoli** (see p94) is a sight in itself but it's also home to a contemporary art gallery that boasts a comprehensive collection of Arte Povera as

Martano

Via Principe Amedeo 29 (011 817 7987/ www.galleriamartano.it). Bus 55, 56, 61/tram 13, 15. Open *3.30-7.30pm Tue-Sat.* No credit cards. Map p243 C1.

A historic character on the Turin art scene who shows painters from the 1960s and '70s, including Boetti, Chiari, Parisot, Reggiani, Soldati, Melotti, Tancredi, Ruggeri, Spagnulo and Gallizio.

Franco Masoero Edizioni d'Arte

Via Giulia di Barolo 13 (011 885 933/fax 011 817 4200/www.francomasoero.it). Bus 30, 55/tram 15, 16. Open *10am-noon, 4-7pm Thur, Fri; 4-7pm Sat.* No credit cards. Map p243 C1.

This small but functional gallery space exhibits some beautiful drawings and etchings by modern and contemporary artists, investing in Turin artists like Nicola De Maria and Carol Rama.

Galleria Maze

Via Mazzini 40 (011 815 4145/www.galleriamaze.it). Tram 9, 16. Open *3.30-7pm Tue-Sat.* No credit cards. Map p243 D1.

Galleria Maze, which opened in 1999 in a converted pinball factory, is dedicated to young international artists. Much of the work is innovative and experimental and the gallery has a fresh feel to it, with a rich calendar of openings and performances.

Franco Noero

Via Giolitti 52A (011 882 208/www.franco noero.com). Bus 61, 68/tram 18. Open *10am-noon, 3-7.30pm Tue-Fri; 3-7.30pm Sat; by appointment at other times.* No credit cards. Map p243 D1.

Franco Noero shows up-to-the-minute international artists and supports video, audio, photography and installation work.

Alberto Peola

Via della Rocca 29 (011 812 4460/www.alberto peola.com). Tram 16. Open *3.30-7.30pm Mon-Sat; mornings by appointment.* No credit cards. Map p243 D1.

Situated in the beautiful via della Rocca in the centre of the city, Peola specialises in international contemporary painting and installation.

Giorgio Persano

Piazza Vittorio Veneto 9 (011 835 527/ www.giorgiopersano.com). Bus 55, 56, 61/tram 13, 15. Open *10am-12.30pm, 4-7pm Tue-Sat.* No credit cards. Map p243 C1.

Persano grew up with Arte Povera in the '70s with the likes of Mario Merz. The gallery today hosts mainly contemporary painting.

Photo & Co

Via dei Mille 36 (011 889 884). Bus 68. Open *3.30-7.30pm Tue-Sat.* No credit cards. Map p243 D1.

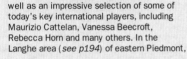

well as an impressive selection of some of today's key international players, including Maurizio Cattelan, Vanessa Beecroft, Rebecca Horn and many others. In the Langhe area (*see p194*) of eastern Piedmont,

the **Palazzo Re Rebaudengo** (piazza del Municipio, Guarene d'Alba, 011 1083 1600/www.fondsrr.org) hosts photographic exhibitions (May to October) as well as part of the Sandretto Re Rebaudengo collection.

Photo & Co dedicates its space to contemporary photographers like Wegman, Nils Udo, Gonzales Palma, Rousse and Tina Barley.

Galleria Sonia Rosso
Via Giulia di Barolo 11H (011 817 2478/ www.soniarosso.com). Bus 30, 55/tram 15, 16. **Open** 3-7pm Tue-Sat. **No credit cards**. **Map** p243 D1.
This small gallery is dedicated to cutting-edge Italian and international art.

Suburbs

E/Static
Via Parma 31 (011 235 140). Bus 19, 68/tram 3. **Open** by appointment only. **No credit cards**. **Map** p243 B2.
E/Static, which opened in 1999, presents visual art, sound design and audio installations, collectively known as Sound Art. Turin-based artists are featured alongside international names.

Out of town

Castello di Rivara
Piazza Sillano 2, Rivara Canavese (0124 31 122). Bus from via Fiocchetto. **Open** 10.30am-6.30pm Sat, Sun. **No credit cards**. **Map** p240.

This huge, magnificent wing of a country castle shows contemporary installation and solo exhibitions of emerging, international artists, especially German artists.

En Plein Air – Arte Contemporanea
Strada Baudenasca 118 (La Tegassa), Pinerolo (0121 340 253/www.epa.it). Bus from via Fiocchetto/train from Porta Nuova station. **Open** By appointment only Mon-Fri; 4-7pm Sat, Sun. **No credit cards**. **Map** p240.
One of the most beautiful countryside galleries in Piedmont, the *associazione culturale* En Plein Air hosts mainly Italian artists of an international status. It has regularly changing exhibitions.

Tucci Russo
Via Stamperia 9, Torre Pellice (0121 953 357/ www.tuccirusso.com). Bus from via Fiocchetto/train from Porta Nuova station. **Open** By appointment only Mon-Wed; 10.30am-12.30pm, 4-7pm Thur-Sun. **No credit cards**. **Map** p240.
This gallery is located in Torre Pellice, a small town near Turin, where it occupies a former textile mill. Artists presented in the gallery have included Sandro Chia, Enzo Cucchi, Mario Merz, Giovanni Anselmo, Jannis Kounellis, Marisa Merz, Luigi Mainolfi, Luigi Stoisa and American and European artists such as Maria Nordman, Thomas Schütte, Richard Long and Tony Cragg.

Arts & Entertainment

Gay & Lesbian

It's easier to be out and proud in Turin than in many other Italian cities, but don't expect much of a lively scene.

When Italy's gay movement emerged from the shadows in the 1970s, Turin was in the vanguard. The first openly gay association was called *Fuori* (Out) and had its national headquarters in Turin; the first national Gay Pride march was held in Turin; as was the first gay cinema festival, Da Sodoma a Hollywood (*see p132* **Turin International Gay & Lesbian Film Festival**); and the Turin office of ArciGay (www.arcigay.it), the largest of the national associations, was set up here in 1986.

With its history of revolution and mould-breaking, Turin has developed a tolerance of 'otherness' that, formally at least, far outstrips that of smaller cities or much of southern Italy. Turin city council, for example, has sponsored initiatives to overcome prejudices based on sexual and personal identity, involving the general public and many of the city's schools. Discrimination in the workplace and harassment either on the streets or by the police seem to be things of the past.

Yet many homosexuals in Turin – as in the rest of Italy, with its strong Catholic conditioning – still find it difficult to come out openly in front of family and friends, showing their 'private' side only occasionally in the seclusion of gay and lesbian venues. It's still rare to see affectionate effusions between men in public. Women, on the other hand, have a slightly easier time from this point of view, as displays of female affection – as long as it's limited to things like hand-holding and hugging – are perfectly acceptable.

Turin has a long history of political associations; there are proportionately more gay, lesbian and, recently, transsexual associations here than in any other Italian city. Turin's lesbian movement was initially strongly political, being closely identified with the city's strong feminist movement. Clubs and saunas, on the other hand, are rarer.

Information, organisations & helplines

Circolo Culturale Maurice
Via Basilica 5, Piazza Castello (011 521 1116/ www.mauriceglbt.org). Bus 3, 27/tram 4, 16. **Open** 9am-noon, 5-7pm, 9-11pm Mon; 9am-noon, 5-7pm Wed; 5-7pm Tue, Thur-Sat. **Map** p242 C3.
This association for gays (Fri evening), lesbians (Tue evening) and transsexuals (Mon evening) offers telephone and face-to-face support as well as organising occasions for debate, get-togethers at cultural and political events and often great parties. It has an extensive library. Everyone involved is very helpful and welcoming.

Davide & Gionata
Via Giolitti 21A, Centro (011 889 811). Bus 61, 68/tram 18. **Open** 9-11.30pm Tue. **Map** p243 D1.

Caffè Leri. *See p147.*

This association of religiously minded gay people offers encounters on religious themes and above all on the relation between homosexuality and faith. Meetings are held every Tuesday.

Informagay

Via Giordano Bruno 80, Suburbs: south (011 304 0934/helpline 011 304 2271/www.informagay.it). Bus 14, 17. **Open** 9.30am-1.30pm Mon-Fri. **Map** p244 C3.

This voluntary work association offers counselling for gays, lesbians and transsexuals. Its helpline operates on Thursdays from 8pm to 11pm. The centre itself is open for psychological support, legal counselling, information on HIV and so on.

Philadelphia

Via Baretti 8, Lingotto (011 658 162). Bus 9, 67/ tram 16, 18. **Map** p245 A1.

Founded in 1996, this association's aims are to defend gay rights and health – with a particular focus on AIDS – offering information, a helpline (8-11pm Thur) and promoting initiatives for prevention.

Bars

Caffè Leri

Corso Vittorio Emanuele II 64, Centro (011 543 075). Bus 9, 12, 52, 61, 67, 68/tram 16, 18. **Open** 6pm-3am Tue-Sun. **No credit cards**. **Map** p243 D1.

This very trendy café and disco-pub is usually jam-packed with a younger, playful crowd.

Il Male Pub

Via Lombardore 10, Suburbs: north (011 284 617). Bus 50/tram 4. **Open** 9pm-2am Mon, Wed-Sun. **No credit cards**. **Map** p242 A3.

There's a real pub atmosphere in this bar with its wooden benches and tables, known for its singles parties and late night events. Lots of delicious hot and cold panini are available.

Vineria Zi Barba

Via Silvio Pellico 13E, Lingotto (011 658 391/ www.zibarba.it). Bus 9, 67/tram 16, 18. **Open** 6pm-2am Tue-Sun. **No credit cards**. **Map** p245 A1.

A more mature set of men frequent this friendly, informal restaurant and wine bar, which is a favourite with bears.

Clubs

Centralino Club

Via delle Rosine 16A, Centro (335 534 9808). Bus 55, 56, 61/tram 15, 16. **Open** midnight-5am Fri, Sun. **Admission** free. **No credit cards**. **Map** p243 C1.

This very central dive, with its deep red decor, is open from Tuesday to Sunday (*see also p152*) and becomes very gay-friendly on Fridays. On Sundays it hosts the dedicated gay-and-lesbian Domenica Zoccola event. There's always a young crowd and lots of house music.

Cruisin'

Autogrill service station at Settimo Torinese (*tangenziale Torino, direzione Milano, map p241*): busy bogs!; you'll need a car; lots of lorry drivers; pretty safe.
Parco del Valentino (*see p80*): the bushes talk by themselves it's so crowded on a summer's night, so watch where you put your feet and be careful of vengeful heterosexuals on the warpath.
Piazza d'Armi park (*map p244 C2*): especially the corso Galileo Ferraris side.
Lungodora Colletta (*map p243 B2*): near the cemetery; you'll need a car.
Parco Pellerina: (*map p241*) on the via Pietro Cossa side – very out of the way, very dark; watch out!

Metropolis

Via Principessa Clotilde 82, Suburbs: north (011 484 116). Tram 3, 16. **Open** 11pm-4am Sat. **Admission** varies. **No credit cards**. **Map** p242 B1.

Commonly known (somewhat unkindly!) as *la necropoli* (the city of the dead), this disco is very popular with an older crowd of men and women.

Notorius

Via Stradella 10, Suburbs: north (347 581 1687/ www.pqdisco.it). Bus 2, 9, 72. **Open** midnight-5am Sat. **Admission** varies. **No credit cards**. **Map** p242 A2.

This big venue, which plays mostly commercial music, is always packed with all kinds of people, though a 20-something crowd predominates.

Saunas

Turin's gay community has traditionally favoured political debate over sweaty camaraderie, but the city's following saunas are popular.

Antares

Via Pigafetta 73D, Suburbs: south (011 501 645). Bus 10, 12, 33, 58. **Open** 1pm-1am Tue-Sun. **Admission** €6.50 Tue-Fri; €8 Sat, Sun. **No credit cards**. **Map** p244 B2.

Free Club

Corso Vigevano 41, Suburbs: north (011 249 0004). Bus 46, 49, 52. **Open** noon-midnight daily. **Admission** €10 Mon-Fri; €13 Sat, Sun. **No credit cards**. **Map** p242 A2.

San Martino

Corso San Martino 8G, Cittadella (011 533 794). Bus 1, 29, 36, 38, 56, 59/tram 13. **Open** 2.30-7.30pm Mon, Wed-Sun. **Admission** €11. **No credit cards**. **Map** p242 C2.

Nightlife & Music

Don't be fooled by appearances... you *can* party the night away in Turin.

At first glance Turin's nightlife may seem non-existent: often even *torinesi* aren't aware of it. But don't be put off: under the apparent calm of evening, a vast current of activity flows and ripples, enveloping anybody willing to party. The important thing is to know the ropes.

WHEN

One of the rules of Italian – and, in particular, *torinese* – nightlife is that it starts late, especially on Fridays and Saturdays. If you were thinking of hitting a club at ten and the sack at midnight, forget it. At ten, *torinesi* are still eating; at midnight they'll be chatting and drinking in a bar; not till after one will they start getting into dance mode. So prepare to reschedule your sightseeing programme.

WHERE

Turin is arranged in such a way as to make going out very easy. A few compact areas are home to a concentrated slew of clubs and *locali*. Select your area, then amble on foot between one venue and another. Remember, though, that there is a striking difference between summer and winter: on summer nights, party people

Get into the mix at **Centralino**. *See p152.*

gravitate towards the **Murazzi** (*see p150* **I Murazzi**), or any other outside venue (*see also p80* **Parco del Valentino**); in winter, they stick to cosier dives in the **Centro** (*see pp69-73*) and **Quadrilatero** areas (*see pp60-63*) and to **Docks Dora** (*see p149* **Docks Dora**).

For something much more *alternativo*, try out one of Turin's many *Centri sociali* – semi-legal squats, some of which offer rich programmes of concerts, debates, film screenings and other events for a decidedly non-conformist 'clientele'. The best-known dives in the **Centro** (*see pp* 47, Lingotto), **Askatasuna** (corso Regina Margherita 47, Centro) and **Gabrio** (via Revello 3, Suburbs: west).

HOW

Kick your evening off by following the time-honoured Turinese *aperitivo* tradition (*see p116* **Aperitivi** *galore*), either in one of Turin's historic cafés or in one of the newer music bars listed below. If you can manage dinner after your *aperitivo* snacks, round your meal off with a glass of Piedmontese wine in a *vineria* (wine bar) before hitting the nightspots.

WHAT

Dance and drink in the venues listed below. Or experience some of the live music that Turin has to offer.

Big names

Most national and international stars pass Turin by. The few that stop off here perform at the **Mazda Palace** (corso Ferrara 30, Suburbs: north-west, 011 455 9090). You're more likely to catch a big name at summer music festivals (*see pp132-4*).

Country, folk & ethnic

For country and folk, head for the **Folk Club** (via Perrone 3bis, Cittadella, 011 537 636). Ethnic music is included in the **Settembre Musica** festival (*see p157* **Torino Settembre Musica**) and at **Big Torino** events (*see p134*).

Electronic

Turin is in the vanguard of electronic music in Italy, with projects like Xplosiva, set up in 1997 by DJs Sergio Ricciardone and Giorgio Valletta; catch them every Friday at the **Officine Belforte** (*see p149* **Docks Dora**) and at summer festivals. Xplosiva explores the boundaries between contemporary dance

Docks Dora

North-west of Porta Palazzo (*see p60*), and hemmed in by the Milan railway line to the west and the River Dora Riparia to the north, Borgo Dora used to be an industrial area, cluttered with railway workshops and slum housing. These days the clank of machinery and wails of hungry children have been replaced by pounding electro, techno and R&B beats. As industry receded from the area in the last few decades, rave organisers and 'alternative' cultural centres moved in to the vast, echoing, unused spaces. The Docks Dora are now home to a number of clubs that are a healthy change from commercial venues elsewhere; many are in the same vast complex in via Valprato and entered either from the street or from the courtyard.

Getting there & getting in

To get into these clubs, you should be a member of the ARCI or AICS cultural associations (membership €10 on the door). However, this rule is generally waived for foreigners, who will be asked to produce ID, after which admission is usually free unless there are special guests playing. (Exceptions to this rule are indicated in the listings below.) Unless otherwise stated, credit cards are not accepted at these venues.

Buses 12, 46 and 77 pass close by but services will probably have already stopped by the time things get going here after 1am… so be prepared to walk or take a taxi. This used to be a tough area and remains so to some extent. Try not to wander off the beaten track, watch your wallet and don't leave valuables in the pockets of coats left in club cloakrooms. **Map** p242 B3.

Café Blue

Via Valprato 68 (011 280 251/ www.cafeblue.it). **Open** 11pm-4am Thur-Sat; 9pm-2am Sun.
If you can get past the aggressive doorman and transsexuals offering free packets of cigarettes, you'll find yourself inside a hangar-like space where part of a railway carriage serves as console area and seating. Rock, punk, hip hop and ska are the usual offerings here, but on Sundays there's a complete change of atmosphere with tango. The entrance to the club is on the street, 50 metres from the main entrance to the coutyard of the docks proper.

Docks8

Via Valprato 68 (011 285 936/335 708 4669/www.docks8.com). **Open** midnight-6am Fri-Sat; 6am-noon Sun.
Lots of videos accompany the beat of techno and electro music on two levels. If you can keep going, Saturday night segues into Scatafashion – the Docks' famous 'after-hours' on Sunday morning.

Docks Home

Via Valprato 68 (011 285 936/ www.dockshome.tiscali.it). **Open** midnight-6am Tue-Wed, Fri-Sat.
Light shows match the lounge, electro and house music in this two-level saloon-type venue, with smaller areas where art is exhibited.

E-lastico Net Café

Via Valprato 76E (011 248 1082/ www.e-lastico.com). **Open** 7.30am-9pm Mon; 7.30am-5am Tue-Sat. **Credit** AmEx, DC, MC, V.
With its friendly sitting-chatting area, its bar, its music and its (free) internet points, E-lastico is welcoming and very civilised. Food is served here at all times of day and there are good *aperitivi*. There are live music sessions – jazz, blues, rock – from Thursday to Saturday, plus a pool table and fruit machines in the back room.

Officine Belforte

Corso Venezia 30 (011 819 4347/ www.barrumba.com). **Open** midnight-6am Fri, Sat. Closed July & Aug.
There's a real buzz at Officine, which has a huge main space with a round central bar, a second smaller bar with seats for resting your weary feet plus a small Arab-style tented room with sofas, cushions and hookahs. On Friday nights, DJs from the Xplosiva crew play acid techno, house and dark groove; Saturdays are organised by Barrumba (*see p152*) with R&B, hip hop and ragamuffin.

On-Gaia

Via Valprato 68 (349 843 0860/335 427 935/www.ongaia.it). **Open** midnight-6am Thur-Sat.
Thursdays mean hip hop, Fridays techno and Saturdays a bit of everything in this large space on two levels. Art exhibits are displayed in the White room.

I Murazzi

Stretching along the banks of the River Po from Ponte Umberto to Ponte Vittorio Emanuele, the Murazzi (see p80) are Turin's party mecca. On summer days, torinesi descend en masse below street level to the waterfront to top up tans, meet up with friends or picnic beside the lapping water. On summer nights, the crush becomes even more immense as a sea of humanity strolls along the water's edge, and hops between the clubs and bars built into the huge arches constructed in the 19th century to hold up the city-level streets above.

To complete the holiday atmosphere, stalls by the water sell everything from jewellery and handicrafts to food.

The Murazzi are heaven for all-night revellers: many of these places stay open until 6am or later, only pulling down their shutters as the sun rises over the lush green Collina (see pp81-3) across the river. They are hell, however, if you forget your mosquito repellent, which should suffice to keep the swarms of riverside blood-suckers off. There are other predators, too, in the shape of very persistent pickpockets, so be sure to keep your wits about you.

Unless stated, there is no admission fee to these venues.

NORTH OF THE BRIDGE

The Beach

Murazzi del Po 18-20 (011 888 777). Bus 55, 30/tram 13, 15. **Open** Feb-Oct 11pm-5am Tue-Sun. **Credit** AmEx, MC, V. **Map** p243 C2.
A beach indeed, with its deckchairs and beach umbrellas set out along the riverbank in summer, this is where smart torinesi come to work on their tans while enjoying a great lunch menu and sipping a fresh mojito by day. By night, there's great dancing (tech-house, electro) courtesy of Turin's Motel Connection, for example, flanked by an ever-changing roster of guest DJs. The high arched brick interior has recently been redesigned with clean contemporary furniture, light installations and video projections on the walls. Also a cultural centre, the Beach often hosts literary meetings or art events.

sounds and the visual arts, performing at fashion and media events, as well as in the brief **Club to Club** (www.clubtoclub.it) happening organised in collaboration with the **Fondazione Sandretto Re Rebaudengo** (see p68). For information on events, check out www.piemontegroove.com, the website (in English) of an umbrella organisation grouping all major players on Turin's electronic music scene.

Jazz & blues

Since 1978 the **Centro Jazz Torino** (011 884 477, www.centrojazztorino.it) has promoted important events like **Linguaggi Jazz** (January-March) and **Blues al Femminile** (autumn and spring): the former brings big and up-and-coming names of every imaginable age and style to the area; the latter focuses on women blues singers. Both are held at the **Piccolo Regio** (see p156) and venues around Piedmont.

There are also many live jazz sessions throughout the winter months in various venues: **Soundtown** (see p152), **Il Magazzino di Gilgamesh** (see p153), **Café Procope** (see p156) or the **Piccolo Regio** (see p156), or, in summer, in parks, including the **Serate al Palazzo** (June-Sept), held in the gardens of **Palazzo Reale** (see p52).

Latin American

Though past its peak as the most fashionable music of the moment, Latin American dance schools are still much frequented and several clubs survive. See p153 **Sabor Latino**.

Unless otherwise stated, there is no admission fee for the venues listed below.

Quadrilatero

DJ bars & clubs

Aquaragia

Via Bellezia 20E (338 299 7000/www.aquaragia.com). Bus 11, 27, 51, 56, 67/tram 4, 13. Open 7pm-2am Mon-Thur; 7pm-3am Fri, Sat. No credit cards. Map p242 C3.
There's an easygoing atmosphere in this locale, which serves food alongside its aperitivi, wines and spirits. It has themed DJ nights on Tuesdays and from Thursday to Saturday.

The Frog

Via dei Mercanti 19 (011 440 7736). Bus 11, 27, 51, 56, 67/tram 4, 13. Open 7pm-3am Tue-Sun. Closed Aug. Admission €9-€16. Credit DC, MC, V. Map p242 C3.

Bokaos

Murazzi del Po 2 (011 812 8931/
www.bokaos.it). Bus 30, 55, 56/tram 13, 15.
Open 8pm-3.30am Tue-Sat. **Credit** DC, MC, V.
Map p243 C2.

This minimalist-decor, Zen-inspired restaurant (average €30) and club attracts large crowds of Turin's smart and well-heeled. Enter from the Murazzi (where there are outside tables in summer), then climb to the lower-level cocktail lounge and bar, then up again into bar and restaurant spaces opening on to piazza Vittorio Veneto.

SOUTH OF THE BRIDGE

Alcatraz

Murazzi del Po 37 (349 805 3516). Tram
16. **Open** *Jan-Apr* 10pm-4am Thur-Sat. *May,*
mid Sept-Dec 10pm-4am Tue-Sat. *June-*
mid Sept 10pm-4am daily. **No credit cards**.
Map p243 D1.

One of the best-known clubs at the Murazzi. It doesn't have a very big dancefloor but can boast a spacious terrace where people cool off in the hot summer nights. It rounds up all

kinds of people, most of them young. Very good for the drum 'n' bass evenings, usually on Fridays or Saturdays. All kinds of cocktails are available, and it's famous for its chupitos.

Giancarlo

Murazzi del Po 49 (011 817 472). Tram 16.
Open *May-Oct* 11pm-7am. **No credit cards**.
Map p243 D1.

This is where the Murazzi's nightlife scene began in the 1980s. More of a pub than a club, Giancarlo (named after its founder) is the haunt of night owls and insomniacs. When everything else has closed, you can always find a drink here.

Jammin'

Murazzi del Po 17-19 (011 882 869).
Tram 16. **Open** *Apr-Oct* 6.30pm-5am daily.
Admission *Outside* free. *Club* varies according to event. **No credit cards**. **Map** p243 D1.

Jammin's outside tables, right on the water's edge, are perfect for sipping *aperitivi*. There's often a long queue to enter the club inside, where dancing (house and dance) doesn't start until after 1am.

In this new club you can linger over *aperitivi* from 7pm onwards, have supper and then dance and party until three in the morning. If you like hip hop and R&B, drop by on Thursday to Saturday.

Late eating & drinking

See also p113 **Hafa Café**.

Luce e Gas

Via IV Marzo 12C (011 436 5483/www.luceegas.it).
Bus 11, 27, 51, 56, 67/tram 4, 13. **Open** 7.30pm-3am
Tue-Sun. Closed Aug. **Credit** MC, V. **Map** p242 C3.

Turin's only 'buddha bar'; a vast, beautifully decorated, trendy restaurant spreads over two floors, serving a mix of Indian and Piedmontese food.

Otium

Via Bellezia 8G (011 436 0738). Bus 11, 27, 51,
56, 67/tram 4, 13. **Open** 8pm-1am daily. **Credit**
DC, MC, V. **Map** p242 C3.

There are a couple of largish rooms in which to discover Siberian, Mongolian or Italian regional specialities in friendly surroundings.

Aperitivi with music

Fusion Café

Via Sant'Agostino 17 (011 436 5022). Bus 11, 27,
51, 52, 56, 67/tram 4, 13, 16. **Open** 6pm-2am Tue-

Thur, Sun; 6pm-3am Fri, Sat. **Credit** AmEx, MC, V.
Map p242 C3.

This stylish bar has high-tech decor on two floors. The music that will accompany your *aperitivo* is a selection of house and lounge.

KM5

Via San Domenico 14-16 (011 431 0032/
www.km5.it). Bus 11, 27, 51, 52, 67/tram
4, 16. **Open** 6pm-3am Tue-Sun. **No credit cards**.
Map p242 C2.

Great *aperitivi* with lots of food. There's a lovely space outside in the summer; inside, it's all red terracotta walls and Mexican hats.

Lobelix

Piazza Savoia 4 (011 436 7206). Bus 11, 27/
tram 4. **Open** 7pm-3am Mon-Sat. **No credit cards**. **Map** p242 C2.

This trendy bar has pavement tables outside on the square in the summer. Whatever the season, a wide range of *aperitivi* and large platefuls of food through the evening mean that it's always packed.

Wine bars

L'Albero di Vino

Piazza della Consolata 9C (011 521 7578). Bus 52,
60/tram 3, 16. **Open** noon-3pm, 7pm-2am Tue-Fri;
7pm-2am Sat, Sun. **Credit** MC, V. **Map** p242 C2.

Arts & Entertainment

Located in beautiful piazza della Consolata, the heart of religious Turin, this is one of many wine bars in the area. There are interesting dishes on the menu if you want to eat.

Cittadella

DJ bars & clubs

Barcode
Corso San Martino 2 (339 526 4712/380 532 9363). Bus 46, 56, 59/tram 1, 10, 13. **Open** 10pm-3am Tue-Thur; 7pm-3am Fri, Sat. **No credit cards. Map** p242 C2.
The decor is great in this friendly disco-bar, which serves *aperitivi* from 7pm and Indian food from 8pm, and stages art exhibitions regularly as part of an imaginative cultural programme. Downstairs there's dancing and themed DJ nights: Tuesdays are for teenage bopping, Wednesdays for guest DJs, Fridays for rock 'n' roll and Saturdays for soul. Films are shown on Thursdays.

Centro

DJ bars & clubs

Barrumba
Via San Massimo 1 (011 819 4347/www.barrumba .com). Bus 55, 56, 61/tram 13, 15. **Open** 11pm-5am Tue, Thur-Sat. Closed July-Aug. **Admission** free; prices vary for live events.
No credit cards. Map p243 C1.
This underground venue offers live events on Tuesdays and clubbing evenings on Thursday to Saturday, with music ranging from rock to crossover and pop. The haunt of university students, it's often very crowded, but its circular dancefloor holds many more people than you would expect. Barrumba also organises summer festivals (*see p133*).

Centralino
Via delle Rosine 16 (335 534 9808). Bus 55, 56, 61/tram 13, 15. **Open** midnight-5am Tue, Thur; midnight-6am Fri-Sun. Closed July-Aug. **Admission** €9; €10 Sat. **No credit cards. Map** p243 C1.
This small club in the centre of town plays excellent techno and electro. Fridays and Saturdays are the hottest evenings, so be prepared for a long wait at the door. On Sundays there's the gay and lesbian event Domenica Zoccola (*see also p147*).

Matilda
Corso Massimo d'Azeglio 3A (393 911 1258/ www.matildafashion.com). Bus 9/tram 16. **Open** 11.30pm-5am Thur-Sat. **Admission** €15-€25.
No credit cards. Map p245 C1.
A big plush club frequented by Turin's *fighetti* (designer-dressed rich kids): it's spacious and well lit but often so crowded that dancing is well nigh impossible. A picky selection policy on the door means that getting in can be quite an ordeal; once inside, you might wonder whether it was worth the struggle/expense. The music is not bad, however, and ranges from house to dance.

Rock City
Corso Dante 17A (011 319 0884). Bus 42. **Open** 11.30pm-5am Thur-Sat. **Admission** €10-€20. **Credit** DC, MC, V. **Map** p245 C1.
House music dominates the scene at this long-running club that offers many interesting evenings, particularly those in collaboration with the organisation Discofever. The place looks like a big cube with a raised privée and two long bars at each end.

Soundtown
Via Berthollet 25 (011 669 6331/www.soundtown.it). Tram 16, 18. **Open** 11am-4am Mon-Sat. **No credit cards. Map** p245 A1.
This cultural association has a large bar on the ground floor, replete with free internet points and secluded spaces for lunch or tea. There are live music nights – there's lots of jazz here – as well as conferences and film screenings, held in the underground room. Comfortable and friendly, this is a great place to meet up with friends.

Transistor
Via Belfiore 24 (339 376 5282). Tram 18. **Open** 11.30pm-5am Thur-Sat. **Admission** ARCI membership card (€10 available at door). **No credit cards. Map** p245 A1.
Transistor is known for its drum 'n' bass nights (Fridays and Saturdays): some of the best in town.

Xò
Via Po 46 (011 817 8329/www.xocafe.it). Bus 55, 56, 61/tram 13, 15. **Open** 8.30am-3am Tue-Sun. **Credit** DC, MC, V. **Map** p243 C1.
A bar by day, this place transforms into one of the favourite meeting places for university students by night. The lower floor becomes a club or live music venue, hosting many parties for Erasmus exchange students too. There's a TV for football matches.

Aperitivi with music

See also p118 **Gran Bar** *and p117* **La Drogheria**.

Damadama
Piazza Madama Cristina 6 (011 655 711/www.damadama.it). **Open** *May-Sept* 11am-1am daily. *Oct-Apr* 6pm-1am daily. **No credit cards**. **Map** p245 A1.
You can start your night here with an *aperitivo* and stay into the small hours. On Thursday evenings musicians and writers man the console.

Imbarchino
Viale Cogni 37 (011 668 9039). **Open** *May-Oct* noon-3am daily. **No credit cards**. **Map** p245 A2.
Turin's summer hang-out *par eccellenza* is deep in the heart of the Parco del Valentino (*see p80*), on a series of terraces descending towards the River Po. From afternoon drinks-in-the-sun to music and cocktails into the small hours.

Sabor Latino.

La Collina

DJ bars & clubs

Hennessy
Strada Traforo del Pino 23, Pino Torinese (011 899 8522/www.hennessyclub.com). *No public transport*. **Open** 11pm-5am Tue-Sat. **Admission** €15-€20. **Credit** AmEx, DC, MC, V. **Map** p241.
One of Turin's biggest (real) discos, playing house and tribal house. Situated on the hill to the east of the city centre, it has an outside dancing space that opens in the summer and an inside dancefloor upstairs.

Zoo Bar
Corso Casale 127 (011 819 4347/www.barrumba.com). *Bus 30, 61*. **Open** 11pm-5am Tue, Fri-Sat. Closed July & Aug. **Admission** free Tue; €9 Fri; €10 Sat. **Credit** AmEx, MC, V, DC. **Map** p243 B3.
As well as live events and cabaret (Thursdays), this trendy disco-bar offers interesting clubbing evenings: R&B on Tuesdays and Fridays, house/dance music on Saturdays. The upper floor resembles a New York loft, the lower a rock café complete with memorabilia.

Lingotto

DJ bars & clubs

Hiroshima Mon Amour
Via Bossoli 83 (011 317 6636/ www.hiroshimamonamour.org). *Bus 14, 74/ tram 18*. **Open** 9pm-4am Tue-Sat; theatre 9.30pm; concerts 10.30pm. **Admission** *Disco* free. *Concerts & cabaret* prices vary. **No credit cards**. **Map** p246 B3.
One of Turin's historic *locali* and cultural centres, HMA started life in 1986 to promote Italian and international music and to stage comic and cabaret theatre. As well as clubbing on Saturday evenings (ska, reggae and pop), Hiroshima offers concerts and theatre shows. It also works with city authorities to organise festivals and big events (*see p155*). A great place for a drink before hitting a dance floor.

Transilvania
Corso Unione Sovietica 353 (011 613 669/ www.transilvania.it). *Bus 63/tram 4*. **Open** 9pm-4am. **Credit** AmEx, DC, MC, V. **Map** p244 D2.
This horror-rock-café is one of a series founded by Italian horror-flick director Dario Argento. Predictably dark and spooky, it's perfect for anyone whose idea of fun is eating on a coffin or drinking Dracula's blood to the sound of heavy metal music.

Suburbs

See also p159 **L'Espace**.

DJ bars & clubs

Sabor Latino
Via Stradella 10, Suburbs: north (011 852 327/ www.saborlatino.it). *Bus 11*. **Open** 11pm-4am Tue-Sun. **Admission** €5-€10. **No credit cards**. **Map** p242 A2.
This disco-pub is Turin's biggest and best-known venue for Latin and Caribbean sounds. There's live music some nights and lots of dancing.

Live music

Il Magazzino di Gilgamesh
Piazza Moncenisio 13B, Suburbs: north-west (011 749 2801/www.gilgameshtorino.it). *Bus 71/ tram 9, 16*. **Open** 8pm-2am Mon-Sat. **Admission** varies depending on concert. **Credit** MC, V. **Map** p242 A3.
This historic *ritrovo* (hangout) for live music lovers – mainly jazz and blues – has never seen a designer make-over. There are tables outside in the square in summer, and there's food too (average €15).`

Performing Arts

From traditional opera to avant-garde theatre, the performing arts scene in Turin is thriving.

Roman Turin had a mighty theatre (*see p58*), erected near the city gate both for ease of access for the whole local populace and to impress visitors on their first glimpse of the city. In later years drama was less democratic but just as demagogic: in the 17th century, in particular, theatre was a monopoly of the crown. Under the veil of 'metaphor' and allegorical 'mystery', precise political agendas were expressed through the 'fêtes, games, water festivals, jousts, similar tournaments and triumphs, ballets and masquerades' described by the artist Federico Zuccari on a trip to Piedmont in 1608.

These attractions were staged at the whim of the monarch inside royal residences for an elite and very restricted courtly public, or in the main piazza Castello (*see pp52-9*) as an expression of dynastic magnificence, ephemeral stage sets being created and dismantled on each occasion. Unlike other Italian cities, Turin had no purpose-built theatre until the first Teatro Regio was inaugurated in 1681, and

theatrical performances continued to be staged only for the court's enjoyment until well into the 18th century.

OPERA

From the start, serious 'theatre' was considered to be drama set to music – what we call opera – which saw its beginnings here in Turin in 1611 at the court of Carlo Emanuele I and has flourished in the city ever since. Opera has been performed in the new Teatro Regio since it was inaugurated in 1740, each opera accompanied by three ballets. Gradually, the season extended beyond the comparatively short period of *Carnevale* and the idea of 'repertoire' (works not written expressly for the particular theatre) took hold, and continues to be a large part of theatre programming today. The 19th century saw productions by the four great Italian composers of melodrama – Bellini, Donizetti, Rossini and the much-loved Verdi – although it was not until 1855 that the first comic opera was staged as part

Ballet has been performed at the **Teatro Regio** for nearly 300 years. *See p156.*

of the official opera season. By the turn of the twentieth century Turin's Regio was synonymous with the names of Wagner and Puccini, Massenet and Richard Strauss, Mercadante and Zandonai.

Today the season runs from October to June and offers at least ten operas (some of them specifically designed for Turin), classical ballet and choral-symphonic concerts. The Teatro Regio also hosts conferences, school initiatives and guided visits, placing it at the centre of the cultural life of the city and the Piedmont region. As the majority of *abbonati* (subscription-holders) tend to renew their subscription every year, it is not easy to get tickets, especially for a first night when the jewels and furs do appear; to avoid disappointment book early. (*See also p158* **Teatri storici.**)

THEATRE

Nowadays, alongside the opera season, the city boasts a rich range of drama and music appreciated by an active and highly knowledgeable theatre- and concert-going public, with each theatre having its share of faithful annual *abbonati*. The **Teatro Stabile di Torino** company (www.teatrostabile torino.it) puts on the great classics of both Italian and foreign prose and includes renowned Italian touring companies in its season. Performances are staged in the **Teatro Carignano** (*see p156*), **Teatro Gobetti** (*see p157*) and sometimes in the **Teatro Alfieri** (*see p156*), and are integrated by at least two annual productions by the TST's present director, the playwright Walter Le Moli.

Theatre on a less grand scale was given a boost recently when City Hall signed an agreement with major theatres to allow flourishing smaller companies an opportunity to stage their productions in prestigious venues. There is also a thriving experimental and avant-garde theatre scene which brings many Italian but also foreign companies on stage, and a small but active sector promoting cabaret.

Now enjoying much success on Italian television, **Hiroshima Mon Amour** (*see also p153*) was the catalyst that relaunched cabaret in Turin back in the late 1980s; it now organises a season from October to May, together with **Zelig Cabaret** from Milan. Since 1995 the **Festival Nazionale del Cabaret** has been held in Turin (www.festival nazionaledelcabaret).

There is also a lot of theatre in the city for children, not least Turin's traditional marionettes. The historical Lupi puppet company originated at the end of the 18th century and is now part of the **Museo della marionetta** (*see p137* **Gianduja**).

Turin's theatre season generally runs from October to May, after which summer festivals kick in. The **Festival delle Colline Torinese** (www.festivaldellecolline.it), for example, stages performances in the gardens of private hillside villas.

MUSIC

The classical music on offer in Turin is of an extremely high level with concert seasons organised by several renowned musical associations.

The national **Rai** symphony orchestra (www.orchestrasinfonica.rai.it) plays twice a week in Renzo Piano's auditorium in the ex-Fiat Lingotto factory (*see p86*) – the first evening always being broadcast live on the Rai3 public radio channel – and is directed by a variety of international conductors. It also holds RaiNuovaMusica, a season of contemporary music, and Domenica Musica, held on Sunday mornings at 11am in the Arsenale della Pace (piazza Borgo Dora 61, Quadrilatero).

Since 1946, the **Unione Musicale** (www.unionemusicale.it) has been organising classical concerts of great Italian and foreign artists, held in the **Conservatorio Giuseppe Verdi** (*see p156*), the **Lingotto Auditorium** (*see p158*) or the **Teatro Piccolo Regio** (*see p156*). In the autumn, the annual month-long festival **Torino Settembre Musica** (*see p157* **Torino Settembre Musica**) is now an event attracting worldwide attention.

The Conservatorio, with excellent acoustics for chamber music, is also home to the **Orchestra Filarmonica di Torino**'s (www.oft.it) season. This orchestra also organises the **Concerti Hicare** series of chamber music concerts (January-May, 9pm Mon) in the delightful surroundings of Palazzo Barolo (via delle Orfane 7, Quadrilatero), a baroque townhouse.

Turin has always been an active centre for jazz (*see also p150*), fostering Italian talent and inviting top international stars.

DANCE

Classical ballet is performed at the **Teatro Regio** (*see p156*) as part of the opera season, a tradition going back to 1740 when three ballets always accompanied every opera. The Regio also organises the **TorinoDanza** contemporary dance festival (011 881 5557/ www.comune.torino.it/torinodanza) held in various venues in February and May, and from September to November. More contemporary dance can be enjoyed at the **Teatro Nuovo** (*see p159*) or as part of the experimental productions at **L'Espace** (*see p159*). Tickets for both genres sell out immediately.

Venues

Castello

Teatro Piccolo Regio

Piazza Castello 215 (011 881 5241/www.teatro regiotorino.it). Bus 55, 56, 61/tram 13, 15. **Box office** at Teatro Regio (*see below*). **Map** p242 C3.
Situated beneath Teatro Regio, this small but comfortable theatre stages 700 events per year, the majority of which are concerts organised by the Unione Musicale (*see p155*) and the Centro Jazz (*see p150*).

Teatro Regio

Piazza Castello 215 (011 881 5241/ www.teatroregiotorino.it). Bus 55, 56, 61/tram 13, 15. **Open** *Box Office* 10.30am-6pm Tue-Fri; 10.30am-4pm Sat; 1hr before show & online. *Shows* 3pm, 8.30pm days vary. **Tickets** *Seasons' subscription* €62.50-€1,162. *Individual performances* €17-€155. **Credit** AmEx, MC, V. **Map** p242 C3.
Located in the Piazza Castello in the heart of Turin, the Teatro Regio is the mecca of Turinese classical music lovers (*see also p158* **Teatri Storici**). Each season sees 100 performances of opera and ballet for 165,000 paying spectators. The Filarmonica '900 Orchestra del Teatro Regio holds a cycle of concerts here from March to June every year with the Regio choir (€90 subscription; €15-€25 per concert; shows 5pm or 9pm, days vary).

Cittadella

Café Procope

Via Juvarra 15 (011 540 675/www.juvarra multiteatro.it). Bus 5, 50, 55, 59/tram 13, 15. **Open** 10pm-2am on performance days, which vary. **Admission** varies depending on event. **No credit cards**. **Map** p242 C2.
This offshoot of the Teatro Juvarra (*see below*) holds concerts, tango and flamenco evenings (€8) on Fridays, book presentations, art exhibitions, live jazz and blues on Wednesdays (€3), disco on Saturdays and experimental theatre (€10).

Tangram Teatro

Via Don Orione 5 (011 338 698/www. tangramteatro.it). Bus 2, 33, 42. **Open** *Box office* at theatre 30mins before show. *Shows* 9pm days vary. **Tickets** €10. **No credit cards**. **Map** p244 B2.
The tiny 75-seater Tangram Teatro shows interesting contemporary theatre not seen on the staider national circuit, with actors and public in close contact. Italian companies perform both Italian and foreign texts.

Teatro Alfieri

Piazza Solferino 2-4 (011 562 3800/www.torino spettacoli.it). Bus 5, 50, 55, 59/tram 13, 15. **Open** *Box office* 10am-10pm Mon-Sat; 2.30-10pm Sun. *Shows* 8.45pm Tue-Sat; 3.30pm Sun. **Tickets** €25-€32. **Credit** DC, MC, V. **Map** p242 C3.

The Alfieri's vast, faithful public of *abbonati* (subscribers) flocks to see prose, musical comedies and commercial productions. The Alfieri's I Concerti del Pomeriggio is a season of light music held from November to May at 4pm on Wednesdays; each concert costs €5.50. The Torino Spettacoli–Teatro Stabile Privato company that runs this theatre organises the following seasons staged in theatres under the same ownership: Eventi d'Autunno in October at the Alfieri and the Gioiello (*see below*); Grande Prosa from October to May at the Alfieri and the Erba (*see p157*); and Fiore all'Occhiello from November to May at the Alfieri and the Gioiello.

Teatro Gioiello

Via Cristoforo Colombo 31 (011 580 5768/ www.teatrogioiello.it). Bus 5/tram 16. **Open** *Box office* 9am-9pm daily. *Shows* 9pm Tue-Sat; 4pm Sun. **Tickets** €22.50. **Credit** DC, MC, V. **Map** p244 B2.
This theatre is home to productions by the Torino Spettacoli–Teatro Stabile Privato company (*see also above* Teatro Alfieri).

Teatro Juvarra

Via Juvarra 15 (011 540 675/www.juvarra multiteatro.it). Bus 5, 50, 55, 59/tram 13, 15. **Open** *Box office* 4-7pm Mon-Sat. *Shows* 8.45pm days vary. **Tickets** varies depending on event. **No credit cards**. **Map** p242 C2.
The Juvarra dates back to 1989 when the anomalous Granserraglio company of artists and musicians from Pistoletto's Zoo revamped this 220-seater theatre. Today it stages interesting modern authors or modern revisitations of the classics, both Italian and foreign, and experimental theatre. The annual Festival del Teatro di Figura event of puppets, marionettes, shadow theatre and masks is held here in September.

Centro

Conservatorio Giuseppe Verdi

Via Mazzini 11 (011 817 8458/www.conservatorio-torino.it). Bus 61/tram 68. **Open** *Box office* at individual organisers of the events. *Shows* days & times vary. **Tickets** varies depending on performance. **No credit cards**. **Map** p242 D3.
On beautiful piazza Bodoni, the Conservatorio Giuseppe Verdi is one of Italy's most famous music schools, attended by over 700 students. It is also the venue for concerts by the Orchestra Filarmonica di Torino (*see p155*) and the Unione Musicale (*see p155*). Every Wednesday afternoon at 5.30pm there are free lesson-concerts with Conservatorio professors and students – a good chance to spot Italy's up-and-coming classical music stars. The acoustics in the Conservatorio are the best in the city for chamber music.

Teatro Carignano

Piazza Carignano 6 (011 517 6246/ www.teatrostabiletorino.it). Bus 56, 61/tram 13, 15, 18. **Open** *Box office* (via Roma 49) 10.30am-7pm

Torino Settembre Musica

When the Torino Settembre Musica classical music festival began in 1977 it was a low-key – if high-quality – affair, held in fabulous baroque churches (many opened specially for the occasion) that you could wander into and out of at your leisure. Though half of the concerts at this September event remain free, times have moved on, and tickets for the rest are hotly contested from June onwards.

The 45-odd dates each year are divided into four strands by the festival's artistic director Enzo Restagno. First, there's a monograph on a composer – Estonia's Arvo Pärt, Japan's Toru Takemitsu and the Italian Salvatore Sciarrino have been recent choices. Then there are truly great orchestras under the batons of truly great conductors: Riccardo Muti and the Orchestra Filarmonica della Scala; Murray Perahia with the Academy of St Martin in the Fields; Colin Davis and the London Symphony Orchestra. Eastern music and dance – from Cambodia, Indonesia, India, China – gets a section to itself; as does the non-classical, with the likes of Brad Mehidau, Uri Caine, Bobby McFerrin and Ornette Coleman performing recently.

To round things off, there are conferences, performances in collaboration with the Teatro Regio (*see p156*) and TorinoDanza (*see p155*) and a host of fringe events.

The festival's original church venues no longer suffice to hold this slew of events, many of which are staged in auditoriums and theatres listed in this chapter. More unusual venues have been added to the list, such as the Borgo medioevale (*see p80*), the Beach at the Murazzi (*see p80 and p150* **I Murazzi**), the beautiful baroque courtyard of the university (*see p75*) and the Sandretto Re Rebaudengo contemporary art foundation (*see p68*).

Torino Settembre Musica

Box office: via San Francesco da Paola 6, Centro (011 442 4777/www.comune. torino.it/settembremusica). Bus 68. **Open** *June-Sept* 10.30am-6.30pm Mon-Sat. **Tickets** €315 festival pass; €4.90 single event. **Credit** DC, MC, V. **Map** p243 D1. There's a 30% surcharge on tickets bought online by credit card. There are many variations of tickets/passes at many different prices. Whatever you opt for, book as early as possible because demand for places is huge.

daily. *Shows* 8.45pm Tue-Sat; 3.30pm Sun.
Tickets €25. **Credit** MC, V. **Map** p242 C3.
This 600-seater theatre is almost 300 years old, the historic twin to the Regio (*see p158* **Teatri Storici**). Reservations can be made online.

Teatro Gianduja

Via Santa Teresa 5 (011 530 238). Bus 5, 14, 55, 59/tram 13, 15. **Open** *Box office* 30mins before shows. *Shows* times vary. **Tickets** €6.30. **No credit cards. Map** p242 C3.
See also p137 **Gianduja**.
The Teatro Gianduja houses the Museo della marionetta, formed around the historic 18th-century collection of puppets and marionettes made by the Lupi family, a tradition that goes back seven generations. There are workshops for children as well as marionette performances.

Teatro Gobetti

Via Rossini 8 (011 815 9132/www.teatro stabiletorino.it). Bus 6, 33, 42. **Open** *Box office* (via Roma 49) noon-7pm daily. *Shows* 3.30pm Sun; 8.45pm days vary. **Tickets** varies depending on performance. **Credit** MC, V. **Map** p243 C1.
Built in the 1840s for the Accademia Filarmonica and reopened in 2001 after restoration, the 230-seater Teatro Gobetti is now the pulsing heart of the Teatro Stabile di Torino (*see p155*).

La Collina

Alfa Teatro

Via Casalborgone 16 (011 819 3529/ www.alfateatro.com). Bus 61, 66. **Open** *Box office* 3.30-7.30pm Tue-Fri. *Shows* 4pm, 8.45pm Fri, Sat; 6pm Sun. **Tickets** €21. **Credit** MC, V. **Map** p243 C3.
The Alfa Teatro's own company stages an annual season of operetta from October to June, as well as plays and marionette shows. Its Giorni di Festa season from November to February (4.15pm Sun) features shows with marionettes, dolls and puppets for adults as well as children by the historic and highly acclaimed Marionette Grilli company (www.marionettegrilli.com). Tickets (€4-€6; free under-3s) for these performances can be ordered on 011 819 7350, or bought at the box office at via Casalborgone 14 (10am-1pm, 2.30-6.30pm Mon-Fri).

Teatro Erba

Corso Moncalieri 241 (011 661 5447/ www.torinospettacoli.it). Bus 47, 66, 67, 73. **Open** *Box office* 9am-10pm Mon-Sat; 3-10pm Sun. *Shows* 9pm Tue-Sat; 4pm Sun. **Tickets** €22.50. **Credit** MC, V. **Map** p243 D2.
The Teatro Erba's programme is run in association with the Alfieri (*see p156*).

Arts & Entertainment

Teatri storici

The first Teatro Regio (*see p57 and p154*) was officially inaugurated in 1681 when the reigning Savoy duke, Vittorio Amedeo I, came of age. It has been constantly in use ever since. Now a rival to Milan's La Scala and the San Carlo in Naples for opera, the present Teatro Regio is a bold 1960s building by architect Carlo Mollino. Walk around the Regio and admire its unashamedly curving sides – a homage to the female body – decorated with stars, a reference to Guarino Guarini's terracotta decoration on the façade of nearby 17th-century Palazzo Carignano (*see p72*).

The first theatre to stand on this site was replaced in 1738-40 with a design by Benedetto Alfieri, which seated 2,500 spectators and included state-of-the-art technology and highly sophisticated decorations. This second theatre was on the first floor, to facilitate direct royal access from the Palazzo Reale (*see p52*). Indeed, the theatre's façade was part of the unified, arcaded street front that linked the key royal, military and governmental buildings around the *'zona di comando'* (*see p53*). When Alfieri's theatre was destroyed by fire in 1936, Mollino rotated the axis of his new design, so that the theatre now no longer runs parallel to piazza Castello, but is perpendicular to it. Inside, Mollino's original plush red colour scheme, '60s lighting, huge window walls and walkways on four floors have been left untouched. The half-open shell shape of the 1,600-seater auditorium is lit by a further cascade of white-indigo lights; the stage is one of the largest in Europe. The acoustics were tweaked in the late 1990s and at the same time architects Gabetti & Isola restyled Mollino's proscenium and refurbished the wood facing and interior. Like its predecessors, Mollino's theatre has no front façade and still blends with the 17th-century street design.

The Teatro Carignano, Turin's other historic theatre, is quite different: small and intimate in feel, it's the only example of an 18th-century Turinese theatre to come down to us (almost) intact, with its horseshoe-shaped interior and tiered boxes... although the decor reflects Carlo Sada's mid 19th-century make-over when gas lighting was introduced. Built in 1711 by the Principe di Carignano (owner of the splendid baroque palazzo of the same name opposite, *see p72*), the theatre was erected on the site of a *trincotto*, the court for a ball game considered to be the forerunner of tennis. When first built the theatre had 56 sumptuously decorated boxes (though, pointedly, no royal box); in the 1750s it was rebuilt to a design by Alfieri who was also responsible for the layout of the piazza in front. Alfieri's version was destroyed by fire – a common occurrence in riotous 18th-century theatres. Rebuilt with great respect for Alfieri's design by Giovanni Battista Feroggio in 1787, it has only undergone external changes since then.

Lingotto

Auditorium Giovanni Agnelli
Via Nizza 280 (www.expo2000.it). Bus 35/tram 1, 18. **Open** *Box office* at individual organisers of the events. *Shows* days & times vary. **Tickets** varies depending on performance. **Map** p247 A2.
Redesigned by Renzo Piano in the ex-Fiat Lingotto factory, this vast auditorium is renowned for its excellent acoustics. It regularly hosts major international conductors and orchestras, as well as the national Orchestra Sinfonica nazionale della Rai (*see p155*). Some of the Settembre Musica festival concerts are performed here too (*see p157* **Torino Settembre Musica**). When it's not being used as a concert hall the auditorium doubles up as a conference facility (*see p86*).

Teatro Agnelli
Via P Sarpi 111 (011 304 2808/www.assembleateatro.com). Bus 62, 63, 74/tram 4, 10. **Open** *Box office* 30mins before performance. *Shows* 9pm days vary. **Tickets** €10; €6 Thur. **No credit cards. Map** p246 B3.
The Agnelli hosts two seasons organised by Assemblea Teatro: Insolito, from January to May, explores 'the unusual'; while in January and February Domenicamattinateatro! will amuse your three-to-six year olds, from 11am each Sunday.

Teatro Colosseo
Via Madama Cristina 71 (011 669 8034/ www.teatrocolosseo.it). Bus 67/tram 9, 16, 18. **Open** *Box office* 10am-1pm, 3-7pm Mon-Sat. *Shows* 9pm days vary. **Tickets** vary. **No credit cards. Map** p245 A1.
The largest theatre in Turin, with 1,600 seats, the Colosseo stages both plays and musical performances. Its November to May season includes big-attraction shows with musicals, dance and performances by renowned TV actors as well as major commercial theatre companies.

The historic **Teatro Carignano**. *See p156.*

Teatro Nuovo
Corso Massimo d'Azeglio 17 (011 650 0211/
www.teatronuovo.it). Bus 45, 67/tram 16, 18.
Open *Box office* 9am-7pm Mon-Sat; 3-7pm Sun.
Shows 4pm, 9pm days vary. **Tickets** vary.
No credit cards. **Map** o245 A2.
This major venue for contemporary dance hosts the
Il Gesto e l'Anima festival – now (2004) in its 25th
year – with shows by the theatre's own company
and other Italian and foreign companies. There's
also an operetta festival in January and February.

Suburbs

Teatro Araldo
Via Chiomonte 3A, Suburbs: west (011 331 764/
www.transeuropetheatre.org). Bus 33, 42, 55/tram
16. **Open** *Box office* 4-7pm Thur-Sat. *Shows* 9.15pm
Fri, Sat; 4.30pm Sun. **Tickets** €4. **No credit cards**.
Map p244 B1.
The resident Teatro del Angolo company produces
contemporary theatrical projects directed by and for
young people and teenagers. It also organises the
national Il Gioco del Teatro festival for Italian children in April, attracting young spectators from all
over the country.

L'Espace
Via Mantova 38, Suburbs: north (011 238
6067/www.salaespace.it). Bus 33, 42, 55/tram
16. **Open** *Box office* 1hr before show. *Shows* 9pm,
10.30pm days vary. **Tickets** €8-€10. **No credit**
cards. **Map** p243 B1.
This was the site occupied by the Arturo Ambrosio
film studios, producing silent films in the early 20th
century. The large spaces, renovated in 2001, are
suitable for all the diverse requirements of experimental and avant-garde theatre. It's home to the
Compagnia Sperimentale Drammatica, founded in
1971 in Amsterdam as the Mobile Action Artists'
Foundation. It stages the experimental theatre and
contemporary dance season Marginalia and also
holds art exhibitions. There are music/DJ nights too.

Teatro Monterosa
Via Brandizzo 65, Suburbs: north (011 284
028/www.teatromonterosa.it). Bus 2, 27, 57, 63,
75/tram 4. **Open** *Box office* 5-7pm Mon-Sat &
during show. *Shows* 9pm Fri, Sat. **Tickets** €8.
No credit cards. **Map** off p243 A1.
The Monterosa doubles up as a cinema and has
many performances for children. Its September-
to-March season is all in Piedmontese dialect: try
it – other Italians don't understand it either.

Sport & Fitness

The *torinesi*'s love affair with food is only matched by their obsession with exercise.

Juventus: black and white magic.

On Sunday mornings the sober, reserved elegance of the *torinese* middle class is replaced by a frivolous disregard for style as it mounts its bike. Inspired, it would seem, by Marvel comics, these bespoked, bespectacled office workers change into their favourite superhero-cum-rock star: catwomen, daredevils and spidermen complete with psychedelic wraparounds can be seen puffing round the city's parks and gardens in displays of tight-fitting ostentatiousness.

Jostling for space are the Sunday morning joggers, in similar attire. They, too, are either working up an appetite, or burning off the previous night's heavy calorie intake. The **Giardino Fausto Coppi** (*see p162* **The best jogging**) is as busy in the morning as the shopping street via Roma is in the afternoon. From December to Easter the parks are less crowded at weekends; you'll find everyone on

the pistes (for skiing information, *see p208* **Ski report**). Some 80 per cent of the city's indigenous population between the ages of six and 60 are competent-to-excellent skiers. (The remaining 20 per cent have had a bad accident and lost their nerve, or are working too hard). Schools close for a week in February to allow families to head off for the annual *settimana bianca* (literally, white week). Roof racks are loaded with a dazzling display of waxed Alpine armoury before being whisked off to high altitudes.

Spectator sports

Football

The draughty high-tech **Stadio delle Alpi** is the battle ground for black and white magic in the form of the **Juventus** football team (www.juventus.com), renowned throughout the world thanks to the on-field antics of some of its better-known players, some of whom have achieved the status of demigod. The same turf is shared by the equally well-loved **Torino Calcio** (www.toro.it; *see below* **Il Grande Toro**), whose *granata* (ox-blood) strip is a metaphor for the purest hot-blooded passion.

Rivalry is intense and very, very serious. Supporting the right team, for example, may be the deciding factor when it comes to promotion in the workplace. On derby day, visitors to the main squares might be led into believing that a medieval jousting tournament is about to be re-enacted: flags, banners, scarves and bunting festoon the arcades and lamp-posts as fans in warpaint taunt each other from the safety of small groups. As the day draws on, ticket-holders make their way to the Stadio delle Alpi, while the rest of the population files into bars, clubs or squares to follow the match on any of the many mega-screens laid on by the local council for the occasion. When the final whistle blows, fans of the winning team grab car keys,

Il Grande Toro

For many, Turin means Fiat cars and Juventus, not necessarily in that order. But there's a staunch band of supporters of Torino, Turin's other football team, for whom Juventus is of minor importance. These days, Torino languishes around the middle of the Second (B) division. In the first half of the last century, Il Grande Toro *was* Italian football.

Like so many sporting associations, Il Toro grew out of a business meeting over a drink in a noisy *birreria*. On 3 December 1906, defectors from the Football Club Juventus, together with some ex-members of the defunct Football Club Torinese, merged to form the Football Club Torino. *Granata* (garnet – an ox-blood colour) was the colour chosen for the new team's strip.

In the early years, Toro's success was overshadowed by the better-established Juventus. But Juventus's run of five successive league championship titles was brought to a stop by the *granata* in the 1935-6 championship games. For his skills, each Toro player received an income of 330 lire a month.

Second World War bombing raids killed a few Toro players, and direct hits on stadiums meant that the venue for matches shifted twice, but the team went from strength to strength. In 1943 a historic victory on Easter Sunday took the team back to the top of the league: the winning goal has been known as the *uovo di Pasqua* (Easter egg) ever since. Later in the same year they achieved an Italian record when they swept both League and Coppa Italia.

In 1944 it was uncertain whether the season could even begin: American troops had landed in Sicily, and sporadic bursts of violent conflict rocked the North. But football is, after all, football, and against this back-drop of near-civil war, a special Northern League was conceived to keep the game alive. In 1944 one of the most arduous return matches in the history of football took place in Trieste: Toro players took eight days to complete the return journey by train, lorry and on foot. Not surprisingly, on their return home Toro was trounced in a long-planned match against firemen from La Spezia.

It was back to relative normality by October 1945, when Italy was invited to play a friendly against Switzerland. The national team included seven Toro players. Fans brought an anthem back from beyond the Alps that would be heard round the Stadio Comunale back in Turin; it had something of the eerie premonition about it:

Torino, oui, oui
Torino, là, là
Torino ne périra pas

Success followed success and in the 1947-8 season the team didn't lose a single match. But this victorious reign was to come to a tragic and abrupt end on 4 May 1949. Italian national captain Valentino Mazzola had organised a friendly match in Lisbon to mark the retirement of Portuguese squad leader Francisco Ferreira, who wanted to end his career playing what was then considered one of Europe's greatest teams. On the way back, Toro's aircraft crashed into the fog-swathed hill behind the basilica di Superga (*see p91*). The shocked city went into mourning.

Why the tragedy occurred is still a matter for debate. Meteorological conditions played their part, clearly. But life was hard in post-war Italy and luxury items scarce. Some say the plane was re-routed from Turin's main airport and sent along a flight path unfamiliar to the pilot to a smaller airfield in order to avoid paying duty on the players' precious cargo of spirits and perfumes.

Arts & Entertainment

friends, neighbours and passers-by and flood into the city centre. The resulting gridlock only begins to disentangle itself in the early hours of the following morning.

Stadio delle Alpi
Strada di Alessano 131, Suburbs: north (011 732 947). Bus 9B (on match days), 29, 72/tram 3. **Tickets** €10-€150. **Credit** depends on outlet. **Map** p241.
Nothing is more eerie and spectacular than this post-modern temple to sport when framed by snow-capped mountains. Tickets can be bought from selected tobacconists, lotto ticket sellers (www.lottomaticaservizi.it) and official club shops (*see below*).

The best Jogging

The Piedmontese predilection for long and elaborate meals has made jogging a necessary evil.

Parco del Valentino
See p80
This picturesque riverside park may soon need traffic lights to regulate the flow of fitness freaks. Full of kiosks selling sugary boosters.

La Pellerina
Map p241
On the outskirts of Turin, this park is popular with adventurous types who can survey the not-too-distant Alps.

From Giardini Fausto Coppi to viale Michelotti
Map p243 C2
The row of monumental plane trees beside the river provides welcome shade during the summer months.

Parco della Colletta
Map p243 A3
Gravel running paths follow the river past workout stations and ad hoc barbecue areas where the smell of grilled meat and sounds of Balkan folk music pervade the park as refugees from ex-Yugoslavia get together to eat, drink and dance in the open air.

Parco Cavalieri di Vittorio Veneto
Map p244 D2
Sports fans are drawn here in the hope of catching a glimpse of the Juventus team practising on the other side of a high security fence.

Tickets & accessories

Official club-related paraphernalia for the devout can be purchased at:

Juventus Store Torino
Via Garibaldi 4E, Centro (011 433 8709). Bus 11, 12, 55, 56, 57, 63/tram 4, 13, 15. **Open** 3.30-7.30pm Mon; 10am-7.30pm Tue-Sat. **Credit** AmEx, MC, V. **Map** p242 C3.
This ultra-modern environment, full of glass cabinets, resembles an airport duty free shop. Flat screens show a continuous loop of past victories, and changing exhibitions bring together private collections of sweaty shirts, boots and other holy relics.

Toro Store
Via Allioni 3, Cittadella (011 521 7803). Bus 29, 55, 56/tram 13. **Open** 3-7pm Mon; 10am-7pm Tue-Sat. **Credit** MC, V. **Map** p242 C2.
The less business-like atmosphere and affable English-speaking shop manager make this the best place to catch up with the *granata*'s (*see p161* **Il Grande Toro**) ups and downs on and off the field.

Active sports & fitness

Climbing & trekking

Club Alpino Italiano
Via Barbaroux 1, Centro (011 546 031/ www.caitorino.it). Bus 55, 56/tram 13, 15. **Open** 2.30-6.30pm Mon-Fri. **Rates** *Annual membership* €38 per person; €56 per couple; €14 under-17s. **No credit cards**. **Map** p242 C3.
If the sight of the nearby Alps gets your feet itching for a wander and your hands craving a sheer rock face, the CAI (Club Alpino Italiano) can provide some useful information to non-members. It also organises a spectacular variety of one-day and weekend excursions with professional guides for members.
On the same phone number, the Giusto Gervasutti climbing school offers advice on climbing anything from brick walls to frozen waterfalls. Specialist courses begin in September.

Cycling

(For **bike hire**, *see p220*.)
The city itself has a 40-kilometre (25-mile) network of cycle paths that are becoming busier every year. Although the inner-city stretches are not always clear of parked cars, it is possible to ride from the Stupinigi (*see p93*) hunting lodge to San Mauro (40 kilometres/25 miles) without encountering major roads or hills. The recently inaugurated route is well signposted and takes you through the Parco delle Vallere, the Parco Valentino and down to the Murazzi (*see p80*), then through the Parco della Colletta from where you head north-east out of the city towards the Monferrato region (*see p186*).

Golf

Golf is an exclusive game in Italy and a good place to do business with local industrialists. Most clubs will ask you to produce a membership card from your home club before letting you loose on their greens and fairways. You can also take advantage of a Torino golf pass. There are two passes valid for 24 hours (€25) or 72 hours (€60) from Monday to Friday. They can be used at several courses near the city. The pass includes the green fee, bag and clubs hire. Apply for one at promozione@turismotorino. org or by fax (011 883 426). Payment can be made in cash, by cheque or by credit card (MC, V). Pick up the pass from any Turismo Torino office (*see p228* **Atrium**), or from most central hotels. To get a pass, non-residents need to produce a document showing their handicap.

Associazione Sportiva i Roveri

Rotta Cerbiatta 24, Fiano Torinese (011 923 5719/ www.iroveri.com). SEAG coach from corso Giulio Cesare. **Open** 8.30am-6.30pm Tue-Sun. **Rates** *Green fee* €65 Mon-Fri; €85 Sat, Sun. *Driving range* €15. *Golf cars* €30. **Credit** AmEx, DC, MC, V. **Map** p241.
The Mandria (*see p89*) is the royal setting for this superb golf course. Designed by Robert Trent Jones, it has been voted the best in Italy. Its chairman is none other than Umberto Agnelli (*see p21* **Whither Fiat?**). If you haven't brought your clubs, don't even think about it, unless, of course, you are a foreign head of state, ambassador or royalty.

Golf Club i Girasoli

Strada Pralormo 315, Carmagnola (011 979 5088/ www.girasoligolf.it). GTT bus for Alba from piazza Marconi (ask driver to let you off at I Girasoli course). **Open** Feb-Dec (depending on snow) 8.30am-dusk Mon, Tue, Thur-Sun. **Rates** *Green fee* €28 weekdays; €40 weekends. *Club hire* €15. **Credit** AmEx, MC, V. **Map** p241.
As well as an 18-hole course par 65, this club offers *agriturismo* (farm holiday) accommodation and an open-air swimming pool. The 15-room guest house (€70 per person per night) is closed in January; golf and accommodation costs €86. A nine-hole par 27 pitch and putt course is open from May to October.

Gyms

Palestra Centro Ginnico Azzurra

Via Boccardo 10, Suburbs: north (011 218 170). Bus 10, 60. **Open** 9am-10pm Mon, Wed, Thur; 10am-10pm Tue, Fri; 10am-1pm, 3.30-6pm Sat. **Rates** €78 for 12 sessions; €7.50 per day. **Credit** DC, MC, V. **Map** p242 A2.
This roomy suburban hothouse is a good place to take virtual mountain bikes out for a spin.

Palestra Gymnica i Club

Via Governolo 36, Cittadella (011 597 951/ www.gymnica.it). Bus 64/tram 5, 15. **Open** 8.30am-

The Po's a good place for a paddle. *See p164.*

9.30pm Mon-Fri; 11am-3pm Sat. **Rates** €70 2wks. **Map** p244 A3.
In winter you may have to move aside a fur coat to get to your locker. The air-conditioning in summer means you probably won't see a bead of sweat on any of the well-heeled clientele, as they get back into shape before the yachting season.

Palestra Il Pardo

Via Accademia Albertina 31, Centro (011 883 900/ www.ilpardo.it). Bus 68/tram 9, 18. **Open** 9am-10.30pm Mon-Fri; 9am-6pm Sat; 9.30am-1.30pm Sun. Closed 2wks Aug. **Rates** €60 1wk. **Credit** DC, MC, V. **Map** p243 C1.
This trendy gym has a special agreement with most hotels in the centre of Turin, which means you can book a session directly through the hotel.

Ice skating

Boisterous driving techniques come in handy on the ice, especially if you are part of the Italian ice hockey team warming up for the Winter Olympics. The **Palaghiaccio Rotelliere** will host the event in 2006 (*see p87* **Olympic venues**).

Palaghiaccio Rotelliere

Via Petrarca 39, Lingotto (011 669 9862). Bus 45, 67/tram 9. **Open** *Ice skating rink* noon-2pm Tue; noon-1pm Thur; 9.30pm-midnight Wed, Fri; 3-5pm,

Arts & Entertainment

9pm-midnight Sat; 10am-noon, 3-6pm Sun. *Roller skating rink* noon-6pm Mon, Tue, Thur; noon-6pm, 9.30pm-midnight Wed, Fri; 10am-noon, 3-6pm Sun. **Admission** €6; €4 under-12s. *Skate hire* €5. **No credit cards**. Map p245 B1.

Massari

Via Massari 114, Suburbs: north (011 220 6211). Bus 21. **Open** *Mid Oct-mid Mar* 9-11pm Fri, Sat; 10am-noon, 9-11pm Sun. **Admission** *Fri* €5; €4 under-15s. *Sat & Sun* €6; €4 under-15s. **Skate hire** €5. **No credit cards**. Map p241.

It's best to call ahead before schlepping all the way to this outdoor rink where opening times depend on weather conditions.

Riding

Mela Cotogna

Parco delle Vallere, Moncalieri (011 677 097). Bus 40, 45 to Maroncelli stop, then walk through park to river/river boat to Mela Cotogna. **Open** 2.30-6.30pm Mon, Tue, Thur, Fri; 9.30am-12.30pm, 2.30-6.30pm Sat, Sun. **Rates** *5 lessons* €72. *30min trips for children with teacher* €6; *1hr riverside treks with teacher* €13; *riverside trips (whole morning)* €36. **No credit cards**. Map p241.

This rather informal centre – run from a couple of rustic log cabins – also organises special courses for beginners and more experienced riders.

Scuderia Cascina Vittoria

La Mandria, Venaria (011 499 3381/3326). Bus 70 to Venaria, taxi to park entrance, then 20min walk. **Open** dawn-dusk daily. **Rates** €13 1hr; €21 2hrs; €25 3hrs. **No credit cards**. Map p241.

The friendly people at the stables are happy to show experienced riders around the park at any time between dawn and dusk. You must book with no fewer than three people in a group. For people without any experience, horse-drawn coach trips are also available. The coach sits up to seven passengers and costs €24 plus €6 per person; trips last one-and-a-half hours and take you past the beautiful neo-Gothic Castello dei Laghi, normally out of bounds.

Rowing

Rowing on the Po dates back to the 1880s; in the 1920s and '30s oarsmen had to steer clear of the seaplane that flew a regular service between the riverbank by the Parco del Valentino *(see p80)* and Venice. Some of the city's most prestigious rowing clubs have changed very little since those days. Nowadays, though, carbon fibre has replaced wood, and clubs are unlikely to let novices out in one of their expensive craft.

Società Canottieri Esperia

Corso Moncalieri 2, Collina (011 819 3013/ www.esperia-torino.it). Bus 56, 61/tram 13. **Courses** *Canoe/kayak* 3.30-5pm Mon, Wed, Fri (5 lessons €120). *Rowing* 1-2.30pm, 7-8.30pm Mon; 1-2.30pm

Wed, Fri; 7-8.30pm Thur; 11am-12.30pm Sat (weekly for 2mths €130). **No credit cards**. Map p245 A2.

Only healthy people need apply. Proof of membership of a rowing club back home entitles you to pats on the shoulder and reams of anecdotes from the club's passionate members, many of whom have raced on the Thames.

Swimming pools

Public swimming pools set aside hours for schools and private coaching; these often take up large chunks of the day. Check the patchwork of opening times before packing towel, costume and shampoo. Swimming hats *(cuffie)* are compulsory in both private and municipal pools.

Centro Nuoto Torino

Corso Sebastopoli 260, Suburbs: south (011 322 448/www.centronuototo.it). Bus 17, 55, 58, 62. **Open** 10.30am-3pm Mon; 12.30-3pm Tue-Fri; 9.30am-6pm Sat. **Admission** €3.73; €3.19 under-16s. **No credit cards**. Map p244 D2.

To keep the splashing down to a minimum, this indoor public pool is only open to over-16s; children beneath that age have a small slot with their parents at 2.30-3.30pm on Saturdays.

Colletta

Via Ragazzoni 5, Parco della Colletta, Suburbs: north-east (011 284 626). Bus 19, 77. **Open** 7.20-9pm Mon, Fri; 12.40-2.20pm Tue, Thur; 10am-noon Sat. **Admission** €3.73; €3.19 under-16s. **No credit cards**. Map p243 A3.

These indoor (open all year) and outdoor (open mid May-Sept, unless temperatures plunge) pools, pleasantly situated in parkland near the confluence of the Po and Dora, are popular with summer sunbathers.

Tennis

Most tennis clubs require you to become a member before using the facilities. But trainers, tracksuits and cash will often suffice to see the rules waived. These two historic riverside clubs, which began life as rowing associations, are well worth visiting just for the *stile Liberty* *(see p26)* decor and view of the river from the terrace. Both have clay courts, a bar, restaurant and lots of bridge tables.

Caprera

Corso Moncalieri 22, Collina (011 660 3816). Bus 52, 56, 61/tram 13. **Open** 8.30am-midnight daily. **Court hire** *Apr-Sept* (outoor) daily 9am-12.30pm, 3-5pm €10.50. *Oct-Mar* (indoor) Mon-Fri 8am-noon €18; noon-10pm €25; 10pm-midnight €18; Sat, Sun €25. **No credit cards**. Map p243 D2.

Esperia

Corso Moncalieri 2, Collina (011 819 3013). Bus 56, 61/tram 13. **Open** 8.30am-11pm daily. **Court hire** €18. **No credit cards**. Map p243 D2.

Arts & Entertainment

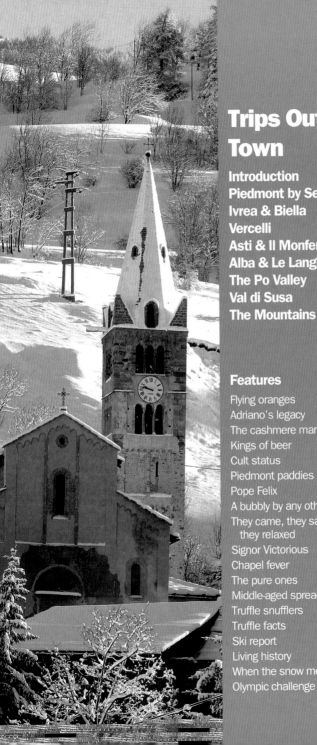

Trips Out of Town

Features

Introduction

From the vast flat expanses of the Po valley to the soaring Alps, Piedmont is a region of dramatic natural contrasts.

The grand northern Italian families that frequented the court of the Savoys (*see p8* **The unstoppable Savoys**) in Turin drew their wealth from huge estates around the region of Piedmont. It was to these country power-bases that the Piedmontese aristocracy withdrew when the pressures of court life grew too great, and here – as in the case of Count Camillo Cavour (*see p10* **The four horsemen of the Risorgimento**) – that they banished their wayward offspring if they became too seditious.

Later it was Turin's industrialists who sought a bolt-hole in the quiet of the countryside. The Agnellis – owners of the Fiat auto maker – have their estate at Villa Perosa on the way to the **Val Chisone** (*see p212*), not to mention their purpose-built ski resort at **Sestrière** (*see p213*); the Feltrinellis – of the eponymous publishing house – kick back in their 18th-century villa at **Villadeati** (*see p188*) in the Monferrato.

Nowadays, frequenters of the region surrounding Turin are more likely to be sports fiends or gastronomes. The former head for the ski resorts of the extraordinary **Via Lattea** (*see p208* **Ski report**) – 400 kilometres (250 miles) of pistes that zigzag between Italy and France through spectacular Alpine landscapes. The latter, on the other hand, find their spiritual home in the **Langhe** (*see p194*) or the **Monferrato** (*see p187*), where they wallow in truffles and some of Italy's greatest wines, including noble Barolo and sparkling Moscato.

Between these two extremes is a little bit of everything, from dramatic medieval abbeys at the **Sacra di San Michele** (*see p204*) and **Oropa** (*see p177*) to hot springs and pampering at **Acqui Terme** (*see p186* **They came, they saw... they relaxed**). There are forts (*see p213* **Fenestrelle**) and New Age temples (*see p178* **Cult status**), industrial hubs around **Ivrea** and **Biella** (*see pp171-9*), and vast expanses of emerald-green rice paddies in **Vercelli** province (*see pp180-83*).

Getting around

We have provided information on how to reach each of the towns and villages covered in the Trips Out of Town section.

The best way of seeing the byways and backwaters of Piedmont is, of course, by car. For information on car hire from Turin, *see p220*.

Train is the best option for travelling between Turin and the larger towns covered in this section. For information on train services, *see p217*. Where there are buses, they tend to be slower and less frequent, but will take you through – and allow you to get off in – interesting places along your route... though don't get off until you've made sure there is another bus later on with which to resume your journey.

Public transport to many of the smaller towns and villages covered in this section is well-nigh non-existent. Keep your wits about you when studying bus timetables – many rural bus services only run on weekdays (*feriali*) and during the school term (*servizio scolastico*). In other places – including the ski resorts (*see pp206-14*) – bus services are frequent and reliable.

The www.regione.piemonte.it/prontotrasporti website provides information on regional transport. The region's toll-free information line (800 990 097 from land lines only) operates from 7am to 9pm daily, with recorded information outside those hours. From mobile phones call 011 691 0000; for information for the hearing-impaired, call 011 882 231.

Vercelli's **Cattedrale di Sant'Eusebio**.
See p182.

Piedmont by Season

Who said the Piedmontese don't know how to party?

Other Italians like to imagine the dour Piedmontese as too wrapped up in their work to take much time off for celebrations, but the stereotype is far from the truth.

In the valleys to the west of Turin, jealously preserved local traditions mean that some festivities date back to pre-Roman days when Celts and Ligurian tribesmen populated the region. They begin – like all good fertility rites – bright and early in the year when the sun's rays return to the narrow valleys after their chilly winter absence.

Around the former Kingdom of Sardinia-Piedmont, pageants that were once performed by loyal flag-waving monarchists have been transformed into more republican-spirited shindigs.

Then there are the gastronomic feasts. Piedmont's food chain begins with its excellent soil: every type of fruit and vegetable originating from it has been honoured with a festival, fair or celebration. This bacchanal spirit naturally extends to the animals that feed on the lush green pastures that stretch up high into the mountains. As well as older food-related festivities, worldwide interest in the region's cooking, promoted by organisations like Slow Food (*see p31* **Slow and steady**), has generated a thriving series of events to celebrate its culinary resourcefulness. (For festivals and events in Turin, *see pp132-4*.)

Winter

Cavour: Tuttomele

Information 0121 68 194/fax 0173 757 730/www.cavour.info. **Date** Nov.
The small town of Cavour, 40km (25 miles) south of Turin, celebrates the produce from its apple orchards with Tuttomele. Adams and Eves are encouraged to crunch into the many varieties and delight in a little taste of Eden.

Carrù: Il Bue Grasso

Information 0173 757 725/www.comune.carru.cn.it. **Date** Dec.
On the second Thursday before Christmas, Carrù groans to the thud of heavyweight hooves and boots as devoted epicureans and the curious alike pay tribute to the mastodontic Piedmontese breed of cattle reared in its environs. Buried deep in folklore, tradition and mud, the town is the home of the Il Bue Grasso (the fattened ox) where not one, but hundreds

of the finest examples of this prized ghostly white beast are paraded and awarded trophies – after rigorous anti-doping tests have been carried out – before falling to the auctioneer's hammer and ultimately the chop. These animals are the stuff of Piedmont's finest *bollito misto* (boiled meats) and tastiest tripe, both of which can be savoured at specially organised tasting sessions.

Val di Susa: Danza della Spada

Information 011 932 8650/www.montagnedoc.it. **Date** Jan-Apr.
While the skiing season is still in full swing, a number of towns in the Susa valley celebrate the Danza delle Spada (sword dance). The valley rings with the sound of tempered steel on stone as *spadari* or *spadolari* (swordsmen), accompanied by the local brass band, prance through the streets wearing ornate flowery hats, stopping periodically to carry out mock fights and perform complex dances. The best place to witness these unique performances are Giaglione (22 Jan) and Venàus (3 Feb). San Giorio has elaborated this ritual to include the performance of a play written in the1930s by a local priest, which tells the story of a local peasant uprising (late Apr). At least one member from every household takes part in the show.

Urbiano di Monpantero, Val di Susa: Ballo dell'Orso

Information 0122 622 323/www.comune.mompantero.to.it. **Date** Feb.
Fertility rites don't come much stranger than the Ballo dell'Orso (bear dance), where a poor bear is flogged and flayed by the town's inhabitants on the first Sunday after Sant'Orso (St Bear; 31 Jan). By unleashing their rage and frustrations upon the unfortunate animal, they hope to be blessed with a bountiful harvest. Animal rights activists need not worry; the luckless victim is a local dressed up for the occasion, who is rewarded for his part by being 'forced' to drink wine through a funnel and dance with the prettiest maiden in town.

Spring

See also above **Danza della Spada**; *p173* **Flying oranges**.

Tonco, nr Asti: La Giostra del Pitu

Information 0141 991 044/www.atasti.it. **Date** Feb-Mar.
Each year as part of Tonco's pre-Lenten *Carnevale* celebrations, a turkey (*pitu* in local dialect) is tried before the town's elders and made to answer for the

town's wrongdoings and misfortunes during the previous year. Sentence is passed, and the luckless bird is hung up in the main square for knights on galloping horses to let fly at with sticks and try to behead it. These days the animal is already dead before it goes on trial.

Castello di Masino, Caravino, nr Ivrea: Tre Giorno per il Giardino
Information 0125 797 900/www.fondoambiente.it. **Date** May.

On the first weekend of May, the landscaped park next to the Castello di Masino (*see p173*) is the lush setting of Tre Giorni per il Giardino. The best Italian nurseries, representing practically each region, rub shoulders with plant enthusiasts from abroad in this garden show with a difference. Here you might find orange trees from Sicily and oaks from Somerset battling it out for one of the coveted prizes. The event also attracts amateur enthusiasts who are invited to display their exhaustive collections of a particular genus. Specially organised exhibitions will instruct you on how to create your own garden à la Russell Page, or how to restore your neglected Roman herb garden.

Cavour: Il Pranzo dei Grassoni
Information La Locanda La Posta, 0121 69 989/ www.locandalaposta.it. **Date** May.

This politically incorrect biennial Fatty of the Year Contest (2006, 2008…) involves climbing on the scales at the entrance to the restaurant before trying to outeat heavyweights from around the world. The person whose weight has increased most after the meal wobbles away with a prize. The meal is on the house. Phone the restaurant to enter.

Summer

Canelli, Asti: Assedio di Canelli
Information www.assediodicanelli.info. **Date** June.

On the third weekend of June, in Canelli, near Asti, a 1613 siege by Mantuan forces is re-enacted by locals in period costume with much quaffing of wine and eating of banquets prepared by local restaurants. You'll need to book well in advance for a table at the victory dinner or for a tour of the besieged cellars of the town.

Fenestrelle, Val di Chisone: Le Fenestrelle
Information 0121 836 00/www.fortedifenestrelle. com. **Date** Aug.

Begun in 1727 to defend Turin from French invaders, the fort of Fenestrelle is now the setting for an extensive programme of outdoor events in August. Festivities include contemporary and traditional music concerts, plays and re-enacted battles. The highlight of the season takes place on 25 August, when both town and fort buzz with dancers, musicians and cauldrons of bubbling polenta covered with a wild boar or ibex sauce.

Back to the Middle Ages at the **Palio d'Asti**.

Rivoli: C'era una Volta un Re
Information 011 956 1043/www.turismovest.it. **Date** Aug-Sept.

C'era una Volta un Re (Once upon a time there was a king…) may sound like the opening line of a fairy tale but this celebration has its roots in a very real event: the abdication of Vittorio Amedeo II in favour of his son Carlo Emanuele III. Rivoli castle provides the majestic backdrop for a bustling array of courtiers, page boys, parading horses and jesters in fine costumes, whose combined effect is a spectacle of exceptional elegance.

Autumn

See also p176 **Ricetto di Candelo**.

Asti: Douja d'Or & Palio d'Asti
Information 0141 530 357/www.terredasti.it. **Date** Sept.

Asti's obvious prosperity is due in no small part to its thriving wine industry, which duly celebrates and promotes local brews at the Douja d'Or fest from the second to the third Sunday of September. Each

Trips Out of Town

Serenading the truffle at the **Fiera Nazionale del Tartufo Bianco d'Alba**.

year about 80,000 visitors descend on the town to take part in the wine and grappa event. Although this fair is dedicated to wine, a fine selection of local cuisine is also always available: park your knees under the table at one of the outdoor kitchens. The event culminates with the Palio d'Asti when the central piazza Alfieri is decked out in medieval trimmings and carpeted with sand and sawdust to become a racetrack for local bareback riders from the town's rival boroughs.

Bra: Cheese – Le Forme del Latte

Information 0172 419 611/www.slowfood.com. **Date** Sept.

Organised by Slow Food (*see p31* **Slow and steady**) the biennial Cheese – Le Forme del Latte festival brings together a massive array of fine Italian and international cheeses on the third weekend of September in odd years (2005, 2007…). At the same time, children aged four to ten can learn about cheese-making, cheesy traditions and shepherds' work conditions at Cheese Bimbi.

Barolo: Festa del Barolo

Information 0173 56 106. **Date** Sept.

Rich, deep red Barolo is a name to set wine connoisseurs' hearts a-flutter. Situated in a natural hol-

low between neatly manicured vineyards, the eponymous town exudes an appealing bouquet of wealth and pride. A modest Festa del Barolo takes place during the second weekend in September. After the grapes have been picked they are ceremoniously borne to the local *cantine*, where trumpeters or a jazz band herald the new arrival.

Alba: Fiera Nazionale del Tartufo Bianco d'Alba

Information 0173 362 807/www.fieradeltartufo. albain.it. **Date** Oct.

The exorbitant fungus *Tuber magnatum* makes its regular appearance in these parts in the late autumn: the white truffle grows beneath dense oak, lime and poplar woods in the Langhe, Monferrato and Astigiano. The Fiera Nazionale del Tartufo Bianco d'Alba takes place from the second to the third week in October with events ranging from concerts by Italian pop faves to specialist courses for tasters. The tuber is also sold at the truffle market in the Alba's cortile della Maddalena every weekend from late September to mid November. From here the fragrant tubers, which range in price from €1,000-€9,000 a kilo are whisked off to Milan from where they are dispatched to European, American and Japanese tables.

Ivrea & Biella

An undiscovered corner of Italy rich in historic monuments and natural beauty.

North-north-west of Turin, the neighbouring areas of Il Canavese and Il Biellese have their main towns, respectively, in Ivrea and Biella. Industrious areas these, but not exclusively: there are hidden gems in this gloriously under-visited corner of Italy.

Il Canavese is a land of manors, churches and castles, steeped in history and tradition. The via Francigena, a medieval super-highway between centres of worship in Canterbury and Rome, brought pilgrims from northern Europe through Ivrea. At many places along this winding road weary, footsore travellers found refreshment for the body and solace for the soul. The Canavese area still shows evidence of this religious devotion in its numerous medieval churches.

Il Biellese is best known for its textile industries – including Zegna (*see p176* **The cashmere man**) – which have been furnishing top-class Italian and international fashion designers for decades. But this wealthy province, almost unspoiled by tourism, has a lot more to offer in artistic and natural beauty.

Ivrea

Just 46 kilometres (29 miles) from Turin along the A5 motorway, Ivrea's fame rests on a citrus-chucking free-for-all (*see p172* **Flying oranges**) during the pre-Lenten *Carnevale*, and on business machinery, in the shape of **Olivetti**, which was founded here in 1908 (*see p175* **Adriano's legacy**).

Small (it has a population of 25,000) but bustling, Ivrea has a historic centre that is easily visited on foot. Via Palestro is the town's main pedestrianised artery, replete with all the familiar retail outlets. Via della Cattedrale leads north from via Palestro to the **Duomo** and **Castello**, an imposing concentration of symbols of religious and temporal power.

Known as *Il castello dalle rosse torri* (the red-towered castle), the castello was built in 1358 by Count Amedeo VI di Savoia. From 1750 to 1970 it was used as a prison. The Duomo (cattedrale di Santa Maria Assunta) was built on the remains of a fourth-century AD Roman temple. Of the original tenth-century church, only the crypt, the bell towers and other small features remain, their Romanesque architecture intact. The rest of the interior was given a

baroque make-over at the end of the 18th century and a pretentious neo-classical façade was added in 1854.

Back down the hill, via Arduino leads towards **Ponte vecchio**, the oldest of the bridges crossing the River Dora Baltea that runs through the town. The bridge was originally built by the Romans around the fifth century AD but has undergone various

Biella's **Duomo**. *See p177.*

The Biellese...

TOURISM, CULTURE, SPORT

a jewel

AND FREE TIME IN THE BIELLESE

to be discovered

In the north of Piedmont, connected by the mountains to the Aosta Valley, where the plains end and the Alps begin, lies the Biellese a real treasure chest to be discovered.

The ideal location for those who love spending a week or some weekends enjoying stunning unspoilt scenery, discovering walled medieval villages or walking in natural oases. All of these unique places are within close proximity of each other and are easily accessible for the disabled. Our province will greet you with warmth and professionalism, the same qualities that have for centuries distinguished us world-wide as a producer of fine woollen textiles.

Candelo: the Ricetto (walled village)

Burcina Park

Biella's Baptistery

Panoramica Zegna

Sanctuary of Oropa

reconstructions and enlargements since then, the last being in 1830 to cope with increasing volumes of traffic crossing the river. On the southern side of the bridge, the medieval Borghetto quarter is a lively neighbourhood with an old-world charm, and is the focal point of Ivrea's exuberant Carnevale (*see below* **Flying oranges**). Slightly further south, the innovative **Museo al cielo aperto dell'architettura moderna** (*see p175* **Adriano's legacy**) offers guided tours of the outstanding architecture of the Olivetti buildings, departing from the railway station.

Some 12 kilometres (7.5 miles) south of Ivrea stands the **Castello di Masino**, one of Il Canavese's most impressive castles. A fortress was first built here in the ninth century; it was destroyed and rebuilt often thereafter,

gradually being transformed from stronghold to stately home. The interior of the castle contains 18th-century furniture and is beautifully decorated with frescoes and stucco. The castle has a 20 hectare (49 acre) park modelled on a mid 19th-century English garden. A three-day garden fair is held here in May (see p169).

Castello di Ivrea
Piazza Castello, Ivrea (0125 44 415). **Open** *May-mid Oct* 10am-noon, 3-6.30pm Sun & public holidays; otherwise groups by appointment. **Admission** €2. **No credit cards.**

Castello di Masino
Masino, Caravino, nr Ivrea (0125 778 100). **Open** *Feb-Sept* 10am-1pm, 2-6pm daily. *Oct-mid Dec* 10am-5pm Tue-Sun. **Admission** €6.50; €3 concessions. **No credit cards.**

Flying oranges

In the 12th century Ivrea's ruthless and highly sexed tyrant Conte Ranieri di Biandrate made a point of asserting his right to *jus primae noctis* on the local blushing brides. But Violetta the miller's daughter had no intention of submitting to the ugly ruler: when her turn came, she lopped off his head and displayed it proudly around the town, sparking off a rebellion that expelled the entire, hated Biandrate family from the city.

This, says local legend, is the event celebrated in what is now one of Italy's most colourful pre-Lenten *carnevale* celebrations, **La battaglia delle arance**.

In fact, the 'battle' first took place in 1808 when French administrators united the many rowdy *carnevale* celebrations that had until then taken place in Ivrea's various quarters. It was probably surplus citrus fruit from French producers around Nice that was first chucked (smaller, earlier battles, it seems, involved beans); and it was the French revolutionary Phrygian cap – a Smurf-like accessory, which at the Ivrea event must be red – that was adopted by non-combatants to signal their unwillingness to be bombarded.

It was not until after World War I that the protocol of Ivrea's orange event was finally established.

In January the town elects the people who are to impersonate the main characters. On Maundy Thursday the *generale* – the master of ceremonies – assumes full power with a proclamation from the town hall balcony. That afternoon, he and his staff arrive on horseback to pay homage to the

Bishop. Later that night he opens the huge masked ball in piazza Ottinetti.

On Saturday night at 9pm the identity of the miller's daughter is revealed, and she's paraded around the town amid torchlight and fireworks. Sunday morning is the time for the *fagiolata*, when a dish made from beans and salami is handed out free. That afternoon the *podestà* (leader of the people) throws a stone into the river from the old Roman bridge to signal the town's contempt for the feudal tyrant, and oranges begin to fly.

Nine teams – a total of about 3,500 orange throwers – gather on foot while more than 30 decorated carts make their way through the streets as moving targets for a hail of oranges. Spectators who don't want to be hit don Phrygian hats; anyone else is fair game over the ensuing three days when some 360 tonnes of citrus are chucked. On Tuesday evening, awards are handed out to the most outstanding teams and carts. Afterwards, the Funeral March is the last act of *carnevale*: the General and his staff reluctantly follow the fifers and drummers to the edge of the piazza where they take their leave.

On the morning of Ash Wednesday the public is served polenta and salt cod in the old Borghetto quarter to mark the beginning of Lent.

Our recommendations: book a hotel months ahead if you want to stay in the city centre; don't try to get here with a car because you won't find parking within a five-mile radius; and get yourself a Phrygian hat! For more information see www.carnevale.ivrea.it.

Trips Out of Town

Duomo (Cattedrale di Santa Maria Assunta)
Piazza del Duomo, Ivrea (0125 424 590).
Open 8am-6pm daily.

Where to stay & eat

Monferrato Residence e Trattoria (via Gariglietti 1, 0125 641 012, closed Sun, average €25) in the heart of the *centro storico* is an authentic trattoria in Piedmontese country style serving *canavesi* dishes made with strictly local ingredients; comfortable mini-apartments with kitchenettes cost €55 per apartment per night.

The **Hotel Sirio** (via Lago Sirio 85, 0125 424 247, €98-€120 double) is located a few minutes from the centre of Ivrea, overlooking Lake Sirio. All the rooms have lovely views and there is a delightful garden. A large but cosy restaurant (average €25) is open for dinner, serving Piedmontese and international cuisine. Guests have access to private lake facilities nearby.

In the countryside outside Ivrea, several castles offer plush, stylish accommodation. **Castello di Borgomasino** (via Arciprete Bonfiglio 2, Borgomasino, 0125 770 181, closed mid Nov-mid Mar, €105 double) provides bed and breakfast in a luxurious 19th-century mansion house with extensive gardens and a

Piazza della Cisterna. *See p175.*

park. Double rooms have fireplaces, finely decorated ceilings and a terrace. ATAP (0158 488 411) operates several bus services from Ivrea railway station Monday to Saturday.

Also doing B&B is the **Castello di Strambino** (via Villanova 20, Strambino, 0125 618 131, €60-€75 double), an elegant 17th-century residence owned by the Scarampi di Villanova family; the marquess still lives there. Surrounded by a park, it also has a sheltered swimming pool. SADEM (011 300 0611, www.sadem.it) buses for Strambino depart from Ivrea railway station every 30 minutes.

Tourist information

Agenzia Turistica Locale del Canadese e Valli di Lanzo
Corso Vercelli 1, Ivrea (0125 618 131/www. canavese-vallilanzo.it). **Open** 9am-12.30pm, 2.30-6pm Mon-Fri; 10am-noon, 3-6pm Sat.

Getting there

By car
Take the A5 Turin–Aosta motorway, exit at Ivrea; alternatively, take the SS11 and SS26. For Masino take the A4/5 link road from Ivrea and exit at Albiano, or local roads to Canavino.

By train
Turin–Aosta services stop at Ivrea, running hourly or half-hourly at peak times.

By bus
SATTI (0125 45 673/49 231/www.satti.it) runs 11 buses daily from via Fiocchetto (map p242 B3) near Porta Palazzo. For Masino, take VITA's (0125 966 546/www.gtt.to.it) Cossano service from Ivrea railway station; several buses a day pass 1km from the castle; the 2.10pm goes to the castle itself.

Biella

A stroll along pedestrianised via Italia at the heart of Biella's *centro storico* will suffice to demonstrate the prosperity of the industrious local community: here, elegant *biellesi* patronise elegant shops hidden beneath lovely baroque porticos.

Off via Italia, piazza del Duomo is home to Biella's key historic monuments. The **Duomo** (cattedrale di Santa Maria Maggiore) dates from 1402, is in Gothic style and has an octagonal dome; the 'Gothick' façade is an 1825 addition. Alongside stands the Romanesque **baptistery** (visits on request at the Duomo), constructed in the second half of the tenth century; it was built of brick, pebbles and bits of ancient masonry, probably from the ruins of the Roman sepulchre over which it stands. The piazza is dominated

Adriano's legacy

Olivetti was founded in Ivrea in 1908 by Camillo Olivetti, but it was his son Adriano (1901-60), who took over as chairman and CEO in 1938, who turned Italy's first, humble typewriter maker into an internationally renowned business machines giant.

An engineer with a passion for urban planning and an industrialist with a strong bent for philanthropy, Adriano was a true Renaissance man whose effects were felt far more widely than provincial Ivrea. Yet it was in this little town that he first put his revolutionary ideas into practice. A fact-finding tour to the US as a young man brought him into contact with the latest theories on stream-lining production, theories that he convinced his father to implement in Ivrea. Employees were involved in the decision-making process and funds were routed towards social programmes. Adriano summoned the best Italian architects and planners to build new factories, and provide housing, crèches, libraries and other social services for workers. Way before anyone else was interested in such matters, he paid particular attention to the environmental and social impact of the new constructions.

In 1956 Olivetti reduced working hours from 48 to 45 hours a week with no drop in salary. Soon other sectors were forced to follow suit. Yet in a highly politicised country, Adriano's unique blend of capitalism and socialism drew fire from both left and right; in return, the Olivetti boss determined to create a society based on local community organisation rather than ideology-driven national politics. With a group of young intellectuals, he founded a publishing house in 1946, producing major international works on sociology, philosophy and politics.

But his intense activity in social and cultural fields never distracted Adriano from his main business. In the 1950s and '60s his firm was acknowledged as a world leader in technology, industrial design and communications. Olivetti spread its activities abroad, most notably to a vast ground-breaking plant in São Paulo, Brazil; its products – including the Lexicon 80 (1948) and the Lettera 22 (1950) typewriters – swiftly became design classics. Olivetti was also one of the first companies to embrace and pioneer the development of the computer, becoming a major player in the electronics market in the 1980s.

Adriano's urban design legacy is visible and visitable today through the **Museo al cielo aperto dell'architettura moderna di Ivrea** (the open-air museum of modern architecture in Ivrea). Opened in 2001, the museum area stretches for two kilometres (1.25 miles) along via Jervis, site of the most significant Olivetti constructions. There are guided tours (*see below*) but if you want to go it alone, pick up a leaflet at the booking centre or follow the signposted path where information points provide the facts about what you're looking at.

Museo a Cielo Aperto dell'Architettura Moderna di Ivrea (MAAM)

Information centre: via Jervis 26 (0125 641 815/www.maam.ivrea.it). **Open** *Apr-Sept 2-6pm Tue-Sat. Oct-Mar 9am-1pm Tue-Fri; 2-6pm Sat.*
Booking centre *for guided tours: Cooperativa Conteverde, via Jervis 77 (0125 43 206).*
Tours *by appointment only.* **Rates** *vary according to route and size of group.*
No credit cards.

by the bell tower of Santo Stefano, which dates from the fifth century. Romanesque in style, it is all that remains of the church of Santo Stefano.

Via Vescovado leads (west) out of the piazza to via Pietro Micca; a short walk south then west again will take you to the church of **San Sebastiano**. Built in the late 15th century, this has a splendid Renaissance cloister, unique in Piedmont. After 20 years of restoration, it now houses the **Museo del territorio biellese**. This important museum complex had still to be completed as this guide went to press. Already open to the public are the *Galleria del territorio*, dedicated to ancient Biellese maps, the *Sezione egizia* with its collection of Egyptian artefacts and the *Sezione storico-artistica* which hosts important local works of art.

Back (north) along via Pietro Micca, piazza Curiel is the terminus for a funicular railway (tickets 70¢), which since 1886 has been shuttling back and forth up to the old hilltop **Borgo del Piazzo**. Dating from the 12th century, this lovely medieval quarter comprises a series of cobblestone streets and winding alleys, all leading to the main **piazza della Cisterna**. Here, surrounded by porticos, noble houses and *palazzi*, there's a definite sensation

of time standing still. Renaissance **Palazzo della Cisterna** (open during exhibitions only), built at the end of the 16th century by the noble family Dal Pozzo, is the square's most imposing building. At the opposite end, the Romanesque church of **San Giacomo** (open 5-7pm Mon-Sat; 9am-noon Sun, depending on the whim of the priest) dates from the 13th century, though it underwent subsequent modifications: the façade and bell tower are from the 14th century, while the portico in front of the façade was added in the 17th century. Inside is a triptych from 1497 by Daniele de Bosis and wooden choir stalls from the 17th century.

On corso del Piazzo, 18th-century **Palazzo La Marmora** (No.19, call 015 352 533 for an appointment) was the residence of a prominent local family, with a magnificent terraced garden overlooking the city. On via Avogadro, the **Porta d'Andorno**, from the first half of the 14th century, was the entrance to Borgo del Piazzo.

Situated five kilometres (three miles) south-east of Biella, **Ricetto di Candelo** is a picturesque late medieval fortified village of roughly 200 uninhabited buildings. Constructed by the local farming community as a bolt-hole in times of war – and doubling up as a wine

The cashmere man

When Ermenegildo Zegna began producing textiles in the first years of the 20th century, the world's wool market was still dominated by rough pre-spun British yarn. But the fabric produced elsewhere from His Majesty's sheep was not good enough for this young industrialist from Trivero, near Biella. In 1910 he founded his own wool mill, the Lanificio Ermenegildo Zegna, in Trivero, with just three looms. Investments in cutting-edge technology and a natural flair for quality and colour brought success; by the 1930s his products were being exported worldwide.

Other locals followed where Ermenegildo led, turning Biella into one of the world's biggest woollen textile fabric-producing hubs, with 2,000 factories turning out 65 per cent of overall Italian output.

Now in its fourth generation, the Zegna family is still at the helm of the company, which supplies fabrics for top fashion houses in Milan, Paris, London and New York as well as producing its own designs: three million ties, 500,000 shirts and 1.8 million metres of fabric are turned out each year.

From the beginning, the philanthropist Ermenegildo opted to reinvest his profits for the good of his people and his land. To ease access to isolated mountain villages he built the Panoramica Zegna road: 65 kilometres (40 miles) of breathtaking beauty, connecting Trivero to Rosazza.

He also created the Centro Zegna health and recreational complex for the local populace. He had old mountain tracks restored and the countryside reforested. In 1993 the Oasi Zegna project was founded to unite and maintain all aspects of the activities initiated by this nature-loving patriarch, protecting and developing 100 square kilometres (39 square miles) of spectacular Alpine environment.

Oasi Zegna

Centro Visite Icemont, Regione Bielmonte 1, Piatto, Biella (015 744 102). **Open** *Aug* 9am-5pm daily. *Sept-July* 9am-5pm Sat, Sun. You'll need a car to get to the Oasi from Biella: follow signs for Valle Mosso and Trivero. The SS232 is the Panoramica Zegna.

and grain warehouse in times of peace – it remains perfectly preserved, its defensive walls intact. The Ricetto hosts the **Museo della vinicoltura** (Museum of wine-making) where you can see old methods of wine-making and sample the results. It's open to all in the first week of October during the wine festival, and can be visited by appointment at other times. Bus 57 from via La Marmora in Biella will get you there.

A UNESCO World Heritage Site, the **Santuario di Oropa** (11 kilometres/seven miles north of Biella) is located 1,200 metres (3,937 feet) up a mountain in a dramatic, unspoiled valley edged by towering Alps.

The original site dates back to the 11th century. It was progressively enlarged, especially in the 16th and 17th centuries, when architects Filippo Juvarra and Guarino Guarini were commissioned by the Savoy family to make 'improvements'.

Today the impressive complex consists of the Basilica Antica, housing a much-revered statue of a Black Madonna that legend says was sculpted by St Luke, and a piazza-like *chiostro* (cloister) with the massive Chiesa nuova at its head. In galleries around the complex are displays of votive offerings, Savoy royal apartments, a library of ancient volumes and the **Museo del tesoro del santuario**. Adjacent to the walled complex is the Sacro monte – 19 mini-chapels dedicated to the life of the Virgin. Although principally used as a religious retreat, Oropa now also offers charming tourist accommodation. Bus 2 from Biella railway station goes to the Santuario twice an hour.

If you want to go deeper into the surrounding Alpine countryside, take a cable-car ride (€8.50) from behind the Chiesa nuova to the **Rifugio Savoia** (Savoy mountain refuge; 1,900 metres/6,234 feet) or further on to **Monte Camino** (2,400 metres/7,900 feet).

Duomo

Piazza del Duomo, Biella (015 22 592). **Open** 8.30am-noon, 3-6pm daily. **Admission** free.

Museo del Territorio Biellese

Via Quintino Sella, Biella (015 252 9345). **Open** 10am-noon, 3-7pm Thur, Sat; 3-10pm Fri; 3-7pm Sun. **Admission** *Museum* free. *Temporary exhibitions* varies. **No credit cards**.

Ecomuseo della Vitivinicoltura

Ricetto di Candelo (information 015 253 6728). **Open** by guided tour (English available) only; book ahead. **Admission** €3;€1.50 concessions. **No credit cards**.
In an incredibly complicated system, would-be visitors have to go to a local bank, pay for admission, then take the receipt to the museum.

Kings of beer

Piedmont's wines are much fêted, but they are not the region's only award-winning brew. Giuseppe Menabrea began making beer in a Biella brewery in 1846, and his descendants are still managing the business today. Maybe it's the Alpine water used, or Menabrea's particular attention to its fresh ingredients, but this beer started to win awards as early as 1899 with a Silver Medal at the Turin Exposition, followed by awards in Dijon, Munich and Ghent. When this micro-brewery swept the Grand Prix at the Universal Exposition in Paris in 1900, its dark Munich-style beer accounted for 90 per cent of sales; nowadays, its lighter Pilsner is the top seller. Production today has reached an annual 80,000 hectolitres, 15 per cent of which finds its way abroad. In recent years, under the guidance of Paolo Thedy – a fourth-generation descendant of the founder – Birra Menabrea can boast three Best Pale Lager and two Best Amber Lager titles from the World Beer Championships in Chicago.

The Menabrea factory and its beer museum can be visited and, more invitingly, the booze can be sampled with local specialities in Menabrea's own *birreria* and restaurant, located in the former stables of the factory.

Museo Menabrea

Via Ramella Germanin 4, Biella (015 252 2320). **Open** Museum visits by appointment only. **Admission** free.

Ristorante Birreria Menabrea

Via Ramella Germanin 6, Biella (015 252 2435). **Open** 7pm-1am Tue-Fri; 7pm-2am Sat. **Average** €20. **No credit cards**.

Santuario di Oropa

Via Santuario di Oropa 480 (015 2555 1200/ www.santuariodioropa.it). **Open** *Basilica Antica* 8am-noon, 2-7pm daily. *Royal apartments & Museo del T+esoro* June-Sept 9am-1pm, 2-6pm Tue-Sun. *Oct-May* 9am-1pm, 2-6pm Sat, Sun. **Admission** *Basilica antica, Chiesa nuova* free. *Royal apartments & Museo del tesoro* €3; €2 concessions. **No credit cards**.

Where to eat, drink & stay

The warm *stile Liberty* **Caffè-Pasticceria Ferrua** (via Italia 43, 015 22 485, closed 2wks Aug) has been in business since 1842; its old

Cult status

In 1975 Oberto Airaudi, the son of a Turin policeman, had a dream of creating a self-sustaining society and began meeting with a group of 20-odd like-minded people to meditate and study philosophy of all descriptions. Today this group has expanded into the Federation of Damanhur, a spiritual community of around 800 members in the Valchiusella valley north west of Ivrea.

The spot was chosen for its special 'energy': it is, members of the community say, one of only two places in the world (the other is in Tibet) where four synchronic lines converge. A slightly more prosaic explanation is that the soil is rich in minerals, which exert a strange gravitational pull.

It is hard to pinpoint an exact belief system for Damanhur. It borrows from Celtic, pagan, New Age and Christian 'beliefs' as well as from psychiatry and philosophy; 'transformation' and 'expansion of awareness' are typical catchwords. Members call each other by animal names such as Butterfly and Octopus, and there are workshops on such themes as 'Astral Travel' and 'Learning to Dream'.

But it isn't all airy-fairy. The 'Federation' is tightly run, with its own constitution, currency and daily paper. It also has schools, farms and all types of craft workshops. Its cashmere and silk factories supply some of Milan's biggest fashion houses, while its wholesale food manufacturer 'Company of the Good Earth' supplies Fortnum & Mason and Macy's.

Damanhur's most extraordinary achievement, however, is its Temple of Humankind – a vast underground network of interlinked halls, corridors and domes (one with a Tiffany glass cupola) studded with gold, silver and mosaics, and carved by hand out of the hillside over the space of 17 years. The project was started in 1978, secretly and without any of the necessary planning permits. Its existence was only revealed in 1992 when a disgruntled former member demanded a huge amount of hush money. Rather than cough up the vast sum the community decided to come clean to the authorities. Fortunately, the official consensus was that the temple was too beautiful to close down and it is now also open to the public. Some 70,000 people – including a few curious souls and countless television crews – are reported to cross the temple's threshold each year.

Whether you're seeking spiritual enlightenment, or just want to ogle the Temple of Humankind, you'll need to make an appointment to visit.

Federazione di Comunità di Damanhur
Baldissero Canavese (0124 512 236/ fax 0124 512 205/www.damanhur.org).

---

coffee- and tearooms are a lovely place to relax with a hot chocolate and a pastry. Friendly staff and good service.

The **Ristorante Alta Italia** (via C Crosa 9, 015 352 529, closed Tue, average €25) serves typical Piedmontese cuisine, all home-made using local ingredients; there's a great selection of wines and impeccable service. From May to September the restaurant moves to the **Circolo del Piazzo** (via Avogadro 29, 015 22 841, closed Mon) where there's an outside patio.

The **Hotel Astoria** (viale Roma 9, 015 402 750, €99 double) is an elegant four-star just 50 metres from Biella's railway station; all bed rooms are en suite and have desk and work facilities. **Hotel Augustus** (via Italia 54, 015 27 554, €100 double) in the heart of the *centro storico* has views of the Alps as well as all mod cons. The **Santuario di Oropa** (*see p177*) also offers accommodation; there are 350 rooms in the complex, with doubles ranging from €30 to €80.

Getting there

By car
Take the A4 Turin–Milan motorway, exit at Santhià, and take the SS143 for Biella for 20km (12.5 miles). Alternatively, head out of Turin on the SS11, which becomes the SS593/SS143.

By train
There are few direct trains from Porta Nuova station. Take one of the hourly Turin–Milan trains, then change at Santhià for Biella.

Tourist information

Azienda Turistica Locale Biella
Piazza Vittorio Veneto 3, Biella (015 351 128/ toll-free 800 811 800/www.atl.biella.it). **Open** 8.30am-1pm, 2.30-6pm Mon-Fri; 8.30am-12.30pm, 2.30-5.30pm Sat.
Opens on Sunday, too, from June to August. Provides information on sightseeing and accommodation.

Ivrea's **Duomo**.
See p171.

Vercelli

There's more to Europe's rice-producing capital than just the white stuff.

Vercelli's **Duomo**.

Driving across the interminable plains of eastern Piedmont, you could easily think the River Po had burst its banks. Closer inspection, however, reveals this to be a neatly irrigated landscape of rice crops under heavy cultivation.

Since the 1400s, Vercelli province has been the centre of rice production in Europe, an activity that has heavily shaped the countryside (*see p181* **Piedmont paddies**). A stroll around Vercelli city, however, reveals that religion has also played an important role in forming the area, as a particularly high density of churches and holy treasures testifies.

The most important of Vercelli's religious buildings and symbol of the city is the **basilica di Sant'Andrea**, built between 1219 and 1227. It's also a splendid example of the transition from Romanesque to Gothic architecture. Behind an imposing green marble façade is a majestic interior of three Gothic aisles leading up to four chapels and a high central transept with a large rose window. A door along the left aisle leads out on to a beautiful, bright, rectangular cloister with vaults and delicate 16th-century brickwork. Off the cloister, the Sala capitolare hosts two magnificent frescoes – a Madonna

and Child, and three instrument-playing angels – by Bernardino Lanino from the same period.

Via Bicheri leads north from the piazza to the **Duomo** (Cattedrale di Sant'Eusebio). Originally built in the 12th century, only the bell tower still survives from that period while the cathedral itself is a mix of styles. The façade is 18th-century neo-classical, the choir stalls, presbytery and sacristy are from the late 16th century, while the dome and the chapel in the right transept – containing, among other things, the mortal remains of Amedeo VII di Savoia, aka anti-pope Felix V (*see p182* **Pope Felix**) – were a 19th-century addition. But perhaps the cathedral's greatest treasure is the crucifix suspended over the third altar of the right aisle: made at the end of the tenth century this huge wooden-based cross measures 3.27 metres (11 feet) in height and is embossed in silver leaf with gold inlays. It's impressive both for the intricate detail of its bas-relief and for the realistic expression on Jesus' face, which seems to be looking at the world with bewilderment and sadness. The archbishop's palace directly behind the cathedral has interesting furnishings, and contains the **Museo del** tesoro del Duomo. Among the treasures of the museum are the fourth-century Codex Evangeliorum, the oldest existing translation of the gospels into Latin by St Eusebius himself, and a 13th-century globe depicting the known world of the time. The highlight of the museum is the Vercelli Book, a tenth-century manuscript in Old English that lay unnoticed in the cathedral library until the late 19th century, probably having been brought to Vercelli in the 13th century. A collection of sermons and poems, the book is considered a vital document for the study of early English.

Via del Duomo leads to the core of the *centro storico*; cut west along via Gioberti and into quaint, recently restored piazza Cavour with its medieval porticos. Overlooking the piazza is the 14th-century Torre dell'angelo. Cafés including **Taverna & Tarnuzzer** (*see p183*) nestling beneath the arcades are good bets for coffee and a cake before ducking down the passageway towards the enclosed piazza Palazzo Vecchio, also known locally as piazza dei Pesci (Fish Square) recalling the fish market that used to be held here. Also revamped recently, this courtyard contains the **Broletto** – the 12th-century town hall – and the **Torre comunale**.

Piedmont paddies

In late spring, when its rice paddies are flooded, the province of Vercelli looks like one huge lake. Water plays a vital role in the cultivation of rice, by far the main agricultural and commercial activity in this corner of Piedmont.

The cereal has been cultivated for at least 5,000 years, was used by the Romans as a cure for upset stomachs and became a fashionable and expensive import around Europe in the 14th century. Cultivation in the Po valley may have begun in the 15th century, when Cistercian monks began to reclaim what until then had been marshy malarial swamps. In this poor, peripheral area of the Savoy kingdom plague, war and famine had been constant threats through the centuries; the development of this highly nutritional cereal was an impelling necessity, not to mention a lucrative one, with every bag of seed rice producing an average of 12 bags of rice for consumption.

For centuries, Piedmontese rice production was a rather haphazard affair. It took the far-sighted organisational zeal of reformer-statesman Camillo Cavour (*see p10* **The four horsemen of the Risorgimento**) to give it a much-needed boost in the early 19th century: Cavour ordered the construction of thousands of kilometres of canals to channel Alpine water to irrigate the plains (sacrificing, as construction advanced, thousands of hectares of forest).

Today, with 220,000 hectares (543,620 acres) of land dedicated to it, Italy produces some 1.3 million tons of rice each year; this may represent a mere 0.25 per cent of world output, but it's almost 42 per cent of the European total.

The key ingredient of that typically northern Italian dish risotto, rice offers ample opportunities for letting your food fantasies go wild. Possible entries in a recipe book entitled '*Risotto con...*' would be endless. From beans to Barolo, most ingredients find a pleasing partner in the creamy-textured potage of a well-stirred risotto.

Short-grained rice is needed to create the creamy-yet-firm texture of the perfect risotto. Arborio, named after a village near Vercelli, is the most commonly used risotto variety. Carnaroli is a pricier version but credited with giving a more balanced consistency, while Vialone Nano is preferred in the Veneto region.

Six centuries of rice-growing are documented at the Principato di Lucedio estate near Trino, 12 kilometres (7.5 miles) south-west of Vercelli, in the heart of rice-growing territory. Exotic red and black varieties are grown alongside the usual Italian staples. This rice farm occupies the premises of a late Renaissance abbey with a high dome and frescoed halls that can be visited on guided tours. Don't forget your mosquito repellent.

Azienda Agricola Principato di Lucedio

Trino (0161 81 519). **Tours** *by appointment only* Tue-Sun. **Admission** *tour only* €4; €8 with *aperitivo*; €18 with risotto tasting; €26 with three-course meal incl wine. **No credit cards**. Tours can be arranged in English for groups of at least ten. By car from Vercelli, take the SS435/SS455 to Trino; in Trino follow directions for Palazzolo, then after 1km turn right for Cigliano/Livorno. There are signs for Lucedio from there. No public transport.

From piazza Cavour, via Verdi leads to the
Museo Leone with collections of archaeology
and applied art. Exhibits range from the
palaeolithic, through the Middle Ages to the
17th century. In the Roman section is the *stele
celto-latina*, a stone tablet inscribed in both
the Celtic and Latin languages.

Further east, the **Museo Borgogna** houses
medieval and Renaissance frescoes detached
from churches in the town, plus a large
collection of paintings from the 16th to the 18th
centuries. There's not a lot to linger for here,
but a Holy Family by Palma il Vecchio and a
Deposition by Titian brighten up the Venetian
collection, while works by Raphael's pupil Il
Sodoma, Gaudenzio Ferrari and Bernardini
Luini are interesting. Parallel to via Borgogna,

Pope Felix

Amedeo VIII (1383-1451) was, by all
accounts, a kind and wise ruler of the
Savoy dominions, so much so that, in
1416, the Holy Roman Emperor
Sigismundo raised this count to the rank
of duke. But after the death of his wife
Maria of Burgundy, Amedeo turned
contemplative, tired of his duties, and
in 1434 retired with five trusty knights to
a hermitage he had founded on the shores
of Lake Geneva, leaving his son Lodovico
to handle the family business.

His retirement lasted just five years,
after which he was shot into the
international limelight when the schismatic
Council of Basle elected him pope. Well,
anti-pope. Because at the time, Pope
Eugene IV was comfortably seated on St
Peter's throne in the Vatican and showed
no intention of relinquishing it.

Sincere as he may have been in his
quest to placate a troubled and divided
Church, Amedeo – now calling himself Felix
V – garnered only patchy support, mainly
from crackpot German mini-states and
reactionary military orders on the fringes
of hereticism. Gradually, as squabbles
broke out over who should enjoy the
benefits of ecclesiastical taxes, even
they withdrew their support.

Amedeo/Felix stuck it out until 1449,
then handed over his anti-papal crown to
Nicholas V, who had replaced Eugene in
the Vatican. Amedeo retired to a quiet life
as an apostolic vicar-general for the Savoy
states, the Church was finally united and
schisms became a thing of the past.

on via Foa, stands the old **synagogue**; built
in 1875 in beautiful Moorish style, it bears
witness to the past wealth of the local Jewish
community but is now closed and sadly in
need of repair. On a nearby street of the same
name is the church of **San Cristoforo** (open
7.30am-noon, 3.30-6.30pm daily) nicknamed the
'Vercelli Sistine Chapel' for its splendid frescoes
(1529-34) by Gaudenzio Ferrari. The ceiling,
walls and chapels are all sumptuously painted
with scenes from the life of the Blessed Virgin;
the Our Lady of the Oranges at the back of the
apse is considered his masterpiece.

Basilica di Sant'Andrea
Piazza Roma 35 (0161 255 513). **Open** *June-Sept*
7.30-11.45am, 3-7pm daily. *Oct-May* 7.30-11.45am,
3-6pm daily.

Cattedrale di Sant'Eusebio
Piazza Sant'Eusebio (0161 252 930). **Open** 7.30-
11.45am, 3-6pm daily.

Museo Borgogna
Via Borgogna 6-8 (0161 252 776). **Open** 3-5.30pm
Tue-Fri; 10am-12.30pm Sat, Sun. **Admission** €5.50;
€4.20 concessions. **No credit cards**.

Basilica di Sant'Andrea. *See p180.*

Museo Leone

Via Camillo Leone 19 (0161 253 204). **Open**
3-5.30pm Tue, Thur, Sat; 10am-noon, 3-6pm Sun.
Admission €4. **No credit cards.**

Museo del Tesoro del Duomo

Piazza d'Angennes 3 (0161 51 650). **Open** 9am-
noon Wed; 9am-noon, 3-6pm Sat; 3-6pm Sun.
Admission €3; €2 concessions. **No credit cards.**

Where to stay & eat

The **Hotel Matteotti** (corso Matteotti 35, 0161
211 187, €75 double) is a warm and comfortable
three-star hotel situated one kilometre from the
city centre; rooms have wooden floors and are
decorated in a mix of fake art nouveau and
Edwardian style. The **Hotel il Giardinetto**
(via Sereno 3, 0161 257 230, €77 double) is
conveniently located in a period building near the
centro storico; there are eight comfortable rooms,
parking facilities and a pretty private garden.

The historic café-pasticceria **Taverna &
Tarnuzzer** (piazza Cavour 7, 0161 253 139) sits
under the porticos of Vercelli's main piazza and
has been supplying the locals with coffees and
cakes since 1830. The interior, with its splendid
wine-pouring counter, is worth checking out.

Just off central piazza Cavour, the
Ristorante Vecchia Brenta (via Morosone
6, 0161 251 230, average €25) is a family-run
restaurant offering all the local rice specialities
including *panissa* (a dish made with rice, beans
and salami) at a reasonable price.

Tourist information

Agenzia Turistica Locale Vercelli

Viale Garibaldi 90 (0161 58 002). **Open** 9am-1pm,
3-7pm Tue, Thur, Fri; 10am-1pm, 2-7pm Sat.

Getting there

By car

Take the A4 Turin–Milan motorway, then the A4-
A26 link road; exit at Vercelli Ovest.

By train

The Turin–Milan service departs every 30mins,
stopping at Vercelli.

By bus

There's no regular bus service from Turin.

Trips Out of Town

Asti & Il Monferrato

Piedmont's gastronomic heartland.

Asti: synonymous with fine food and wine.

An imaginary line running east–west through the town of Asti divides the Monferrato area of Piedmont into southern *alto* (high) and northern *basso* (low) Monferrato. This is not as counterintuitive as it seems: the adjectives refer to topography. Basso Monferrato's (*see p187*) low hills and flatlands unravel into the vast Lombardy plain; Alto Monferrato (*see p189*) is in hilly, almost mountainous country at the foothills of the Ligurian Apennines.

The castle strongholds and fortified hill towns of Alto Monferrato bear witness to the conflicts that ravaged the area over the centuries. Romans, Ligurians, Lombards and French all held sway over the Monferrato – and in particular over Asti – at one time or another in the past. The area's historical attractiveness has little to do with its (unquestionable) natural beauty. The Monferrato is a gateway where the rich agricultural plains of Lombardy meet the foreboding Apennines separating northern Italy from the Mediterranean. Like any crossroads, over time the territory has been enriched by the passage of cultures, faiths and influences.

Today Asti and the Alto Monferrato are synonymous with excellent cuisine. Asti is one of Italy's largest exporters of wine; its famous Asti spumante (*see p32* **Regional wines**) pops the cork on parties the world over. On the table, you'll find Piedmont ravioli, called *agnolotti*, stuffed and doused in a hundred different ways. Truffles, excellent meats and strong cheeses all play a part in a cuisine recognised by Italians as one of the best in the country. Come to the table hungry.

Spring and autumn are good times to visit. Spring is more beautiful, with an endless array of greenery and blossom. But aesthetics apart, autumn is better: many of the local *sagre* (feasts) and festivals are held in the harvest months. **Sette Giorni della Gastronomia Astigiana** (seven days of Asti cuisine) takes place in mid September; the **Sagra d'Asti** is held on the second weekend in September. Entry is free, though you'll have to pay for your dinner. Asti's **Mostra-Mercato di Tartufi** (truffle fair), which attracts hordes of tourists and epicureans, is held over two weekends in the second half of November.

Asti

The town of Asti is one of the most beautiful *città d'arte* in Piedmont. Its historic centre is defined by narrow medieval streets and *case-forti* (fortified houses), which were constructed for security-conscious nobles until the 12th century.

Corso Vittorio Alfieri is named after Asti's most famous son, writer Vittorio Alfieri (*see p14* **Literary Turin**). Many of the town's most beautiful 17th-century houses are on this street, including the **Palazzo di Bellino** (No.357) and **Palazzo Ottolenghi** (No.350, visits on request: 0141 399 391). The **Palazzo di Bellino** houses the Museo del Risorgimento and the Pinacoteca (art gallery), which were both closed indefinitely for renovation when this guide went to press. The narrow side-streets between corso Alfieri and via XX Settembre are lined with attractive medieval and Renaissance buildings.

At the western end of town is the **Cattedrale di Santa Maria Assunta**, one of Piedmont's most important Gothic monuments. Built between 1309 and 1354, the edifice was remodelled over successive centuries, most notably in 1450 when three Gothic portals were opened in its façade. On the right wall of the exterior is a splendid *protiro* (entrance) in flamboyant Gothic style. Among the mainly 17th-century frescoes that cover walls and vault – many of them by local dabbler Gandolfino d'Asti – an *Adoration of the Shepherds* and *Adoration of the Magi* by Defendente Ferrari stand out in the sacristy. The cathedral treasury holds important religious artefacts including a monstrance dating from 1446.

Back towards the central piazza Alfieri, **San Secondo** is an attractive Gothic church with some fragments of early 15th-century frescoes. The Romanesque bell tower remains from a tenth-century church, while beneath the church the crypt may date as far back as the eighth century. **Piazza Alfieri**, a square surrounded by attractive 19th-century *palazzi*, is where the yearly **Palio d'Asti** (*see also p169*) – a horse race not unlike the more famous Palio in Siena – is staged. Held on the third Sunday of September, the Asti version has the advantage of being less famous, and therefore more accessible, than its over-hyped, over-crowded Tuscan cousin. The race has been held yearly off and on since 1275, and includes 21 participants – 14 horses from Asti's *rioni* (neighbourhoods) and the others from outlying provinces.

At the easternmost end of corso Alfieri in piazza 1° Maggio, the octagonal Romanesque **Rotonda di San Pietro** was built in 1280. When the sun is shining, the combination of filtered sunlight and darker walls is beautiful enough to impress even the most world-weary heathen. The same complex houses both the **Museo archeologico** and the **Museo paleontologico**, containing a rather sparse if well-presented collection of prehistoric artefacts from the region, as well as Egyptian items.

Cattedrale di Santa Maria Assunta
Piazza Cattedrale (0141 592 924). **Open** 8.30am-noon, 3.30-5.30pm daily.

Collegiata San Secondo
Piazza San Secondo (0141 530 066). **Open** 10.45am-noon, 3.30-5.30pm daily.

Rotonda di San Pietro (Museo Archeologico & Museo Paleontologico)
Corso Alfieri 2 (0141 353 072). **Open** *Apr-Oct* 10am-1pm, 4-7pm Tue-Sun. *Nov-Mar* 10am-1pm, 3-6pm Tue-Sun. **Admission** €2.50; €1.50 concessions. **No credit cards**.

A bubbly by any other name...

Wine buffs may turn up their sensitive noses at the fizzy wines produced around Asti but that doesn't stop some 80 million bottles a year of the stuff being snapped up – slightly more than 70 per cent of it on foreign markets – for the kind of parties where by 10.30pm no one's looking too closely at the label.

But this spumante can claim distinguished – even noble – origins. The same sweet grapes used to create Asti spumante were first used to produce its cousin Moscato – a lower-alcohol, higher-sugar dessert wine – as early as the 13th century, according to public records of the town of Canelli, south of Asti. In the late 16th century Giovan Battista Croce, a Milanese jeweller and goldsmith to the duke of Savoy, took these delicate white grapes and perfected their filtration to create the dessert wine Moscato d'Asti, a superheated version of which would eventually become today's well-known and much-derided descendant. His creation was such a success at court that he published a book on the process, rather laboriously entitled *On the Excellence and Diversity of the Wines Made on the Mountains of Turin and How to Produce Them*.

Where to stay & eat

In a region where food and fine cuisine has an almost religious significance, it's hard to go wrong when you pick a restaurant. Book ahead to get a table at **Gener Neuv** (Lungo Tanaro Pescatori 4, 0141 557 270, closed Sun dinner & Mon, average €50), a family-run restaurant that specialises in the local *cucina astigiana*. Make sure you try its *agnolotti alle tre carne*. **Angolo del Beato** (via Guttuari 12, 0141 531 668, www.angolodelbeato.it, closed Sun, average €35) is a fine restaurant in an attractive 13th-century palazzo. Specialities include *cardi con fonduta* and an excellent *brasato*. **Convivio Vini e Cucina** (via Giuliani 4-6, 0141 594 188, www.turismodoc.it, closed Sun, average €27) is located right in the heart of the *centro storico* and serves wonderful home-made pasta dishes.

Palio (via Cavour 106, 0141 34 371, www.hotelpalio.com, closed Aug, €140 double) is a straightforward, modern hotel located just off the piazza where Asti's Palio horse race is celebrated every September. Romantic it's not, but it's oh-so-convenient. The **Hotel Lis** (via Fratelli Rosselli 10, 0141 595 051, www.salera-lis.com, €95-€98 double) is also conveniently located in the heart of Asti and most rooms look out over the town's public gardens. The **Hotel Reale** (piazza Alfieri 6, 0141 530 240,www.hotel-reale.com, €110-€140 double) is located in a beautiful palazzo in the *centro storico*, and has a tradition of entertaining guests that dates all the way back to 1793.

Tourist information

Asti Turismo ATL
Piazza Vittorio Alfieri 29 (0141 530 357/ www.terredasti.it). **Open** 9am-1pm, 2.30-6.30pm Mon-Sat; 9am-1pm Sun.

Getting there

By car
Take the A21 motorway (exit Asti Ovest) or the SS10.

They came, they saw… they relaxed

The Romans were no slouches when it came to kicking back and taking a load off their feet. If there was a hot spring to be found anywhere along their conquering route, they wasted no time tracking it down, harnessing its hot waters and building marble and mosaic baths to relax in.

Roman **Acqui Terme** (*see also p190*) was called Acqui Statiellae, after the Ligurian Statielle tribe that occupied this territory before the conquerors arrived. Pliny and Seneca wrote about the town's health-giving waters, some of which came to the surface right in town, while more was channelled here from the surrounding countryside by soaring aqueducts, the remains of which can still be seen outside the town. Recent archaeological digs have brought much of the Roman baths complex to light, including a pool that dates to the imperial period. While not everything that has been unearthed is open to the public, free tours of several sites are organised through the local tourist office (*see p191*), and recovered artefacts are on display in the **Museo civico archeologico** in the Castello dei Paleologi.

In piazza della Bollente stands the scalloped marble fountain where wondrous waters bubble forth. All year round, the Bollente spring supplies some 560 litres (148 gallons) of water per minute, spilling out over the marble fountain at an average temperature of 75°C. Springs outside the town include a small one known as the acqua marcia (rotten water), where stinky, strongly sulphuric water issues forth at 28.4°C.

Throughout the latter half of the 20th century, Acqui Terme was a popular destination with ailing Italians who came to steep themselves in the town's curative waters subsidised by the national health service. With clients like these, its attractiveness as a tourist mecca waned. When the health service stopped shelling out for water cures, many larger hotels and spa complexes closed.

The health and beauty-conscious 1990s brought a surge of interest in spas, and Acqui set to work renovating many of its existing thermal bath complexes, the majority of which are located in the town's centre.

Castello dei Paleologi-Museo Civico Archeologico
Via Morelli 2 (0144 57 555/ www.acquimusei.it/archeo). **Open** 9.30am-12.30pm, 3.30-6.30pm Wed-Sat; 3.30-6.30pm Sun. **Admission** €5; €3 concessions. **No credit cards.**

By train
Frequent services from Porta Nuova station (40mins).

By bus
ATAV (011 856 545/www.vigobus.it) buses run 3-4 times a day from Turin (corso San Maurizio) to Asti, but it's a 2-3hr trip with a change at Castelnuovo.

Il Monferrato

With Le Langhe (*see p194*), Il Monferrato forms part of a promised land for *enogastronomia* – the study, production and conservation of wine (*enologia*), and the fine art of preparing and consuming food (*gastronomia*). Of course, the area is rich in churches, *palazzi* and castles too (though the vast majority of its castles are in private hands and difficult to visit). But more often than not, your most memorable experiences will not involve art, architecture or history; they will occur at the table.

Over the centuries, various families acquired the marquisate of Monferrato. Legend has it that some time in the late tenth century a certain Aleramo was given three days in which to ride his horse as far and wide as he could, after which the land encompassed by this wild gallop would be his. The Aleramici family became the first marquises of Monferrato, followed by the Paleologi (1305-1533) and then the Gonzagas (1559). In 1703 the lands passed to Turin's ruling Savoy family.

The area is divided into Alto (high) and Basso (low) Monferrato. Although there is no clear demarcation line between the two, the *monferrini* generally consider the lands between the Po and Tanaro rivers as the Basso Monferrato and those from the Tanaro to the Ligurian border as the Alto Monferrato.

Writer Vittorio Alfieri. *See p185.*

Basso Monferrato

There's something rather Tuscan about parts of the Basso Monferrato, where compact hilltop towns dot the rolling landscape. The similarities end in the north, where the hills sink into rice paddies in the south-western tip of the vast Po valley plain that occupies most of the next-door region of Lombardy. In spring water and fresh rice shoots create a bright-green mirrored tableau that stretches as far as the eye can see.

Casale Monferrato, the main town of Basso Monferrato, is a busy place, with a flourishing agricultural industry. Past the ugly industrial outskirts lies a well-preserved *centro storico*.

In piazza Castello, the squat castle looks out over the River Po. Used as a military storehouse until a few years ago, it is currently being renovated. Note the Paleologi, Gonzaga and Aleramici escutcheons in marble on the façade.

But perhaps the most interesting building at this western end of town is the nearby **Palazzo Anna d'Alençon** (the palazzo is closed to the public, but you can wander into the courtyard). This residence of the marquis of Monferrato is an excellent example of late 14th-century architecture, and has remained largely intact. The courtyard has charming multicoloured frescoes. On the first floor are portraits of various marquises.

Via Alessandria leads east towards the **Sinagoga**, constructed in 1595 and radically restructured in 1857. The building's exterior is deliberately nondescript: *monferrini* rulers forbade the synagogue to be recognisable externally or to have direct access to a principal street. But inside the contrast could not be more striking; the synagogue's interior is opulently decorated with wood carvings, baroque stuccoes and gilding. Also inside is the **Museo d'arte e storia ebraica**, which houses sacred artefacts from the 18th and 19th centuries. In the 18th century the area around the synagogue was a Jewish ghetto. Despite the restrictions imposed on the community, the Jews continued to thrive. A 1761 census counted 673 inhabitants in the ghetto, making this Jewish community the second largest in Piedmont after the one in Turin.

Further east on via Cavour, the **Museo civico** houses a number of minor Renaissance paintings and an extraordinary *gipsoteca* – a collection of plaster models for statues – by local sculptor Leonardo Bistolfi. Bistolfi was born in Casale Monferrato in 1859, and went on to study at Milan's renowned Brera art academy. A champion of the *stile Liberty* that was all the rage at the beginning of the 20th century, and creator of numerous monuments for major Italian cities, Bistolfi was all but forgotten by art history for many decades but has recently been re-evaluated as one of the foremost Italian symbolist sculptors. The collection extends beyond plaster, and includes terracotta, bronze and marble sculpture.

Casale Monferrato's main drag is via Mameli, which crosses via Cavour. At Nos.27-9 is **Palazzo Gozzani di Treville** (not open to the public, but the courtyard is usually visible), a building designed in 1710 by Giuseppe Scapitta. The palazzo has an extremely elegant atrium and courtyard, complete with refined stuccoes and marble columns. Note the trompe l'oeil frescoes on the vaults above the entry.

On the second Sunday of every month, Casale Monferrato hosts a major antiques market.

Thirty kilometres (18 miles) west of Casale Monferrato on the SS590 rises the **Santuario di Crea** (*see p190* **Chapel fever**), an extraordinary church and nature park. Further west is the small town of **Villadeati**, perched on a hilltop overlooking the valley and home to the Villa-Castello Belvedere, a late 18th-century building that was bought and completely renovated by the Feltrinelli family, of the eponymous publishing company and bookstore chain (*see p121*). The Feltrinellis took pains to restore the original look and feel of the building, recreating the romance of its extensive towers, balconies and large terraced garden. The castle remains a private residence, but the custodian will usually provide a brief tour upon request.

South and east of Casale Monferrato lie a number of attractive towns. South on the SS31 is **Occimiano**, a village of Roman origins that gained prominence in the Middle Ages; its pretty medieval architecture remains. The town's church, **San Valerio** (10am-1pm; 4-6pm daily), was rebuilt in the 16th century, but has retained its original Romanesque bell tower.

A narrow lane from Occimiano leads southwest to **Conzano**, a tiny *borgo* dominated by a single Roman tower. Hamlets of this size in Italy have a habit of dying out. Not so Conzano, where relations with locals who emigrated to Australia earlier in the 20th century buoys the place not only economically – with investments in property – but also socially. The main square is called piazza Australia. Thanks largely to subsidies from Down Under, Conzano holds a crafts fair around Easter, when the streets fill up with *conzanesi* both Aussie and Italian.

Some eight kilometres (five miles) north-east of Occimiano on the same lane, you'll hit the River Po and the **Parco fluviale del Po** (Po river park), a natural reserve created to protect riverbank woodland and wetlands that are home to countless bird species, including various kinds of heron (which can be seen prowling the nearby rice fields), Peregrine falcons and cormorants. The town of **Frassineto Po** lies at the epicentre of Italy's poplar industry. This species was first farmed in plantations along the river here.

Museo Civico, Pinacoteca & Gipsoteca Bistolfi

Via Cavour 5, Casale Monferrato (0142 444 309). **Open** by appointment Mon-Fri; 10.30am-1pm, 3-6.30pm Sat, Sun. **Admission** €2.70; €1.60 concessions. **No credit cards**.

Sinagoga & Museo d'Arte e Storia Ebraica

Vicolo Salomone Olper 44, Casale Monferrato (0142 452 076). **Open** *Synagogue & museum* By appointment Mon-Sat; 10am-noon, 3-5pm Sun. Closed Jan, Aug. **Admission** €4.

Where to stay & eat

In an area where even your car mechanic will wax lyrical about the subtle odours of porcini mushrooms and the delicate bouquet of an aged Barbera, just about any local restaurant can be counted on to provide top-flight fare.

Midway between Casale Monferrato and Murisengo, just off the SS590, lies the tiny hilltop hamlet of **Mombello Monferrato**. Here you will find **Dubini** (via Roma 36, 0142 944 116, closed 2wks Jan, 2wks Aug, average €25); run by the same family since 1888, it continues to surprise with its sumptuous *monferrina* cuisine. Come hungry: your *antipasti* alone will number in double digits. Current owners Cesare and Marisa Dubini have added a quaint, four-bedroom B&B (€75 double).

In Casale Monferrato proper, **La Torre** (via Caroglio 3, 0142 70 295, www.ristorante-latorre.it, average €42) offers fine, innovative local cuisine, including excellent *vitello tonnato* *all'antica*. In nearby **Moncalvo**, the **Locanda dell'Orsolina** (via Caminata 28, 0141 921 180, www.cascinaorsolina.com, €130-€145 double) is in a renovated 18th-century farmhouse; country-style rooms look out over a garden and vineyards owned by the **Locanda**'s patrons.

Getting there

By car

For Casale Monferrato, take the A21 motorway to Alessandria, then switch to the A26 (exit Casale Monferrato Sud). Alternatively, take the SS11 (becomes the SS31bis). You'll need your own transport to reach most of the small towns in the area, along generally well-signposted local roads.

By train

Local services for Casale Monferrato from Turin's Porta Nuova station leave approximately every hour. The trip averages 1hr 30mins and requires a change of trains in either Asti or Alessandria.

By bus

Stat Autoticino (0142 452 854) buses leave from Turin (via XX Settembre) daily. The journey takes about 1hr 50mins with many stops in smaller towns.

Tourist information

IAT

Piazza Castello (0142 444 330/www.comune.casale-monferrato.al.it/www.monferrato.org). **Open** 8am-6pm Mon-Sat; 10am-12.30pm, 3-6.30pm Sun.

Parco Fluviale del Po

Park information office *Cascina Belvedere, SS494, km70, Frascarolo (0384 84 676/ www.parchi.it).*
Call Carmela Caiazzo from 8.30am-3.30pm Mon-Fri for information or to make an appointment to visit the information centre.

Alto Monferrato

Nizza Monferrato (15 kilometres/9 miles south-east of Monferrato as the crow flies, but the road is less direct) has been an important market town since the 16th century, when animals, silk and cotton were traded here. Its importance as a trading town was due in large measure to the vicinity of the nearby navigable Belbo river and drew tradesmen from Piedmont, Liguria and Lombardy. Today the town clearly

Signor Victorious

In Casale Monferrato's **Museo civico** (*see p188*) hangs the only existing portrait of Giovanni Battista Boetti (1743-94), a Dominican priest from Monferrato who strove to unite Christianity and Islam, conquering territory stretching from the Black Sea to the Caspian in his own private Holy War.

Born in 1743 in Piazzano del Monferrato, Giovanni was at first forced by his father to study medicine, but then opted for theology, became a Dominican missionary and set out to convert heathens in the Far East. A gifted linguist, he would pick up Arabic, Persian and many other eastern languages on his travels. He also took time out to study Islam.

In Bira, on the banks of the Euphrates, the monk used his rudimentary medical skills to save the life of the local pasha's daughter. On the strength of this 'miracle' he was later ordered by the pasha to assist an important Turkish dignitary suffering from a stomach ailment. Giovanni prepared a potion that the Turk promptly drank, promptly dying afterwards. The *monferrino* was banished to Kurdistan, where he began to have visions. Islam was perfectable, he told a growing band of enthusiastic disciples, and the religions of Europe and Asia could be merged.

With some 3,000 followers, Giovanni engaged and routed a Turkish regiment near Akhaltsikhé. In the wake of the battle Giovanni was renamed *Al-Mansûr* – the Victorious. His fame spread, and 40,000 soldiers rallied to his cause. Not content with threatening the Ottomon Empire, Signor Victorious turned his attention to the Russian one, leading his forces into Georgia, where he forged an alliance with the Kurds and Chechens, and hacked his way to victory over tsarist troops in the Sunzha river valley.

But his biggest victory turned out to be the beginning of the end. News of the massacre of Russian soldiers reached the court in St Petersburg, and what had until then been mountain folklore was now seen as a serious threat.

Convinced God was firmly on his side, *Al-Mansûr* led his small army against the impenetrable Russian fortress of Giyorgivesk, and was defeated. His aura of invincibility gone, Signor Victorious saw the fervour that had kept his followers behind him evaporate. Boetti was captured by the Russians in 1791 and locked up in a monastery at Solovetsk by the White Sea, where he died three years later.

Trips Out of Town

still has a mercantile mindset and hosts a variety of itinerant markets and fairs, including a *mercato antiquario* (antiques market) on the third Sunday of each month and a truffle fair in the beginning of November. Nizza's main drag, via Carlo Alberto, has been pedestrianised (though that's a relative concept in Italy); its brightly coloured 18th- and 19th-century *palazzi* make this a pleasant walk. In piazza Dante is the **Museo Bersano delle contadinerie e stampe antiche sul vino** (0141 720 211, open by appointment only), with a range of wine-making instruments from the 1700s and later.

East of here is Mombaruzzo, home of the amaretto. This almond-flavoured biscuit was invented by Francesco Moriondo, master pastry chef for the Savoy court during the early 18th century. Combining a mix of ground almonds and whipped egg whites, Moriondo's invention was an immediate success and he chose Mombaruzzo to host the first amaretto factory. Today Mombaruzzo's pastry shops still proudly display their noble *biscotto* in their windows. Head south from Nizza on SS456 for **Acqui Terme**, a hotspot in every sense dating back to

Asti's **Santa Maria Assunta**. *See p185.*

Chapel fever

Legend has it that St Eusebius escaped persecution in the fourth century by hiding in a rustic chapel where the **Santuario di Crea** now stands. It was not until 1589, however, that local prior Costantino Massino applied to the then ruler of the Monferrato region Vincenzo Gonzaga for permission to emulate the saint, and create a *sacro monte*.

Dear to northern Italians, who began building them in the 15th century, a *sacro monte* is a collection of chapels dotted around a hillside, usually representing the Stations of the Cross. Gonzaga was taken with the idea of having one on his own territory, and immediately constructed a chapel at his own expense. Additional chapels were to be built with funds from other noble families in the region.

Soon competition had replaced devotion as the driving force behind the project. In 1598 new plans for the *sacro monte* foresaw no fewer than 40 chapels. The entire community became involved in the project. Work continued until 1612, when war broke out in the Monferrato. The project was not taken up again until 1820, continuing into the early 20th century.

Forty chapels proved to be more ambitious than realistic. Today the **sacro monte di Crea**

is composed of 23 chapels and five hermitages. Many of the chapels are relatively unimpressive, but several are worth noting, including No.5, the original chapel built for Gonzaga,which includes statuary by Melchiorre d'Enrico and frescoes by Giuseppe Moncalvo; and chapel 23, also known as the paradise chapel, which has a collection of more than 300 figures attached to its vault. There's a basilica, too – a largely Romanesque building with a bold baroque façade.

A nature reserve has been made in 470 square kilometres (181 square miles) of woodland around the Santuario (open dawn to dusk daily). There are walking tracks and a wide variety of animals to be spotted, including foxes, owls, hawks, hares, salamanders and green woodpeckers.

Santuario di Crea

Piazzale Santuario, Serralunga di Crea (0142 940 109). **Open** 7am-noon, 2-6pm daily. **Admission** free.
The Santuario also offers clean – if rather spartan – accommodation. Thirty recently renovated rooms are available. A double room costs €35, but may be reduced if you're staying for more than one night.

ancient Roman times (*see p186* **They came, they saw... they relaxed**). The *centro storico* of this elegant and thriving spa town has been turned into a pedestrian zone that can easily be explored on foot. In central piazza della Bollente, a shell-shaped marble fountain marks the spot where Acqui Terme's Bollente hot water springs hit daylight at a searing 75°C. During the Middle Ages, this area was home to a host of artisans, merchants and healers who gravitated towards the hot springs and their lounging, moneyed frequenters. The **Duomo**, consecrated in 1067, has a large, intricately carved marble lunette over its main doors. East of the Duomo, the **Castello dei Paleologi** dates from the 11th century, but was significantly renovated and enlarged in the 1480s by the Paleologi family, who ruled over large portions of the Monferrato throughout the second half of the 15th century. In 1967 the local government put the **Museo archeologico** (closed for restoration as this guide went to press) inside the castle and turned the surrounding gardens into a small, in-town nature reserve. The museum houses locally-found prehistoric and Roman artefacts.

Duomo
Piazza Duomo, Acqui Terme (0144 322 381). **Open** 9am-noon, 3-6.30pm daily.

Where to stay & eat

In Nizza Monferrato, the family-run **Le Due Lanterne** (piazza Garibaldi 52, 0141 702 480, average €28) provides a pleasant, classic *monferrino* dining experience in a charming rustic setting; chocoholics should order double helpings of its *bonet al cioccolato*.

In Acqui Terme the **Grand Hotel Nuove Terme** (piazza Italia 1, 0144 58 555, www.anticadimore.com, €130-€180 double) continues the town's centuries-old health spa tradition, combining elegant hostelry with thermal baths and hot springs in a 19th-century palazzo that was recently remodelled from top to toe. The **Talice Radicati** hotel (piazza Conciliazione 12, 0144 328 611, www.antichedimore.com, €103-€201 double) is a 17th-century home-turned-hotel conveniently located in the city centre.

Tourist information

For **Nizza Monferrato**, *see p186* **Asti Turismo ATL**.

IAT di Acqui Terme
Via Magiorino Ferraris 5, Acqui Terme (0144 322 142). **Open** 9.30am-12.30pm, 3.30-6.30pm Mon-Sat; 10am-1pm Sun.

Getting there

By car
Local roads from Asti are well signposted.

By train
Local services for Nizza Monferrato from Turin's Porta Nuova station leave approximately every hour. Travel time is approximately 1hr; change in Asti or Alessandria.

Alba & Le Langhe

Truffle country.

Shopping on Alba's **via Vittorio Emanuele II**.

Midway between Turin and Genoa, nestling between the Rivers Tanaro and Bormida, the Langhe area is a rural treasure trove of picturesque villages and agricultural landscapes, from the rolling vineyards of Langa Bassa in the south, where some of Italy's finest wines are produced, to the pine forests of the Langa Alta highlands in the north and east, where the soft hazel-nut of Piedmont grows.

Alba

Alba, the capital of Le Langhe, lies 62 kilometres (39 miles) south of Turin in the Tanaro valley. There was already a settlement here during the neolithic period but it first entered history books as Alba Pompeia following its conquest by Rome in the first century BC. Barbarians brought turmoil when they streamed through after the fall of Rome in the fifth century. Stability returned to the town under the rule of Otto I in 967.

Between 1100 and 1500 the commune fought repeatedly against neighbouring Asti (*see pp184-91*; still a rival, though now on the

gastronomic front) to extend its territory, and suffered rule by many different overlords. Alba was finally declared the domain of Turin's Savoy family in 1628. During World War II the area was at the centre of partisan activity; for 23 days at the end of the conflict, when partisans had liberated it from German occupation, the town was declared an independent republic, an event documented in the book *I ventitre giorni della città di Alba* by Beppe Fenoglio.

Alba today is a prosperous town, buoyed by flourishing local industry – including the Ferrero empire of Nutella fame (*see p194* **Middle-aged spread**) – and by the tourists and buyers who flock to the city during October to purchase, indulge in or merely choke over the prices of Alba's most famous product, the white truffle (*see p198* **Truffle facts**).

Once known as the town of 100 towers, Alba now has about 20 of these reminders of medieval vulnerability scattered around its centre; you'll notice several as you walk along the town's main shopping artery, via Vittorio Emanuele II. On the corner of the main drag and via Paruzza, the baroque **church of the Maddalena** (9am-

8pm daily) has a colourfully painted interior.
Inside is the chapel of Blessed Margherita di
Savoia, her body conserved in a silver urn.
The **Museo civico archeologico e di
scienze naturali**, with its collection of local
prehistoric and Roman finds, is next door.

Parallel (east) to via Vittorio Emanuele II,
via Accademia leads to the Gothic church of
San Domenico, built at the end of the 13th
century by Dominican friars and reworked
frequently since. It has regained much of its
original splendour, however, thanks to recent
restoration work. During its term as a stable
under French occupation in the early 19th
century, many of the church's 15th-century
frescoes were painted over, though one of the
Madonna and Child with Saints remains in the
lunette. A marble statue group by Leonardo
Bistolfi was commissioned by President Luigi
Einaudi in 1949 to commemorate Alba's
glorious Resistance movement.

Vie Vittorio Emanuele II and Accademia both
end in central piazza Risorgimento, where Alba
Pompeia's forum stood. It's now home to the
Palazzo Comunale (visits by appointment
only, call 0173 292 244), the oldest parts of
which date from the eighth century. Inside are
works by local artist Pinot Gallizio (1902-64; in
his spare time he was a chemist and partisan),
an altarpiece by Macrino d'Alba (1501) and, in
the Sala della Resistenza, photos and
documents relating to the wartime Resistance.

On the eastern side of the piazza is the
crumbly red-brick **Duomo** (cattedrale di San
Lorenzo). A church has stood here since the first
half of the seventh century; the Romanesque
church was replaced by a Gothic one in 1484,
when the bell tower was added, though remains
of a Romanesque tower can be seen inside.
Many revamps have taken their toll since then,
most significantly in 1652, following major
earthquake damage to the vault and nave in
1626. It was at this time that the church was
given its current Latin cross shape with the
addition of two side-chapels. Between 1868
and 1878 the church was again 'restored' and
the façade rebuilt, though the three 11th-
century doors remain.

West of the piazza, via Cavour has more
defensive towers, and a medieval loggia at No.5.

Duomo

Piazza Risorgimento (0173 440 000). **Open** 7am-
noon, 3-6.30pm daily. Closed for restoration as this
guide went to press.

Museo Civico Archeologico e di
Scienze Naturali

Via Vittorio Emanuele II 19 (0173 290 092). **Open**
3-6pm Tue-Fri; 9.30am-12.30pm, 3-6pm Sat, Sun.
Admission €4; €2.50 concessions. **Credit** MC, V.

Where to eat & drink

For tasty local specialities try **Enoclub** (piazza
Savona 4, 0173 33 994, taster menu €30) and
Enotria (corso Enotria 24, 0173 441 330, taster
menu €26). **Osteria Vento di Langa** (via
Pertinace 20, 0173 293 282, average €31) is an
intimate and tastefully decorated *osteria*. The
chic **La Brasilera** (via Roma 2, 0173 290 086,
average €15) is good for lunch. **Osteria del
Vincafe** (via Vittorio Emanuele II 12, 0173 364
603, closed Mon, average €20) has a rustic but
elegant environment and is popular with locals.

Shopping

Alba's Saturday market in **via Vittorio
Emanuele II** (open 8am to 1pm) is not to be
missed: they've been selling local produce and
gastronomic specialities here since 1171. This
is also the street to buy local food and wine.

The pure ones

Between the 11th and 14th centuries
the Cathars were one of Europe's most
powerful religious sects, concentrated
mainly in southern France and northern
Italy. Their faith rested on the concept of
Dualism, which at its simplest translated
into a battle between spiritual good (God)
and material evil (Satan). The name Cathar
derives from the Greek 'Katheroi', meaning
'pure ones': the sect believed all material
matter to be evil because it was created by
Satan, and its aim was an apostolic life of
piety and ascetism; spiritually advanced
members, known as 'perfecti', ate no meat
and abstained from sex. Materialistic,
rich Catholic priests and nobles were
considered to be servants of the devil. The
Cathars found support among the poor who
resented paying high taxes and tithes to
support the excesses of the Catholic clergy.

The perceived threat of the Cathar (aka
Albigensian) heretics to the mainstream
Church was deemed to be so great that
in 1209 Pope Innocent III proclaimed
a crusade against them. Cathars who
refused to renounce their belief were
often burnt at the stake. The Cathars of
Monforte were some of the earliest victims
of Catholic wrath, burnt to death at the
hands of the army of the bishop of Milan
in 1028. Despite their persecution Cathar
communities survived through the 14th
century, only dying out in the 15th century.

Trips Out of Town

I Piaceri del Gusto (via Vittorio Emanuele II 23A, 0173 440 166, closed Sun Jan-Aug) is great for mushroom and truffle products; it also has a restaurant and wine cellar. *See also p31* **Morra**.

Where to stay

The **Hotel Savona** (via Roma 1, 0173 440 440, fax 0173 364 312, €96 double) is a luxurious three-star hotel in the heart of town with a traditional restaurant (taster menu €25-€30, closed Mon lunch & Sun) and swish café that does great *aperitivi*. **Hotel I Castelli** (corso Torino 14, 0173 361 978, fax 0173 361 974, €110 double) is a newly built four-star with a great terrace overlooking the old town. **Albergo San Lorenzo** (piazza Rossetti 6, 0173 362 406, fax 0173 366 995, €70 double) is in a refurbished 19th-century house and a real gem of a place. For tighter budgets, the **Leon d'Oro** (piazza Marconi 2, 0173 440 536, €42-€58 double) is a reasonable two-star option.

Getting there

By car

Take the A6 Turin–Savona, exit at Marene, then take the SS231 to Alba. Alternatively, take the A21 Turin–Piacenza, exit at Asti Est, then take the SS231 to Alba. For destinations in Le Langhe, local roads are generally well signposted.

By train

For Alba, you'll have to change at Bra, Asti or Carmagnola; there is a direct service from Porta Nuova station in October when the truffle fair on.

By bus

SATTI (011 521 4703, www.satti.it) buses leave every 30 minutes from Turin's piazza Marconi for Alba and Barolo.

Tourist information

ATL – Ente Turismo Alba

Piazza Medford 3 (0173 35 833/www.langheroero.it). **Open** 9am-12.30pm, 2.30-6.30pm Mon-Fri; 9am-12.30pm Sat.

During the truffle fair in October, the office opens regular weekday hours at weekends too. It also organises themed cycling tours around Le Langhe; bikes are provided.

Consorzio Turistico Langhe Monferrato Roero

Via Vittorio Emanuele II 19 (0173 362 562/www.turismodoc.it). **Open** 9am-1pm, 2-6pm Mon-Sat; 10am-1pm, 2-6pm Sun.

Organises cycling tours around Le Langhe; bikes are provided.

Ufficio Turistico Città di Alba

Via Vittorio Emanuele II 19 (0173 362 562/www.comune.alba.cn.it). **Open** *Jan, Feb* 9am-1.30pm, 2-6pm Mon-Sat. *Mar-Dec* 9am-1.30pm, 2-6pm daily.

Le Langhe

Every Sunday from May to October, many of southern Piedmont's splendid (but generally closed) castles are opened to the public in an event called **Castelli aperti** (Open Castles). For information, see www.castelliaperti.it.

Middle-aged spread

It may have seemed a nutty idea at the time, but when pastrymaker Pietro Ferrero couldn't get enough cocoa in food-rationed post-war Alba (*see p192*), he added local hazel-nuts, sugar, powdered milk and vegetable oils to come up with a novel sweet spread that has since taken the world by storm.

Nutella turned 40 in 2004, the mainstay of a confectionery dynasty that is tightly controlled and still run by the very guarded and secretive Ferrero family.

An earlier version of the spread with the boastful name of Supercrema Gianduja was sold by the smear to hordes of *ragazzi* clutching slices of white bread in corner shops. As the pimple-inducing product took off, an international name was needed: thus Nutella was born in 1964. Its ascent rivals that of Fiat as a symbol of the economic miracle that gripped Piedmont in the 1950s and '60s. Ferrero now pumps out 179,000 tons of the stuff a year, and claims that it outsells peanut butter.

Now endowed with cult-like status, the spread dubbed 'mother-love in a jar' gets gobbled around the globe morning, noon and night and has fostered many themed gatherings, from innocent kiddy birthday parties to disco licking events where Nutella gets spread in places its inventor would never have imagined.

The sweet smell of roasting hazel-nuts and cocoa wafts over the Ferrero plant in Alba, where Nutella finds its way into another world-beating confection, Ferrero Rocher. Some Italian chefs who were raised on the stuff can't resist adding this homey bit of nostalgia to pizzas, pastas and ice-cream.

Alba once had 100 towers. *See p192.*

Langa Bassa

Five kilometres (three miles) south-west of Alba, the village of **Roddi** has a castle and tower with a finely decorated upper section; the castle was the property of Renaissance humanist Francesco Pico della Mirandola. At Roddi's 'university' for truffle dogs, founded in 1880, man's best friend is trained to become an expert sniffer-outer of the Langhe's much-sought-after truffles (*see p197* **Truffle snufflers**).

Continuing south, the imposing bulk of the 13th-century castle of **Grinzane Cavour** (six kilometres/four miles) is visible from afar. In 1832, this was the operational headquarters of Camillo Cavour (*see p10* **The four horsemen of the Risorgimento**). Inside the castle, you can still see the great man's bed and a small collection of artefacts in the ethnographical museum. Also in the castle is an *enoteca* (closed Tue and Jan) where you can taste the local nectar of Bacchus.

Near Grinzane, at Gallo d'Alba, the road splits to follow the deep valleys of the Langa Bassa; crossing laterally from one valley to the next is well nigh impossible.

In the westernmost valley, **La Morra** affords magnificent views over Le Langhe from piazza Castello. In the nearby (north) village of **Annunziata**, the former Benedictine abbey of San Martino is today the **Museo Ratti dei vini d'Alba**. Every last Sunday in August, people gather outside the Ratti museum to take

a gastronomic walk through the vineyards, and past farms and ancient chapels, with music and dancing rounding off the day.

You can track across country from La Morra to the heart of Le Langhe and Barolo country (a fast road – the E74 – direct from Alba gets you there more quickly). **Barolo's** castle stands lord and master over rolling hills covered with vineyards of nebbiolo grapes. The castle, first built around 1000, was home to the noble Falletti family before passing to Mantua's Gonzagas, then Turin's Savoys in 1631. It was Giulia Colbert, the last of the Fallettis, who invented the technique still used today to make Barolo's prestigious wines. In the castle cellars is an *enoteca* and wine museum.

South of Barolo, **Novello** is a heady mix of art, history, cuisine and wines, with the peak of Monviso (*see p201*) providing a dramatic backdrop. In Roman times the *albesi* built their summer residences here. The castle (now a restaurant) that dominates the town was built in 1880 by Gran Battista Schellino in flamboyant neo-Gothic style. The wine shop in piazza Marconi sells Branda di Novello, the local tipple.

Further east, **Monforte d'Alba** is reportedly full of the ghosts of Cathar heretics burnt at the stake here (*see p193* **The pure ones**). They probably won't bother you, though, as you watch one of the summer concerts in the Horszowski auditorium (information 0172 438 324, www.langadellevalli.it), inaugurated in 1986 by the pianist. A backdrop consisting of

the 18th-century Palazzo Scarampi (not open to the public), the baroque oratory of Santa Elisabetta and the façade of the 17th-century church of the Disciplinati makes a concert in the auditorium a real treat.

South of Monforte, **Dogliani** is the birth-place of Luigi Einaudi, the first president of the Italian Republic and home to the best Dolcetto wine in the Langhe.

Across the valley floor to the south-west, **Farigliano**'s main square is dominated by the church of **San Giovanni** (open 8am-noon, 3.30-7pm daily) built at the end of the 19th century; shops have local wines at good prices. On the road to Carrù the sanctuary of Mellea is said to have witnessed apparitions of the Virgin.

In valleys further to the east stand the fortresses of **Serralunga d'Alba** and **Castiglione Falletto**. The former dates back to the early Middle Ages and was originally a lookout tower. In 1340 the tower was extended into a castle by feudal lord Pietro Falletti. Houses were built clustered round the castle to make it easy for villagers to take shelter in times of war. Restored in the 1950s, it's now state owned and is one of the few castles in the Langhe that you can visit. Barolo Chinato – a mix of Barolo wine, sugar, spices and quinine, served hot as a remedy for colds and malaria – was first whipped up here.

The Falletto family received the area around Castiglione as a fiefdom in 1225 and added their surname to the town's moniker to make sure no one ever forgot who was in charge. The castle here is not open to the public.

Langa Alta

The Langa Alta includes the area east of Alba and the hazel-nut-filled valleys to the south-east of the town.

Just outside Alba, **Barbaresco** is notable not only for its wines but also for its distinctive red tower in the centre of town, constructed at the beginning of the 11th century as a defence against the Saracens.

A short drive to the east is the perfect centre of **Nèive**, founded by the Romans but with stunning medieval, Renaissance and baroque highlights too. Fought over by local families for centuries, this town only passed under the control of the Savoys after Napoleon's occupying troops withdrew in 1815. Nèive's castle is now home to a fine wine cellar. Each year on 22 December, freshly fattened cockerels are turned into Christmas dinner fare at the **Fiera dei Capponi**, one of the oldest festivals in the Langhe. The remains of the 'operation' are used in a sauce to cover *tarjarin*, a finely cut pasta and speciality of the region.

Nebbiolo grapes in **Barolo**. See p195.

In the nearby village of **Borgonuovo**, all that is left of the church of Santa Maria del Piano is a five-floor bell tower built on the remains of an ancient temple dedicated to Diana.

South-east of Alba and sitting astride the River Bormida, **Cortemilia** is famous for its hazel-nuts, and holds a fair every August to celebrate its crop. At the heart of the old town are medieval houses, each with its own porch. A 13th-century tower rises above the town.

South from Cortemilia, **Bergolo** is a pretty town built of sandstone. A short walk uphill from Bergolo's town square to the highest point of the village stands the 12th-century chapel of **San Sebastiano** (open 7.30am-noon, 3.30-6.30pm daily) from where there's a splendid view over the Bormida and Uzzone valleys. The façades of many of Bergolo's houses have been decorated with frescoes and mosaics by art school students who take part in the annual

(July-Aug) Concorso d'Arte Bergolo competition. In May the town hosts the Cantè Magg music and dance festival (www.langadellevalli.it).

Castello di Grinzane Cavour
Via Cavour 5 (0173 262 159). **Open** *June-Sept* 10am-12.30pm, 2.30-6.30pm Mon, Wed-Sun. *Sept-Nov* 9am-noon, 2-6pm daily. *Dec, Feb-May* 9am-noon, 2-6pm Mon, Wed-Sun. **Admission** €3.50. **Credit** AmEx, MC, V.

Castello dei Marchesi Falletti di Barolo
Piazza Falletti, Barolo (0173 56 277). **Open** 10am-12.30pm, 3-6.30pm Mon-Wed, Fri-Sun. Closed Jan. **Admission** €3; €2.50 concessions. **Credit** MC, V.

Castello di Roddi
Piazza Castello, Roddi (0173 615 001). **Open** *May-Oct* 11am-1pm, 2-5.30pm Sun; other times by appointment only. **Admission** €2.60; €1.90 concessions. **No credit cards**.

Truffle snufflers

Jolly may be an unassuming-looking little mongrel with a pointed muzzle and an extra-ordinarily fleshy nose but she is worth her weight in gold. She is fiercely loyal to her master, Ezio, a tall, slim salt-of-the-earth type with intense brown eyes and a gentle manner. Ezio is a *trifolau* (truffler) and encourages Jolly in her work of seeking out precious tubers with a secret language of softly spoken half words and half sounds that make no sense to anyone but the two of them. In one pocket of his jacket he holds a store of little 'treats' to reward his dog with, while another holds the special tool he uses for digging. When Jolly smells something interesting, man and dog work together at carefully unearthing the prize, she with fast working paws and he finishing the job with his little spade; dogs are inclined to eat truffles, so he must get to it first.

A great deal of mystique surrounds the business of truffling. It is a *mistero* that is passed down through generations; Ezio's father was a *trifolau* and his son is carrying on the family tradition. Certain dogs seem to be born with a predisposition for the business, but need careful training nonetheless. Their search takes place by night or at dawn, when they are less likely

to be seen by rivals and there are few sounds to distract the working animals.

Due to the lack of rain, 2003 was a disastrous year for truffles and the prices soared to as high as €350 per 100 grams, more than double the going rate in 2002. Like most *trifolau*, Ezio does not rely exclusively on truffles for his livelihood. With his wife Clelia, he runs a wonderful restaurant, **Tra Arte e Querce** (Località Monchiero Alto 11, Monchiero, 0173 792 156), near Barolo, where you can sample the fruits of his labours. Clelia cooks (superbly), Ezio does front of house. The price for a vast set meal is €25 (excluding truffles and wine); booking is essential. They also have six neat, elegant bedrooms (€70-€100 double).

Truffle facts

The truffle is a hypogeous fungus, that is, it grows below the ground. Inside it's meaty; outside it's tough and bark-like, though its consistency depends on the soil in which it grows. Soft earth makes it more rounded, while compact soil produces a more rutted, knobbly fungus. The surrounding plant life and quality of water have a bearing on the truffle, too, determining its colour and perfume.

The search for this pricey fungus takes place under the cover of darkness from late September to late December. Specially trained truffle-sniffer dogs are used to locate these gastronomic jewels and to extract them delicately from the earth with their paws.

In Alba's 2003 auction, 100 grams of white truffles sold for an average of €260; at this kind of price, you'll want to make the most of them.

In order to maintain the truffles' particular taste and aroma, they must be consumed as soon as possible, though you can wrap them in fabric or paper to keep them fresh for a couple of days. Truffles come complete with clogs of earth; these must be removed before eating (you don't want to be grating clumps of soil on to your pasta) with delicate brushing movements but NEVER by washing. Truffles are best served raw, grated or thinly sliced on to steaming pasta with melted butter or tomato sauce. They are also great eaten with *fonduta* (fondue), *carne cruda all'albese* (a local take on steak tartare), simple risotto or fried eggs. Few truffles can take cooking.

There are many truffle varieties; the following are some of the better-known ones:

Tuber magnatum Pico
(**Tartufo bianco pregiato**)
This fungus has a soft exterior, which is pale ochre in colour. The flesh is pinky-white with a white grain. The strong smell is gives off is faintly garlicky. It matures between October and December.

Tuber melanosporum Vitt.
(**Tartufo nero pregiato**)
The blackish-brown exterior of this fungus has rusty-coloured scarring. The flesh is purple-black with a fine white vein. It has a fruity scent and a pleasant taste that remains even after cooking. It matures between October and November.

Tuber brumale Vitt.
(**Tartufo nero invernale**)
The black exterior of this fungus hides brown and white flesh that has a pleasant taste. It's sometimes confused with the *tartufo nero pregiato*, but it matures between January and March.

Tuber macrosporum Vitt.
(**Tartufo nero liscio**)
This globular fungus has a lumpy reddy-brown exterior and purply-red flesh that develops a dark vein when it comes in contact with air. It has a pungent taste and smells slightly garlicky like the *tartufo bianco*. It matures in October.

Castello di Serralunga d'Alba
Viale del Castello di Serralunga 1 (0173 613 358).
Open *Apr-Oct* 9am-noon, 2-6pm Tue-Sun. *Nov-Mar*
10am-noon, 2-5pm Tue-Sun. **Admission** free.

Museo Ratti dei Vini d'Alba
Frazione Annunziata 2, La Morra (0173 50185).
Open 8.30am-noon, 2.30-6pm Mon-Fri; by
appointment Sat, Sun. **Admission** free.

Where to eat & drink

In La Morra, **Vineria San Giorgio** (via
Umberto 1, 0173 509 594, closed Mon, average
€20) is in the restored cellar of a historic house.
In Barolo, **Osteria La Cantinella** (via
Acqua Gelata 4A, 0173 56 267, closed Mon
dinner, Tue dinner, average €27) is an authentic
wine cellar with a cosy atmosphere.
In Monforte d'Alba, **Osteria dei Catari**
(vicolo Solferino 4, 0173 787 256, www.
osteriadeicatari.com, closed Mon lunch & Tue,
average €28) is in a medieval building and offers
langarole recipes that vary with the season.
In Serralunga d'Alba, **Vineria Café
Ravanin** (piazza M Cappellano, 0173 613 010,
closed Tue, average €20) is set in one of the
most picturesque villages in the Langhe. The
rural atmosphere of this restaurant-cum-wine
bar makes it a warm and cosy place to eat;
meals are served in the courtyard in summer.

Shopping

Bottega del Vino Dolcetto di Dogliani
(piazza San Paolo 10, Dogliani, 0173 742 260,
open 9.30am-12.30pm, 3-7pm Mon-Thur, Sat, Sun;
3-7pm Fri) has a great selection of the local tipple.
Occelli Agrinatura (regione Scarrone 2,
Fariglione , 0173 746411, www.occelli.it) sells
both typical and rare varieties of local butters
and cheeses from the Langhe and Farigliano.
Enoteche (wineries) in many of Le Langhe's
wine-producing centres offer tours of the
cellars and wine tasting, as well as the chance
to buy some local bottles. It's best to book in
advance. Admission is free.

Enoteca Regionale Piemontese Cavour
Via Castello 5, Grinzane Cavour (0173 262 159).
Open 9.30am-12.30pm, 2.30-6.30pm Mon, Wed-Sun.
Closed Jan.

Enoteca Regionale del Barolo
Piazza Falletti, Barolo (0173 56 277). **Open** 10am-
12.30pm, 3-6.30pm Mon-Wed, Fri-Sun. Closed Jan.

Enoteca Regionale del Barbaresco
Via Torino 8A, Barbaresco (0173 63 5251). **Open**
9.30am-1pm, 2.30-6pm Mon, Tue, Thur-Sun. Closed
Jan, 1wk Aug.

Where to stay

Just outside La Morra, the **Ca' Nelide** (frazione
Santa Maria, borgata Onorati 81, 0173 50 288,
€52 double) is in a lovingly restored family
home; there's a swimming pool too.
In Barolo, **L'Angolo di Nonno Felice**
(piazza Eraldo Cabutto 6, 0173 613 100, €80
double) is a two-room apartment conveniently
located in the centre of town, suitable for
families or groups.
In Novello, **Barbabuc** (via Giordano 35,
0173 731 298, www.barbabuc.it, €73-€88
double) has an enchanting garden and
terrace with fantastic views over the
surrounding countryside.
In the *centro storico* of Dogliani, the **Albergo
Fiorito** (piazza Confraternita 25, 0173 70 582,
€50 double) has a veranda affording wonderful
views over the surrounding countryside; there's
a restaurant too (average €31).
The lovely **Italia** (piazza M Cappellano 3A,
0173 613 114, €70 double) in Serralunga d'Alba
is a beautiful rustic hotel and restaurant
(average €30) in the *centro storico*.
The **Hotel dei Quattro Vini** (località
Fausoni 7, 0173 679 874, www.hoteldei-
quattrovini.com, €90-€110 double) in Nèive
is an old farmhouse in the heart of the
northern Langhe hills.
In Bergolo, there's a good **youth hostel**
(via Roma 22, 0173 87 222, €15 per person;
breakfast €2.50 extra).

Tourist information

Ufficio Turistico Dogliani
*Piazza Luigi Einaudi 9, Dogliani (0173 70 210/
www.comune.dogliani.cn.it).* **Open** 9am-12.30pm, 2.30-
7pm Wed, Thur; 2.30-7pm Fri, Sat; 9am-noon Sun.

Ufficio Turistico di Cortemilia
*Palazzo Comunale, corso Luigi Einaudi 1, Cortemilia
(0173 81 027/www.comunecortemilia.it).* **Open**
8.30am-12.30pm Mon, Wed, Sat; 8.30am-12.30pm,
2.30-5.30pm Tue, Fri.

Getting there

See p194.

Getting around

The best way to get to grips with Le Langhe
is by car. If driving yourself doesn't appeal,
Albarent (0173 363 964, www.albarent.com)
will provide taxis and drivers who will
do it for you.
Fogliati (0173 440 216) operates local bus
services from piazza Medfort in Alba.

The Po Valley

Trace the River Po to its source via Alpine peaks and historic towns.

Savigliano.

The River Po wends its way for over 600 kilometres (370 miles) across northern Italy, playing an integral part in the culture and mythology of the regions through which it flows. Its source lies in the Alps to the west of Turin at the foot of Monviso, a peak of child's-drawing sharpness.

The trip to the source starts on a dull note, through the drear, anonymous hinterland to the south of Turin. A turn to the west, however, brings you abruptly face to face with the breathtaking sight of the western Alps, presided over by Monviso itself. Roads cross and recross the Po, never losing sight of the imposing heights.

A vast plain separates the city from the Alps. In winter crows wheel above groves of black trees; in summer green fields are strewn with wild flowers. Autumn sees the oxblood walls of the Piedmontese farmhouses stacked with drying corn cobs in shades of red and old gold; falcons and buzzards hunt for prey by the roadside and the occasional heron lifts itself in stately fashion from the hedgerows. Three towns – Moretta, Savigliano and Saluzzo – provide interesting stopovers en route to the river's source.

The Po plain

Forty kilometres (25 miles) south of Turin, pretty little **Moretta** (*more* means blackberries; one features on the town's crest) was first established as a rest stop and place of worship by Benedictine monks in the 11th century; all trace of their chapel has gone, but the town does boast a baroque church, **San Giovanni Battista** (opening hours vary; 0172 94 148), with a classic *cotto* façade in its main square. If Moretta's sights don't detain you long, its food may: the porticoed streets are home to many great cafés serving home-made ice-cream and *pasticceria*. If you turn up in the last week of May, you can challenge your arteries at **Maggioformaggio**, a cheese festival and all-in dairy binge. The festival, held in the grounds of the Santuario della Beata Vergine del Pilone (built between 1684 and 1786), provides a rare opportunity to visit the extensive lawns and gardens of the *santuario*, which now houses the food science faculty of Turin University. Salami is also produced locally, and along with Moretta's dairy products can be sampled at the weekly (Monday) market or in the town's eateries.

The evening sunlight gives a rosy glow to the red Gothic-Roman brickwork of the **Abbazia di Staffarda**, a few kilometres north of Moretta. Founded by Cistercian monks in the 12th century, this majestic complex houses the splendid three-nave abbey and the monks' refectory and outbuildings in its extensive grounds. Cross the road outside the abbey to picnic in the **Parco del Po** by the river (which can dry up unattractively in summer).

The ancient town of **Savigliano** was capital number two of the Savoy kingdom, and has fine examples of Renaissance and baroque art and architecture to underscore its own importance. The 17th-century fresco cycle celebrating the heroic deeds of Vittorio Amedeo I di Savoia in the royal hall of Palazzo Taffini d'Acceglio is a case in point.

But the real jewel of Savigliano is **piazza Santorre di Santarosa** in the *centro storico*, one of the best-preserved medieval squares in Italy. Originally laid out in the 12th century, it's a fascinating mishmash of medieval and Renaissance, with glorious *cotto* embellishments. Overlooking the piazza are the 17th-century Torre Civica (not open to the public) and 16th-century *arco di trionfo* (triumphal arch) built in honour of the House of Savoy. Complete your leisurely stroll around the square with an *aperitivo* or a pastry in the **Pasticceria Magliano** (No.50); the town's oldest bakery, it's an art nouveau treasure, still with its original painted windows.

Completing the triangle of towns on the plain is **Saluzzo**, a medieval centre known as the 'Siena of the Alps'. It was the stronghold of the marquesses of Saluzzo and capital of a feisty independent state for four centuries until handed to Turin's Savoy rulers in a treaty with France in 1601. Much 14th-century charm remains in the old quarter built on the hillside, where the cobbled streets leading towards the castle (closed for restoration) are lined with medieval houses, their gardens full of roses in summer.

Beneath the castle in via San Giovanni, the **Museo civico di casa Cavassa** occupies a 15th-century nobleman's house and is a fine example of a Renaissance dwelling (right down to the lack of heating in winter… go well wrapped). Amid a host of lesser artworks from the 15th to the 19th centuries Hans Clemer's exquisite golden Madonna della Misericordia (1499) stands out in the large reception hall.

Also by Hans Clemer is the 15th-century polyptych in the **Cattedrale** in corso Italia. The 82 metre-long (269 foot) interior with a nave and two aisles houses many works of art including a high baroque altar decorated with statues in 1721 by Carlo Giuseppe Plura and a 13th-century crucifix.

Abbazia di Staffarda

Piazza Roma, frazione di Staffarda, Revello (0175 273 215/www.mauriziano.it). **Open** *Apr-Sept* 9am-12.30pm, 2-6pm Tue-Sun. *Oct-Mar* 9am-12.30pm, 2-5pm Tue-Sun.

Cattedrale di Saluzzo

Corso Italia, Saluzzo (0175 42 962). **Open** 3-6pm daily.

Museo Civico di Casa Cavassa

Via San Giovanni 5, Saluzzo (0175 41 455/ cavassa@comune.saluzzo.cuneoCN.it). **Open** *Apr-Sept* 10am-1pm, 2-6pm; guided visits only 11am & 3pm Tue, Wed. *Oct-Mar* 10am-1pm, 2-5pm Thur-Sun. **Admission** €4; €2 concessions; €8 family. **No credit cards.**

Palazzo Taffini d'Acceglio

Via Sant'Andrea 53, Savigliano (0172 717 185). **Open** 10am-12.30pm, 2-6pm Sat, Sun guided tours only, leaving from tourist office. *See p202* **Tourist information**.

Monviso

Twenty kilometres (12.5 miles) west of Saluzzo, the road begins to climb almost imperceptibly at first. The local industry is slate mining; the road (SS662) passes through the town of **Barge** and by many quarries and showrooms, their courtyards heaped with great slabs of dark grey slate left outside to harden further in winter's sub-zero temperatures. Villages become smaller

Savigliano.

Paths on **Monviso** are well marked.

as the road narrows, winding ever more steeply up hair-raising bends. But as you round the curve after Paesana and suddenly find yourself face to face with Monviso in all its lofty glory, the white-knuckle driving all seems worth it. The town of **Crissolo** is about as far as you can get in the winter when snow makes the tortuous road impassible.

Here the Po is a gushing torrent of crystal-clear water, tumbling over boulders… a far cry from its muddy manifestation downstream in Turin. In summer, the Alpine walks beyond Crissolo are a joy: maps and information are available from the Crissolo and Saluzzo tourist offices (*see below*) or the bar at **Ristorante Monviso** (*see below*), and in winter skiers slalom off-piste through snow-laden woods. After some bracing activity in this sparkling air try the local specialities: rib-sticking polenta and *cervo* (venison)… but avoid the surly service in the restaurant at the top of the town and try the friendlier trattoria in the centre.

The Po bubbles to life at **Pian del Re** seven kilometres (4.5 miles) beyond Crissolo; it's walkable (following the signposted routes) even in winter, weather permitting.

Where to stay & eat

For good-value local cuisine, an extensive wine list and a fervent foodie chef (he's an expert in rare rice varieties) try **La Veja Moretta** in

Moretta (via Torino 69, 0172 94 229, closed Sun, average €25). Next door, the cosy and reasonably priced **Hotel Italia** (via Torino 71, 0172 911 184, €36 double) has been offering accommodation since 1881.

In Saluzzo try **Osteria dei Mondagli** (piazzetta dei Mondagli 1, 0175 46 306, closed Wed, average €25) for the usual *piemontesi* specialities including home-made gnocchi; there are tables outside in the summer.

Get your circulation going again with rustic goodies such as polenta and wild mushrooms at the **Ristorante Monviso** in Crissolo (piazza Umberto I 153, 0175 94 940, closed Tue, average €20, no credit cards), a pretty place with jovial staff; it's a hotel too (€50 per person full board, €35 per person B&B, minimum stay three nights, no credit cards).

Tourist information

IAT
Corso Roma 36, Savigliano (0172 710 247/ fax 0172 710 320/www.comune.savigliano.cn.it). **Open** 8.30am-12.30pm, 2.30-5.30pm Mon-Thur. The IAT runs guided tours of the town: these happen on request – just turn up at the office between 10am-12.30pm, 2.30-5.30pm Saturday and Sunday – take about one hour and include a visit to Palazzo Taffini d'Acceglio (*see p201*). €3.10 per person; under-14s free.

IAT
Piazzetta dei Mondagli 5, Saluzzo (0175 46 710 /fax 0175 46 718/iat@comune.saluzzo.cn.it). **Open** *Apr-Sept* 9am-12.30pm, 3-6.30pm Tue-Sun. *Oct-Mar* 9am-12.30pm, 2-5.30pm Tue-Sun. Also has information on the Crissolo and Pian del Re areas.

Ufficio Turistico
Via Umberto 1, Crissolo (0175 940 131). Opening times are unpredictable.

Getting there

By car
Take the Torino–Savona A6 south of Turin, exit at Marene and follow signs for Savigliano and Saluzzo (35km/22 miles). Moretta is 10km (6 miles) north of Saluzzo; Monviso is about 20km (12.5 miles) west – follow local signs.

By train
There are regular (hourly) trains to Savigliano from Turin's Porta Nuova station – change in Savigliano for Saluzzo (60mins).

By bus
ATI (0175 43 744, www.atibus.it) buses run hourly from Turin (largo Marconi, map p245 A1) to Saluzzo (1hr 30mins) via Moretta (1hr). Regular services from Saluzzo (via Circonvallazione 19) to Crissolo.

Val di Susa

Italy's mountainous border with France is steeped in history.

Sacra di San Michele. *See p204.*

There are two main reasons why people go to the Val di Susa: one is to reach the ski resorts in the upper valley (*see pp206-14*) and the other is to cross the border into France. While skiing as a sport is a mere 100 years old, people have been using the valley as an Italy–France highway for millennia.

In 218 BC Carthage's General Hannibal descended the valley heading for Rome, leading an army of 50,000 soldiers and a few dozen elephants. One can only picture the faces of the valley's original Celtic inhabitants at the sight of these gigantic pachyderms with their swaying trunks. Hannibal was eventually packed off home by the Romans, who in turn took this same path a few years later, on their way to conquer Gaul. But the Celtic king Cozio was no pushover and his army fought bravely until Augustus gave way in 13 BC and agreed to an alliance between his forces and the local Celts.

After the fall of the Roman Empire, the valley was fought over until the tenth century, when the powerful House of Savoy (*see p8* **The unstoppable Savoys**) took over the Piedmont region. In the 16th century they made Turin

their territory's capital and fortified the valley with castles and forts to defend themselves against, guess who?… the French. At the end of the 18th century another belligerent monsieur called Napoleon couldn't resist sending a few hundred thousand soldiers down the valley and on to Rome to conquer the Italian peninsula. In 1805 the man himself passed through this neighbourhood on his way to Milan to be crowned king of Italy. Nowadays, passers-through have less bellicose intentions and the inhabitants of the valley are peaceful and welcoming.

Avigliana & San Michele

Avigliana, with its medieval centre, is 25 kilometres (16 miles) due west of Turin. Cobbled streets lead up to the porticoed piazza Conte Rosso; nearby, a ruined castle looms. The Romanesque-Gothic church of **San Pietro** (open 10am-12.30pm, 3-6pm Sat, Sun, or by appointment 011 932 8300) in Borgo San Pietro still has 12th- and 13th-century frescoes. But the main attraction here are Avigliana's two

Susa. *See p205.*

complex itself. At the top of the Scalone della morte (deceased monks were immured here) is a magnificent 12th-century door carved with zodiac signs and scenes from the stories of Samson, and Cain and Abel. The main church is a lesson-in-stone on the transition from Romanesque to Gothic; 24 illustrious Savoys are buried here. Stairs lead down from the central nave to the crypt, which was probably part of the original tenth-century construction.

Sacra di San Michele
Via alla Sacra 14, Sant'Ambrogio (011 939 130/ www.sacradisanmichele.com). **Open** *Mid Mar-June, Sept-mid Oct* 9.30am-12.30pm, 3-6pm Tue-Sat; 9.30am-noon, 2.40-6pm. *July-Aug* 9.30am-12.30pm, 3-6pm daily. *Mid Oct-mid Mar* 9.30am-12.30pm, 3-5pm Tue-Sat; 9.30am-noon, 2.40-5pm Sun. **Admission** €2.50; €3.50 3-6pm Sun; €1.50 concessions. **No credit cards**.

Where to stay & eat

In Avigliana, the **Hotel Chalet del Lago La Magnolia** (via Monginevro 26, 011 936 9225, €70 double) is a small three-star only 30 metres (98 feet) from the lake, providing sunbathing and water sport facilities, a bar, restaurant and disco; while the **Hotel Hermitage** (strada Sacra San Michele 12, 011 936 9230, €75 double) is a small castle with nine rooms with terraces overlooking the Lago Grande. Eat in the baroque-style restaurant, which serves typical Piedmontese cuisine.

volcanic lakes, now part of a nature reserve. The **Lago Grande** is a favourite spot for swimming, sunbathing and boating, while the less-developed **Lago Piccolo** is popular with twitchers. The local tourist office (*see below*) has information on hikes and tours.

Beyond Avigliana, the massive silhouette of the **Sacra di San Michele**, perched on the peak of Monte Pirchiriano (962 metres/ 3,156 feet), is visible for miles around. One of Piedmont's most important historical sites, the Sacra's nucleus dates back to the tenth century (though legend has it that a chapel dedicated to the archangel Michael was built here by angels in the fifth century). A penitent knight by the name of Ugo di Montboissier began construction of the abbey in 983 for the Benedictine order, which enlarged the site several times until it was forced out in 1622. Since 1836 the Sacra has been in the hands of Rosminian Fathers. A major restoration in the 1990s set centuries of wear and tear to rights and the Sacra is now back to its former glory. It's a long, steep climb to the entrance, inside which a terrace affords spectacular views across the mountains and of the monastery

Tourist information

IAT
Piazza del Popolo 2, Avigliana (011 932 8650/ fax 011 934 1584/avigliana@montagnedoc.it). **Open** 9am-noon, 3-6pm Mon-Fri; 9am-noon Sat. Provides information on mountain biking, hiking and riding in the reserve around the lakes.

Getting there

By car
SS24/SS25 (aka E70) or A32 Torino–Fréjus motorway, exit at Avigliana.

By train
The Turin–Modane service runs hourly and stops at Avigliana.

By bus
The Turin–Rubiana service operated from Porta Susa station by SATTI (011 521 4703, www.satti.it) stops at Avigliana. Peak times every 10mins, otherwise every half-hour.
There's no public transport from Avigliana to Sacra di San Michele: the 14km (8.5 mile) taxi ride (011 932 0819/337 204 700) will cost around €20.

Susa & Exilles

Ancient Segusium, **Susa** was for centuries
the key to control of this much-invaded valley.
The **Porta Savoia** gate was part of the third-
century AD Roman defence system.
Immediately to the north of it stands the 11th-
century cathedral of **San Giusto** with its
massive Romanesque bell tower, gothic apse
and unique 14th century wooden choir stalls.
In the sacristy is *Nativity* by Defendente
Ferrante (1518).

Back outside the walls, the nearby **Parco
di Augusto** – once the site of the Roman
forum – slopes gently uphill to the **Arco di
Augusto**, erected in 9 BC to mark the pact
between the Romans and the Val di Susa
Celts. Further up the rise are the ruins of the
Terme Graziane, an aqueduct (or manybe
part of the town's defence system) constructed
in AD 375 by Emperor Gratian. On the peak
of the rise stands the medieval **Castello di
Adelaide**, which has proudly guarded over
Susa since the tenth century. Formerly a Savoy
residence, it now hosts a library, a museum
(open 2.30-5pm daily) and historical archives.

Twelve kilometres (7.5 miles) further up
the valley, tiny **Exilles** is a jewel from a
time long past, situated in a rocky valley with
an imposing fort guarding over the entrance
to the village.

It's easy to miss this old Celtic stronghold,
a fact that has kept mass tourism away and
left Exilles largely and blissfully untouched.
A fort has stood here protecting this vital
passage between Italy and France since the
12th century or earlier, but the prime example
of military architecture visible today was first
erected in the 18th century. Little wonder, then,
that Napoleon had Exilles's fort levelled to the
ground in 1796. The Piedmontese rebuilt it
stone by stone in 1815, using it as a military
base until 1946 after which it was abandoned.

In 2000, after extensive restoration, the fort
opened its doors to the public as the grandly
named **Musei delle truppe alpine e delle
fortificazioni delle alpi occidentali**.
Having inspected the defences, lose yourself
in the narrow cobbled streets that meander in
and out of the village's network of tunnels and
work your way down towards the River Dora
Riparia. For even more tranquillity, head for
the nearby **Salbertrand Natural Forest
Park** (*see p212*); or don your skis and head for
the slopes of the upper Susa valley (*see pp206-
14* **The Mountains**).

Cattedrale di San Giusto

Piazza San Giusto 12, Susa (0122 622 053).
Open 7am-6pm Mon-Sat; 7am-noon, 2.30-6pm Sun.

Museo delle Truppe Alpine e delle Fortificazioni delle Alpi Occidentali

*Forte di Exilles, via degli Alpini, Exilles (0122 58
270).* **Open** *Mid Apr-Sept* 10am-7pm Tue-Sun.
Oct-mid Apr 10am-2pm Tue-Sun. **Admission** €5;
€3.50 concessions. **No credit cards**.

Where to stay & eat

In Susa, the **Susa & Stazione Hotel** (corso
Stati Uniti 4-6, 0122 622 226, €65 double) is
handily placed opposite the railway station.
All rooms are cosy and en suite. It serves local
Piedmontese cuisine in its restaurant. The 62-
room **Hotel Napoleon** (via Mazzini 44, 0122
622 855, €75 double) is neat and comfortable,
despite the grim exterior. The elegant
Ristorante Meana (piazza IV Novembre 2,
0122 32 359, average €30) has an impressive
list of wines to go with its local specialities.
The **Cantina del Ponte** (via Mazzini 7, 0122
32 869, average €20) is a family-run trattoria
and rustic wine bar. For a taste of the wonderful
local confectionery, try **Pietrini** (piazza
Enrico de Bartolomei 10, 0122 622 303),
which has been producing traditional *dolci*
of the region since 1958.

In Exilles, **Il Sole e la Luna** (via degli
Alpini 1, 0122 58 244, www.casadiexilles.it,
€10 per person, €13 B&B, €25 full board)
has friendly hostel-style accommodation; its
restaurant (€10 fixed price) serves mountain
specialities. **Da Laura al Cels** (Rif 3, Cels,
Exilles, 0122 58 260/348 056 5791, €44 double)
situated one kilometre before Exilles, is a
comfortable family-run B&B with en suite
double rooms.

Tourist information

Associazione Pro Susa

*Corso Inghilterra 39, Susa (0122 622 470/333 416
2136).* **Open** *May-Sept* 3-6pm Mon; 9am-12.30pm,
3-6pm Tue-Sat; 9am-12.30pm Sun. *Oct-Apr* 9am-
1pm Mon-Sat.

Getting there

By car

SS24/SS25 (aka E70) or A32 Turin–Fréjus motorway;
exit at Susa Est and continue on SS24 for Exilles.

By train

The hourly Turin–Modane service stops at Susa; for
Exilles take the local SAPAV bus (*see below*) from
Susa station.

By bus

SAPAV (0122 622 015) runs 1 bus daily (8.25am)
from Turin's corso Inghilterra to Susa and Exilles,
and a local service (6 daily) between Susa and Exilles.

Trips Out of Town

The Mountains

Whether you're visiting in summer or winter, the lure of the Alps is hard to resist.

There's skiing for all levels in **Bardonecchia**. *See p207.*

Imposing as they are, the mountains that separate Italy and France to the west of Turin have proved no barrier to invaders over the ages – from Hannibal and his elephants in 218 BC, to the Romans in 58 BC, Saracen pirates through the Middle Ages and the empire-building Spanish and French later.

Perhaps it's this history of repeated conquest that makes locals initially diffident toward outsiders. Once a rapport has been established, however, Alpine hospitality shines through. Like their inhabitants, these valleys are full of contrasts. In isolated spots such as **Cesana Torinese** (*see p210*), nothing much has changed in the past 100 years (give or take a plasma-screen TV and a mobile phone or two). **Sestrière** (*see p213*), on the other hand, is resolutely 21st century. Towering above it all are the ageless Alps, their natural splendour untarnished by the passing of time.

The upper Susa and Chisone valleys are best visited in summer or winter, not because there's anything wrong with spring and autumn here – indeed, they're wonderful – but you're likely to find many hotels, restaurants and shops closed.

The winter season starts, unofficially, on 8 December, the Feast of the Immaculate

Conception, and draws to a close at the end of the Easter break. The season peaks over the Christmas holidays – a good time to avoid the slopes here if you don't like crowds. Road conditions can be treacherous in winter; you'll need chains if you're planning to cross the mountain passes to Clavière and Sestrière.

The summer season runs from early June to mid September. The period around Ferragosto – 15 August – is the busiest time.

Apart from the accommodation options mentioned in this chapter, another excellent resource for places to stay is the Club Alpino Italiano (www.cai.it/www.cai.rifugi.it; *see also p162*), which has hundreds of mountain refuges (*rifugi*) all over the country. These range from simple mountain huts to plush hotels, and many are open year-round. To identify *rifugi* located in the Turin province on the CAI website, look for a 'TO' next to the name of the refuge.

The upper Val di Susa

You know you've reached the upper Susa valley (for the lower valley, *see p212*) when the road really begins to wind. The SS24 climbs past **Exilles** (*see p205*) and then descends to

Salbertrand and Oulx where the valley splits: to the north-west there's Bardonecchia and the Fréjus tunnel to France; to the south-west, a narrow valley leads to **Cesana Torinese** (*see p210*) and then forks again, westward to Clavière and the Monginèvre pass to France, and eastward to Sestrière and the Val Chisone.

Tiny medieval **Salbertrand** is not only the gateway to the Gran Bosco nature reserve (*see p212* **When the snow melts...**) but also home to a recognised linguistic minority that is part of the undeclared nation of Occitania (*see p211* **Living history**). The upper Susa valley marks the north-eastern reaches of this territory.

Keep your wits about you if you're driving along the SS335 to **Bardonecchia**: deer, chamois and fox tend to amble across the road.

Located on the banks of the Dora river, the Bardonecchia area was already inhabited when Caesar's soldiers passed through in 58 BC. Attacks by Barbarians and Saracens took their toll; in the tenth century the area passed into the hands of the De Bardonnèche family, whence the town's name. Turin's Savoy rulers took control in 1713.

The tree-lined streets near the pistes are filled with small hotels, while more modern resort hotels have been built right at the foot of the runs. Beyond the main skiing area at Campo Smith, the tiny hamlet of **Melezet** has a ski station and a handful of houses, one of which contains the **Museo d'arte sacra** in the Cappella Madonna del Carmine with a wealth of sacred art and frescoes from local churches.

Bardonecchia's main drag, via Medail, has scores of stores including workshops where intricate wood carvings are made and displayed. Via Medail climbs up into the old town, a maze of narrow medieval streets; note the names, written both in Italian and Occitan.

In piazza Sant'Ippolito in the old town centre is the 19th-century church of **Sant'Ippolito** (open 8.30am-6pm daily). The fountain in the square dates back to 1651. In nearby via des Geneys, the **Museo etnografico** contains old farm implements from the valleys around. A good way to take a tour of the old town is to follow the *Sentiero* (path) *del borgo* created by Bardonecchia's schoolchildren, which meanders around the winding streets and past piazzas and historic chapels.

Between the ski pistes and the old town is the recently revamped 18th-century **Palazzo delle feste**, which has a brightly frescoed courtyard; it's open to the public only when hosting events such as the **Festa nazionale del vino della montagna** (information: www.comune.bardonecchia.to.it), which takes place in mid March.

Museo d'Arte Sacra

Cappella Madonna del Carmine, frazione Melezet (0122 622 640/www.centroculturalediocesano.it). **Open** by appointment only. **Admission** €3; €2 concessions; under-12s free. **No credit cards**.

Museo Etnografico

Via des Geneys 6, Bardonecchia (0122 902 612). **Open** *July-Aug* 5-7.30pm Tue, Wed, Fri-Sun. *Sept-June* by appointment only. **Admission** donations accepted.

Where to stay & eat

After you've explored the Gran Bosco nature reserve (*see p212* **When the snow melts...**), stop for lunch at the **Antica Locanda Due Bandiere** (piazza Martiri Libertà 2, Salbertrand, 0122 854 640, closed Sat lunch, Mon and Sept, average €20), which provides delicious meals in an intimate mountain setting.

In Bardonecchia, the **Albergo La Genzianella** (via des Geneys 12, 0122 999 897, closed May, Oct & Nov, €83 double) is an intimate little hotel in the old town. If you want to be close to the slopes, try **La Quiete** (viale San Francesco 26, 0122 999 859, €75 double) in a tranquil spot among the trees. **La Betulla** (viale della Vittoria 4, 0122 999 846, €75 double) is centrally located. For good local food produced with organic farm products try **Bardosteria** (via Medail 33, 0122 99 862, average €15). **Biovey** (via Generale Cantore 2, 0122 999 215, closed Tue, average €35) provides a lighter version of traditional cuisine. A favourite with the locals, **Etable** (via Medail 82, 0122 96 973, closed Mon-Thur, average €27) is an intimate restaurant in a rustic setting. Also high on their list is **Ristorante La Ciaburna** (frazione Melezet 48, 0122 999 849, closed Wed, May & Oct, average €30) in the hamlet of Melezet south-west of Bardonecchia. **L' Crot de Ciulin** (via des Geneys 20, 0122 96 161, closed Thur) is a great wine bar in the old town.

Getting there & around

By car

Take the A32 and exit at Bardonecchia. Alternatively, follow the SS24 past Salbertrand, then take the SS335.

By train

About 6 direct trains depart from Porta Nuova station to Bardonecchia daily. Alternatively, change at Bussoleno for local train services to Bardonecchia.

By bus

Sapav (800 801 901/www.sapav.it) runs infrequent services between Oulx and Bardonecchia. There are no buses from Turin to Bardonecchia. A local service in Bardonecchia does a circular route downtown, as well as runs to the ski slopes.

Trips Out of Town

Ski report

The upper Susa and Chisone valleys are part of the Via Lattea (Milky Way) system: 400 kilometres (250 miles) of ski runs that zigzag between Italy and France. A *Via Lattea Internazionale* day pass costs €35 (€48 2 days low season, €54 2 days high season; €116 5 days low season, €130 5 days high season; €158 1wk low season, €177 1wk high season. High season includes the Christmas holidays and from the end of January to mid March).

Ski-hire prices given below are per day. Skiing lesson prices are per hour.

BARDONECCHIA
(*See p207*)
Not linked to the Via Lattea, Bardonecchia still offers a wealth of downhill skiing and snowboarding. From the majestic Mount Jafferau, which takes you 2,750 metres (9,000 feet) up and allows you to descend on blue and red runs, to the extensive choice offered by the Colomion and Melezet slopes, the area caters to all levels and is particularly popular with families.

Vital statistics
110km (68 miles) of pistes; 3 black runs, 12 red runs, 16 blue runs; 9 chair lifts, 14 drag lifts; snowmobiles, 10km (6 miles) of cross-country tracks, skating rink, snow-shoeing, ice climbing.

Ski hire
De Marchi Outdoor
Campo Smith (0122 96 075). **Rates** €14; €11 children. **Credit** MC, V.

Ski school
Scuola di Sci Bardonecchia
Campo Smith (0122 999 253/ www.scuolascibardonecchia.it). **Rates** €30. **Credit** MC, V.

SAUZE D'OULX
(*See p210*)
Skiing in Sauze d'Oulx is an experience, both for the view of the mountains and the extravagant dress (and outrageous behaviour) of the skiers. This young crowd will carry on on the slopes during the day, then continue partying into the night in the resort's dozens of bars and pubs. This is a particularly popular destination with British holiday-makers. Part of the Via Lattea, it also offers heli-skiing.

Vital statistics
Access to 400km (250 miles) of pistes; 42 black runs, 117 red runs, 52 blue runs; 3 cable cars, 39 chair lifts, 49 drag lifts; snow park, excursions on snowmobiles, 13km (8 miles) of cross-country tracks, skating rink, snow-shoeing.

Ski hire
Besson Sport
Via Clotes 10 (0122 850 786). **Rates** €20; €10 children. **Credit** MC, V.

Ski school
Scuola di sci Sauze d'Oulx
Via Monfol 1 (0122 858 084). **Rates** €30. **Credit** MC, V.

CESANA-SAN SICARIO
(*See p210*)
San Sicario is a small resort area at 1,700 metres (2,735 feet). Popular with families. It's part of the Via Lattea and is directly linked to Sauze d'Oulx and Sestrière. Skiers staying at Cesana Torinese have access to San Sicario's runs as well as the slopes of Monti della Luna, which lead to Clavière and France.

Vital statistics
Access to 400km (250 miles) of pistes; 42 black runs, 117 red runs, 52 blue runs; 3 cable cars, 39 chair lifts, 49 drag lifts; snow park, excursions on snowmobiles, and with sled dogs, snow-shoeing and heli-skiing at San Sicario.

Ski hire
Besson Sport
Centro Commerciale San Sicario (0122 811 546). **Rates** €15; €13 children. **Credit** MC, V.

Ski school
Scuola di Sci San Sicario Cesana
Centro Commerciale San Sicario (0122 811 201). **Rates** €32. **Credit** MC, V.

CLAVIERE
(*See p210*)
Close to the French border, Clavière is a tiny community at the base of the Monti della Luna. It is the Via Lattea's jump-off point to France.

Vital statistics
Access to 400km (250 miles) of pistes; 42 black runs, 117 red runs, 52 blue runs;

3 cable cars, 39 chair lifts, 49 drag lifts; 16km of cross-country tracks, skating rink, snow-shoeing.

Ski hire

Noleggio Seas
Strada Gimont (0122 878 818). **Rates** €13; €10 children. **No credit cards**.
Sci Fondo Clavière
(cross-country)
Via Nazionale 43bis (tel/ fax 0122 878 646).
Rates €10; €7 children. **Credit** MC, V.

Ski schools

Scuola Italiana Sci Clavière
(downhill)
Strada Valle Gimont 4 (0122 878 818). **Rates** €32. **Credit** MC, V.
Sci Fondo Clavière
(cross-country)
Via Nazionale 43bis (tel/fax 0122 878 646). **Rates** €32. **Credit** MC, V.

SESTRIERE

(*See p213*)
On the Via Lattea, Sestrière offers access to the area's most challenging slopes, with the largest number of black runs, some above 2,800 metres (9,200 feet). It's the most expensive destination and its clientele reflects this.

Vital statistics

Access to 400km (250 miles) of pistes; 42 black runs, 117 red runs, 52 blue runs; 3 cable cars, 39 chair lifts, 49 drag lifts; snow park, excursions on snowmobiles, night skiing, 10km of cross-country tracks, outdoor ice rink, snow-shoeing, ice climbing, heli-skiing and two-seater paragliding.

Ski hire

Marcellin Sport
Via Lauset 8 (0122 77 597). **Rates** €15; €10 children. **Credit** MC, V.

Ski school

Scuola di Sci Sestrière
Piazza Kandahar 3A (0122 77 060). **Rates** €32. **Credit** AmEx, MC, V.

PRAGELATO

(*See p213*)
Pragelato is a cross-country skier's heaven, with the longest series of trails in the area. It also promotes snow-shoeing. With Occitan and Weldesian (*see p211* **Living history**) touches, Pragelato has a particular cultural feel. The community will be linked to the Via Lattea by 2006.

Vital statistics

50km (30 miles) of pistes; 1 black run, 12 red runs, 5 blue runs; 2 chair lifts, 4 drag lifts; 40km (25 miles) of cross-country tracks, outdoor ice rink, snow-shoeing, ice climbing, driving on ice.

Ski hire

Noleggio Sci Roman Bruno
Piazzale della Seggiovia Clot de la Soma (0122 78 864). **Rates** €10 downhill; €7.50 children downhill; €8.50 cross-country; €7 children cross-country.
No credit cards.

Ski school

Scuola Sci Pragelato
Via Wembach Hahn (0122 78 960). **Rates** €30. **No credit cards**.

Trips Out of Town

Cesana Torinese: popular with families.

Tourist information

IAT

*Viale della Vittoria 4, Bardonecchia (0122 99 032/
www.comune.bardonecchia.to.it).* **Open** *July, Aug,
Dec-Mar* 9am-12.30pm, 2.30-7pm daily. *Apr-June,
Sept-Nov* 9am-noon, 3-6pm daily.

From Oulx to Clavière

At the confluence of the Dora di Bardonecchia
and the Dora Riparia river valleys on the SS24
is the small town of Oulx. From Oulx, a road
leads up a stomach-churning series of hairpin
bends to **Sauze d'Oulx**, aptly known as the
balcone degli Alpi. The old centre is a maze of
17th-century stone houses. Sauze is known for
its fountains; dotted around the old town you'll
find simple concrete ones as well as elaborate
ones with carved wooden columns.

In piazza Europa, the church of **San
Giovanni Battista** (open 5.30-6.30pm Mon-
Sat; 8-11am, 5.30-6.30pm Sun) is a Romanesque-
Gothic structure built between the 14th and
15th centuries; note the elaborately carved and
gilded altar. Outside the church is one of the
town's hallmark fountains and a terrace from
where the view over the valley is spectacular.

That's about it for sights in Sauze d'Oulx.
The *centro storico* is a pedestrian zone; if you
need to drive in to get to your hotel, buzz the
establishment at the intercom by the bar that
blocks vehicle access.

The SS24 continues winding along by the
Dora Riparia river. The nine kilometres (five
miles) to Cesana Torinese are glorious: keep

your eyes turned to the right for the best of the
scenery. The valley narrows and then, past the
turn-off for Mollières, widens up again to reveal
mountain hamlets perched on the crests of hills
or along the walls of side valleys. Peering down
from the peak of Monte Chaberton is the 19th-
century **Forte Chaberton** (*see below*).

Cesana Torinese is a series of 14 hamlets,
only seven of which are inhabited year-round.
Cesana proper is the heart of the community. Life
was hard in this isolated place – inaccessible for
months and with a very short growing season.
It continues to be a challenge for the 900-odd
people who live here, heating their homes with
wood-burning stoves and making a living
producing liqueurs and cheeses.

Most of Cesana's shops and restaurants are
located along the pedestrianised main drag, via
Roma. Check out **Ferragut** (No.16) which has
Alpine specialities such as Cesana's herbal
liqueur, local honey and deer sausages.

Five kilometres and 350 metres (three miles
and 1,150 feet) above Cesana on Monte Fraitève,
the hamlet of San Sicario fills with skiers
during the winter season.

In the six short kilometres (four miles) from
Cesana Torinese to Clavière the road climbs
more than 400 sinuous metres (1,200 feet),
making it a challenging drive, particularly
in the winter months.

A tiny place with fewer than 200 inhabitants,
Clavière is the last Italian stop before the
Monginèvre pass into France, where Hannibal
and his elephants may have crossed. In the 14th
century the poet Francesco Petrarca extolled
Clavière's beauty. The town was French until
1713 when it passed to Piedmont.

Clavière was one of the first Alpine towns
to develop as a ski resort, and maybe it's this
head start that makes it somehow less brash
than more recent additions to the tourist trail.
It's part of the 400-square-kilometre (150-
square-mile) Via Lattea ski area (*see p208*
Ski report), and has dozens of cross-country
ski runs too. In summer you can hike from here
to **Forte Chaberton**, at 3,124 metres (10,250
feet) the highest fort in the Italian Alps.
Construction began in 1898 and was completed
in 1906. The tourist information office will
provide information on the routes.

Where to stay & eat

Finding accommodation can be a challenge
in these parts in the skiing season, when tour
operators block-book rooms.

In **Sauze d'Oulx**, the most pleasant choice
for independent travellers is the refurbished
18th-century **Chalet Faure** (via Chaberton 4,
0122 859 760, www.faure.it, closed May-mid

June, mid Sept-Nov, €120-€150 double); below the hotel is a 'wellbeing centre' and tearoom. **Hotel Monte Genevris** (via Assietta 12, 0122 858 086, www.hotelmontegenevris.it, closed Apr-June, Sept-Nov, €70-€85 double), in the old part of Sauze d'Oulx, offers cosy, rustic rooms and two meals daily for hotel guests (€50 for two meals). For a bit of an adventure, choose the **Capricorno** (Case Sparse 21, Località le Clotes, 0122 850 273, www.chaletilcapricorno.it, closed Apr-mid June, Sept-Dec, €135-€150 double): an isolated chalet, it's only accessible on skis or by snowmobile in the winter. The rustic but elegant restaurant (€45 average) is renowned. For a delicious Piedmontese meal in a beautiful mountain setting visit **Il Cantun del Barbabuc** (via Luigi Faure 3, 0122 858 593, open evenings only) where the four-course set menu (€30) allows you to taste a bit of everything. Prince Albert of Monaco chose **Ristorante del Falco** (via Assietta 6, 0122 858 063, closed May & Oct, average €30) when he visited Sauze d'Oulx; make sure you book. For pizza try the **Ristorante del Borgo** (via Assietta 30, 0122 850 329, closed May and Mon-Fri Oct & Nov, average €20).

In **Cesana**, the **Hotel Chaberton** (via Roma 10, 0122 89 147, €60-€80 double) is the nicest of the few that aren't block-booked. The **Edelweiss** (piazza des Escartons 6, 0122 89 450, closed May-mid June, mid Oct-Nov, €110 per person half-board) is elegant with cosy rooms but its meals are hit and miss. For a delicious pizza in a casual mountain setting try **Al Brusacheur** (via Roma 57, 0122 89 254, closed Wed, average €15). **La Sirena** (via Roma 39, 347 682 3541, closed Thur, average €20) provides simple mountain fare in a refurbished stable. There's a fantastic spread of snacks at the cosy wine bar **La Nata** (via Roma 48, 0122 89 433, closed lunch daily & all Thur).

In the lower hamlet of San Sicario is the **Circolo Olimpiadi del Gusto** (San Sicario Borgo, 0122 832 475, closed May & Oct-Nov, average €30) is a club for connoisseurs of Piedmontese cuisine. You have to become a member – at no cost – to eat the delicious multi-course meals: come with an empty stomach.

In **Clavière**, the **Piccolo Chalet** (via Torino 7, 0122 878 806, closed mid Apr-Dec, €55 per person half-board) has spartan rooms, but the food (for hotel guests only) is delicious and the

Living history

Stretching from the Spanish border, through southern France to the Alpine reaches of north-western Italy, Occitania is (and always has been) an ideal rather than a political entity, united by a language – known as Provençal, Languedoc or Occitan – that differs but little across that swathe of the Continent. It has remained largely unchanged since the Middle Ages and is still widely spoken in some areas today.

From the *occitani* came the troubadours, the lyrical poets of the Middle Ages: while most of continental Europe was bent on penitence and austerity, the people of Occitania were singing the praises of *jovent* (youth), *jòi* (joy) including erotic joy, *paratge* (equality) and *mercés* (tolerance). This *joie de vivre* resulted only in persecution; by the end of the 13th century, the vitality of the *occitani* was snuffed out by the Inquisition.

Later, in the 16th century, when the Protestant Waldenses were persecuted by the Catholic Church and forced to leave their homes (mainly in France) or face massacre, the spirit of medieval Occitania reawoke. Hundreds of Waldensian refugees fled to Occitan safe-havens, including the upper Susa and Chisone valleys, where they were welcomed by the tolerant locals and formed a community that remains strong to this day.

The 19th century saw a rebirth in Occitan culture; its literature flourished thanks to writers such as Fédéric Mistral and 1904 Nobel literature laureate Theòdor Aubanel.

The blood-red and gold cross that symbolises *d'Òc* territory is still seen in these valleys, and the language is widely spoken. In **Cesana Torinese** (*see p210*) and beyond to the Chisone valley they speak Provençal Occitan; in **Bardonecchia** (*see p207*) and **Salbertrand** (*see p206*) the Alpine variety.

Salbertrand, in particular, works hard to preserve its Occitan culture. The language is taught in primary schools and celebrated in special events through the year. In the town hall, most signs are in both Italian and Occitan. When the municipality makes requests to the Piedmont regional council, it does so in the centuries-old tongue.

(Occitan–*Italian*–**English**)
bunjù *buon giorno* **good day**
salù' *salute* **hello**
aruar *arrivederci* **goodbye**
bun'aptì *buon appetito* **bon appétit**
l'ità *estate* **summer**
sàndë *sabato* **Saturday**

When the snow melts...

The upper Susa and Chisone valleys are popular destinations in the summer months.

White water rafting

From **Fenils** near Cesana Torinese (*see p210*) you can do a 6km (4-mile) white water run to Oulx. The excursion doesn't require prior experience but you should be a strong swimmer and very fit.The trip takes an average of three hours. Book in advance.

OK Adventure Company
Frazione Fenils, Cesana Torinese (335 628 2728/www.okadventure.it). **Departure times** *May-July* 9.30am, 12.30pm, 3.30pm daily. **Rates** €50. **No credit cards**.

Biking

From Sauze d'Oulx (*see p210*) rent a bike (*see below*) and follow the **via Saracena** (Saracens' way), the route purportedly taken by the Saracens as they plundered the lower Susa valley. It's 38.5km (24 miles) through the Gran Bosco nature reserve (*see above*). Or try the **Giro Assietta** (Assietta tour) from Sauze d'Oulx to the Colle delle Finestre (2,176m/7,195ft) mountain pass.

Besson Sport
Via Clotes 10, Sauze d'Oulx (0122 850 786). **Open** *July-Aug* 8.30am-12.30pm, 3-7.30pm daily. **Bike hire** Prices vary from season to season. **Credit** MC, V.

Hiking

The three nature reserves in the Val di Susa and Val Chisone each have many kilometres of well-marked tracks.

Parco Naturale Gran Bosco di Salbertrand

Information: *Via Monginevro 7, Salbertrand (0122 854 720)*. **Open** *Mid Sept-mid June* 9am-noon, 1.30-3.30pm Mon-Fri. *Mid June-mid Sept* 8am-12.30pm, 1-3.30pm Mon-Sat.

Parco Naturale Orsiera Rocciavrè

Information: *Sede di Fenestrelle, località Pra Catinat, Fenestrelle (0121 83 757)*.

Parco Naturale Val Troncea

Information: *via della Pineta, frazione La Ruà, Pragelato (0122 78 849)*. **Open** *Jan-July, Sept-Nov* 8am-12.30pm, 2-4.30pm Mon-Fri. *Aug, Dec* 8am-12.30pm, 2-4.30pm daily.

---

hotel is right at the foot of the ski slopes; make sure you're on time for meals as the cook doesn't hang about. The **Hotel Pian del Sole** (via Nazionale 28, 0122 878 085, closed May, €50-€70 per person half-board) in the town centre is also reliable. The excellent 'I **Gran Bouc** (via Nazionale 24A, 0122 878 830, closed May & mid Sept-mid Dec, average €35) serves typical local dishes. The **Gallo Cedrone Ristorante** (via della Fontana 8, 0122 878 817, closed Sun dinner, average €17 lunch, €30 dinner) does a self-service lunch and an elegant dinner. For good pizza try the **Pizzeria Ristorante Kilt** (via della Fontana 1, 0122 878 051, closed Mon, mid Apr-July & mid Sept-Dec, average €15).

Tourist information

For information on the whole area, and to see how it's gearing up for the 2006 Winter Olympic Games check the website www.montagnedoc.it.

IAT

Piazza Assietta 18, Sauze d'Oulx (0122 858 009/www.comune.sauzedoulx.to.it). **Open** *Dec-Mar, July-Aug* 9am-12.30pm, 3-6.30pm daily. *Apr-June, Sept-Nov* 9am-noon, 3-6pm daily.

IAT

Piazza V Amedeo 3, Cesana Torinese (0122 89 202/www.comune.cesana.to.it). **Open** 9am-12.30pm, 3-6pm Mon-Fri; 9am-12.30pm, 3-6.30pm Sat, Sun.

IAT

Via Nazionale 30, Clavière (0122 878 856/www.claviere.it). **Open** 9am-noon, 3-6.30pm Mon-Fri; 9am-12.30pm, 3-6.30pm Sat, Sun.

Getting there & around

By car

From the A32 exit at Oulx Est and take the SS24 along the Dora Riparia valley. Alternatively, take the SS25 (becomes the SS24) all the way from Turin.

By train

There are about half a dozen direct trains from Turin's Porta Nuova station to Oulx daily. Alternatively, change at Bussoleno for a local train to Oulx.

By bus

One **Sapav** (800 801 901/www.sapav.it.) bus runs daily from Turin to Cesana and Clavière. Five buses run daily from Turin to Cesana and Clavière while 10 buses run daily from Turin to Oulx and Sauze d'Oulx. There are also French minibuses that depart from the Oulx train station to Cesana and Clavière.

The Val Chisone

Parallel to, and south of, the Val di Susa, the Val Chisone has been shaped to a large extent by its original Occitan inhabitants and by the Waldensian Protestants (*see p211* **Living history**) who fled persecution in France in the 16th century and took refuge here. The valley is also rich in natural beauty.

The Sestrière mountain pass divides the Susa and Chisone valleys. The SS23 road from Cesana Torinese (*see p210*) is steep and winding; you'll need chains for your tyres in winter.

If you're looking for something quaint and intimate, keep your foot on the accelerator and give Sestrière a miss. Once a bucolic sheep-rearing area, **Sestrière** the resort was the brainchild of Giovanni Agnelli, founder of Fiat (*see p21* **Whither Fiat?**). The first hotel went up in 1930 and development hasn't stopped since. Home to the area's only Club Med, Sestrière is the epitome of a chi-chi ski resort, with its white tower blocks and slew of apartments. But Sestrière does provide the most challenging pistes of the Via Lattea ski area (*see p208* **Ski report**) to a very sophisticated clientele. The resort boasts Europe's highest golf course at over 2,000 metres (6,500 feet) – only open, naturally, when the snow melts.

Ten kilometres (six miles) north-east of Sestrière, **Pragelato** is made up of a series of hamlets along the base of the valley. It's famous for its cross-country skiing and its promotion of snow-shoeing, and it's also a good place to stock up on Ramie di Pomaretto wine and Genepì liqueurs made from a mountain herb.

In the heart of Pragelato, the quaint **Museo del costume e delle tradizioni delle genti alpine** provides a glimpse into daily life in the Alps, with authentic objects in re-creations of a stable, a kitchen, a bedroom and a 'bread room'.

A symbol of Val Chisone is its *meridiane* (sundials). There are around 140 of them in this valley, the oldest dating back to the 17th century. To learn about their history and how they work stop off in Pragelato's **L'ombra del tempo centro di documentazione sulla meridiana**. In Balboutet, off the SS23 just west of Fenestrelle and its fort, there are a record 20 *meridiane* on village houses

As the largest fortification in Europe and the most extensive wall construction after the Great Wall of China, **Forte di Fenestrelle** is an imposing example of human ingenuity.The fort was built by Savoy Duke Vittorio Amedeo II; construction began in 1708. There are three fortifications: San Carlo (the lower fort), the Tre Denti and delle Valli (the upper forts), joined by a staircase with some 4,000 steps. The structure is about five kilometres (three miles) long and

climbs 700 metres (2,300 feet) up the mountain. Inside, a gallery of military uniforms has reconstructions of battle scenes from the Italian Risorgimento (*see p10* **The four horsemen of the Risorgimento**) to World War II.

Forte di Fenestrelle

Fenestrelle (0121 83 600/ www.fortedifenestrelle.com). **Open** *July-Aug* 9.30am-12.30pm, 2.30-6pm daily. *Oct-May, Sept-June* 9.30am-12.30pm, 2.30-6pm Mon, Thur-Sun. **Admission** *Fort* €2. *Galleria dell'uniforme del regio esercito italiano* €5. **No credit cards**.
The fort offers the following guided tours:
1hr departs 10am, 3pm (2.30pm Nov-Mar); €3.50.
3hrs departs 10am, 3pm (2.30pm Nov-Mar); €6, €5 concessions, free under-7s.
1 day departs Apr-Nov 9am; €10, €8 concessions, free under-7s.
Evening departs 9pm; €5.

Museo del Costume e delle Tradizioni delle Genti Alpine

Via San Giovanni, Borgata Rivet, Pragelato (0122 78 800). **Open** *Sept-July* 3-6pm Sat; 10am-12.30pm, 3-6pm Sun; weekdays by appointment. *1-24 Aug* 10am-12.30pm, 3-6pm daily. *25-31 Aug* 3-6pm daily. **Admission** €2.50; free under-8s. **No credit cards**.

L'Ombra del Tempo – Centro di Documentazione sulla Meridiana

Viale Cavalieri di Vittorio Veneto, frazione Ruà, Pragelato (0122 78 800). **Open** 3-6pm Sat, Sun; weekdays by appointment only. Closed mid Sept-Oct. **Admission** €2.50; free under-8s. **No credit cards**.

Where to stay & eat

In **Sestrière**, the **Hotel Savoy Edelweiss** (via Fraitève 7, 0122 77 040,www.hotelsavoy sestriere.com, €75-€200 double) is conveniently located in the town centre. The cosy rooms are in Alpine style. The **Hotel Biancaneve** (via Cesana 12, 0122 755 176, closed Apr-June & Sept-Nov, €60-€68 per person half-board) on the SS23 just before the town centre is also reliable. The family-run **Hotel Sud-Ovest** (via Monterotta 17, 0122 755 222, www.hotelsud-ovest.it, closed May-June & Sept-Oct, €60-€160 double) serves typical Piedmontese meals in its restaurant (average €25) and has a fitness centre.

For a delicious meal in **Sestrière**, try **La Gargote** (via Sauze di Cesana 1bis, 0122 76 888, average €30). **Ristorante Last Tango** (via della Gleisa 5A, 0122 76 337, average €30) specialises in local dishes. The view from the **Ristorante Colombiere** (via Monterotta 23, 0122 76 323, closed Tue dinner & Wed lunch, average €30) is quite something.

There are few beds available in **Pragelato**. For Alpine simplicity try the **Albergo Passet** (via Nazionale 5, frazione Grange, 0122 78 948,

€94 per person half-board), which has been doing business since 1932, or **Il Fouia** (frazione la Ruà, 0122 78 884, closed Apr & Nov, €47 double) which also has a restaurant (closed Wed, average €20) offering delicious local and Occitan dishes for groups by appointment. In a refurbished stable, **'l Teit** (via Roma 25, frazione La Ruà, 0122 78 448, closed Mon, May & Oct, average €17) is a restaurant in the evening and a disco-pub later at night.

If you really want to pamper yourself, continue on the SS23 toward **Fenestrelle** and stay at the lakeside **Lago Laux** (via al Lago 7, frazione Laux, 0121 83 944, closed 2wks Apr & 2wks Sept, €124 double). The stone structure houses a restaurant (average €40) and cosy bedrooms. Also en route to Fenestrelle, in **Usseaux**, **La Placette** (via della Chiesa 5, 0121 83 073, closed Thur, average €20) is a great place for lunch.

Tourist information

IAT
Via Louset, Sestrière (0122 755 444/ www.sestriere.it). **Open** *Dec-Mar, July, Aug* 9am-12.30pm, 2.30-7pm daily. *Apr-June, Sept-Nov* 9am-12.30pm, 3-6pm daily.

IAT
Piazza Lantelme, Pragelato (0122 741 728/ www.comune.pragelato.it). **Open** 9am-noon, 3-6pm daily.

Getting there & around

By car
Take the A32 motorway, exit at Oulx Est and continue along the SS24. Alternatively, take the SS25 (becomes SS24) all the way to Cesana Torinese, then the SS23 for Sestrière and the Val Chisone. To reach the valley from the east, take the SS23 direct from Turin.

By train
The nearest station to the Val Chisone is Oulx... and it's not very near. There are, however, buses onwards from Oulx (*see below*).

By bus
Four **Sapav** (800 801 901/www.sapav.it) buses depart daily from Turin (corso Vittorio Emanuele II 125) to Sestrière and Pragelato. There are also local services from Oulx which make stops all along the Val Chisone.

Olympic challenge

For 17 days, from 10 to 26 February 2006, tens of thousands of athletes, judges and journalists – not to mention an estimated million spectators – will be descending on Turin and the Susa and Chisone valleys to be part of the 20th edition of the Winter Olympic Games, and the Paralympic Games (10-19 March).

Seven communities in the two valleys, along with the host city Turin, are preparing the venues for competitions, training and accommodation. The opening and closing ceremonies will be held in Turin at the **Stadio Comunale** (*see p162*).

In December 1999 the Turin Organising Committee XX Olympic Winter Games (TOROC) was set up to get things ready for the 2006 event; despite having been hampered by political in-fighting, its success in preparing for 2006 has been remarkable. Its website (www.torino2006. org) provides up-to-the-minute information on the Games.

Another organisation, Montagnedoc, was created to promote the Olympic area. Its website (www.montagnedoc.it) provides an overview of the towns involved.

Below are listed the events that each community will be hosting:

COMPETITION HOSTS

Val di Susa
Bardonecchia (*see p207*)
Snowboarding, Olympic Village.
Clavière (*see p210*)
Training facilities for downhill and cross-country skiing.
Sauze d'Oulx (*see p210*)
Freestyle skiing.
Cesana Torinese & San Sicario (*see p210*)
Biathlon, women's downhill skiing, bobsleigh, luge and skeleton.

Val Chisone
Pinerolo (*map p240*)
Curling.
Pragelato (*see p213*)
Cross-country skiing, ski jumping and nordic combined.
Sestrière (*see p213*)
Downhill skiing, Olympic Village.

Turin
(*See p86* **Olympic venues**)
Ice hockey, figure skating, speed skating, short-track competitions, Olympic Village, five media Villages, and the media centre.
Torre Pellice (*map p240*)
Ice hockey training facilities.

Directory

Directory

Getting Around

Arriving & leaving

By air

Aeroporto Internazionale Sandro Pertini, Caselle

Strada San Maurizio 12, Caselle Torinese (011 567 6361/fax 011 567 6420/www.turin-airport.com). **Open** 6am-midnight daily.
Turin Airport is located 16km (ten miles) north of the city centre.

From the airport

The **express rail service** (information toll-free 800 990 097/011 691 0000/www.gtt.to.it) between the airport and Dora station (*map p242 A2*) takes 19 minutes and runs every 30 minutes from 5.13am until 7.43pm (6.49am-9.19pm to the airport). Some carriages have access for wheelchair users (*see also p222*). A €3 ticket is valid for 70 minutes and allows you to use buses and trams in the city too. Tickets can be bought with cash or major credit cards from automatic machines in the airport lobby and rail stations. You must stamp your ticket in the machines on the station platform before boarding. When this guide went to press, the train service terminated at Dora station; the line was being extended to the more central Porta Susa station.

Bus is the best way to reach central Turin. **Sadem** (011 300 0611/fax 011 309 8995/ www.sadem.it) runs blue buses from outside the airport's arrivals lounge to Porta Nuova railway station (*map p242 D3*) approximately every 30 minutes, from around 5am to midnight daily. Tickets cost €5 from automatic machines, newsstands, the ticket office in the airport and bars around the bus terminus at Porta Nuova station. There's a 50¢ surcharge if you buy your ticket on board. The service takes approximately 40 minutes and stops at Caselle, Borgaro and Turin Porta Nuova.

Rates on all the above services are discounted for holders of the Torino Card, available at Turismo Torino's Info Point at the airport.

A **taxi** (*see also p218*) from the airport to central Turin should cost between €26 and €42 and take 30 minutes. The taxi rank is located at

the arrivals level by the exit. **CTA** (011 996 3090) offers a 24-hour private taxi/limousine service.

Car rental company offices are located at the arrivals level in front of the terminal exit, inside the multistorey car park. (*See also p220.*)

Milano Malpensa International Airport

Malpensa Aeroporto, Varese (information 02 7485 2200/ T1 lost luggage 02 5858 0070/ T2 lost luggage 02 7485 4215/www.sea-aeroportimilano.it). **Open** 24hrs daily.
Malpensa is Milan's main international airport. It is located around 50km (31 miles) north-west of Milan and 130km (81 miles) from Turin, and has two terminals linked by a shuttle bus.

Sadem (011 300 0611/fax 011 309 8995/www.sadem.it) runs three buses daily (11.30am, 3.30pm, 8.30pm) from both terminals to Turin's long-distance bus station at the junction of corso Vittorio Emanuele II with corso Inghilterra (*map p242 D1*). Tickets cost €17.50.

Alternatively, the **Malpensa Shuttle bus** service (tickets €4.13) runs every 20 minutes, connecting Malpensa with Linate airport (*see below*) and the Milano Centrale railway station; it takes around 50 minutes to reach the station, from where trains leave frequently for Turin's Porta Susa station.

Milano Linate International Airport

Linate Aeroporto, Milano (information 02 7485 2200/ lost luggage 02 7912 4451/ www.sea-aeroportimilano.it). **Open** 24hrs daily.
Linate is 7km (4.5 miles) east of Milan and 155km (96 miles) from Turin.

Buses (information 02 717 106) run every 30 minutes from the airport to Milano Centrale railway station, from where trains leave frequently for Turin. Bus tickets cost €4; the bus journey takes about 20 minutes.

Orio al Serio International Airport

Via Aeroporto 13, Orio al Serio, Bergamo (information 035 326 323/lost luggage 035 326 352/

ticket office 035 326 324/ www.sacbo.it). **Open** 24hrs daily.
Orio al Serio is 45km (28 miles) from Milan and 180km (112 miles) from Turin.

Autostradale (035 318 472/02 3391 0794) provides a frequent bus service from 8.30am to 12.30am daily between Orio al Serio airport and Milano Centrale railway station, from where trains leave frequently for Turin. Bus tickets cost €6.70; the journey takes around 50 minutes.

Major airlines

Air One

Information & booking 199 207 080/ www.flyairone.it. **Open** 7am-11pm daily. **Credit** AmEx, DC, MC, V.

Alitalia

Information & booking domestic flights 848 865 641/international flights 848 865 642/www.alitalia.it. **Open** 24hrs daily. **Credit** AmEx, DC, MC, V.

British Airways

Booking 199 712 266/www. britishairways.com/italy. **Open** 8.30am-7.30pm; 9am-5pm Sat. **Credit** AmEx, DC, MC, V.

Ryanair

Booking 899 899 844/ www.ryanair.com. **Open** 24hrs daily. **Credit** AmEx, DC, MC, V.

By bus

Coach terminal

The coach station is located at the junction of corso Vittorio Emanuele II and corso Inghilterra. *(011 433 2525. Bus 9. Map p242 D1).*
Most international and national coach lines operate their services from this terminal.

By train

There are two mainline Trenitalia-Ferrovie dello Stato (**FS**; state railways) stations in Turin. **Stazione Porta Nuova** in corso Vittorio Emanuele II 53 (*map p242 D3*) is the main one. Most long-distance trains arrive at Porta Nuova, which is also the hub of the city bus network. The station is a pickpocket's paradise, so watch your wallets and luggage carefully. If you arrive at Porta Nuova after midnight, it's advisable to take a taxi to your final destination.

Some trains – including many Milan and other east/west-bound services – stop at **Stazione Porta Susa** (map p242 C1).

For further information on trains and tickets, see below.

Public transport

For a transport map, see p248. For transport outside Turin, see p167.

City-centre transport

Turin's first metropolitan railway line (Collegno-Porta Nuova) is under construction and is due for completion by 2006. Work was scheduled to begin on a second line (Porta Nuova-Lingotto) in 2004. This ambitious project has transformed the city's generally efficient and user-friendly transport system into a nightmare of changing numbers and altered and re-routed lines; getting hold of an up-to-date bus map (available free from tobacconists and newsagents) may help to some extent, but be prepared to do some lateral thinking and/or footwork to reach your destination.

Turin's transport system is co-ordinated by GTT (Gruppo Trasporti Torinesi; information toll-free 800 019 152/www.gtt.to.it). Its Trambus buses are mainly orange (though new ones are grey and blue, including the zippy new supertrams and bendy buses). Regular Trambus services run between about 5am and midnight daily, with a frequency of between ten to 45 minutes, depending on the route. The doors for boarding (usually front and rear) and alighting (usually centre) are clearly marked. Each bus stop shows the lines that

stop there, and lists the stops each line should make along its route.

Twenty electric minibuses also ply the centre. The Star 1 connects car parks in the city centre (see also p219).

GTT is also responsible for the lift to the top of the Mole Antonelliana (see p77), the boats on the Po (see p218) and the Sassi-Superga cable car (see p91 **La Cremagliera**).

GTT

Corso Turati 19E, Cittadella (information toll-free 800 019 152/www.gtt.to.it). **Phone line** with operator 6.30am-7.30pm Mon-Sat; recorded information 24hrs daily.

Fares & tickets

See also p51 for information on the Torino Card, which allows unlimited use of public transport.

The same tickets are valid on all city bus and tram lines. They must be bought before boarding and are available from automatic ticket machines, tobacconists and newsagents.

When you board, you must stamp your ticket in the machines by the rear and/or front doors. Children less than one metre tall travel for free, after which they pay the adult fare for single, daily and weekly tickets, as do pensioners. Students, pensioners and the disabled pay lower rates for monthly and yearly passes.

If travelling without paying seems an easy option, bear in mind that there are ticket inspectors around: if you are caught you will be fined €36 on the spot.

Ordinario urbano

Valid for 70 minutes, during which you can use an unlimited number of buses and trams in the urban area; 90¢. These can be bought in a carnet of 15 tickets; €12.50.

Giornaliero

Valid 24hrs from when it is stamped; €3.

Shopping

Valid for 4hrs between 9am to 8pm; €1.80.

Viaggiare insieme

Valid from 2.30pm to 8pm on Sat or Sun for maximum four people; €4.

Settimanale formula U

Valid one calendar week on all bus and tram routes; €8.50.

Abbonamento mensile

Valid one calendar month for unlimited travel on the entire metropolitan transport system; €32.

Ordinario suburbano

Valid for 60 minutes in the suburban area; 90¢.

Trains

All Italian stations now have the same phone number for information: 892 021; lines are open between 7am and 9pm daily. From 9pm to 7am there are automatic recordings of train schedules.

Train timetables can be purchased at any edicola (newsstand). The website www.trenitalia.com gives complete schedule information (in English).

Mainline trains are operated by **Trenitalia-Ferrovie dello Stato** (FS). Tickets can be bought at stations (over the counter or at machines; all major credit cards are accepted at both), or from travel agents with an FS sign. They can also be booked on the **Trenitalia** website by credit card (you'll need to register, after which you'll be given a password) and picked up from machines in stations.

Children under 12 pay half fare; children under four travel free. For information on taking wheelchairs on trains, see p222.

Slower trains (diretti, espressi, regionali and interregionali) are very cheap; a system of supplements means that faster services – **InterCity** (IC), **EuroCity** (EC), **Eurostar Italia** (ES) – are closer to the European

Directory

norm. The first two cost up to 50 per cent more than slower trains; Eurostar (not to be confused with Channel tunnel trains of the same name) cost more than double.

Advance reservation is obligatory and free on ES trains on Fridays and Sundays, and all week at certain peak times of year. An R inside a square on train timetables indicates this; check when purchasing your ticket. Booking a seat on IC and internal EC routes costs €3, and is well worth it even when not obligatory, to avoid standing in a packed corridor at peak times. If your ES, IC or EC train arrives more than 30 minutes late – it rarely will – and you have a seat booking, you can have the supplement reimbursed at the booth marked *rimborsi*.

You must stamp your ticket and supplements in the yellow machines at the head of each platform before boarding the train. You will be fined if you don't.

Turin's main stations are:

Porta Nuova
Corso Vittorio Emanuele II 53, Centro (011 532 427/www.torino portanuova.it). Bus 5, 12, 14, 33, 34, 35, 50, 52, 57, 59, 63, 64, 65, 67/ tram 4, 9, 15, 18. **Map** p242 D3.

Porta Susa
Piazza XVIII Dicembre 8, Cittadella (011 538 513). Bus 1, 46, 51, 52, 55, 59, 65/tram 10, 13. **Map** p242 C1.

Lingotto
Via Pannunzio 1, Lingotto (011 317 3897). Bus 14, 34, 35, 45, 74/tram 1, 18. **Map** p247 B1.

Stazione Dora
Via E Giachino 10, Suburbs: north (toll-free 800 990 097/011 691 0000/www.gtt.to.it). Bus 11, 46, 49, 52, 57, 63, 77/tram 10, 16, 18. **Map** p242 A2.

Tour buses

GTT and **Turismo Torino** run a 'hop-on, hop-off' tour bus, TurismoBus Torino (July-

mid Sept hourly 10am-6pm daily; mid Sept-June hourly 10am-6pm Sat, Sun). The bus leaves via Villa della Regina (*map p243 D3*) and stops at piazza Gran Madre, piazza Vittorio Veneto, piazza Castello, piazza Solferino, corso Re Umberto, corso Vittorio Emanuele II, corso Galileo Ferraris, via Cernaia, via Santa Teresa, via Roma, piazza Castello, via Accademia delle Scienze, via Lagrange, corso Massimo d'Azeglio and via Villa della Regina. You can join the service at any point along its route. Tickets cost €5 (€3 under-12s; free with Torino Card, *see p51*). Tickets can be bought on board or at Turismo Torino information points (*see p228* **Atrium**), many hotels and GTT information points at Porta Nuova station and Corso Francia 6 (*map p242 C1*).

Suburban transport

For a transport map, *see p248*. For details of transport to out-of-town destinations, *see p167*.

Water transport

GTT (bookings 011 888 010/ information 011 581 1900/ toll-free 800 019 152) runs two boats on the River Po. Services leave from the Imbarco Murazzi on the riverbank at the end of piazza Vittorio Veneto, south of the Vittorio Emanuele bridge (*map p243 C2*) at 3pm, 4.15pm, 5.45pm Tue-Fri; 3pm, 4.15pm, 5.45pm, 7pm, 9.30pm, 10.45pm Sat; 10.30am, 3pm, 4.15pm, 5.45pm, 7pm, 9.30pm, 10.45pm Sun. They depart from the Borgo medioevale (*see p80; map p245 B2*) and stop 15 minutes later.

Taxis

Authorised taxis are white, have the city's emblem on the front doors and rear licence plate, and have a meter.

Fares & surcharges

When you pick up a taxi at a rank or hail one in the street, the meter should read €3.10. There's a 50¢ charge for each item of luggage placed in the boot and, from 10pm to 7am, a night charge of €2 on top of the fare.

Most of Turin's taxi drivers are honest workers, but if you suspect you're being ripped off, make a note of the driver's name and number from the metal plaque inside the car's rear door. The more ostentatiously you do this, the more likely you are to find the fare returning to its proper level. Report complaints to the drivers' co-operative (its phone number is shown on the outside of each car) or, in serious cases, the police (*see p226*).

Taxi ranks

Ranks are indicated by an orange sign with 'Taxi' written in black. In the central area there are ranks at piazza Vittorio Veneto near the junction with via Po; piazza Solferino near the junction with via Santa Teresa; piazza San Carlo; via Sacchi (by Porta Nuova railway station); via Nizza (by Porta Nuova railway station); piazza Palazzo di Città; piazza Castello; piazza Savoia; piazza XVIII Dicembre (Porta Susa railway station); piazza Statuto; via Cernaia.

Phone cabs

You can phone for a taxi from any of the following companies at any time of day or night. When your call is answered you'll be given the taxi code-name (which is always a location followed by a number) and a time, as in *Bahamas 69, in tre minuti* (Bahamas 69, in three minutes). A radio taxi will start the meter from the moment your phone call is answered.

Pronto Taxi 011 5737
Radio Taxi 011 5730/011 3399
Turin Airport Taxi 011 991 4419
Torino Porta Nuova Taxi 011 547 331/011 657 139
Torino Porta Susa Taxi 011 562 2535

Driving

Turin's rigid grid-pattern streets make it easy to navigate in the city; its rush-hour traffic, however, may make you wish you'd left your vehicle elsewhere.

If you do use a car, some tips to be borne in mind are listed below. Short-term visitors should have no trouble driving with their home licences, although if they are written in different scripts or less common languages an international licence can be useful.

Remember the following:

● You are required by law to wear a seat belt at all times and to carry a warning triangle in your car.

● Outside urban areas, you must drive with your headlights on.

● Keep your driving licence, vehicle registration, vehicle insurance and personal ID documents on you at all times.

● Do not leave anything of value in your car. Take all your luggage into your hotel when you park.

● Flashing your lights in Italy means that you will not slow down (contrary to British practice).

● If traffic lights flash amber, you should stop and give way to the right.

● Watch out for death-defying mopeds and pedestrians.

Restricted areas

Large sections of the city centre are closed to non-resident traffic from 7.30am to 10.30am and sometimes in the evening. Police and electronically activated video cameras stand guard over these areas; any vehicle without

the required pass will be fined €68.25 if it enters at restricted times.

Your vehicle may be wheel-clamped if left where it is not allowed or not properly parked, in which case you'll have to pay a fine, plus a charge to have the clamp removed. If your car is in a dangerous position or blocking trams and buses, it will be towed away immediately (*see p220* **Car pounds**). If you need to reach accommodation in the restricted area, you should make arrangements with your hotel before your arrival. As this guide went to press, plans were afoot to ban all vehicles without catalytic converters from the city centre. The first Sunday of most months is designated a no-car day: this is rigidly enforced in the city centre.

Breakdown services

It is advisable to join a national motoring organisation, like the AA or RAC in Britain or the AAA in the US, before taking a car to Italy. They have reciprocal arrangements with the Automobile Club d'Italia (**ACI**), which offers assistance in the case of a breakdown, and can provide useful general information. Even for non-members, ACI is the best number to call if you break down.

If you require extensive repairs and do not know a mechanic, pay a bit more and go to a manufacturer's official dealer, as the reliability of any garage depends on long years of building up a good client-mechanic relationship. Dealers are listed in the Yellow Pages under *auto*, along with specialist repairers such as *gommista* (tyre repairs), *marmitte* (exhaust repairs) and *carrozzerie* (bodywork repairs).

Automobile Club d'Italia (ACI)

Via Giolitti 15, Centro (information 011 57 791/24hr emergency line 116/24hr information line 803 000/traffic report in Italian 1518/www.acitorino.it). Bus 55, 56, 61, 68, 70/tram 13, 15, 16. **Open** 8.30am-1pm, 2-4pm Mon-Fri. **Map** p242 D3.
The ACI has English-speaking staff and provides a range of services for all foreign drivers, which are either free or at low prices. Members of associated organisations are entitled to basic repairs free and to other services at preferential rates. Non-members will be charged, but prices are generally reasonable.

Touring Club Italiano (TCI)

Via San Francesco d'Assisi 3, Cittadella (travel agency 011 562

7070/bookshop 011 562 7207/24hr members' emergency line 800 337 744/www.touringclub.it). Bus 12, 50, 51, 55, 56, 57, 58, 59, 61, 63/tram 4, 13, 15, 18. **Open** 9am-7pm Mon-Fri; 9am-1pm Sat. **Map** p242 C3.
The TCI bookshop has a good selection of travel titles.

Parking

A system in which residents park free and visitors pay has recently been introduced to many areas of the city and is efficiently policed: watch out for tell-tale blue lines. Parking fees are paid at pay-and-display ticket dispensers, at the rate of €1 per hour. Fees don't always apply round-the-clock, so check the instructions on the machine before feeding it with coins. For longer stays, a €25 parking card, available from *tabacchi (see p228)*, allows you to deduct parking fees gradually and saves having to search your pockets for small change.

Where there are no blue lines, anything resembling a parking place is up for grabs, with some exceptions: watch out for signs for entrances saying *Passo carrabile* (access at all times), *Sosta vietata* (no parking), and disabled parking spaces marked by yellow stripes on the road. The sign *Zona rimozione* (tow-away area) means no parking, and is valid for the length of the street, or until the next tow-away sign with a red line through it denoting the end of the restricted area. If a street or square has no cars parked in it, you can safely assume that it's a seriously enforced no-parking zone. In some areas, self-appointed *parcheggiatori* ('garagemen') will 'look after' your car for a small fee; though it is illegal and a ridiculous imposition, it's worth coughing up to ensure that your tyres remain intact.

Although cars are fairly safe in most central areas, you may prefer to pay the hefty rates charged by underground car parks to ensure the vehicle is not tampered with. The following are centrally located.
Bodoni
Piazza Bodoni, Centro (011 577 9354). Bus 34, 52, 67, 68/tram 9, 16. **Open** 7am-1am Mon-Sat; 2pm-1am Sun. **Map** p242 D3.
Bolzano-Porta Susa
Corso Bolzano, Cittadella (011 506 9989). Bus 36, 38, 55, 56, 59, 60, 65, 71/tram 1, 10, 13, 15, 16. **Open** 24hrs daily. **Map** p242 D1.
Galileo Ferraris
Corso Galileo Ferraris, Cittadella (toll-free 800 019 152). Bus 5, 14, 50, 52, 64, 65, 68/minibus Star 1/tram 1, 10, 15. **Open** 24hrs daily. **Map** p242 D2.

Giardino della Cittadella
*Piazza Albarello, Cittadella (toll-free
800 019 152). Bus 12, 36, 46, 49,
52, 55, 56, 59, 67/tram 1, 10, 13.*
Open 24hrs daily. **Map** p242 C2.
Palagiustizia
*Via Cavalli 12, Suburbs: west
(toll-free 800 019 152). Bus 36, 38,
55, 56, 60, 71/tram 9, 15, 16.*
Open 24hrs daily. **Map** p242 D1.
Re Umberto
*Corso Re Umberto, Cittadella (toll-
free 800 019 152). Bus 5, 14, 33,
42, 58, 59, 63, 64/tram 4, 10, 12.*
Open 24hrs daily. **Map** p242 B3.
Via Roma
*Piazza Carlo Felice, Centro (011 577
9354). Bus 5, 14, 33, 34, 35, 50, 52,
57, 59, 63, 64, 65, 67/tram 4, 9, 12,
15, 18.* **Open** 7am-1am Mon-Sat;
2pm-1am Sun. **Map** p242 D3.

Car pounds

If you don't find your car where you
left it, it has probably been towed
away. Phone the municipal police
(Vigili urbani; 011 812 3422 7.30am-
7.30pm Mon-Sat; 011 460 6060
7.30pm-7.30am daily) and quote
your number plate to find out which
of the two car pounds it has been
taken to: via Fontanesi 2bis C (011
883 122; map p243 B2) or via
Giordano Bruno 1 (011 319 6012;
map p244 D3). You'll be fined €78.70
if your car was towed away between
7am and 7.30pm Monday to
Saturday, or €103 if it was towed
away between 7.30pm and 7am
Monday to Saturday or any time
on Sunday. You'll also be charged
€5.15 for each day your vehicle
remains in the pound.

Petrol

Petrol stations sell unleaded petrol
(*senza piombo* or *verde*) and diesel
(*gasolio*). Liquid propane gas is GPL.
Most petrol stations offer full service
on weekdays; pump attendants
do not expect tips. At night and on
Sundays many stations have
automatic self-service pumps that
accept €10, €20 and €50 notes in
good condition.

Vehicle hire

Car hire

To hire a car you must be over
21 – in some cases 23 – and
have held a licence for at least
a year. You will be required to
leave a credit card number or
a substantial cash deposit. It's
advisable to take out a

collision damage waiver
(CDW) and personal accident
insurance (PAI) on top of basic
third party insurance when
you hire a car. Companies that
do not offer a collision damage
waiver are best avoided.

Car City Club
*Corso Cairoli 32, Centro
(information 848 788 888/bookings
848 787 787/011 813 7811/fax 011
813 7809/www.carcityclub.it). Bus
30, 53, 56, 61, 66, 70, 73/tram 13,
15, 16.* **Open** 8.30am-6pm Mon-Fri.
Credit AmEx, DC, MC, V.
Map p243 D1.
848 numbers function 24hrs daily.

CAARP Car & Bus Services
*Corso Regio Parco 41, Suburbs:
north (011 247 2072/fax 011 247
5387/www.caarp.it). Bus 30, 55, 68,
75, 77/tram 3, 15, 16.* **Open** 9am-
1pm, 3-7.30pm Mon-Fri. **Credit**
AmEx, DC, MC, V. **Map** p243 B1.

Avis
*Airport (011 470 1528/
www.avisautonoleggio.it).* **Open**
7.30am-11.30pm Mon-Sat; 8.30am-
11.30pm Sun. **Credit** AmEx,
DC, MC, V.
Other locations: Porta Nuova
railway station, Centro (011 567 8020).

Hertz
*Airport (011 567 8166/
www.hertz.it).* **Open** 8am-11.30pm
Mon-Fri; 9am-3.30pm, 4.30-11pm Sat,
Sun. **Credit** AmEx, DC, MC, V.
Other locations: via Magellano 12,
Cittadella (011 502 080).

Maggiore
*Airport (011 470 1929/
www.maggiore.it).* **Open** 8am-
11.30pm Mon-Sat; 8.30am-11.30pm
Sun. **Credit** AmEx, DC, MC, V.

SixtWin Rent
*Airport (011 470 2381/www.e-
sixt.it).* **Open** 8am-11pm Mon-Fri;
8.30am-1pm, 3.30-7pm Sat, Sun.
Credit AmEx, DC, MC, V.

Target Rent
*Airport (011 567 8090/
www.targetrent.it).* **Open** 7.30am-
11.30pm Mon-Sat; 8.30am-11.30pm
Sun. **Credit** AmEx, DC, MC, V.

Moped, scooter & cycle hire

To hire a scooter or moped
(*motorino*) you'll need a credit
card, photo ID and/or a cash

deposit. Helmets are required
on all motorbikes, scooters
and mopeds and the police
are very strict about enforcing
this. To ride a moped up to
50cc you need to be over 14;
a driver's licence is required
for anything over 50cc. For
hiring bicycles, you can
normally just leave an
identity document rather
than pay a deposit.

Mopeds
Ruotò-GTT
*Palagiustizia car park entrance (011
744 892/fax 011 750 9024). Bus 30,
55, 68, 75, 77/tram 3, 15, 16.* **Open**
9am-7pm Mon-Fri. **Credit** AmEx,
DC, MC, V. **Map** p242 D1.
Rents scooters and electric bikes.
As this guide went to press a new
outlet was planned at Atrium (*see
p228* **Atrium**).

Bike hire
Through the summer months
(roughly April-September, depending
on weather conditions), bike-hire
stands set up outside many of
Turin's parks.

Parco del Valentino
(*see p80*)
Viale Ceppi, Centro. **Map** p245 B1.
Parco Colletta
Via Carcano, Suburbs: north-east.
Map p243 A3.
Parco Mario Carrara
*Corso Appio Claudio 106, Suburbs:
north-west.* **Map** off p242 B1.

Amici della Bicicletta
*Via Principe Amedeo 21, Centro
(347 405 4810/011 561 3059).
Bus 1, 65/tram 10.* **No credit
cards. Map** p243 C1.
Bici & Dintorni
*Via Andorno 35B, Suburbs:
east (011 888 981/www.
biciedintorni.org). Bus 68, 77/
tram 15.* **Map** p243 B2.
Not a bike-hire outfit but an
association of keen cyclists with
an excellent website containing
everything you could ever want to
know about bike-riding in and
around Turin.
Risciò
*Viale Virgilio, Centro (338 763
6964). Bus 30, 53, 56, 61, 66, 70,
73/tram 13, 15, 16.* **No credit
cards. Map** p245 B1.
If you have no style qualms about
peddling your own rickshaw,
this is the place to pick one up for
a leisurely tour of Parco del
Valentino (see p80). Risciò is open
only in the summer (April-
September depending on the
weather) and at hours that change
from year to year.

Resources A-Z

Accommodation

See p228 **Atrium**.

Age restrictions

Cigarettes and alcohol cannot legally be sold to under-16s. Anyone over 14 can ride a moped or scooter of 50cc; no licence is required.

Business

Turin is a popular conference venue. The city is well equipped for these events, with three conference centres: **Lingotto**, **Torino Incontra** and the **Unione Industriale**.

Information on doing business in and around Turin can be had from **Investimenti a Torino e in Piemonte** (ITP; www.itp-agency.org), from **Finpiemonte** (www.finpiemonte.it) and from the **Centro Estero Camere Commercio Piemontesi** (www.centroestero.org).

The public-private Torino Convention Bureau will fix you up with translators, caterers and all your conference needs, as well as arranging the venue.

Torino Convention Bureau

Via Bogino 9, Centro (011 81 831/fax 011 812 8545/www.torino convention.it). Bus 55, 56, 61, 68/tram 13, 15. **Map** p243 C1.

Conference centres

Centro Congressi Lingotto–Expo 2000
Via Nizza 280, Lingotto (011 631 172/664 4111/fax 011 312 1697). Bus 35/tram 1. **Map** p247 A2.
Centro Congressi Unione Industriale
Via Fanti 17, Cittadella (011 571 8246/www.ui.torino.it). Bus 5, 12, 14, 33, 42, 58, 63, 64/tram 4, 10, 16. **Map** p242 D2.
Torino Incontra – Centro Congressi Camera di Commercio

Via San Francesco da Paola 24, Centro (011 557 6800/561 7300/fax 011 561 7039). Bus 53, 55, 56, 61, 68, 70/tram 13, 15, 16. **Map** p243 D1.

Conference organisers

CCI – Centro Congressi Internazionale
Via Cervino 60, Suburbs: north (011 244 6911/fax 011 244 6900/www.congressiefiere.com). Bus 50/tram 2, 4. **Map** p242 A2.
ACTA
Via Caboto 44 (011 591 871/fax 011 590 833/www.actacongress.com). Bus 12, 68/tram 4, 10, 16. **Map** p244 B2.
MAF Servizi
Via GB Vico 7, Cittadella (011 505 900/fax 505 976/www.mafservizi.it). Bus 5, 33, 64/tram 16. **Map** p244 B3.
Selene
Via Sacchi 58, Cittadella (011 568 3534/fax 011 568 1010/www.seleneweb.it). Bus 12, 63/tram 4, 16. **Map** p244 A3.

Couriers (international)

DHL toll-free 199 199 345/www.dhl.it.
Federal Express toll-free 800 123 800/www.fedex.com.
TNT toll-free 803 868/www.tnt.it.
UPS – United Parcel Service toll-free 800 877 877/www.ups.com.
SDA 800 016 027/www.sda.it.
Executive toll-free 800 331 393/www.executivegroup.com.

Couriers (local)

Pony Express 011 2466/www.pony.it.
Defendini 011 883 04/www.defendini.it.

Interpreters

COPAT
Via Gropello 16 (011 440 0111/fax 011 440 0222/www.copatitalia.com). Bus 36, 65, 71/tram 1, 13, 16. **Map** p242 C1.

Customs

EU citizens do not have to declare goods imported into or exported from Italy for personal use, as long as they arrive from another EU country and respect the following limits:
• 800 cigarettes or 400 small cigars, or 200 cigars, or one kilo (35.27oz) of tobacco.
• ten litres of spirits (over 22 per cent alcohol), 90 litres of fortified wine (under 22 per cent alcohol) or 110 litres of beer. For non-EU citizens, the following limits apply:
• 200 cigarettes or 50 small cigars or 50 cigars or 250 grams (8.82oz) of tobacco.
• One litre of spirits (over 22 per cent alcohol) or two litres of fortified wine (under 22 per

---

Travel advice

For up-to-date information on travel to a specific country – including the latest news on safety and security, health issues, local laws and customs – contact your home country government's department of foreign affairs. Most have websites packed with useful advice for would-be travellers.

Australia
www.dfat.gov.au/travel

Canada
www.voyage.gc.ca

New Zealand
www.mft.govt.nz/travel

Republic of Ireland
www.irlgov.ie/iveagh

UK
www.fco.gov.uk/travel

USA
http://www.state.gov/travel

Directory

cent alcohol); 50 grams (1.76oz) of perfume.

There are no restrictions on the import of cameras, watches or electrical goods. Visitors are also allowed to carry up to €10,329.14 in cash.

Disabled travellers

Information

Centro Informazione Disabilità della Provincia di Torino

Corso G Lanza 75, Collina (011 8613141/3143/www.provincia. torino.it/cid). Bus 52, 53, 64, 66, 70. **Open** 9am-5pm Mon-Fri. **Map** p243 D2.

Informa Handicap

Via Palazzo di Città 11, Piazza Castello (011 442 1631/ www.arpnet.it). Bus 12, 50, 51, 63/tram 4, 13, 15, 18. **Open** 9am-12.30pm, 1.30-4pm Mon-Fri. **Map** p242 C3.

Transport

Turin is in the process of making the whole of its bus network accessible to wheelchairs. Trams 4, 10 and 30 can take wheelchairs. Most taxi drivers will carry wheelchairs (they have to be folded); if possible, phone and book a cab rather than hail one in the street (see p218). GTT runs a taxi service for the disabled; ring 011 58 116 (open 8am-4.45pm Mon-Thur; 8am-3.45pm Fri) to book.

To ascertain which trains have wheelchair facilities, call (or visit) the *Ufficio disabili* (office for the disabled) at the station from which you plan to depart, or consult the official timetable, which shows a wheelchair symbol next to accessible trains. Twenty-four hours prior to departure, the disabled traveller or someone representing him/her must phone or send a fax to the *Ufficio disabili* of the appropriate station and go, before boarding the train, to fill in and sign a form requesting assistance. Reserve a seat when buying a ticket, and make sure you arrive three quarters of an hour before departure time.

Turin airport has facilities such as adapted toilets. Inform your airline of your needs: it will contact the office at Caselle, where you will be able to use special facilities and waiting rooms on arrival and departure.

Sightseeing

Well-designed ramps, lifts and toilets have been installed in many museums. Among sites with full facilities are the Castello di Rivoli (see p94), Galleria d'arte moderna e contemporanea (see p68), Museo nazionale del cinema (see p78), Museo Egizio (see p71), Fondazione Sandretto Re Rebaudengo (see p68), Palazzo Accorsi (see p77), Palazzo Bricherasio (see p70), Palazzo Cavour (see p71) and Pinacoteca Marella e Giovanni Agnelli (see p88).

Toilets

Public toilets accessible to wheelchair users are numerous in central areas… though there's no guarantee that they'll be in working order or open when you need them.

Where to stay & eat

The number of accessible hotels has increased recently: Turismo Torino (see p228 **Atrium**) has details. Local by-laws now require restaurants to have disabled access and toilets; in practice, few have made the necessary alterations. But if you phone ahead and ask for an appropriate table, most will do their best to help. In summer, the range of outdoor restaurants makes things easier. Getting to toilets, though, can be difficult or impossible.

Most bars open on to the street at ground level, and/or have tables outside in summer. Again, though, most bar toilets are tiny dark holes down long flights of steps.

Wheelchair hire

Ortopedia Sanitaria

011 675 417/337 211 968/ www.ctosas.it/info@ctosas.it. **Open** 9am-12.30pm, 3-7.30pm Mon-Fri; 9am-12.30pm Sat. **No credit cards.** Wheelchairs are delivered.

Officina Ortopedica Zumaglini

Corso Turati 45bis, Cittadella (011 581 8864/fax 011 568 1796/ info@zumaglini.it). Bus 12, 33, 58, 63/tram 4, 10. **Open** 9am-12.30pm, 3-7pm Mon-Fri. Closed July or Aug. **Credit** AmEx, DC, MC, V. **Map** p244 B3.

Drugs

If you are caught in possession of drugs of any type, you will be taken before a magistrate. If

you can convince him or her that the tiny quantity you were carrying was for purely personal use, you will be let off with a fine or ordered to leave the country. Habitual offenders will be offered rehab. Anything more than a tiny amount will push you into the criminal category: couriering or dealing can land you in prison for up to 20 years. It is an offence to buy or sell drugs, or even to give them away. Sniffer dogs are a fixture at most ports of entry into Italy; the customs police take a dim view of visitors entering even the smallest quantities of narcotics, and those caught are nearly always refused entry.

Electricity

Most wiring systems work on 220V, which is compatible with British-bought appliances. With US 110V equipment you will need a current transformer. Adaptors can be bought at any electrical or hardware shop (look for *elettricità* or *ferramenta*).

Embassies & consulates

Listed below are addresses and phone numbers of embassies (in Rome). Britain has a consulate in Turin.

Australia Embassy
Via Alessandria 215, Rome (06 852 721/www.australian-embassy.it).
British Embassy
Via XX Settembre 80A, Rome (06 4220 0001/fax 06 4220 2334/ www.britain.it).
Canadian Embassy
Via GB de Rossi 27, Rome (06 445 981/www.canada.it).
New Zealand Embassy
Via Zara 28, Rome 06 441 7171/ www.nzembassy.com).
South African Embassy
Via Tanaro 14, Rome (06 852 541/ www.sudafrica.it).
United States Embassy
Via Vittorio Veneto 119, Rome(06 46 741/www.usembassy.it).
British Consulate (Turin)
Via Madama Cristina 99, Centro (011 650 9202/bcturin@yahoo.com). **Map** p245 A1.

Emergencies

See also p227 **Safety & security;** *below* **Health;** *p226* **Police;** *p225* **Money.**

Thefts or losses should be reported immediately at the nearest police station (*see p226*). You should report the loss of your passport to your consulate or embassy (*see p222*). Report the loss of a credit card or travellers' cheques immediately to your credit card company (*see p225*).

Emergency numbers

Police *Carabinieri* (English speaking helpline) 112
State police 113
Fire service *Vigili del fuoco* 115
Ambulance *Ambulanza* 118
Car breakdown *Automobile Club d'Italia (ACI)* 116

Domestic emergencies

If you need to report a malfunction in any of the main services, the following emergency lines are open 24 hours a day.
Electricity *Aem* 800 910 101
Gas *Italgas* 800 900 777
Telephone *Telecom Italia* 187
Water *Smat* 800 239 111

Health

Emergency healthcare is available for all travellers through the Italian national health system and, by law, hospital accident and emergency departments (*see below*) must treat all emergency cases free of charge.

If you are an EU citizen, obtain an E111 form from your local health authority or post office before leaving home: this entitles you to a free consultation with any doctor. Non-EU citizens should consider taking out private health insurance (*see p224*). For an ambulance, call 118.

Consulates (*see p222*) can provide lists of English-speaking doctors and dentists.

Accident & emergency

If you need urgent medical care, go to the *pronto soccorso* (casualty department) of one of the hospitals listed below, all of which offer 24-hour casualty services.

Azienda Sanitaria Ospedaliera OIRM-Sant'Anna

Via Ventimiglia 1, Lingotto (011 313 4444/toll-free 800 274 673/ www.oirmsantanna.piemonte.it). Bus 1, 34, 35, 42, 74, linea H/ tram 18. **Map** p247 A3.
Specialises in obstetrical and children's emergencies.

Azienda Sanitaria Ospedaliera

Molinette San Giovanni Battista di Torino, corso Bramante 88-90, Lingotto (011 633 1633/ www.molinette.piemonte.it). Bus 1, 34, 35, 42, 45, 47, 66, 67, 74/ tram 18. **Map** p245 C/D1.

Ospedale Amedeo di Savoia-Birago di Vische

Corso Svizzera 164, Suburbs: west (011 439 3111/fax 011 439 3785). Tram 3, 9. **Map** off p242 B1.
For the treatment of infectious diseases.

Ospedale Infantile Regina Margherita

Via Zuretti 23, Lingotto (011 313 4444/toll-free 800 274 673/ www.oirmsantanna.piemonte.it). Bus 1, 34, 35, 42, 74, linea H/ tram 18. **Map** p245 D1.
A children's hospital.

Ospedale Umberto I

Largo F Turati 62, Lingotto (011 508 1111/www.mauriziano.it). Bus 14, 42, 63/tram 4. **Map** p244 B3.

Presidio Ospedaliero CTO

Via Zuretti 29, Lingotto (011 693 3111/www.cto.to.it). Bus 1, 17, 18, 34, 35, 42, 74. **Map** p245 D1.

Ospedale Maria Vittoria

Corso Tassoni 46, Suburbs: west (011 439 3111). Bus 36, 38, 55, 56, 59, 60, 65, 71/tram 1, 3, 9, 10, 13, 15, 16. **Map** off p242 B1.

Ortopedia Sanitaria

Via Cellini 28, Lingotto (011 675 417/337 211 968/www.ctosas.it /info@ctosas.it). Bus 1, 35, 45,

67/tram 18. **Open** 9am-12.30pm, 3-7.30pm Mon-Fri; 9am-12.30pm Sat. **Map** p244 C3.

Complementary medicine

Homeopathic remedies are available from most pharmacies (for addresses, *see p224*).

Contraception & abortion

Condoms (*preservativi*) are on sale near checkouts in supermarkets, or over the counter in pharmacies. The contraceptive pill is available on prescription. Abortion is available on financial hardship or health grounds, and is legal only when performed in public hospitals.

Local councils run *consultori famigliari* (family-planning clinics). EU citizens with an E111 form are entitled to use them, paying the same low charges as locals; to locate your nearest one, check in the phone directory under *USL* (or *ASL*) – *Consultori famigliari.*
ANCED
Corso Racconigi, Suburbs: west (011 337 734). Bus 33, 42, 55, 56, 64/tram 15, 16. **Open** 9am-noon, 3pm-7pm daily. **No credit cards.** **Map** p241.
This private non-profit association provides good, low-cost gynaecological care.

Dentists

Most dentists (see *Dentisti* in the Yellow Pages) in Italy work privately. You may wait for months for a dental appointment in a national health service hospital. Dental treatment in Italy is not cheap and may not be covered by your health insurance. For serious dental emergencies, make for the hospital casualty departments listed above.

Doctors

EU nationals with an E111 form (obtain this before leaving home from your local health authority or post office) can consult a national health service doctor free of charge. Drugs that he/she prescribes can be bought at pharmacies at prices set by the Health Ministry. If you need tests or specialist out-patient treatment, this, too, will be charged at fixed rates. Non-EU nationals who need to consult health service doctors will be charged a small fee at the doctor's discretion.

Hospitals

Public hospitals (*see p222* **Accident & emergency**) offer good-to-excellent treatment for most ills, though nursing standards can appear rather slack to anyone used to Anglo-Saxon hospitals.

Opticians

See p128.

Pharmacies

Pharmacies (*farmacia*, identified by a green cross; for addresses *see p129*) will give informal medical advice for straightforward ailments, as well as making up prescriptions from a doctor. Most pharmacies also sell homeopathic and veterinary medicines, and all will check your height/weight/blood pressure on request. If you require regular medication, make sure you know the chemical (generic) rather than brand name of your medicines: they may only be available in Italy under different names.

Normal opening hours are from 8.30am to 1pm, 4pm to 8pm Monday to Saturday. Outside of normal hours, a duty rota system operates. A list by the door of any pharmacy indicates the nearest ones that will be open at any time. The daily rota is also published in local papers.

ID

You are required by law to carry photo ID with you at all times. You will be asked to produce this if you are stopped by traffic police (who will demand your driving licence, which you must have on you whenever you are in charge of a motor vehicle). ID will also be required when you check into a hotel. Smaller hotels may try to hold on to your passport/ID card for the length of your stay; if you have no other form of photo ID, you are completely within your rights to ask for it back.

Insurance

See also p223 **Health**; *p226* **Police**.

EU nationals are entitled to reciprocal medical care in Italy, provided they have an E111 form, available in the UK from health centres, post offices and Social Security offices. This will cover you for emergencies, but using an E111 naturally involves having to deal with the intricacies of the Italian state health system, and for short-term visitors it's better to take out health cover under private travel insurance. Non-EU citizens should take out private medical insurance for all eventualities before setting out from home.

Visitors should also take out adequate property insurance before setting off for Italy. If you rent a vehicle, motorcycle or moped, make sure you pay the extra charge for full insurance cover and sign the collision damage waiver when hiring a car.

Internet & email

Most budget hotels will allow you to plug your modem into their phone system; more upmarket establishments should all have PC points in bedrooms. You can caper in cyberspace or check your email at ever more internet points around the city.

A number of Italian providers offer free internet access, including **Fastwebnet** (www.fastwebnet.it), **Caltanet** (www.caltanet.it), **Libero** (www.libero.it), **Tiscali** (www.tiscalinet.it), **Kataweb** (www.kataweb.com) and **Telecom Italia** (www.tin.it).

There are many internet points around the city, and the number keeps growing. The following are very central:

1pc4you
Via Verdi 20G, Centro (011 835 908/www.1pc4you.it). Bus 55, 56/tram 13, 15, 18. **Open** 9am-10pm Mon-Sat; noon-10pm Sun. **Map** p243 C1.

Internet Train, American Stars
Via Pietro Micca 3A, Castello (011 543 000/www.internettrein.it). Bus 55, 56/tram 13, 15, 18. **Open** 10am-2am Mon-Sat; noon-2am Sun. **Map** p242 C3.

Left luggage

If you're staying in a hotel, staff are generally willing to look after your luggage for you during the day, even after you have checked out. There's no left luggage office at Turin airport.

Legal help

The first stop if you need legal advice should be your embassy or consulate; *see p222.*

Libraries

Other specialist libraries can be found under *biblioteche* in the phone book. It is always useful to take ID with you; in some cases, a letter from your college or tutor stating the purpose of your research will also be required.

Archivio di Stato
Piazza Castello 209, Piazza Castello (011 540 382/562 4431/fax 011 546 176). Bus 12, 27, 50, 51, 55, 56, 57, 61, 63/tram 11, 13, 15, 18. **Open** 8am-6.30pm Mon-Fri; 8am-2pm Sat. **Map** p242 C3.
See also p53. Turin's historical archive, designed by Filippo Juvarra, contains documents relating to Savoy (*see p8* **The unstoppable Savoys**). rule in the Kingdom of Sardinia-Piedmont.

Biblioteca Internazionale di Cinema e Fotografia Mario Gromo
Via Montebello 20, Centro (011 812 5658/fax 011 812 5738). Bus 15, 55, 56, 61, 68/tram 13, 16. **Open** *by appointment only* 9am-1pm Tue-Fri. **Map** p243 C1.
Some 25,000 books and 75,000 periodicals on the history of the moving image are housed in this library inside the Museo nazionale del cinema (*see p78*).

Biblioteca del Museo Egizio
Via Eleonora Duse, Centro (011 561 7776). Bus 11, 12, 27, 50, 51, 55, 56, 57, 61, 63/tram 11, 13, 15, 18. **Open** 9am-1.30pm Mon, Wed, Fri; 9am-5pm Tue, Thur. **Map** p242 C3.
With its 6,000-plus tomes relating to all things Egyptian, this library is one of Europe's most important of its kind; prior permission from the management is needed to gain access.

Biblioteca del Museo Nazionale del Risorgimento Italiano

Palazzo Carignano, via Accademia delle Scienze 5, Centro (011 562 1147/fax 011 56 46 95/ risorgimento.to@libero.it). Bus 11, 12, 27, 50, 51, 55, 56, 57, 61, 63/tram 11, 13, 15, 18. **Open** 9am-1pm, 2-5pm Mon-Wed, Fri; 9am-1pm, 2-6.45pm Thur. **Map** p242 C3.
Some 137,000 tomes and pamphlets cover Italy's political, military, diplomatic and social history from the late 18th century to World War I. Many of the periodicals were published during the Risorgimento (*see p12*).
Biblioteca Reale
Piazza Castello 191, Piazza Castello (011 543 855). Bus 12, 27, 50, 51, 55, 56, 57, 61/tram 11, 13, 15, 18. **Open** 10am-5pm Tue-Sat. **Map** p242 C3.
This beautiful wood-panelled library contains some 200,000 volumes, manuscripts, drawings, maps and photographs from the Savoy and Savoy-Carignano family collections.

Lost property

For items lost on public transport, go to the **GTT** (*see p222*).
Oggetti rinvenuti
Via Vigone 80, Suburbs: west (011 442 9246). Bus 56. **Open** 9am-noon Mon, Wed, Fri. **Map** p244 A1
Anything lost around town may (but probably won't) turn up at this municipal lost property office.

Media

Magazines

Panorama and *L'Espresso* provide a generally high-standard round-up of the week's news, while *Sette, Venerdì* and *Specchio* – respectively the colour supplements of *Corriere della Sera* (Thursday), *La Repubblica* (Friday) and Turin's *La Stampa* (Saturday) – have nice photos, though the text often leaves much to be desired; *La Repubblica*'s *D* supplement on Saturdays is the best of the lot.
For tabloid-style scandal, try *Gente* and *Oggi* with their weird mix of sex, glamour and religion, or the execrable *Eva 3000, Novella 2000* and *Cronaca Vera*.
Internazionale (www. internazionale.it) provides an excellent and readable digest of interesting bits and pieces gleaned from the world's press over the previous week. *Diario della Settimana* (www.diario.it) is informed, urbane and has a flair for investigative journalism.
But the biggest-selling magazine of them all is *Famiglia Cristiana* –

available from newsstands or in most churches – which alternates Vatican line-toeing with Vatican-baiting, depending on relations between the Holy See and the idiosyncratic Paoline monks who produce it.

Newspapers

National dailies

Italian newspapers can be a frustrating read. Long, indigestible political stories with very little background explanation predominate. On the plus side, Italian papers are delightfully unsnobbish and happily blend serious news, leaders by internationally known commentators, and well-written crime and human-interest stories. Sports coverage in the dailies is extensive and thorough, but if you're not sated there are the mass-circulation sports papers *Corriere dello Sport, La Gazzetta dello Sport* and *Tuttosport*.
Corriere della Sera (*www.rcs.it*). To the centre of centre-left, the solid, serious but often dull Milan-based *Corriere della Sera* is good on crime and foreign news.
La Repubblica (*www.repubblica.it*). The centre-ish-left-ish *La Repubblica* is good on the Mafia and the Vatican, and comes up with the occasional major scoop on its business pages.
La Stampa (*www.lastampa.it*). Part of the massive empire of Turin's Agnelli family, *La Stampa* has good (though inevitably pro-Agnelli) business reporting.
Il Sole 24 Ore A highly regarded business paper with an excellent cultural supplement each Sunday.

Local dailies

La Stampa and *La Repubblica* (*see above*) print local editions with news and listings for Turin and around. *Torino Sera* and *Torino Cronaca* are low-brow locals, as is *Leggo Torino*, which is handed out free in bars and stations.
For listings of cinema, music and other events, check out *Torino Sette*, which comes with *La Stampa* on Fridays, or the free monthly *011*, which you'll find lying about in bars, clubs and cinemas.

Foreign press

The *Financial Times, Wall Street Journal, USA Today, International Herald Tribune* (with its Italy daily supplement) and most European dailies can be found on the day of issue at most central newsstands; US dailies can take 24 hours to appear.

Listings & small ads

Tutto Affari *La Stampa*'s Sunday supplement is essential reading for

anyone looking for a place in Turin (to rent or buy). Place ads free on 011 5152.
Secondamano More essential reading for anyone looking to rent or buy a place in Turin. Published twice a week (Tuesday and Friday), it also has sections on household goods and cars. Place ads free on 011 5651.

Radio

The three state-owned stations (**RAI 1**, 89.7 MHz FM, 1332 KHz AM; **RAI 2**, 91.7 MHz FM, 846 KHz AM; **RAI 3**, 93.7 MHz FM, 1107KHz AM/www.rai.it) play classical and light music, and have chat shows and regular news bulletins.
For UK and US chart hits, mixed with home-grown offerings, try the following:
Radio Capital 95.8 MHz FM/www.capital.it
Radio 105 96.1 MHz FM/www.105.net
Radio 24 105.0 MHzFM/www.radio24.it
Radio Montecarlo 105.5 MHz FM/www.radiomontecarlo.it
Radio Deejay 106.90 MHzFM/www.radiodeejay.it

Local radios

Radio Torino Popolare 97.0 MHz FM/www.rtp97.it
Radio Flash 97.6 MHz FM/www.radioflash.to
Radio Energy 93.9 MHz FM/www.radioenergy.to
Radio Grp 99.300 MHz FM/www.radiogrp.it

Television

Italy has six major networks (three owned by state broadcaster **RAI**, three belonging to Silvio Berlusconi's **Mediaset** group), together with two channels operated across most of the country: **La7** and **MTV**. When these have bored you, there are any number of local stations to provide hours of compulsively awful channel-zapping fun.
The standard of television news and current affairs programmes varies; most, however, offer a breadth of international coverage that makes British TV news look like a parish magazine.
RAI 3 supplements its 2pm, 7.30pm and 10.30pm news programmes with regional round-ups. La7 broadcasts a CNN news programme in English, beginning at around 4am.

Money

See also p229 **Tax**.

The Italian currency is the euro. There are banknotes of €5, €10, €20, €100, €200 and €500, and coins worth €1 and €2 plus 1, 2, 5, 10, 20 and 50 cents (*centesimi*). Coins and notes from any Eurozone country are valid tender in Italy.

ATMs

Most banks have 24-hour cashpoint (*Bancomat*) machines, though some may shut down late at night on weekends. The vast majority of these accept cards with the Maestro and Cirrus symbols. Most cashpoint machines will dispense the daily limit of €250.

Banking hours

Most banks are open from 8.30am to 1.30pm and 2.45pm to 4.30pm, Monday to Friday. Some central branches now have extended hours, staying open until 6pm on Thursdays and from 8.30am to 12.30pm on Saturdays. All banks are closed on public holidays, and staff work reduced hours the day before a holiday, usually closing around 11am.

Bureaux de change

Banks usually offer better exchange rates than private bureaux de change (*cambio*). It's a good idea to take a passport or other identity document whenever you're dealing with money, particularly to change travellers' cheques or withdraw money on a credit card. Commission rates vary considerably: you can pay from nothing to €5 for each transaction. Watch out for 'no commission' signs, as the rate of exchange will almost certainly be terrible.

Many city-centre bank branches have automatic cash exchange machines, which accept notes in most currencies. Notes need to be in good condition.

Main post offices also have exchange bureaux. Commission is €2.58 for each transaction of up to €1,000. Travellers' cheques are not accepted. (*See also below* **Postal services**.) Major international exchange bureaux such as American Express and Thomas Cook do not have branches in Turin.

Credit cards

Nearly all hotels of two stars and above accept at least some of the major credit cards.

If you lose a credit or charge card, phone one of the emergency numbers listed below. All lines have English-speaking staff and are open 24 hours daily.
American Express 06 722 803 71/82; US cardholders 800 874 333.
Diners' Club 800 864 064.
Eurocard/CartaSi 800 018 548.
MasterCard 800 870 866.
Visa 800 877 232.

The addresses of the *Polizia di stato* and the *Carabinieri* are listed in the telephone directory under *Polizia* and *Carabinieri* respectively. Incidents can be reported to either force.

Postal services

Big improvements have been made recently in Italy's once notoriously unreliable postal service (www.poste.it) and you can now be more or less sure that your letter will arrive in reasonable time.

Italy's equivalent to first-class post, *posta prioritaria*, generally works very well: it promises delivery within 24 hours in Italy, three days for EU countries and four or five for the rest of the world; more often than not, it succeeds. A letter of 20g or less to Italy costs 60¢ and to any EU country 62¢ by *posta prioritaria*; outside the EU the cost is 80¢ or €1 depending on destination; special stamps can be bought at post offices and *tabacchi*; letters can be posted in any box.

Stamps for slower regular mail are also sold at post offices and *tabacchi*.

Most postboxes are red and have two slots, *per la città* (for Turin) and *tutte le altre destinazioni* (for everywhere else).

The **CAI-Posta Celere** service (available only in main post offices) costs more than *posta prioritaria* and allows you to track the progress of your letter on its website

(www.poste.it) or by phone (160 8am-8pm Mon-Sat). It can, however, be painfully slow. Registered mail (*raccomandata*) costs €2.80 over the normal rate.

Parcels can be sent from any post office.

For postal information of any kind, phone the central information office on 160.

Ufficio Postale Centro (Central Post Office)
Via Alfieri 10, Cittadella (011 506 0280). **Map** p242 D3.
Other post offices:
Via Nizza 10, Centro (011 657 562).
Via Bligny 8, Quadrilatero (011 436 5458). **Map** p242 C2.
Via Maria Vittoria 24, Centro (011 812 5667). p243 C1.
Via Montebello 23, Centro (011 835716). p243 C1.
Piazza Gran Madre 14, Collina (011 819 2364). 243 D2.

Queuing

Though torinesi are more disciplined than Italians from further south, the scrum at, for instance, a shop counter or market stall may not seem like an orderly queue to Anglo-Saxon eyes. On the whole, though, queuers have a knack for remembering who arrived when and queue-jumpers will be given short shrift. However, hanging back deferentially is taken as a sure sign of stupidity: you'll have a long wait if you don't make your desires known loudly in a crowded bar.

Religion

None of Turin's 200-plus Catholic churches has mass in English, and neither do most of the 50-odd churches belonging to other denominations, with the exception of the Evangelical church listed below.
Casa Valdese
Via Principe Tommaso 1, Centro (011 650 9467). Bus 34, 52, 67, 68/tram 9, 16. **Map** p245 A1.
Pastor Rob McKenzie leads a service in English at 10.30am on Sunday.

Relocation

Anyone staying here is obliged by the Italian state to pick up a whole series of forms and permits. The basic set is described below. EU citizens should have no difficulty getting their documentation once they are in Italy, but non-EU citizens are advised to enquire at an Italian embassy or consulate in their own country before travelling. There are agencies that specialise in obtaining documents for you if you can't face the procedures yourself – for a price (see *Pratiche e certificati – agenzie* in the Yellow Pages).

Paperwork

Carta d'Identità (Identity card)

Resident foreigners should have an ID card. You'll need three passport photographs, a *permesso di soggiorno* (*see below*), and a special form that will be given to you at your *circoscrizione* – the local branch of the central records office, which will eventually issue the card. To find the office for your area, look in the phone book under *Comune – servizi comunali – anagrafe*.

Codice Fiscale (tax code) & Partita IVA (VAT number)

A *codice fiscale* is essential for opening a bank account or setting up utilities contracts. Take your passport and *permesso di soggiorno* (*see below*) to your local tax office (*ufficio delle entrate, see below*), fill in a form and return a few days later to pick up the card. It can be posted on request.

The self-employed or anyone doing business in Italy may also need a *Partita IVA*. The certificate is free. Most people pay an accountant to handle the formalities. Take your passport and *codice fiscale* to your nearest tax office (*ufficio delle entrate*) and be prepared for a long wait. Make sure you cancel your VAT number when you no longer need it: failure to do so may result in a visit from tax inspectors years later.

Information on *uffici delle entrate* (revenue offices) can be had by calling the Finance Ministry's information line (848 800 444) or consulting its website at www.finanze.it; addresses are also in the phone book under *Ministero delle finanze*. Which office you should go to depends on the *circoscrizione* (city district) in which you live.

Permesso/Carta di Soggiorno (permit to stay)

EU citizens need a *permesso di soggiorno* if they're staying in Italy for over three months; non-EU citizens should (but usually don't) apply for one within eight days of their arrival in Italy. Take three passport photographs, your passport, and proof that you have some means of supporting yourself and reason to be in Italy (preferably a letter from an employer or certificate of registration at a school or university) to the nearest *commissariato* (police station; see the phone book under *Polizia di stato*) between 8.30am and noon (people start queuing before 7am). For information call the Questura centrale on 011 558 8111. The *carta* (card) *di soggiorno* is similar to the *permesso* but allows you to stay in Italy indefinitely, though it has to be renewed every ten years. EU citizens who have been in Italy for at least five years and who also have a renewable *permesso di soggiorno* can request the card. Those married to a foreigner who already has a card can request one for themselves at the Questura centrale.

Permesso di Lavoro (work permit)

In theory, all non-Italians employed in Italy need a work permit. Application forms can be obtained from the **Ispettorato del lavoro**. The form must be signed by your employer; you then need to take it with your *permesso di soggiorno* and a photocopy back to the *Ispettorato*. Don't rush: often the requirement is waived, or employers arrange it for you.

Residenza (residency)

This is your registered address in Italy, and you'll need it to buy a car, get customs clearance on goods brought from abroad and many other transactions. Take your *permesso di soggiorno* (*see above*; it must be valid for at least another year) and your passport to your local *circoscrizione* office (*see above, carta d'identità*). Staff will check that rubbish collection tax (*nettezza urbana*) for your address has been paid (ask your landlord about this) before issuing the certificate.

Bank accounts

To open an account you'll need a valid *permesso di soggiorno* or *certificato di residenza*, your *codice fiscale* (*see above*), proof of regular income from an employer (or a fairly substantial sum to deposit) and your passport.

Work

Casual employment can be hard to come by, so try to sort out work before you arrive. English-language schools and translation agencies are mobbed with applicants, so qualifications and experience count.

The classified ads papers *Secondamano* and *Tutto Affari* have lots of job advertisements. For serious jobs, check *La Stampa* and *La Repubblica*, or try one of the following agencies.

Adecco

Piazza Solferino 8C, Cittadella (011 530 505). Bus 5, 29, 55, 56, 59/tram 13. **Open** 9.30am-1, 3-6.30pm Mon-Fri. **Map** p242 C3.

Euro Interim

Via Gioberti 63D, Centro (800 020 303/011 508 6079/fax 011 595 103/www.eurointerim.it). Bus 63/tram 4. **Open** 9.30am-1pm, 2.30-5.30pm Mon-Fri. **Map** p244 A3.

Accommodation

The best places to look for accommodation are *Secondamano* and *Tutto Affari* (*see p225*). Look out for *affittasi* (for rent) notices on buildings, and check classifieds in *La Stampa*.

When you move into an apartment, it's normal to pay a month's rent in advance plus two months' deposit, which should be refunded when you move out, although some landlords create problems over this. You'll probably get a year's contract, normally renewable. If you rent through an agency, expect to pay the equivalent of two months' rent in commission.

Safety & security

Muggings are fairly rare in Turin, but pickpockets and bag snatchers are particularly active in train and bus stations. You will find that a few basic precautions greatly reduce a street thief's chances:

● Don't carry wallets in back pockets, particularly on buses. If you have a bag or camera with a long strap, wear it across the chest and not dangling from one shoulder.

● Keep bags closed, with your hand on them. If you stop at a pavement café or restaurant, do not leave bags or coats on the ground or the back of a

Directory

chair where you cannot keep an eye on them.

● When walking down a street, hold cameras and bags on the side of you towards the wall, so you're less likely to become the prey of a *scippatore* (motorcycle thief).

● Avoid groups of ragged children brandishing pieces of cardboard, or walk by quickly, keeping hold of your valuables. They'll wave the cardboard to confuse you while accomplices pick pockets or bags.

If you are the victim of crime, call the police helpline (*see p223*) or go to the nearest police station and say you want to report a *furto* (theft). A *denuncia* (written statement) of the incident will be made for you. It is unlikely that your things will be found, but you will need the *denuncia* for making an insurance claim.

Smoking

Smoking is not permitted in public offices (including post offices, police stations, etc),
on public transport or in restaurants except those with special smoking areas. A growing number of bars operate a no-smoking policy too. For where to buy cigarettes, *see below* **Tabacchi**.

Study

See also p224 **Libraries**.

The **Università degli Studi di Torino** and the **Politecnico di Torino** offer exchanges with other European universities through the EU's Erasmus programme.

All EU citizens have the same right as Italians to study in Turin's universities, paying the same fees. You'll need to have your university certificates translated and validated by the Italian consulate in your own country before lodging your application at the *ufficio stranieri* (foreigners' department) of the university of your choice. You will also need to provide evidence that you can support yourself financially during your stay in Turin.

Politecnico di Torino
Corso Duca degli Abruzzi 24, Cittadella (011 564 6111/ www.polito.it). **Map** p244 A2.
Università degli Studi di Torino
Via Verdi 8, Centro (011 670 6111/ www.unito.it). **Map** p243 C1.

Bureaucracy & services

Foreigners studying on any type of course in Italy must obtain a student's permit to stay (*see above*).

Tabacchi

Tabacchi or *tabaccherie* (identified by signs with a white T on a black or blue background) are the only places where you can legally buy tobacco products. They also sell stamps, telephone cards, tickets for public transport, lottery tickets and the stationery required when dealing with Italian bureaucracy.

Most *tabacchi* keep proper shop hours; many, however, are attached to bars and, through that outlet, can satisfy your nicotine cravings well into the night. Many also have 24-hour cigarette dispensers.

Atrium

In the run-up to the 2006 Winter Olympics, Turin's authorities have streamlined their information services inside two striking structures made of wood, brushed steel and glass in central piazza Solferino. Designed by Giorgetto Giugiaro – best known as creator of some of the most immediately recognisable cars on our streets – the two Atrium 'pods' provide 2,000 square metres (21,500 square feet) of exhibition space over three floors, inside 2,400 square metres (25,800 square feet) of glass wall. **AtriumCittà** is dedicated to the changing shape and look of Turin; **Atrium2006**, on the other hand, charts preparations for the Winter Olympics and hosts conferences on the forthcoming Games.

On the first floor of Atrium2006, the Turismo Torino info-point provides tourist information, sells the Torino Card (*see p51*) and the TurismoBus Torino pass (*see p218*),

organises guided tours and arranges hotel and B&B bookings, though only if you contact it in advance (48 hours for hotels, a week for B&Bs). Also inside AtriumCittà, **Vetrina Torino Cultura** provides information on cultural events and shows.
Atrium Torino
Piazza Solferino, Cittadella (011 516 2006/ www.atriumtorino.it). Bus *5, 12, 14, 29, 33, 34, 35, 50, 52, 57, 59, 63, 64, 65, 67/tram 13, 15, 18.* **Open** *9.30am-7pm daily.*
Map *p242 C3.*
Turismo Torino *(011 535 181/531 327/ fax 011 530 070/www.turismotorino.org).*
Open *9.30am-7pm daily.* **Credit** *MC, V.*
Other locations: *Porta Nuova railway station, by platform 17 (011 531 327); Turin airport, arrivals hall (011 567 6361/6362/6420).*
Vetrina Torino Cultura *(011 506 6667/toll-free 800 015 475).* Open *9.30am-7pm Mon-Sat; 11am-7pm Sun.*

Tax

Sales tax (IVA) is charged at varying rates on most goods and services, and is almost invariably quoted as an integral part of the price. Occasionally top-end hotels will quote prices without IVA. Some trades people will also offer you rates without IVA, the implication being that if you are prepared to hand over cash and not demand a receipt in return, then you'll be paying around 19 per cent (the amount you would have spent on IVA) less than the whole fee.

Telephones

Dialling & codes

All Turin land-line numbers begin with the area code 011, and this must be used whether you call from within or outside the city. Phone numbers within Turin generally have eight digits, although some of the older numbers may have seven or fewer. If you try a number and cannot get through, it may have been changed to an eight-digit number. If you have difficulties, check the directory or ring enquiries (412).

All numbers beginning with 800 are toll-free lines. For numbers beginning 840 and 848 you will be charged at low set rates, regardless of where you're calling from or how long the call lasts. These numbers can be called from within Italy only; some only function within one phone district.

Mobile phone numbers begin with 3; until recently they began with 03 and you will still sometimes find them written as such. Don't dial the 0.

Rates

Pressure of competition has brought Telecom Italia charges down, though they still remain some of Europe's highest, particularly for international calls. Calls cost more from public phones. Keep costs down by phoning off-peak (6.30pm-8am Mon-Sat; all day Sun). Avoid using phones in hotels, which may carry extortionate surcharges.

Public phones

Most public phones only accept phone cards (*schede telefoniche*); a few also accept major credit cards.

Telephone cards cost €1, €2.50, €5 and €7.75 and are available from *tabacchi* (*see p228*), some newsstands and some bars. Beware: phone cards have expiry dates (usually 31 December or 30 June), after which you won't be able to use them, however much credit remains. To use public coin phones you will need 10¢, 20¢, 50¢ or €1 coins. The minimum charge for a local call is 10¢.

International calls

To make an international call from Turin, dial 00, then the appropriate country code: Australia 61; Canada 1; Irish Republic 353; New Zealand 64; United Kingdom 44; United States 1. Then dial the area code (for calls to the UK, omit the initial zero of the area code) and the number.

To phone Turin from abroad, dial the international code (00 in the UK), then 39 for Italy and 011 for Turin, followed by the individual number.

Operator services

To make a reverse charge (collect) call, dial 170 for the international operator in Italy. Alternatively, to be connected to the operator in the country you want to call, dial 172 followed by a four-digit code for the country and telephone company you want to use (for the UK and Ireland this is the same as the country code; for other countries see the phone book). If you are placing a collect call from a phone box, you will need to insert a 10¢ coin, which will be refunded after your call.

The following services operate 24 hours daily:
Operator and Italian Directory Enquiries 12
International Operator 170
International Directory Enquiries 176
Communication problems on national calls 187
Communication problems on international calls 176
Wake-up calls 114; an automatic message will ask you to dial in the time you want your call, with four figures on a 24-hour clock, followed by your phone number.

Mobile phones

Italian cellphone numbers begin with 3 (formerly 03).

Owners of GSM phones can use them on both 900 and 1800 bands; British, Australian and New Zealand mobiles work without problems. US mobiles work on a different frequency and cannot be used in Italy.

Fax

Faxes can be sent from most large post offices (*see p226*), which will charge you for the number of sheets sent. Faxes can also be sent from some photocopying outlets. In all cases, the surcharge will be hefty.

Telegrams & telexes

These can be sent from main post offices. Alternatively, you can dictate telegrams over the phone. Dial 186 from a private phone and a message in Italian will tell you to dial the number of the phone you're calling from. You will then be passed to a telephonist who will take your message.

Time

Italy is one hour ahead of London, six ahead of New York, eight behind Sydney and 12 behind Wellington. Clocks are moved forward by one hour in early spring and back in late autumn, in line with other EU countries.

Tipping

Foreigners are expected to tip more than Italians, but the ten per cent customary in many countries is considered generous even for the richest-looking tourist. Most locals leave 10¢-20¢ on the counter when ordering drinks at a bar and, depending on the standard of the restaurant, €1 to €5 for the waiter. Many larger restaurants now include a ten to 15 per cent service charge. Tips are not expected in family-run restaurants, although even here a couple of euros is always appreciated. Taxi drivers will be happy if you round the fare up to the nearest whole euro.

Toilets

If you need a toilet, the easiest thing is usually to go to a bar (which won't necessarily be clean or provide toilet paper). There are modern lavatories at or near most of the major tourist sites; most have attendants, and you must pay a nominal fee to use them. Fast food joints and department stores also come in handy.

Tourist information

See p228 **Atrium**.

Water & drinking

Turin's water comes from underground aquifers and is excellent and safe for drinking.

When to go

See also pp132-4 **Festivals & Events** and *pp168-70* **Trips Out of Town: Piedmont by Season**.

Climate

Situated far from the mitigating effects of the sea, Piedmont's climate is continental, with large changes in temperature daily and annually. Summers are cool in the hills and hot on the plains; winters are cold and mainly dry, though you might not think so as you struggle through the thick fog that tends to linger on plains. Heaviest rainfall is recorded between October and April.

Public holidays

On public holidays (*giorni festivi*) virtually all shops, banks and businesses are closed, although (with the exception of May Day, 15 August and Christmas Day) bars and restaurants tend to stay open.

Limited public transport runs on 1 May and Christmas afternoon. Holidays falling on a Saturday or Sunday are not celebrated the following Monday; however, if a holiday falls on a Thursday or a Tuesday, many people will take the Friday or Monday off as well. Public holidays are:

New Year's Day (*Capo d'anno*) 1 January
Epiphany (*La Befana*) 6 January
Easter Monday (*Pasquetta*)
Liberation Day (*Festa della Liberazione*) 25 April
May Day (*Primo maggio*) 1 May
Patron saint's day (*San Giovanni*) 24 June
Feast of the Assumption (*Ferragosto*) 15 August
All Saints (*Tutti santi*) 1 November
Immaculate Conception (*Festa dell'Immacolata*) 8 December
Christmas Day (*Natale*) 25 December
Boxing Day (*Santo Stefano*) 26 December

Women

Turin is a safe city for women, and as long as you stick to central areas you can walk alone late at night without wishing you'd brought your mace. Women can feel daunted, however, by the sheer volume of attention they receive. If you do find yourself being hassled, take comfort in the fact that Italian men are generally all mouth and no trousers.

For women on their own, common sense will usually be enough to keep potential harassers at bay. If you're not interested, ignore them and they'll probably go away. Alternatively, duck into the nearest bar: they'll give you up as a lost cause and look for a new victim.

Health

See also p223 **Health**.
Women suffering gynaecological emergencies should head for the nearest *pronto soccorso* (accident & emergency department, *see p222*). Tampons (*assorbenti interni*) and sanitary towels (*assorbenti esterni*) are cheaper in supermarkets, but you can also get them in pharmacies and *tabacchi*.

Visas

EU nationals and citizens of the US, Canada, Australia and New Zealand do not need visas for stays of up to three months. For EU citizens, a passport or national identity card valid for travel abroad is sufficient, but all non-EU citizens must have full passports. In theory, all visitors have to declare their presence to the local police within eight days of arrival. If you're staying in a hotel, this will be done for you. If not, contact the **Questura centrale**, the main police station, for advice (*see p227*).

Average monthly climate

	High Temp	Low Temp	Rainfall	Humidity
Jan	5°C (41°F)	0°C (32°F)	44mm (1.7in)	82%
Feb	8°C (46°F)	2°C (36°F)	60mm (2.4in)	73%
Mar	13°C (55°F)	6°C (43°F)	77mm (3in)	65%
Apr	18°C (64°F)	10°C (50°F)	94mm (3.7in)	57%
May	23°C (73°F)	14°C (57°F)	76mm (2.9in)	59%
June	27°C (81°F)	17°C (63°F)	118mm (4.6in)	56%
July	29°C (84°F)	20°C (68°F)	64mm (2.5in)	61%
Aug	28°C (82°F)	19°C (66°F)	91mm (3.6in)	58%
Sept	24°C (75°F)	16°C (61°F)	69mm (2.7in)	63%
Oct	17°C (63°F)	11°C (52°F)	125mm (4.9in)	73%
Nov	10°C (50°F)	6°C (43°F)	122mm (4.8in)	80%
Dec	6°C (43°F)	2°C (36°F)	77mm (3in)	89%

Directory

Glossary

Amphitheatre – (ancient) oval open-air theatre

Apse – large recess at the high-altar end of a church

Atrium – (ancient) courtyard

Baptistery – building – often eight-sided – outside church used for baptisms

Baroque – artistic period from the 17th-18th century, in which the decorative element became increasingly florid

Basilica – ancient Roman rectangular public building; rectangular Christian church; church built as the result of a vow

Bas-relief – carving on a flat or curved surface where the figures stand out from the plane

Cardine – (ancient) secondary street, usually running north–south

Castellated – (building) decorated with battlements or turrets

Choir – area of church, usually behind the high altar, with stalls for those singing sung mass

Cloister – exterior courtyard surrounded on all sides by a covered walkway

Column – upright architectural element, can be round, square or rectangular, usually structural but sometimes merely decorative, usually free-standing, conforms to one of the classical orders (qv); (cf. pilaster – rectangular column projecting slightly from a wall: pillar – upright element, always free-standing but not conforming to orders)

Crypt – vault beneath the main floor of a church

Cupola – dome-shaped roof or ceiling

Decumanus – (ancient) main road, usually running east–west

Ex-voto – an offering given to fulfil a vow; often a small model in silver of the limb/organ/loved one cured as a result of prayer

Fresco – artistic technique in which paint is applied on to wet plaster; by extension, a painting done using this technique

Futurism – artistic and literary movement of the early 20th century that strove to express growth and movement through innovative (and often scandalous) techniques

Gothic – architectural and artistic style of the late Middle Ages (from the 12th century), of soaring, pointed arches

Greek cross (church) – in the shape of a cross with arms of equal length

Latin cross (church) – in the shape of a cross with one arm longer than the other

Loggia – gallery open on one side

Lunette – semicircular area, usually above a door or window

Mannerism – High Renaissance style of the late 16th century; characterised in painting by elongated, contorted human figures

Monstrance – receptacle, usually ornate and in silver or gold, with a glass section in which the consecrated host is exposed

Nave – main body of a church; the longest section of a Latin cross church (qv)

Necropolis – (ancient) literally, city of the dead, graveyard

Neo-classical – late 18th-century artistic movement advocating rigid classical standards in reaction to the frivolous rococo (qv)

Ogival – (of arches, windows etc) curving in to a point at the top

Orders – rules governing the proportions and decoration of columns, the most common being the very simple Doric, the curlicue Ionic and the Corinthian with stylised acanthus leaves

Palazzo – large and/or important building (not necessarily a palace)

Piazza (or largo) – square

Pietà – a picture or sculpture of the Virgin Mary holding the dead body of Christ in her arms

Pilaster – *see* column

Pillar – *see* column

Polyptych – a painting – usually and altarpiece – made up of several panels

Portal – imposing door

Portico – open space in front of a church or, in Turin, lining a street, with a roof resting on columns

Prie-dieu – a narrow desk at which to kneel for prayer

Pronaos – roofed temple vestibule with closed sides and columns in its open front

Rationalism – Italian movement founded in 1926 by architects including Marcello Piacentini; founded when its close relationship with the Fascist regime forced it to abandon its strong, massive lines for a more eclectic style drawing on classical influences

Reliquary – receptacle – often highly ornate – for holding or displaying relics of saints

Rococo – highly decorative style fashionable in the 18th century

Romanesque – architectural style of the Middle Ages (c500 to 1200), drawing on Roman and Byzantine influences

Sacristy – room in church, usually off choir (qv), where vestments are stored

Stile Liberty – Italian take on art nouveau

Stucco – plaster

Theatre – (ancient) semi-circular open-air theatre

Transept – shorter arms of a Latin cross church (qv)

Tromp l'oeil – decorative painting effect to make surface appear three-dimensional

Further Reference

Books

Fiction & literature

(*See also p15* **Literary Turin**.)

Calvino Italo *The Watcher and Other Stories*
The Watcher is a fantasy story set in Cottolengo, a city within the city of Turin.

De Amicis Edmondo *Cuore: the Heart of a Boy*
This sentimental, patriotic school-boy story has been jerking tears ever since it was first published in 1886.

Eco Umberto *The Name of the Rose*
The abbey setting for Eco's bestselling medieval detective yarn is probably based on the Sacra di San Michele (*see p204*) in the Val di Susa.

Ginzburg Natalia *Things We Used to Say*
This highly autographical novel by the acclaimed Jewish Italian author charts a woman's childhood and youth in Turin.

Gozzano Guido *The Colloquies; Journey Towards the Cradle of Mankind*
Exquisite, gently decadent verse paying homage to Turin and Piedmont's air of gentle melancholy.

Lucentini Franco, Fruttero, Carlo *The Sunday Woman*
This early detective novel by the writing duo is set in Turin.

Non-fiction

Barzini Luigi *The Italians*
Insightful look into the Italians and how they run their lives and country.

Chamberlain L *Nietzsche in Turin: The End of the Future*
Examines the most creative year in Nietzsche's life, and his last sane one.

Ginsborg Paul *A History of Contemporary Italy*
Excellent introduction to the ups and downs of post-war Italy.

Ginsborg Paul *Italy and its Discontents 1980-2001*
A coherent analysis of contemporary Italy structured around the continuing importance of the family in Italian society.

Levi Carlo *Christ Stopped at Eboli*
Torinese Levi recounts his year's internal exile in a backwards village in pre-war southern Italy.

Levi Primo *The Periodic Table; If This be a Man; If Not Now, When?*
Levi's powerful writing is strongly coloured by his wartime experiences in Auschwitz.

Rousseau Jean-Jacques *Confessions*

Several chapters of this famous work recount the author's experiences in Turin in the mid 18th century.

Thomson Ian *Primo Levi: A Biography*
A voluminous and meticulously researched biography of *torinese* Levi that's also a great read.

Varriano John *Italian Baroque and Rococo Architecture*
A good introduction to these architectural styles.

Vassalli Sebastiano *My Piedmont*
A homage to Piedmontese culture and history, complemented by beautiful photos of the region.

Wilson Ian & Schwortz Barrie *The Turin Shroud: Unshrouding the Mystery*
An overview of the shroud, its history and its (debatable) origins.

Wittkower Rudolf *Art and Architecture in Italy 1600-1750*
Everything you ever wanted to know about the baroque.

Food & Wine

Kramer Matt *A Passion for Piedmont*
Local recipes and an excellent section on regional wines.

Film

Cabiria (1914)
Set in the Punic Wars of the third century BC, and made during Turin's golden age of cinema, this film was shot partly on location in the Italian Alps.

Così ridevano (1998)
A story of devotion and sacrifice involving two poor Sicilian immigrant brothers living in Turin during the late 1950s and early '60s.

La donna della domenica (1975)
A satirical crime drama set in Turin that makes interesting observations about Italian bourgeois society.

The Italian Job (1969)
The planning and execution of a Turin bullion heist takes a back seat to the infamous stunt-riddled getaway.

Non ho sonno (2001)
A gory thriller set in Turin starring Max von Sydow.

Il partigiano Johnny (2000)
This epic story of the Italian Resistance was filmed in the Langhe (*see p194*).

Profumo di donna (1974)
Remade as *Scent of a Woman* in 1992 starring Al Pacino, the Italian original is set in Turin and Naples.

Riso amaro (1948)
This neo-realism classic is an earthy drama of human passions among women rice workers in the Po valley.

Santa Maradona (2002)
Two 20-something graduates sharing a bachelor pad in Turin get their first taste of grown-up life.

La seconda volta (1995)
A Turin university professor develops a relationship with a woman who it transpires tried to kill him 12 years earlier in a terrorist attack.

Time to Love (1999)
Three contrasting but intertwined love stories, one of which is set in modern Turin.

War and Peace (1956)
The Savoy residences of Palazzo Reale (*see p54*), Castello del Valentino (*see p80*) and Stupinigi (*see p93*) were used for exterior shots in King Vidor's megabucks epic starring Audrey Hepburn and Vittorio Gassman.

Music

Subsonica Turin's lively music scene is spearheaded by Subsonica, whose melodic brand of techno is now gaining a reputation abroad as well as at home.
Africa Unite One of the growing number of bands emerging from the city's large immigrant community.
Mau Mau This Turinese band have been purveying their particular brand of ethno-techno-trance since 1991.

Websites

www.beniculturali.it
The first port of call for information on museums and archaeological sites is the Cultural Heritage Ministry's excellent (but alas Italian-only) site.
www.comune.torino.it
www.provincia.to.it.
www.regione.piemonte.it
The official sites of various councils around the region. Contain everything from local news to information on the music and theatre scene in Turin and Piedmont.
www.sindone.org/en
The official Turin Shroud website has everything you need to know about the holy relic.
www.turismotorino.org
Excellent website with a thorough overview of sights, hotels and restaurants, and advice on creating an itinerary for your visit.
www.torino2006.org
www.montagnedoc.it
Information on the upcoming 2006 Winter Olympics.
www.piemontegroove.com
News on musical novelties and events all over the region.

Vocabulary

The *torinesi* always appreciate attempts at spoken Italian, no matter how incompetent. In hotels, and all but the most spit-and-sawdust restaurants, you're likely to find someone with at least a basic grasp of English.

There are two forms of address in the second person singular: *lei*, which is formal and should be used with strangers and older people; and *tu*, which is informal. The personal pronoun is usually omitted.

Italian is pronouced as it is spelt.

PRONUNCIATION

a – as in ask.
e – like a in age or e in sell.
i – like ea in east.
o – as in hotel or in hot.
u – as in boot.
Remember that c and g both go soft in front of e and i (becoming like the initial sounds of check and giraffe respectively). An h after any consonant makes it hard. Before a vowel, it is silent.
c before a, o and u: as in cat.
g before a, o and u: as in get.
gl like lli in million.
gn like ny in canyon.
qu as in quick.
r always rolled.
s has two sounds, as in soap or rose.
sc like the sh in shame.
sch like the sc in scout.
z can be sounded ts or dz.

USEFUL PHRASES

hello and goodbye (informal) *ciao, salve*
good morning – *buon giorno*
good evening – *buona sera*
good night – *buona notte*
please – *per favore, per piacere*
thank you – *grazie*
you're welcome – *prego*
excuse me, sorry – *mi scusi* (formal), *scusa* (informal)
I'm sorry, but... – *mi dispiace...*
I don't speak Italian (very well) – *non parlo (molto bene) l'italiano*
can I use/where's the toilet? – *posso usare/dov'è il bagno/la toilette?*
open – *aperto*
closed – *chiuso*
entrance – *entrata*
exit – *uscita*

FEMALE SELF-DEFENCE

no thank you, I can find my way by myself – *no grazie, non ho bisogno di una guida.*

can you leave me alone? – *mi vuole* (or *vuoi* – informal – if you want to make it clear you feel very superior) *lasciare in pace?*

TIMES & TIMETABLES

could you tell me the time? – *mi sa (formal)/sai (informal) dire l'ora?*
it's – o'clock – *sono le (number)*
it's half past – *sono le (number) e mezza*
when does it (re-)open? – *a che ora (ri)apre?*
does it close for lunch? – *chiude per pranzo?*

DIRECTIONS

(turn) left – *(gira a) sinistra*
(it's on the) right – *(è a/sulla) destra*
straight on – *sempre diritto*
where is...? – *dov'è...?*
could you show me the way to the Pantheon? – *mi potrebbe indicare la strada per il Pantheon?*

TRANSPORT

car – *macchina*
bus – *autobus, auto*
coach – *pullman*
taxi – *tassi, taxi*
train – *treno*
tram – *tram*
plane – *aereo*
bus stop – *fermata (d'autobus)*
station – *stazione*
platform – *binario*
ticket/s – *biglietto/biglietti*
one way – *solo andata*
return – *andata e ritorno*
(I'd like) a ticket for – *(vorrei) un biglietto per...*
where can I buy tickets? – *dov'è si comprono i biglietti?*
I'm sorry, I didn't know I had to stamp it – *mi dispiace, non sapevo che lo dovevo timbrare*

COMMUNICATIONS

phone – *telefono*
fax – *fax*
stamp – *francobollo*
can I send a fax? – *posso mandare un fax?*
can I make a phone call? – *posso telefonare?*
letter – *lettera*
postcard – *cartolina*
courier – *corriere, pony*

SHOPPING

I'd like to try the blue sandals/black shoes/brown boots – *vorrei provare i sandali blu/le scarpe nere/gli stivali marroni*
do you have it/them in other colours? – *ce l'ha in altri colori?*
I take (shoe) size... – *porto il numero...*

I take (dress) size... – *porto la taglia...*
it's too loose/too tight/just right – *mi sta largo/stretto/bene*
can you give me a little more/less? – *mi dia un po' di più/meno*
100 grams of... – *un etto di...*
300 grams of... – *tre etti di...*
one kilo of... – *un kilo/chilo di...*
five kilos of... – *cinque chili di...*
a litre/two litres of... – *un litro/due litri di...*

ACCOMMODATION

a reservation – *una prenotazione*
I'd like to book a single/twin/double room – *vorrei prenotare una camera singola/doppia/matrimoniale*
I'd prefer a room with a bath/shower/window – *preferirei una camera con vasca da bagno/doccia*
can you bring me breakfast in bed? – *mi porti la colazione al letto?*

EATING & DRINKING

I'd like to book a table for four at eight – *vorrei prenotare una tavola per quattro alle otto*
that was poor/good/delicious – *era mediocre/buono/ottimo*
the bill – *il conto*
is service included? – *è incluso il servizio?*
I think there's a mistake in this bill – *credo che il conto sia sbagliato*
See also p98 The menu.

DAYS & NIGHTS

Monday *lunedì*; Tuesday *martedì*; Wednesday *mercoledì*; Thursday *giovedì*; Friday *venerdì*; Saturday *sabato*; Sunday *domenica*; yesterday *ieri*; today *oggi*; tomorrow *domani*; morning *mattina*; afternoon *pomeriggio*; evening *sera*; night *notte*; weekend *fine settimana, weekend*

NUMBERS & MONEY

0 *zero*; 1 *uno*; 2 *due*; 3 *tre*; 4 *quattro*; 5 *cinque*; 6 *sei*; 7 *sette*; 8 *otto*; 9 *nove*; 10 *dieci*; 11 *undici*; 12 *dodici*; 13 *tredici*; 14 *quattordici*; 15 *quindici*; 16 *sedici*; 17 *diciassette*; 18 *diciotto*; 19 *diciannove*; 20 *venti*; 30 *trenta*; 40 *quaranta*; 50 *cinquanta*; 60 *sessanta*; 70 *settanta*; 80 *ottanta*; 90 *novanta*; 100 *cento*; 200 *duecento*; 1,000 *mille*; 2,000 *duemila*.
how much is it/does it cost? – *quanto costa/quant'è/quanto viene?*
do you take credit cards? – *si accettano le carte di credito?*
can I pay in pounds/dollars/travellers' cheques? – *posso pagare in sterline/dollari/con i travellers?*

Index

Advertisers' Index

Please refer to the relevant sections for contact details

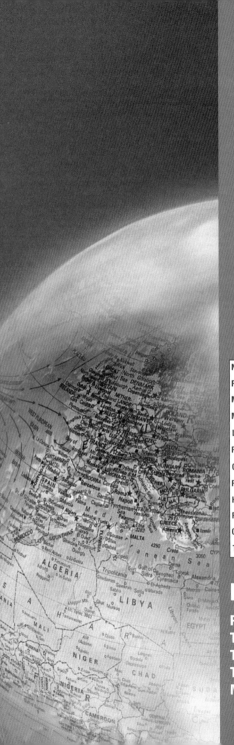

National border	- - - -
Province border	....
Motorway (*autostrade*)	═══
Main road	....
Lake/River/Canal	▨
Place of interest	▨
Church	⊞
Park	▨
Hospital/university	▨
Pedestrianised area	▨
Car park	🅿
Tourist information	ⅈ

Maps

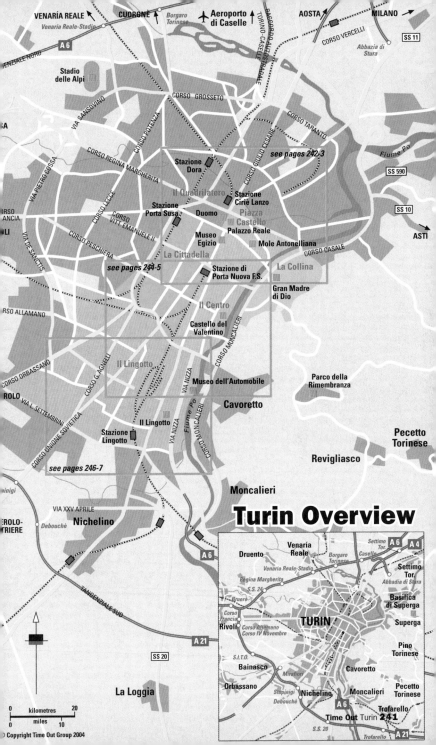

Turin Overview

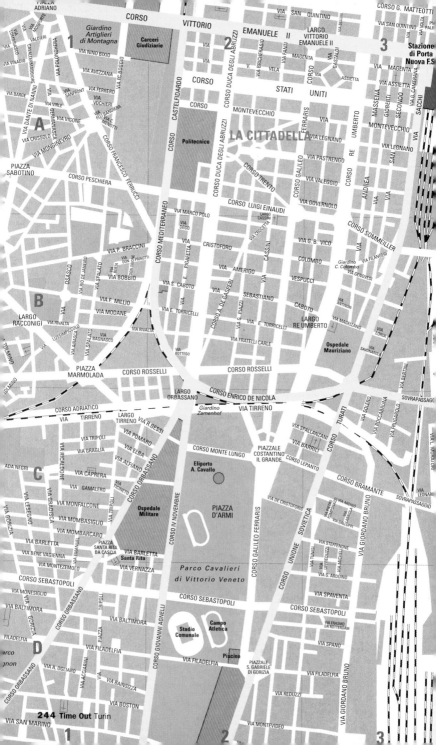

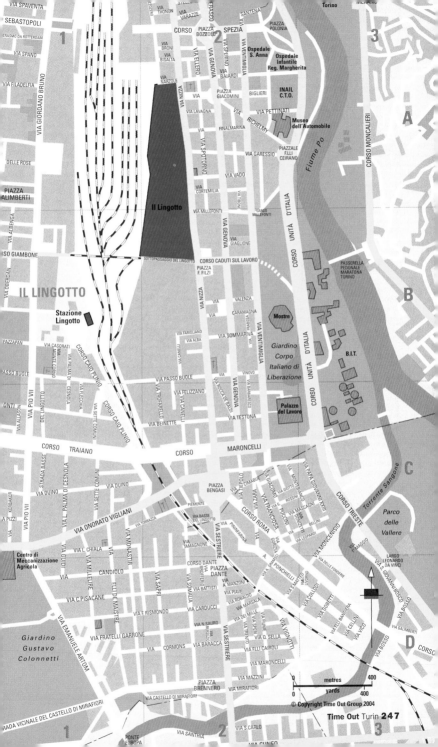

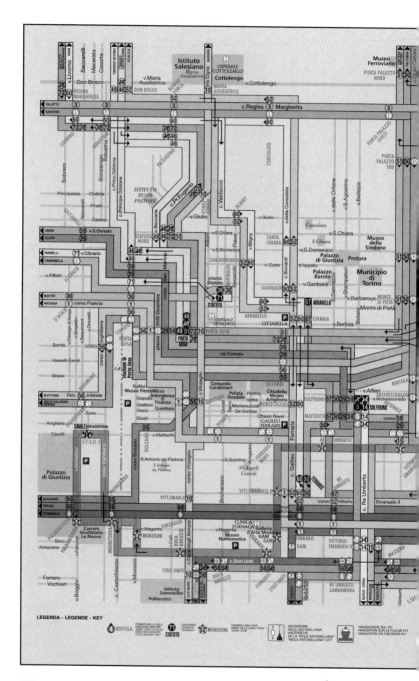

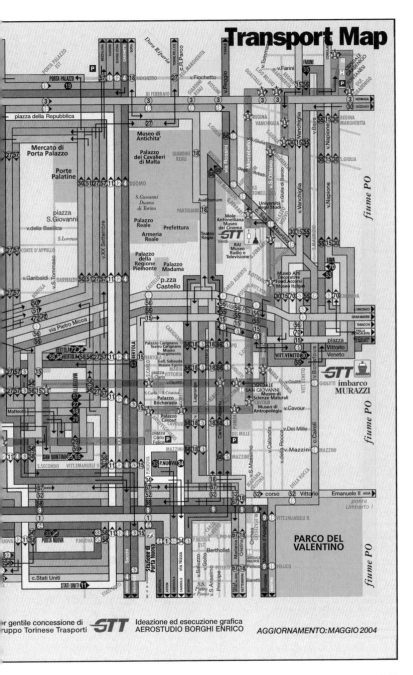

Transport Map

Street Index

TRAIANO CSO 246 C3	TRINCEE DELLE VIA 242 A1/A2	
TRENTO VIA 244 A2	TRIPOLI VIA PZA 244 D1	
TRENTO VIA 247 D2	TRIPOLI VIA 244 C1	
TRIESTE CSO 247 C3	TROFARELLO VIA 247 C2	

Turin Please let us know what you think

About this guide...

1. How useful did you find the following sections?

	Very	Fairly	Not very
In Context	☐	☐	☐
Where to Stay	☐	☐	☐
Sightseeing	☐	☐	☐
Eat, Drink, Shop	☐	☐	☐
Arts & Entertainment	☐	☐	☐
Trips Out of Town	☐	☐	☐
Directory	☐	☐	☐
Maps	☐	☐	☐

2. Did you travel to Turin...?

Alone ☐   With children ☐
As part of a group ☐   On vacation ☐
On business ☐   To study ☐
With a partner ☐   I live here ☐

3. How long was your trip to Turin? (write in)

_____ days

4. Where did you book your trip?

Time Out Classifieds ☐
On the Internet ☐
With a travel agent ☐
Other (write in) _____

5. Where did you first hear about this guide?

Advertising in Time Out magazine ☐
On the Internet ☐
From a travel agent ☐
Other (write in) _____

6. Is there anything you'd like us to cover in greater depth?

_____
_____
_____

7. Are there any places that should/ should not* be included in the guide? (*delete as necessary)

_____
_____
_____

8. How many other people have used this guide?

none ☐   1 ☐   2 ☐   3 ☐   4 ☐   5+ ☐

9. What city or country would you like to visit next? (write in)

_____
_____

About other Time Out publications...

10. Have you ever bought/used Time Out magazine?

Yes ☐   No ☐

11. Do you subscribe to Time Out London?

Yes ☐   No ☐

12. Have you ever bought/used any other Time Out City Guides?

Yes ☐   No ☐

If yes, which ones?
_____

13. Have you ever bought/used other Time Out publications?

Yes ☐   No ☐

If yes, which ones?
_____

About you...

14. Title (Mr, Ms etc): _____
First name: _____
Surname: _____
Address: _____
_____
Postcode: _____
Email: _____
Nationality: _____

15. Date of birth: ☐☐/☐☐/☐☐

16. Sex: male ☐   female ☐

17. Are you...?
Single ☐☐
Married/Living with partner ☐☐

18. What is your occupation? _____

19. At the moment do you earn...?

Under £15,000 ☐
Between £15,000 and £19,999 ☐
Between £20,000 and £24,999 ☐
Between £25,000 and £39,999 ☐
Between £40,000 and £49,999 ☐
Over £50,000 ☐

☐ Please tick here if you'd like to hear about offers and discounts from Time Out and relevant companies.

Time Out Guides

FREEPOST 20 (WC3187)
LONDON
W1E 0DQ

Time Out Subscriptions
FREEPOST NAT2971
Somerton
TA11 6ZA